THE DEAD SEA SCROLLS
IN THEIR
HISTORICAL CONTEXT

THE DEAD SEA SCROLLS IN THEIR HISTORICAL CONTEXT

Edited by
Timothy H. Lim
with
Larry W. Hurtado, A. Graeme Auld,
Alison Jack

T&T CLARK
EDINBURGH

T&T CLARK LTD
59 GEORGE STREET
EDINBURGH EH2 2LQ
SCOTLAND

www.tandtclark.co.uk

First published 2000

ISBN 0 567 08707 7 HB
ISBN 0 567 08759 X PB

British Library Cataloguing-in-Publication Data
A catalogue record for this book is available from the British Library

Typeset by Fakenham Photosetting Limited, Fakenham, Norfolk
Printed and bound in Great Britain by Bookcraft Ltd, Avon

CONTENTS

NOTES ON CONTRIBUTORS

GRAEME AULD, Professor of Hebrew Bible, University of Edinburgh, is author of *Kings Without Privilege* (1994) and *Joshua Retold* (1998), and co-author of *Jerusalem I: From the Bronze Age to the Maccabees* (1996). He is preparing commentaries on the Hebrew and Greek texts of Joshua, and on the standard and Qumran texts of Samuel.

GEORGE J. BROOKE is Rylands Professor of Biblical Criticism and Exegesis, University of Manchester, and co-director of the Manchester–Sheffield Centre for Dead Sea Scrolls Research.

CALUM M. CARMICHAEL is Professor of Comparative Literature, Adjunct Professor of Law at Cornell University. His most recent books are *The Story of Creation: its Origin and its interpretation in Philo and the Fourth Gospel* (1996); *The Spirit of Biblical Law* (1996); and *Law, Legend, and Incest in the Bible* (1997). He is the Editor of the *Collected Works of David Daube*.

JOHN J. COLLINS is Holmes Professor of Old Testament at Yale University. His books include the commentary on *Daniel* in the Hermeneia series, *The Scepter and the Star, Jewish Wisdom in the Hellenistic Age, Apocalypticism in the Dead Sea Scrolls, The Apocalyptic Imagination* and *Between Athens and Jerusalem*. He is co-editor of *The Encyclopedia of Apocalypticism*. He has served as editor of the *Journal of Biblical Literature* and as president of the Catholic Biblical Association. He is president-elect of the Society of Biblical Literature for 2002.

PHILIP R. DAVIES is Professor of Hebrew Bible at the University of Sheffield and co-director of the Manchester–Sheffield Centre for Dead Sea Scrolls Research.

JAMES R. DAVILA is Lecturer in Early Jewish Studies at the University of St. Andrews. He is a member of the international team responsible for publishing the Dead Sea Scrolls, and his edition of Qumran manuscripts of Genesis and Exodus was published in *Discoveries in the Judean Desert* vol. 12 (1994). He is also co-editor of *The Jewish Roots of Christological Monotheism. Papers from the St. Andrews Conference on the Historical Origins of the Worship of Jesus* (1999).

CHARLOTTE HEMPEL, Sutasoma Research Fellow, Lucy Cavendish

College, University of Cambridge, is author of *The Laws of the Damascus Document: Sources, Tradition, and Redaction* (1998).

LARRY W. HURTADO, Professor of New Testament, Language & Theology, University of Edinburgh, is the Director of the Centre for Christian Origins.

ALISON JACK, PhD in New Testament (1996) at the University of Edinburgh, is author of *Texts Reading Texts, Sacred and Secular* (1999) and is a Church of Scotland minister.

TIMOTHY H. LIM is Reader in Hebrew and Old Testament Studies and New Testament Studies, University of Edinburgh, where he teaches undergraduate, honours and postgraduate courses in the Hebrew Bible, Qumran Scrolls and New Testament. He is author of *Holy Scripture in the Qumran Commentaries and Pauline Letters* (1997) and main editor of *The Dead Sea Scrolls Electronic Reference Library* (1997).

J. IAN H. MCDONALD is Honorary Fellow and formerly Reader in Christian Ethics and New Testament Studies at the University of Edinburgh, where he taught in several Departments. His recent publications include *Biblical Interpretation and Christian Ethics* (1993), *Christian Values* (1995) and *The Crucible of Christian Morality* (1998).

E. P. SANDERS, Arts and Sciences Professor of Religious Studies, Duke University, is author of *Paul and Palestinian Judaism, Jesus and Judaism*, and *Judaism: Practice and Belief*. He previously held positions at McMaster University and the University of Oxford.

LAWRENCE H. SCHIFFMAN is Edelman Professor of Hebrew and Judaic Studies; Chair, Skirball Department of Hebrew and Judaic Studies, New York University.

SACHA STERN is Senior Lecturer and Head of Department of Jewish Studies at the London School of Jewish Studies. He is author of *Jewish Identity in Early Rabbinic Writings* (Brill, 1994) and has published many articles on ancient Jewish calendars.

JULIO TREBOLLE-BARRERA is Professor in the Departmento de Hebreo y Arameo, Facultad de Filologia, Universidad Complutense de Madrid.

HÅKAN ULFGARD is Senior Lecturer in Biblical Studies at Linköping University, Sweden.

EUGENE ULRICH, John A. O'Brien Professor of Hebrew Bible in the Department of Theology, University of Notre Dame, is Chief Editor of the Qumran Biblical Scrolls. One of the translators of the New Revised Standard Version, he is the principal editor for six volumes in the series *Discoveries in the Judaean Desert*, author of *The Dead Sea Scrolls and the Origins of the Bible* (1999), and co-author of *The Dead Sea Scrolls Bible* (1999).

JAMES C. VANDERKAM, John A. O'Brien Professor of Hebrew Bible in the Department of Theology, University of Notre Dame; teaches in the undergraduate, masters, and doctoral programs. He has edited several parabiblical and poetic volumes in the *Discoveries in the Judaean Desert* series, is one of the editors-in-chief for the *Encyclopedia of the Dead Sea Scrolls*, and has written, among other books, *The Dead Sea Scrolls Today* (1994) and *Calendars in the Dead Sea Scrolls* (1998).

ABBREVIATIONS

CRC *The Community of the Renewed Covenant: The Notre Dame Symposium on the Dead Sea Scrolls* edited by E. Ulrich and J. VanderKam. Notre Dame: University of Notre Dame Press, 1994.

DSSFYR *The Dead Sea Scrolls: Forty Years of Research* edited by D. Dimant and U. Rappaport. Leiden: E. J. Brill, 1992.

LTLI *Legal Texts and Legal Issues. Proceedings of the Second Meeting of the International Organization for Qumran Studies. Cambridge 1995. Published in Honour of Joseph M. Baumgarten* edited by M. Bernstein, F. García Martínez, and J. Kampen. Leiden: Brill Academic Publishers, 1997.

MQC *The Madrid Qumran Congress: Proceedings of the International Congress on the Dead Sea Scrolls, Madrid, 18–21 March 1991* edited by J. Trebolle-Barrera and L. Vegas Montaner. 2 volumes. Leiden: E. J. Brill, 1992.

NQTS *New Qumran Texts and Studies* edited by G. J. Brooke with F. García Martínez. Leiden: E. J. Brill, 1994.

SSQFYA *The Scrolls and the Scriptures. Qumran Fifty Years After* edited by S. E. Porter and C. A. Evans. Sheffield: Sheffield Academic Press, 1997.

TPWW *Time to Prepare the Way in the Wilderness. Papers on the Qumran Scrolls by Fellows of the Institute for Advanced Studies of the Hebrew University, Jerusalem, 1989–1990* edited by D. Dimant and L. W. Schiffman. Leiden: Brill Academic Publishers, 1995.

INTRODUCTION

On 5–6 May 1998, the Faculty of Divinity of the University of Edinburgh hosted an international conference entitled 'The Dead Sea Scrolls in their Historical Context' at the historic site of New College on Mound Place in Edinburgh. Five months after the Jubilee of the discovery of the Dead Sea Scrolls (in 1947), and in the wake of numerous fiftieth anniversary celebrations worldwide, this gathering sought to begin the second half-century of scholarly research by situating these most important ancient manuscripts within the context of Judaism in the Second Temple period.

The guiding issue around which the theme of the conference revolved was the marginality or centrality of the Dead Sea Scrolls. In particular, two aspects were addressed. First, how central or marginal was the community that owned these scrolls? Most scholars, though certainly not all, believe that the Qumran community who owned these scrolls are to be identified with the Essene sect known from the classical sources – primarily those of Philo, Pliny and Josephus. Is this community one of several fringe sectarian groups, about whom we now happen to know more than we do about others? Formulating the question this way also begs the question of what we know in the first place about the religious practices and theology of the ordinary Jew in Second Temple Judaism. Was the sacrificial system of the Jerusalem cultus 'normative' or 'common'?

A corollary of the question about the character of the sectarian community is the marginality or centrality of the corpus of Qumran scrolls. It is widely held that the eight hundred or so scrolls found in the eleven caves by the Dead Sea belong to the 'library' of the Qumran community, in the sense that they constitute a heterogeneous collection. Like New College Library that includes in its collection books by staff members, past and present, as well as copies of different versions of Hebrew, Greek and Aramaic Bibles and other extra-canonical texts, so the Qumran library also contains works that were not composed or even copied by the sect, but brought in by those – presumably volunteers – who joined the community.

For example, the biblical texts, comprising some one quarter of the total number of the corpus, were not composed (though some believe that they were copied) by the Qumran community, but their presence within this library has allowed scholars to marginalize them as sectarian copies. If this were true, then the pluriformity evident in the Qumran biblical scrolls cannot be extrapolated to the textual status of scripture in Second Temple period generally. Though this view is not held by any of the speakers of the conference, several of them have explicitly or tacitly addressed the marginality/centrality of the non-sectarian Qumran texts.

Second, the phenomenon of the Dead Sea Scrolls, fuelled as it is by concentrated academic interest and widespread media coverage, raises historiographical issues that are not normally part of the study of other ancient documents. With the sustained publication of numerous articles and books about the scrolls, one might inadvertently slip into the mistake of assuming that all Jews in the Second Temple period were carved in the image of the Qumran-Essene sectarian. Has our picture of nascent Judaism been skewed as a result of the chance discovery and intensive research into the Dead Sea Scrolls?

The papers presented here are grouped into sections, addressing four broad areas of research, namely the Qumran community itself, biblical texts and interpretation, sectarian and normative Jewish law, and teaching and theology. The plenary papers by Ed Sanders, Eugene Ulrich, Lawrence Schiffman, and John Collins provide broad brush strokes on the canvas of Second Temple Judaism. These papers are intended as summary statements of the *status quaestionis*, although all of them also carry forward and extend particular topics of research.

Thus while Sanders describes the nature of sub-groups, the walls of which are a little porous allowing ideas to flow between it and the main group, he also provides an extended treatment of purities, engaging in dialogue with the recent work of Albert Baumgarten. After a methodological preamble, Ulrich argues for the terminology of 'scripture' to replace 'biblical', and suggests that the rabbis did not select the proto-Masoretic text, but rather 'received it'. Schiffman combines a history of scholarship approach with a digest of important legal issues found particularly in the *Damascus Document*, the *Temple Scroll* and 4QMMT, and balances his view of the Sadducean features of Qumran halakha with a discussion of how the community wore phylacteries in common with other Jews in the Second Temple period. Collins summarizes the biblical and Qumran evidence for messianism, and interacts with recent suggestions of communal messianism (by Hartmut Stegemann and Annette Steudel) and of a non-Davidic messiah (by Kenneth Pomykala).

The other eleven papers confine themselves to specific topics within the four areas, contributing as they do to biblical and Qumran scholarship. I query the common restoration of 'the wicked priest' in column one of the Habakkuk Pesher and suggest the alternative reconstruction of the lacuna with 'the liar'. J. Ian McDonald compares the teaching of John the Baptist to the Qumran community and outlines his distinctiveness in matters of purification and immersion, righteousness, interaction with crowds on the edge of the wilderness, the proclamation of the Day of the Lord, and political significance.

Julio Trebolle-Barrera charts a course between biblical and parabiblical texts, advancing the view that scriptural texts were preserved, edited, ordered and interpreted according to two different groups: one consisting of the Torah, Isaiah, the Twelve, Psalms and Job, and the other including Joshua, Judges, 1–2 Samuel, 1–2 Kings, Jeremiah, Ezekiel and Daniel. George J. Brooke discusses examples of how the Qumran community tolerated a plurality of biblical text forms, but required a single, definitive interpretation.

Calum Carmichael explains why the *Book of Jubilees*, a work considered authoritative by the Qumran community, announces the Year of Jubilee on the Day of Atonement. James VanderKam explores how biblical demarcations of time, namely those of the sabbath and Jubilee, are used in 11QMelch, 4Q180–181, and 4Q384–90. Sacha Stern argues that the Qumran calendars, including the 364-day calendar, are all impractical, because there is no accompanying system of intercalation found that will align them to the astronomical year. Charlotte Hempel amasses the manuscriptal and citational evidence to draw attention to the special status of *Jubilees* at Qumran.

Philip Davies examines detailed references to 'messiah' and argues that the Damascus Document represents a single messianic figure, and not the dual pattern suggested by Collins. Håkan Ulfgard traces the motifs of branch and shoot from the Qumran texts to the New Testament. And James Davila updates the topic of Dead Sea Scrolls and merkavah mysticism by a discussion of recently published and released Qumran texts.

Coinciding with the conference, Geza Vermes gave his series of Gunning Lectures on 'Jesus the Jew and the Dead Sea Scrolls' at New College. And Kelvingrove Art Gallery and Museum in Glasgow hosted the Scrolls from the Dead Sea exhibit, for which participants of the conference were invited to a reception and private viewing.

Many contributed to the planning, funding, organization and execution of the conference. Funding was provided by the University of Edinburgh Faculty Group of Arts, Divinity and Music and the Interdisciplinary Symposium Fund.

Thanks are due to all those who helped in organizing the conference, particularly Alison Jack and Christopher Grundke. The conference also received support from Stewart J. Brown, convener of the Gunning Fund,

Duncan Forrester, Dean of Divinity, John Richardson and Frances Dow, successive Provosts of the Faculty Group, and Stewart Sutherland, Vice-Chancellor and Principal of the University of Edinburgh who opened the proceedings with a welcome to the participants.

This conference was organized under the aegis of the newly founded University of Edinburgh Centre for Christian Origins.

TIMOTHY LIM

PART I

The Qumran Community, Essenes and other Sects

1

THE DEAD SEA SECT AND OTHER JEWS: COMMONALITIES, OVERLAPS AND DIFFERENCES

E. P. Sanders

Introduction: Groups and Sub-groups

Of the overlapping themes of the conference at which these papers were presented, I shall address primarily the question of agreements and disagreements between the sect and other Jews, but I shall comment on the other questions at the end, especially the relationship between the Essene party and the Dead Sea Scrolls.*

I imagine groups in human society as being in some ways like groups in nature.[1] To simplify, life-forms are divided into two kingdoms, animal and vegetable; animals are chordata or not; chordata are verte- brate or not; vertebrate animals are subdivided into mammals, birds, reptiles, amphibians and fish; some mammals are primates, some primates are homidae, and so on. At each stage, there are both common and distinguishing characteristics of each group. Some very basic factors are common to all life forms, though vegetables are in most ways different from animals. Skipping a few stages, we note that the females of all mammals nurse their young, but there are significant differences between primates and other mammals. After we reach species and sub- species, at the end of this systematic arrangement of life-forms, we find individual differences and similarities. All humans are like other humans in many important respects, but no two humans are precisely alike.

There are some parallels between human societies and life-forms. In the ancient world, for example, we find Jews and non-Jews. Both were humans, and both were ancient, which means that they were all alike in numerous ways. Our ability to say that some ancient people but not others were Jews, however, indicates that there were some distin- guishing characteristics. Moreover, Jews might be divided into sub-groups. The members of a sub-group of Jews must be like other Jews in identifiable ways, but there should also be some distinctive

---

*I am very grateful to Albert I. Baumgarten for reading this essay and discussing several points with me. These discussions were extremely helpful – not least when we continued to disagree.

[1]Jonathan Z. Smith has more than once used 'taxonomy' (often called 'systematics') in discussing religion. See recently 'A Matter of Class: Taxonomies of Religion', *HTR* 89 (1996) 387–403.

characteristics of the sub-group. The members of each sub-group of Jews shared some characteristics with other mammals, other primates, other humans, other Jews, and other members of their sub-group. And, needless to say, all the members were individuals.

The question of common and distinctive characteristics, however, which is frequently complicated in botany and biology, becomes even more complex when we consider human social groupings. There will sometimes be no one decisive feature that places people in one group or sub-group rather than another. We cannot say that all Jews were monotheists, that all Jews observed the sabbath, that all Jews avoided pork, or that all male Jews were circumcised. In the ancient world, *most* people whom we can identify as Jews *were* monotheists; most observed the sabbath in one way or other; most would not consume pork, shellfish or blood; and most Jewish males were circumcised. These were extremely *frequent* characteristics, but we could not insist on a single one of them as a completely definitive distinguishing mark. Who were Jews? In general, they were people who were born of a Jewish mother or who converted to Judaism. Another general way of defining ancient Jews fixes on perception: Jews were people who regarded themselves as Jewish and who were so regarded by other people.

I do not intend, however, to probe the topic of Lawrence Schiffman's book, *Who was a Jew?*[2] This requires considering marginal cases, such as apostates. As a practical matter, we can be much more specific about identity markers. The vast majority of Jews in the ancient world had these characteristics: (1) they believed in and worshipped the God of Israel; (2) they accepted the Hebrew Bible (often in translation) as revealing his will; (3) consequently they observed most aspects of the Mosaic law; (4) they identified themselves with the history and fate of the Jewish people. If we ignore marginal cases (such as the apostate Tiberius Julius Alexander), these four points will serve to identify ancient Jews. I insist on saying 'ancient' in order to eliminate some modern issues, such as atheism and agnosticism. In general, then, leaving aside a few difficulties and exceptions, I propose that most Jews believed in God and the Bible, thought of themselves as belonging to the people of Israel, and followed a way of life that was in general conformity with the Jewish law.

Jews sometimes formed sub-groups. Clubs and societies were a strongly marked feature of the ancient world. In fact, the voluntary formation of relatively small groups is a general human characteristic,

---

[2]Lawrence Schiffman, *Who Was a Jew? Rabbinic and Halakhic Perspectives on the Jewish-Christian Schism* (Hoboken NJ: KTAV, 1985).

and there may be an evolutionary explanation of this tendency.[3] In any case, Jews shared it. Voluntary groups necessarily have a good number of the characteristics of the surrounding society: they cannot be entirely unique. Even when they are deliberately counter-cultural societies, they still share characteristics with the larger whole of which they are a part.[4] American hippies were, and American militia are, strongly American. No matter how radical they intend to be, people cannot escape the circumstances that fashion them.

It follows that in the Graeco-Roman period Jewish sub-groups were Jewish. They shared enough of the common Jewish identity markers (e.g. belief in the God of Israel, acceptance of the Mosaic law) that a learned and perceptive student in the ancient world, had he or she found the writings of a Jewish sub-group, would have been able to recognize it as Jewish. And, in fact, today scholars have few problems deciding whether or not an ancient document was composed by a Jew.

A sub-group may form because of one over-riding issue, but if it endures, and if it is to function as a cohesive unit, it will broaden its interests. In the US today, there are a good number of one-issue voters – that is, people who will vote in an election purely on the basis of one topic, such as abortion. Some people will always vote for a candidate who wishes to make abortion illegal, no matter what other views the candidate holds. There can be an *alliance* of such people, who may band together for the limited purpose of campaigning for their cause, but I do not think that there can be a *continuing cohesive social group* in which only one conviction is common to all members. Other issues will arise. Staying with our US example, we could suppose that some people who wish to outlaw abortion would also like to ban guns, while others would favour using guns (and bombs) in support of the anti-abortionist cause. Anti-abortionists might also divide on such questions as supporting the UN, extending the North American free-trade agreement to include South America, admitting eastern European countries to NATO, and destroying all nuclear weapons. A one-issue group is inherently unstable, since disagreements on other issues will sub-divide or destroy it. If a sub-group endures, to repeat, its concerns will spread. Moreover, those concerns will to an appreciable degree reflect issues in the larger society. It is not possible for a sub-group to be so isolated that is has a whole range of concerns that are completely different from the

---

[3]Families, clans and tribes are much more ancient than nations. The tendency to form groups and clubs may reflect the need to revert to relatively small groupings. Students of baboons and chimpanzees have noted that these primates can relate to a small number of other animals.

[4]See Albert I. Baumgarten, *The Flourishing of Jewish Sects in the Maccabean Era: An Interpretation* (SJST 55, Leiden: Brill, 1997) 34, 55–8.

topics at issue in the larger group. This also means that there will be overlapping concerns among sub-groups.

I shall briefly make three more general points about sub-groups. (1) I have just been proposing that the walls around a sub-group must be at least a little porous, which means that issues in the larger group will filter into the sub-group. On the other hand, however, the sub-group can take minority positions on those issues in order to reinforce its distinctiveness over against the larger society or over against other sub-groups. (2) The longer the sub-group endures, and the more it attempts to isolate itself from the larger group, the more it has to imitate the scope of the activities, institutions and offices of the larger group. I shall give a brief example. In England, the Methodist movement remained a sub-group within the Church of England longer than was the case in America. In the New World, Methodists soon expanded into areas where there was no Anglican church. Consequently, at an early point the Methodists in America became a full church, which meant that they had to face issues ignored in the English Methodist movement, such as ordination and the sacraments. Eventually Methodism in both countries became a fully separate church, and it had to take on all or most of the roles exercised by its parent. The longer it endured, and the more separate it became, the more functions it had to assume. Its functions were still those of surrounding Christianity, but it had to establish its own particular rules regarding ordination, baptism, communion, expulsion, de-frocking, and the like.

(3) The longer a sub-group endures, and the bigger it becomes, the more diversity will emerge within it. In a small, relatively isolated sub-group, education and drill can produce considerable uniformity; but, still, human nature being what it is, diversity will emerge.

The Dead Sea Sect

I think that studying the material recovered from the caves around Qumran is just about the best activity that one can pursue who wishes to understand either ancient Judaism or sub-groups. And, it follows, it is the best thing one can do if one wants to understand sub-groups in ancient Judaism. This is true, however, only if the student of the Dead Sea Scrolls also knows enough about Jews in general and about one or more other sub-groups to put information from the Scrolls in perspective. In the years immediately after the publication of some of the major scrolls, when New Testament scholars found agreements between the Scrolls and the New Testament, they sometimes regarded these as proving the dependence of early Christianity on the Qumran community. These suggestions were sometimes based on ignorance of other Jewish literature. Views and practices that seemed to constitute striking agreements between the Scrolls and the New Testament often turn out to be common within Judaism. There are other explanations of why scholars have not infrequently misperceived the relationship between the Scrolls and the rest of Judaism, of which I shall name two: Some have thought of Judaism as *consisting of* the small parties named in Josephus, and thus have not thought of elements common to all or most Jews. Others have not considered the facts that on any given issue there can be only a few possible positions, and that on some legal issues there can be only two possible positions. These failings have sometimes led to mis-positioning Qumran vis-à-vis the Sadducees, the Pharisees, and the majority of Jews. We should expect there to be a good number of agreements between any two of the parties; such agreements do not necessarily prove a close connection between the groups as wholes. Enough agreements between two sub-groups, of course, would lead us to speak of family resemblances.[5]

It is not my purpose, however, to criticize the work of others, and especially not the efforts of scholars in the early days of research on the Scrolls. Often they had to make sense of the new finds in the absence of a broad perspective, based on sound knowledge of the rest of Judaism. It was commonly thought that rabbinic literature as a whole represented Pharisaism and that Pharisees controlled Jewish life and thought. Thus rabbinic literature equalled 'Judaism', except for a few odd groups, such as the Sadducees and a handful of apocalyptic conventicles. The main textbooks – Schürer, Bousset and Moore – did not create this view, but they certainly fostered it.[6] This general misperception of Judaism

---

[5]Since I shall not discuss the Sadducees below, I shall note here that Lawrence Schiffman has pointed out agreements between Sadducean positions according to Rabbinic literature and some of the DSS (4QMMT, 11QTemple and CD). I have not studied this issue closely enough to justify having a clear opinion, but my opening assumption would be that there might be some family resemblances between Qumran and the Sadducees, especially since it is possible that both included Zadokite priests. This seems to be more likely than the obvious alternative, namely that there were Sadducees or Sadducean documents at Qumran. See Schiffman, 'Miqsat Ma'aśeh ha-Torah and the Temple Scroll', RQ 14 (1990) 435–57; 'Pharisaic and Sadducean Halakhah in Light of the Dead Sea Scrolls. The Case of Tevul Yom', DSD 1 (1994) 285–99 and elsewhere.

[6]W. Bousset, Die Religion des Judentums im neutestamentlichen Zeitalter (Berlin 1903, frequently reprinted). G. F. Moore, Judaism in the First Centuries of the Christian Era, 3 vols. (Cambridge, MA: Harvard University Press, 1927–1930, frequently reprinted). E. Schürer, Geschichte des jüdischen Volkes im Zeitalter Jesu Christi, 2nd ed., 1886–1890; 3rd and 4th eds. 1901–1909 (frequently reprinted, once translated, and once revised and translated): Schürer, The Jewish People in the Time of Jesus Christ, 6 vols., ET of the 2nd German ed. (Edinburgh: T&T Clark, 1885–1891); Schürer, The History of the Jewish People in the Age of Jesus Christ (175 B.C.–A.D. 135), rev. and ed. by Geza Vermes, Fergus Millar and others, 3 vols. in 4 parts (Edinburgh: T&T Clark, 1973–87).

naturally skewed efforts to see the Qumran material in the right perspective.

Similarities and Differences: General Features

Now we should strive to give better accounts of the relationships between Qumran and other Jews. This paper is intended to be a small contribution to this effort. I shall begin by discussing the relationship between the Dead Sea Scrolls and other Jewish material in general terms and then turn to a few specific points. For the purposes of the first part of this discussion, I have constructed an alter ego. This alter ego has the view of human society and especially of sub-groups that I have just presented, and it also has my knowledge (or lack of knowledge) of Judaism in the late second-temple period, approximately 63 BCE to 66 CE. In two very important ways, however, the alter ego is quite different from me. It is highly intelligent and it is prescient. My More Intelligent and Prescient Alter-ego, or Professor MIPA for short, has just been told that a library has been found in a remote area near the Dead Sea, that it is from the Graeco-Roman era, and that it is the library of some Jewish group or other that seems to have lasted for more than one generation. Professor Mipa now makes the following predictions:

1. The library will reflect the *general* characteristics of ancient Jews; it will be seen (a) that the people believed in and worshipped the God of Israel; (b) that they accepted the Hebrew Bible as revealing his will; (c) that they observed most aspects of the Mosaic law; and (d) that they identified themselves with the history and fate of the Jewish people.

2. The material from the Dead Sea will reveal both agreements and disagreements with what is known of other Jewish groups, especially major groups, the Sadducees, the Pharisees and the Essenes (as described by Josephus and Philo).[7] It will contain both agreements and disagree-ments *even if* it turns out to be the library of a section of one of these three parties. If the library (for example) turns out to be Pharisaic, it nevertheless will not coincide precisely with what we learn about Pharisaism from Josephus and Rabbinic literature, since any enduring social group will contain disagreements as well as agreements. After all, other information about the Pharisees does not reveal perfect uniformity.

3. Professor Mipa's third (and last) prediction is that the library will include a range of material. This is a long and complicated prediction that will require a few pages. It is based on these views: (a) a socially cohesive group that endures cannot be only a one-issue group; (b) a

---

[7]See Baumgarten, *Jewish Sects*, 34, 55–8.

sub-group will expand its interests to include several of the topics that are important in the larger group; (c) the closer a sub-group is to isolation, the more elements of the wider society it includes. Since Qumran was fairly isolated and endured for well over a century, it must have had its own version of a lot of the aspects of Judaism in general.

In terms of genre, Professor Mipa predicts, there will be legal material, historical treatises, exegetical treatments of the Bible, and devotional material (such as prayers). There may be liturgical material (besides prayers); that is, the group may have had views about what to do when sacrificing. There might also be wisdom collections.[8] There will probably not be any book of prophecy (modelled on Isaiah or other prophetic books). Professor Mipa, having foreknowledge of the work of Rebecca Gray,[9] knows that prophecy as an activity had not ceased, but that the role and office of publicly recognized prophets had ceased, and consequently that the production of prophetic books such as Isaiah was unlikely, though not impossible.

He next predicts that there will probably be some speculative literature. Not all Jews were interested in eschatology, but if the Dead Sea group did have this interest, some of its members will have speculated about a new age. Or they could have produced non-eschatological speculations about heavenly secrets, such as the chariot of Elijah or the wheels of Ezekiel.

Of the legal material, there might be two forms: it could be like the Mishnah, arranged by topics, or like the halakhic midrashim, arranged as commentary on the legal books of the Bible. There might also be commentaries on non-legal biblical books. There will probably not be any systematic treatises of theology, and especially not philosophical theology. Philo wrote such treatises, but apart from Philo it is hard to think of any examples – unless Romans counts, and in his view it does not.

The legal views (our prescient professorial sage continues) will cover many of the topics of biblical law (topics that were common to most Jews). If the group was in contact with Gentiles, the members may have discussed idolatry. If not, probably not. The same applies to food laws. They will almost certainly have discussed the sabbath and purity. On the legal topics, they will have some positions that are at least partly different from others. But the topics, as well as many of the specific

---

[8]Since Qumran's contribution to the study of wisdom is not yet very well known, I shall cite two recent studies: Daniel J. Harrington, *Wisdom Texts from Qumran* (London: Routledge, 1996); John J. Collins, *Jewish Wisdom in the Hellenistic Age* (Louisville, KN: Westminster John Knox Press, 1997), ch. 7.

[9]Rebecca Gray, *Prophetic Figures in Late Second Temple Jewish Palestine. The Evidence from Josephus* (Oxford: Oxford University Press, 1993).

issues (not necessarily the conclusions), will be those known from other Jewish material. The issues of the larger society will have filtered into the sub-group, and there will also be overlaps with other sub-groups, which will have dealt with the same issues. (In this paragraph, Professor Mipa applies predictions 1 and 2 above to legal issues.)

Though the library will probably not have any systematic theological treatises, there will be theology in it, partly expressed and partly implied. We shall learn from the newly discovered literature something about God, and possibly about angels, the afterlife (or lack thereof), providence, and freewill – that is, the topics mentioned by Josephus when he discusses the Jewish parties, plus a few others.[10] We shall find the theology of the Bible in some form or other: grace, election, love of God, repentance,[11] punishment, atonement, treatment of other human beings, and the like. There will not be one narrow but predominating theological conviction, such as those postulated by Protestant scholars when they discuss the ancient world. Here I must digress to explain Professor Mipa's point.

One of the faults of Protestant scholarship has been the retrojection of the issues of the Protestant reformation into earlier history, and the allied assumption that ancient religious groups formed around a theological slogan that arose from the reformation or that was prominent in reformation polemics. Many Protestant NT scholars are fundamentalists at heart, and so these views are often supported by one-line quotations from the New Testament. According to the gospel of John, the law was given through Moses, but grace and truth came through Jesus Christ (1:17). This tells us all we really need to know about ancient Judaism and Christianity, namely, that Jews believed in law, that Christians believed in grace, and that the two are opposed to each other. Other NT texts help support this erroneous and regrettable view. Thus Paul's attack on other Christians in Galatians, we are often told, was really an attack on Jewish and specifically Pharisaic soteriology, which held the legalistic view that individual humans must save themselves by doing more good than evil deeds. Christianity is based on love, grace and faith, and it excludes self-righteous works. When scholars (not necessarily Protestants, since the issues as stated by Protestant biblical scholars have been very influential) who dreamt that ancient religions really divided into these categories read the Dead Sea Scrolls, they responded as one would expect. One scholar, writing on the *Thanksgiving Hymns* (1QH), proposed that the view of Qumran

---

[10]*J. W.* 2.119–166; *Ant.* 18.11–25.

[11]The noun 'repentance' (*teshûvah*) is not a biblical word, but the idea is present in various ways, including use of the verb *shûv*, 'return'.

was completely different from the Pharisaic idea of 'justification by human works'.[12] That is, this scholar found reformation theology (justification by grace) in the Qumran *Hymns* and contrasted it with Pharisaism, which he supposed was organized around a slogan from Protestant polemics, justification by works. A different scholar, taking into account more of the Qumran literature, wrote that we should 'allow ... for different "philosophies" within Qumran itself', the two philosopies being 'a legalistic puritanism or perfectionism' and belief in the 'doctrine of "grace" or divine help'.[13] In this scholar's mind, 'grace' and 'works' are competing and incompatible theologies, and what was surprising about the Scrolls was that the competition between them went on within Qumran; legalism is found in 1QS (*The Rule of the Community*), grace in 1QH.

Anyone, such as Professor Mipa, who had actually studied the Jewish material that was known prior to the discovery of the Scrolls, would have known that these are not two contradictory theologies, and that all forms of Judaism – and, for that matter, all forms of Christianity, including especially Pauline Christianity – combine the view that God saves by grace with the view that humans are accountable for their deeds.

I return now to Professor Mipa's general prediction: the newly discovered sub-group will not have had only one theological idea, and it will not have divided from other Jews because it accepted or renounced one of the slogans of the Protestant reformation.

Professor Mipa would make all of these and other guesses, too numerous to be listed here, because he had studied all the other Jewish material of the period and because he knew that an enduring group would have its own version of many of the topics, themes, literary genres, etc. that characterized the larger society. Moreover, since the Qumran sub-group was geographically remote, it could be assumed to duplicate Jewish society more than would have been the case had it been in close contact with the larger group. It might have its own priests, Levites, judges, etc. The genres and themes would have their specific characteristics, but they would be generally like those in the rest of Palestinian Judaism. The sub-group cannot have invented everything. In fact, it cannot have invented very much that was not available in the broader culture. Most people are about as inventive as the folk who imagined new beasts, such as a horse with a single horn or a creature half lion and half eagle.

When we read the Scrolls, we find that Professor Mipa, whose views

---

[12]M. Delcor, *Les Hymnes de Qumran (Hodayot)* (Paris: Letouzey et Ani, 1962) 48.
[13]Matthew Black, *The Scrolls and Christian Origins* (New York: Scribner, 1961) 124–6.

were entirely based on his knowledge of other Jewish material, was mostly right.[14] This establishes that there was a lot in common between the group at Qumran and the rest of Judaism, and even more in common between the Dead Sea sect and the rest of Palestinian Judaism. We also know, at least in general, that Qumran was in some or many ways distinctive. Now we bid adieu to Professor Mipa and take up a few issues in more detail.

Five Cases

Since the Qumran community was a sub-group, there were many features of belief and practice that set the members apart from other Jews, even though the topics were the same. I shall comment briefly on five points, three that are legal and practical, and two that are theological.

Temple, priests, sacrifices and festivals

Virtually all Jews believed that God required sacrifices, that he had specified that they must be offered in the Temple in Jerusalem, that he appointed hereditary priests, and that he designated certain days during certain seasons as times of festivals. The Qumran sectarians entirely agreed. They remained true, however, to the high priestly family mentioned in the Bible, the Zadokites, which was overthrown by the Hasmonean family as a consequence of the successful revolt against the Seleucids.[15] Moreover, the sectarians thought that festivals should never fall on the sabbath, and to accomplish this end they followed a calendar that was different from the one accepted by other Jews. The upshot was that the community at Qumran did not worship at the Temple in Jerusalem. It is this complex of disagreements on common topics that

[14]A few of his predictions are not supported by the finds: for example, there are no halakhic midrashim; historical treatises after the pattern of 1 and 2 Kings are absent, though CD does have a kind of history of the sect and there are historical allusions in 1QpHab and elsewhere. I am leaving out of account retellings of biblical stories, such as are found in the Genesis apocryphon and parts of 4Q382 (DJD XIII 363–416).

[15]The Zadokites are prominent in 1QS, 1QSa, 1QSb, 4QFl, and CD. They are missing, however, from fragments that parallel parts of 1QS (4QSᵇ and 4QSᵈ), which raises the question of whether or not at Qumran Zadokites always had the same position as they have in 1QS. Geza Vermes first called attention to these fragments ('Preliminary Remarks on Unpublished Fragments of the Community Rule from Qumran Cave 4', *JJS* 42 (1991) 250–5). Albert Baumgarten has suggested that originally the sect was egalitarian and that the emphasis on governance by Zadokites represents a stage when leaders wished partially to replace egalitarianism with hierarchy ('The Zadokite Priests at Qumran: A Reconsideration', *DSD* 4 [1997] 137–56).

made the sect *exclusivist*. Though the sectarians agreed in general on temple, priests, sacrifices and festivals, they disagreed to such an extent that they did not have community of worship with other Jews. This is a fact of enormous importance for understanding the unique place of the Qumranians in second-temple Judaism.[16] They cut themselves off from the way in which Jews had always worshipped God and from one of the main sources of world-wide Jewish solidarity.[17]

The Sabbath

The word 'sabbath' occurs in pre-exilic biblical material, but the exile added a lot to its observance. Nehemiah forbade buying and selling in Jerusalem on the sabbath, even by Gentiles (Neh 13:15–22). This seems to have been a previously unknown rule. As everyone knows, sabbath law posed a problem during the wars against the Seleucid kingdom, since the idea had arisen that Jews should not fight on the sabbath[18] – a view that never appears in the stories of warfare in the days of the judges and the pre-exilic kings. Josephus confirms the fact that warfare on the sabbath was a problem and required a special rule: Jews could respond to direct but not to indirect attacks on the sabbath. This emerges from the story of Pompey's conquest of Jerusalem.[19] Travelling and carrying were also restricted on the sabbath.[20] The Pharisees created the idea of 'erûbîn, which permitted some families to carry pots and thus dine together on the sabbath, and which simultaneously shows that most Jews would not carry dishes outside of the house on the day of rest.[21] The Rabbis and others debated whether or not minor cures were permissible on the sabbath,[22] and the Pharisees and early Rabbis also worried about how to prepare food if a festival day – which was a

---

[16]On this vital point, CD (*The Covenant of Damascus*) stands apart from the other Scrolls. If (as many scholars think) the DSS are Essene, CD comes from a group that was not monastic (note the reference to a member's child in 11:11), that lived in towns and cities (and possibly near Gentiles, 11:14f.), and that took offerings to the temple and sacrificed there (11:17–20). CD is considered more fully below.

[17]See the fuller discussion in my *Judaism: Practice and Belief* (London: SCM Press; Philadelphia: Trinity Press International, 1992), 53, 352, 362f. (hereafter cited as *P&B*). See further, Baumgarten, *Jewish Sects* 68f.

[18]1 Macc 2:29–41.

[19]*J. W.* 1.145–7 (cf. Dio Cassius 37.16.2f.). See further *J. W.* 1.157–60; 2.517; *Ant.* 13.252; 14.237.

[20]The prohibition of carrying predates the exile, being first attributed to Jeremiah, who banned carrying pots outside of one's house on the sabbath (Jer 17:21–24). Limitations on sabbath travel are discussed below.

[21]See *m. Erub.*, especially 6:2, which reflects the Sadducees' opposition to Pharisaic practice.

[22]For Rabbinic views on minor cures, see *m. Šabb.* 14:3f.; *t. Šabb.* 12:8–14. It is probable that these passages are from the second century, but the topic was earlier; see n. 24.

semi-sabbath – immediately preceded the seventh day of the week.[23] Thus we know that there was a lot of discussion of sabbath law within Judaism during the Graeco-Roman period.[24]

Consequently we are not surprised when we see a range of prohibitions in the *Damascus Document*. The following summary is provided by Geza Vermes:

> The sectary was not only to abstain from labour 'on the sixth day from the moment when the sun's orb is distant by its own fullness from the gate (wherein it sinks)' (CD 10:15–16), he was not even to speak about work. Nothing associated with money or gain was to interrupt his Sabbath of rest (CD 10:18–19). No member of the Covenant of God was to go out of his house on business on the Sabbath. ... He could not cook. He could not pick and eat fruit and other edible things 'lying in the fields'. He could not draw water and carry it away, but must drink where he found it (CD 10:22–23). He could not strike his beast or reprimand his servant (CD 11:6, 12). He could not carry a child, wear perfume or sweep up the dust in his house (CD 11:10–11). He could not assist his animals to give birth or help them if they fell into a pit; he could, however, pull a man out of water or fire with the help of a ladder or rope (CD 11:12–14, 16–17).[25]

It is instructive to note that the *Damascus Document* also prohibits any sacrifice on the sabbath except the sabbath offering (CD 11:17–18). That is, when a festival fell on the sabbath, only the sabbath offerings were to be sacrificed, not the festival offerings as well. We noted above that at Qumran a different calendar was observed, so that festivals and

---

[23]See *m. Beṣa* (or *Yôm Tôv*) and *t. Yôm Tôv*. Much of the material in the early chapters of *m. Beṣa* is attributed to the Houses of Hillel and Shammai. The legal problem is this: on a 'festival day' (days of 'holy convocation', Lev 23:7f., 21, 24, 27, 35f., 39, or 'solemn assembly', Exod 12:16), work was prohibited, except for preparation of food to be eaten that day (Exod 12:16). Since on a festival day people could not prepare food for the next day, and since sabbath food had to be prepared the previous day, it was hard to know what to do about sabbath food when a festival day came on Friday.

[24]Although *m. Šabbat* reveals that sabbath rules were much discussed after the destruction of the Temple, all the topics in the present paragraph can be dated before 70 CE. Prohibitions of buying, selling and carrying pots are biblical; the prohibition of warfare is at least as early as the Hasmonean period; there is a limitation on travel in CD10:21; *m. 'Erub.* 6:2 relates a story about Rn. Simeon b. Gamaliel (who was active before and during the first revolt) and the Sadducees; discussion of minor cures on the sabbath appears in CD 11:10 and in the Gospels; the problem of festival days that fell on Friday is debated by the Houses (or Schools) of Hillel and Shammai (e.g. *m. Beṣa* 2:1). The Houses are usually dated *c.* 90–110, the period in which R. Joshua and R. Eliezer the Great flourished, but they could not have invented very many of the topics that they debated (because of the general limits of human inventiveness). The related problem of festival days that fell *on* the sabbath is a fairly major point in the Scrolls, and the legal problem (see the previous note) of how to prepare food for the sabbath if a festival day fell on Friday would have been an important issue prior to 70.

[25]Geza Vermes, *The Dead Sea Scrolls. Qumran in Perspective* (London: Collins, 1977) 101.

sabbath would not overlap. CD's prohibition of festival sacrifices on the sabbath points in the same direction.[26]

The sabbath rules from CD allow us to illustrate some of the earlier remarks about overlapping topics among groups. CD prohibits festival sacrifices when the festival falls on the sabbath, while Rabbinic literature attributes to Hillel the decision to sacrifice the Passover lamb even when Passover fell on the sabbath.[27] CD prohibits pulling animals out of a pit on the sabbath, while according to Luke 14:5 Jesus found general agreement with the view that even on the sabbath an owner should rescue his animal if it fell into a pit. Thus topics that were current in Palestinian Judaism also appear in CD. The specific conclusions of CD are not the same as the conclusions of other Jews, and in general they are stricter, but the topics fit perfectly. I should again point out (as in n. 16) that the relationship between the *Damascus Document* and the Dead Sea sect is a somewhat vexed question. We cannot settle it comprehensively, but we shall return to it in the last section of this paper.

Purity

Here there are three sub-topics. The first is *immersion*. From at least the days of the later Hasmoneans, either some, many or all Palestinian Jews immersed in order to rid themselves of the impurities mentioned in Leviticus 12 and 15, and also as part of the purification required in Numbers 19.[28] The impurities in question are childbirth and various forms of contact: with semen, menstrual blood, other discharges from the genitals (e.g. those caused by miscarriage or gonorrhoea), and with corpses. Though the purpose of the pools at Qumran has been debated, there is no doubt in my mind that some of them were for the purpose of religious purification.[29] The pools are neither bathtubs, cisterns nor

---

[26]CD does not presuppose the Qumranian calendar, but it shows the same desire not to allow festival sacrifices on the sabbath. The sabbath rules of CD 10 and 11 are supported by fragments from the Qumran caves. See DJD XVIII: *Qumrân Grotte 4*, vol. XIII (ed. Joseph Baumgarten; 1996) 160f. (4Q270 Frg. 6 v), 180–82 (4Q271 Frg. 5 i).

[27]*T. Pisha'* 4:12f.

[28]On immersion pools (in rabbinic Hebrew, *miqva'ot*), see Sanders, *Jewish Law from Jesus to the Mishnah* (London: SCM Press; Philadelphia: Trinity Press International 1990) 31f.; 38; 105; 214–27 (hereafter *JLJM*); *P&B* 222–9 and plates.

[29]In support of this view, we may note (1) that 1QS 5:13 mentions 'entering the water' before partaking of the Purity (the Pure Meal); (2) that CD refers to pools of water large enough for immersion, which were used for purification (10:11–13); (3) that immersion is implied in 4Q512 Col. X Fr. 11, Col. VIII Fr. 27, Col. VII line 5, and Col. VIII Fr. 16 (as restored by Joseph Baumgarten) and (4) that Josephus says that the Essenes bathed their *bodies* before meals (*J. W.* 2.129), which implies immersion. Several other references to water in the

swimming pools; therefore they are immersion pools.[30] Some of them –
like some *miqva'ôt* found elsewhere in Palestine – have ways of
separating the people entering the pool from those leaving, which fits
perfectly with the view that they were for purification. The Qumran
pools are like other immersion pools in two important respects: a lot of
the total space of the pool is taken up by steps; the pools are cut into
bedrock, and so cannot be drained. There is a lot of variation among
immersion pools, but the Qumranian pools share these fundamental
characteristics with other pools of the period. As in the case of sabbath
law, there were common features and some differences.

The second subject under the heading 'purity' is *purity and eating*.
This is a very large and complicated topic. I shall try to be brief, but I
shall give it more space than the other topics receive. We first note that
the Bible requires purity when eating holy food: (a) The priests in the
Temple ate some of the sacrifices while on duty, obviously in a state of
purity (Num 18:8–10). (b) The priests could bring home some of the
sacrificial meat, which they and their families ate in purity (Num 18:11).
(c) Similarly, when the priests ate first-fruits and tithes, they and their

---

Scrolls might be only metaphorical (e.g. 1QS 3:4f; 3:8f.). The problems of using Josephus on
the Essenes when discussing the activities of the community at Qumran, like the problem of
using CD, will be discussed below. On the fragments (3 above) see Joseph M. Baumgarten,
'The Purification Rituals in *DJD* 7', *The Dead Sea Scrolls. Forty Years of Research*, ed.
Devorah Dimant and Uriel Rappaport (STDJ 10; Leiden: Brill, 1992) 199–209, here 201f. The
crucial phrase is 'while standing': after bathing, the one being purified prays 'while standing',
which is best understood as meaning 'before leaving the immersion pool'. 'While standing' is
clear in 4Q512 Col. VIII fr. 27, and Baumgarten proposes this restoration in Col. X Fr. 11. In
Col. VII line 5, the relevant phrase is 'and prays there', that is, in the water. (In Baumgarten,
p. 202, the reference to 4Q502 is an error for 512.)

[30]Some scholars are sceptical about the identification of stepped pools as immersion pools,
partly because they have not compared the stepped pools with bathtubs and cisterns, and
partly (I suspect) because they have not appreciated how much work was involved in digging
a pit in bedrock. Bathtubs were small and stood above the ground, so that they could be
emptied. Cisterns – which were essential to life – were dug in bedrock. They were large
caverns, with a very small opening, from which people drew water by using a rope and bucket.
People did not walk down into their drinking water. Thus stepped pools were neither cisterns
nor bathtubs, which leaves immersion as their purpose. The pools vary a good deal in size, but
a typical pool was 12 ft. × 7 ft. at the surface, and about 7 ft. deep (*c.* 3 m. × 2 m. × 2 m.).
Steps usually went all the way across one end and all the way to the bottom, occupying
perhaps 25–30% of the total space. Immersion pools are not infrequently found immediately
next to a cistern, while in the houses of the aristocrats in upper Jerusalem they are sometimes
part of a bathing complex that also contains a bathtub. Only a strong motive could account
for digging such large pits in bedrock – a need almost as important as having water in the dry
season. I have frequently dug holes 2 ft. × 2 ft. × 2 ft. in clay, using hardened steel (*c.* .6 m³).
Scholars who believe that the stepped pools in Palestine were bathtubs should sometime try
digging an 8 cubic foot hole in clay – which is child's play compared to a 588 cubic foot hole
in bedrock (12 cubic metres), using ancient iron. On cisterns, bathtubs and immersion pools,
see further *JLJM* 216f.

families dined in purity (Num 18:12–20; 20:26).[31] (d) All Jews observed purity rules when eating sacrificial food and second tithe (the Deuteronomic tithe, set aside by farmers to be eaten in purity in Jerusalem).[32]

This list makes it clear that in common Judaism purity when eating was usually connected with the Temple. Tithes and first-fruits could be contributed apart from the Temple, as the strong Rabbinic interest in tithing, much of which can be dated to the second century, makes clear (see the tractates *Demai* and *Maʿaseroth*). But ordinary people ate in purity only during the festivals, when they had some meat from the sacrifices as well as their own second tithe. Since the Qumranians did not worship at the Temple, one might imagine that they never ate in purity. On the other hand, this was an extremist group, and so one might also imagine that they made up new purity rules, possibly including eating in purity when not in Jerusalem, and observed them. The latter is the case.

The *Community Rule* several times refers to 'the Purity', which included food and possibly the dishes and vessels. Thus there was a pure meal. Most scholars take 'the Purity' to be the average, everyday meal of the sect, and they also equate the daily meal with the meal described in 1QS 6:4f. I have argued elsewhere that these equations may not be correct.[33] Here I mention just two points: (a) In the section on punishments in 1QS, exclusion from the Purity (which I shall hereafter call the Pure Meal) is distinguished from a reduction in the food allowance. (So also 4QS^g. See Philip S. Alexander and Geza Vermes, *Qumran Cave 4. Serekh Ha-Yahad and two Related Texts* (Oxford: Clarendon Press, 1998) pp. 177–8.) A member of the community, for example, could be excluded from the Pure Meal for a year and also lose one-fourth of his 'bread', that is, his basic daily sustenance (1QS 6:24f.). This might mean that there were two daily communal meals at Qumran: one the Pure Meal, eaten by full members in good standing, the other a common meal eaten by probationers and members who were being punished. But the simplest explanation is that the Pure Meal was a special meal, rather than the daily meal of members. (b) The meal described in 1QS 6:4f.

---

[31]I use 'first-fruits' here as a general term including the first produce, first-born animals, etc. The tithe that priests and their families ate is called 'a tithe of the tithe' in Num 18:26 and 'heave-offering of tithe' by the Rabbis. In theory, first tithe went to the Levites, who in turn tithed to the priests. On purity rules as applied to food eaten by priests and their families, see further *P&B* 107–12, 146–57, 221f.

[32]E.g. Lev 15:31 (purity required for entering the Temple); Num 9:10–12 (participants in the Passover festival could not have corpse impurity); Deut 26:14 (purity when handling second tithe); Josephus, *Against Apion* 2.198 (purifications were prescribed 'in view of the sacrifices'). On ordinary people, food and purity, see further *P&B* 71f., 113, 133, 134, 157.

[33]*P&B* 353–6.

appears to be a festival meal. The passage mentions the 'first-fruits of bread' *or* the 'new wine'. This seems to be a general description that covers two types of 'first-fruits', either new bread or new wine. While we cannot achieve absolute certainty, I am inclined to identify the Pure Meal with the meal of 1QS 6:4f. (a festival meal) and to distinguish this from the ordinary daily meal. In this case, exclusion from the Pure Meal for a year would mean that the member who was being punished was excluded from a small number of special meals, while reduction of the food allowance would apply to all of his meals.

Even if accepted, this proposal does not prove that the Qumranians did not eat their daily meals in some sort of purity. On the contrary, it appears that they did. A fragmentary text from Cave 4 discusses the case of a man who has a flux or discharge from his genitals (a *zav*) and who is therefore impure for seven days (Lev 15:1–15). The Bible requires such a man to wait for seven days after the flow stops, bathe and wash his clothes (15:13). The Qumran text (4Q514) states that he may not eat until he has begun to be purified (line 4).[34] It then repeats the point by saying that he may not eat while he is is in his 'first impurity' (line 7), which is to be understood as 'the *initial* impurity of a person "who has not begun to cleanse himself" '.[35] The text allows the man to eat 'his bread' after he has begun purification by bathing and washing in water (lines 6, 9). The standard rule of purification was that it required washing and the setting of the sun (though Lev. 15.13 does not mention the setting of the sun). It appears that the sectarian who had a genital discharge immersed on the first day (rather than waiting seven days) and was pure enough to eat his ordinary meal, called his 'bread', even before the sun set. The text makes it clear that the man would remain partially impure for seven days, but it does not indicate whether or not immersion was required before each meal.

Joseph Baumgarten has pointed out the similarity of the Qumranian view in 4Q514 to the Rabbinic view of the *tevûl yôm*, an impure person who had immersed but upon whom the sun had not yet set.[36] Such a person was partially pure and therefore did not convey impurity to the same degree as did one who had not yet immersed (see e.g. *m. T. Yom* 4:1). The Rabbis, it should be noted, did not require people to be even half-pure in order to eat their ordinary food or conduct any other normal daily activities. Prior to the publication of this Scroll, we had known of the existence of a group stricter than the Pharisees or Rabbis,

---

[34]For the text, see *Discoveries in the Judaean Desert VII: Qumrân Grotte 4*, vol. III (ed. Maurice Baillet; Oxford: Oxford University Press, 1982) 295–8.

[35]Joseph M. Baumgarten, 'The Purification Rituals in *DJD* 7' (n. 29), p. 205 n. 10.

[36]See the previous note.

the 'morning immersers', who criticized the Pharisees (*perûshîm*) because they pronounced the divine name in the morning without immersion (*t. Yad.* 2.20). We now have certain knowledge of a pre-70 Jewish group that exceeded the Pharisees' concern with purity and food by a wide margin.

Thus it appears that the Qumranians ate all of their meals in some degree of purity. I think it likely that partially pure sectarians could eat *only* their basic daily allotment of food (their 'bread'), not the festival meal that is described in 1QS 6:4f. The community seems to have been highly conscious of degrees of rank, whether based on seniority or on knowledge and ability (e.g. 1QS 2:19–23). It agrees with this that its leaders would have allowed the partially pure person some privileges, especially his daily bread, but have reserved others, such as 'the Purity' or festival meals, for the entirely pure. Whatever the correct resolution of this question concerning the Pure Meal and the meal of 1QS 6:4f., we see that, like other Jews, the sectarians required purity before some meals. They may have been almost unique in requiring some degree of purity before all meals.

Many scholars, however, have proposed that the Pharisees ate all their meals in purity, and they have more-or-less equated the Pharisees and the Qumranians in this respect. A frequently repeated version of this opinion is that the Pharisees treated their own tables like the altar and ate in the same state of purity as did the priests in the temple.[37] I wish here to offer a digression on Pharisaic views about eating in purity. There are three reasons for including this discussion: it provides the opportunity to give concrete examples of what it would mean to eat food in purity; it allows clarification of an often misunderstood topic; it will help us put the Qumranian group in perspective.

There are two faults with the view just cited (that the Pharisees ate in purity in imitation of the priests in the Temple). The first is that it would have been impossible for lay people, and especially married lay people, routinely to eat in full priestly purity. Since most purifications require washing *and* the setting of the sun (see Leviticus 15), and since contact with semen results in impurity, married people could eat in purity only if they had sexual intercourse early enough to immerse before sunset. If a farmer and his wife had sexual relations after sunset, they would be impure all the next day and therefore should neither handle nor eat food. On a small farm, this would be difficult – to put it mildly. Moreover, when the wife was menstruating, or during the period after childbirth, she would be forbidden to prepare the food or eat with her

---

[37]E.g. Jacob Neusner, *Judaism. The Evidence of the Mishnah* (Chicago: University of Chicago Press, 1981) 226. For brief discussions of representative scholars, see *JLJM* 152–66.

husband. He would have to grind, mix, knead and bake, as well as plow, sow, hoe, harvest etc. – which is not humanly possible. Extended families would not solve the problem, since if several women lived in the same house, they would probably all menstruate at the same time. Actually, if Pharisees could not eat with menstruants, their domestic situation would be even more difficult than just described. As Talmudists have observed, eating in purity would require that a menstruant (or a woman after childbirth) be expelled from the house[38] (that is, from a small house; a sufficiently large house could have separate quarters).

Even if male Pharisees had been willing to expel menstruants from the house (and no evidence suggests that they were) it would still have been impossible for Pharisees and their familes to solve all the purity problems of daily life: how to have sexual relations, how to find more hours in the day so that men could prepare the food, and where to build the housing that would hold one-fourth of the post-puberty, pre-menopausal wives of Pharisees at any given time.[39]

The question of the possibility of perpetual purity can be clarified by considering the priests and their families. They did not eat all their meals in purity. Priests were on duty only two weeks out of every year, plus extra service during the festivals. As we have already noted, when serving in the Temple priests ate some of the meat from sacrifices. They could also take other categories of meat home from the Temple, in which case they and their families had to eat it in purity. Further, they received some food from the offerings of tithes and first-fruits, which they and their families also ate in purity.[40] These three categories supplied only part of their food; we have no idea how much, since we cannot quantify any of this free food. In any case, whenever they had sacred food to eat, they could eat it in purity without too much inconvenience. Priests were not farmers, and so they did not have to worry about some problems that would have faced Pharisaic farmers. The priestly families could simply immerse before nightfall and then eat tithes, etc. after nightfall. They could have non-sacred food during the course of the day, and so would not have to fast even when they were to eat sacred food in the evening. Lay people would have followed the same routine when eating sacrificial meat and second tithe during

---

[38]See I. M. Ta-Shma, 'Niddah', *Encyclopaedia Judaica* 12, cols. 1141–8, quoted in *JLJM* 155f.

[39]In theory, Pharisees could have required members to immerse after sexual relations and then have allowed them to handle and eat food when partially pure (see the discussion of the *tebûl yôm*, above). But no such rules can be attributed to the Pharisees or later to the Rabbis.

[40]On the categories of sacred food eaten by priests, see *P&B* 107–12, 146–57, 221f.

the festivals. Saying that the Pharisees always ate in purity 'like the priests', therefore, actually requires them to outdo the priests by a very large margin, since the priests by no means always ate in purity.

Secondly, there is no evidence that the Pharisees wished to eat all their food in priestly purity. My review of the rabbinic passages on the Pharisees that Jacob Neusner used in his work on this topic revealed that he had misinterpreted them.[41] Most of the rabbinic passages on handling food in purity refer either to food that is destined for the priesthood or to second tithe, which lay people ate in purity (as previously noted). The rabbinic passages on the Pharisees *distinguish* how tithe and second tithe were to be handled from how ordinary food was to be handled, thus making it clear that lay Pharisees ordinarily ate food that was not handled in purity. There is in fact *no* evidence that indicates that Pharisees wanted to eat in priestly purity, or that they wished to eat only food that would be suitable for priests – to say nothing of the much higher state of purity that was required of priests and their food when they ate in the Temple. We should especially note the complete absence of material discussing the topics that the Pharisees/Rabbis would have had to discuss if they ate their ordinary meals in purity: what to do about sexual intercourse; where to sequester menstruants and nursing mothers; what to do about a chair on which a menstruant or nursing mother had sat, or the bed on which she lay; what to do with the farm when the Pharisaic family went to Jerusalem for a week to be purified after attending a funeral.

Unlike the scholars who have proposed that the Pharisees lived like priests in the Temple, the Pharisees themselves were well aware of gradations in the purity of food and the people who ate it: (a) At the high end there was food eaten by priests in the priests' court of the Temple. (b) Next came the priests' portion of first tithe (see n. 31) and first-fruits, which were eaten in purity by priests and their families outside the Temple. During the festivals, lay people ate sacrificial food and second tithe in the same state of purity. (c) The Pharisees ate in a higher level of purity than the ordinary people, but it was not equal to that of the priests, even outside the Temple. (d) At the bottom end, most lay people observed no purity laws in connection with their own food (except during the festivals). I shall expand on (c) briefly by giving two examples of Pharisaic practice (continuing to rely on the passages chosen by Neusner).[42] First, they tried to avoid inadvertently contracting corpse impurity. They did

---

[41]Jacob Neusner, *Rabbinic Traditions about the Pharisees Before 70*, 3 vols. (Leiden: Brill, 1971); *A History of the Mishnaic Law of Purities*, 22 vols. (Leiden: Brill, 1974–77). My analysis is in *JLJM* 131–254; more briefly in *P&B* 431–40.

[42]These examples come from *JLJM* 131–254. I have omitted the probability that Pharisees tried to minimize contracting *midras* impurity (for a brief account, see *P&B* 436f.).

not follow the priestly rule, namely to contract corpse impurity only when a member of their close family died, but they did try to avoid some cases of corpse impurity. I regard this as a 'minor gesture' towards a higher level of purity than that of the ordinary person. Secondly, since the Shammaites and Hillelites disagreed about proper procedure in handwashing before sabbath and possibly festival meals,[43] we may suppose that the Pharisees washed their hands before such meals. This should also be classed as a minor gesture. The Bible does not require anyone to wash hands before any meal, but by the first century this was a known practice within Judaism, possibly being more widespread in the Diaspora than in Palestine.[44] The Pharisees seem to have washed hands only before sabbath or festival meals. In any case, handwashing does not result in priestly purity, but is a token gesture towards purity. My study of the numerous Pharisaic passages on purity indicates that *m. Hag* 2:7 (on purity of garments) applies to purity in general, including purity when eating. According to this passage, different groups maintained various degrees of purity. From low to high, the list reads: ordinary people, Pharisees, those who eat heave-offering (priests and their families outside the Temple), those who eat Holy Things (priests inside the temple), those who occupy themselves with the sin-offering water (required for the removal of corpse impurity).[45] In general, we may say that the Pharisees intended to attain a higher level of purity than the ordinary lay person. As noted above, they did *not* require a person to immerse and therefore be half-pure before eating ordinary food. The Pharisaic minor gestures towards purity were not the equivalent of the Qumranian requirement of immersion, discussed above, which was that the impure sectarian should take the first step towards full purity as defined in the Bible before eating ordinary food. Nor did the Pharisaic gestures come close to making Pharisees as pure as priests in the Temple.

We now return to the question of purity and food at Qumran. I hope that the digression on the Pharisees illustrates what eating in purity would require and also makes it clear that there was a range of possibilities regarding food and purity. If the Qumranians were a male monastic group, several of the possible sources of impurity were

---

[43]They argued about when to mix the cup and when to wash the hands before meals on sabbaths and other holy days (*m. Ber.* 8:2,4; *t. Ber.* 5:25–8). Here I have in mind not meals that included meat from sacrifice, which required full purity, but meals on festival days when the family had no sacrifical meat to eat – for example, when the family was not able to go to Jerusalem for a festival.

[44]See *JLJM* 30, 39f., 228–31 (Pharisaic passages), 260–63 (Diaspora).

[45]*Hatta't* here refers to the mixture of water and the ashes of the red heifer, needed to purify the corpse-impure: see Chanoch Albeck, *Sishah Sidre Mishnah (The Six Orders of the Mishnah)*, 6 vols. (Bialik Institute: Jerusalem and Tel Aviv, 1958–1959) 2. 396. This usage is established by *m. Para*; see e.g. 4:1; 10:1.

eliminated: semen (except for nocturnal emissions), menstrual blood, other flows from female genitalia (e.g. miscarriage) and childbirth. This would leave them with the following sources of impurity: nocturnal emission (Lev 15:16f.); an abnormal emission from the penis (a *zav*, Lev 15:2–15); corpses (Num 19). It is quite possible that they added some sources of impurity, such as defecation.[46] 1QS, unfortunately, says little about sources of impurity and means of purification. We have seen that the Qumranians used immersion pools, but was this all? Ordinarily, two of the impurities just listed – abnormal emission from the penis and corpse-impurity – required the temple and priests. With regard to the former, Lev 15:14 requires the offering of two birds. With regard to the latter, Num 19 requires a priest and the ashes of a red heifer. Since the Qumranians could not have brought sacrifices and could not have accepted purification at the hands of a Jerusalem priest, what did they do?

I have been unable to find any text that addresses the problem of sacrifices for purification. We know that the sectarians held the theological view that their community and its activities atoned for sin (e.g. 1QS 8:3f.), and we may suppose that this view eliminated the need for sacrifices of purification – especially since the few purification texts that we have contain references to atoning as well as cleansing.[47] We saw above a fragmentary text (4Q514) that gives part of the ritual for purifying a *zav*, and we must assume that at the end of the text the man is considered pure even though he did not take the required two birds to the temple. Support for this comes from another fragmentary text from the same cave, 4Q512.[48] This is the ritual for the purification of a man who had contracted corpse impurity. Col. 12 (fragments 1–6) does not contain any complete sentences, but we find the words 'on the third day' (line 1, cf. Num 19:19), 'holy ash' (line 3, referring to the ashes of the red heifer, Num 19:9f.), and 'sprinkle' (line 7, as in Num 19:19). We do not know who sprinkles,[49] but it is evident that the sect carried out a version of the ritual of the red heifer, its burning, and the use of its ashes. In this text, by the way, the themes of atonement and sanctification are marked (atonement, lines 3, 14; sanctification, line 10).

We conclude from this that the Qumranians had their own means of

---

[46]According to Josephus (*J. W.* 2.148f.), Essenes chose remote areas for defecation, and afterward they washed themselves 'as if defiled'. On defecation, see further below, at n. 51 and on pp. 36–41.

[47]Joseph Baumgarten, 'The Purification Rituals in *DJD* 7' 199–201, 207f.

[48]For the text, see DJD VII: *Qumrân Grotte 4*, vol. III (ed. Baillet) 272; see also J. Baumgarten (previous note).

[49]Similarly in 11QTemple 49:18 'they sprinkle', and in 50:14 'he sprinkles'. Num 19:18f. specifies only a 'pure person' as the sprinkler.

removing all the biblical impurities, including those that ordinarily required the temple and its priests. They seem not to have had their own sacrifices of animals and birds, but they did have their own ashes of a red heifer, which they used in removing corpse-impurity. One assumes that one of their own priests killed and burnt the heifer. We have also learned that the sectarians required the impure to begin purification before they were allowed to eat their daily rations. This is a much more ambitious requirement than those followed by the Pharisees.

I have dedicated so much space to food and purity because it is the legal topic that is least understood – for the very good reason that it is more complex than most other legal topics (such as sabbath law). I shall summarize my view of food and purity at Qumran: 1QS 6:2–5 refers to a special periodic meal, not to every meal; we do not know what purity rules were followed when the sectarians ate 'the Purity', but I think it likely that they required full purity; the impure had to begin purification before they could eat their daily bread; their own rituals were adequate to remove impurities that ordinarily required the Temple; the Qumranians, like the Pharisees, had their own distinctive policies with regard to the common subject of food and purity, and they were here as elsewhere much more radical.

The third sub-topic under purity is the *purity of Jerusalem*. In general, Jews thought that Jerusalem was holier and purer than other parts of Israel. According to the *Temple Scroll* (11QTemple), when the sectarians occupied Jerusalem, menstruants and several other classes of impure people would be banned from the city and would have to live in camps outside the walls.[50] Further, the sectarians would have to go outside the city walls in order to defecate.[51] On the sabbath, they would not be able to defecate at all, since their sabbath rules would forbid them to walk far enough beyond the walls.[52] This is clearly an extreme

[50]11QTemple 46:16–18: lepers, men with irregular discharge from their genitals, men who had nocturnal emissions; 48:14–17: people with the following conditions are to be expelled from all Jewish cities, not just Jerusalem: leprosy, plague, males with irregular genital discharge, menstruants and women after childbirth. For discussion see Yigael Yadin, *The Temple Scroll*, 3 vols. + supplementary plates (English ed., Jerusalem: Israel Exploration Society, 1983) 1. 304–7.

[51]11QTemple 46:13–16 (latrines had to be 3,000 cubits outside Jerusalem); cf. 1QM 7:6f. (latrines had to be 2,000 cubits outside the military camps during the war). See Yadin, *The Temple Scroll* 1. 294–304. (A cubit was approximately 1/2 yard or metre.)

[52]Note the distances in the previous note (2,000 or 3,000 cubits). According to CD 10:21, a sabbath's day journey could be no more than 1,000 cubits. The Rabbis allowed sabbath journeys of 2,000 cubits. Josephus also comments that the Essenes did not defecate on the sabbath (*J. W.* 2.147). As Albert Baumgarten notes, this could be because they could not carry their mattock on the sabbath or dig with it after they reached a secluded space: Baumgarten, 'The Temple Scroll, Toilet Practices, and the Essenes', *Jewish History* 10 (1996) 9–20, here 16 n. 14.

form of a common view: Jerusalem should be purer than other cities. This paragraph partly conceals some difficulties, which I shall consider in the final section of the paper. It will remain highly probable that the Qumranians wished to eliminate from Jerusalem more impurities than would have occurred to most Jews.

Providence and freewill

We shall now consider providence (which may be called determinism or predestination) and freewill, the first of our two theological topics. This is one of the major defining characteristics mentioned by Josephus in his summaries of the Jewish parties (probably relying on Nicolaus of Damascus; see n. 58 below). According to Josephus, the Essenes believed in providence (or predestination), the Sadducees believed in free will, and the Pharisees believed in both.[53] My own view is that probably they all believed in both, though there may have been differences of emphasis. We should also note that Paul believed in both and that he had been a Pharisee.[54] Jews had not been through the debates of Medieval Christianity, nor had they read Calvin, and so they did not know that providence and freewill are mutually exclusive.

It is easy to believe in both because one applies them somewhat differently. This is brilliantly clear in the Dead Sea Scrolls. Typing out all the passages that emphasize divine control of events *or* human choice *or* both requires somewhere between six and ten pages.[55] I shall mention only one point: membership in the community. One of the names that the sectarians called themselves was 'the chosen' or 'elect' (e.g. 1QS 9:14; 1QpHab 5:4). In agreement with this, according to one passage, God himself, from the beginning, determined the 'lot' of every individual. He created the righteous person (*ṣaddîq*) and 'established him *from the womb* for the time of goodwill, that he might be preserved in God's covenant'. Similarly he created wicked people (*resha'îm*) for the time of wrath and vowed them *from the womb* for the Day of Massacre (1QH 15:13–19).

Other passages lay equal stress on human decision and will. Those who enter the covenant are called 'volunteers' or, in Geza Vermes' translation, 'those who have freely devoted themselves' (1QS 1:7). Contrast this statement of entry to the earlier statement, that God decides on a person's 'lot':

---

[53]*J. W.* 2.163, 165; *Ant.* 18.13, 18.

[54]Rom 9:1–18 and 10:9–16.

[55]For fuller discussion, see Sanders, *Paul and Palestinian Judaism* (London: SCM Press, 1977) 257–70.

Every man of Israel, who freely vows to join the Council of the Community, shall be examined by the Guardian at the head of the Congregation concerning his understanding and his deeds. If he is fitted to the discipline, he shall admit him into the Covenant that he may be converted to the truth and depart from all falsehood; and he shall instruct him in all the rules of the Community. And later, when he comes to stand before the Congregation, they shall all deliberate his case, and according to the decision of the Council of the Congregation, he shall either enter or depart. (1QS 6:13–16, Vermes)

The explanation of these two ways of discussing membership in the community is this: when one thinks of God, one naturally attributes to him foreknowledge and power. Imagine the opposite: could pious Jews think that God does not know what is happening or what will happen, and that he is not in charge of what he created? I think that to the monotheist in particular, belief in divine determinism is easy and simple, and that this is the thought that comes to mind when thinking of God or addressing him in prayer. But when a group of people gathers to discuss rules that will govern the group, they naturally think of human ability to make decisions and to take responsibility for their actions. Thus a person who betrays the group is treated as a traitor, not as a poor victim of God's caprice. As we noted above, the same individual, such as Paul, can hold both views on the same day, since they apply to slightly different points.

Righteousness

The second theological point is that the sectarians believed that people can be *righteous only as the gift of God* and that they are able to be *righteous by their own effort*.[56] This is the supposed grace/works dichotomy beloved by Protestants. I again shall give only two passages:

Righteousness, I know, is not of man, nor is perfection of way of the son of man: to the Most High God belong all righteous deeds. The way of man is not established except by the spirit which God created for him to make perfect a way for the children of men, that all His creatures might know the might of His power, and the abundance of His mercies towards all the sons of His grace. (1QH 4:29–33)

On the other hand, members do not enter the community unless they are perfect of way (1QS 8:10). If a member deliberately transgresses – which he is free to do – he is not readmitted until 'all his deeds are purified and he walks in perfection of way' (8:18; cf. 10:21). Thus a member should be perfect of way, but he can transgress, in which case he can again become perfect of way if he has 'the right stuff'.

---

[56]See Sanders, *Paul and Palestinian Judaism*, 305–12.

The explanation of this apparent dichotomy is basically the same as in the previous case: when the members compared themselves *to God*, they said that only he was righteous and that only he could give them perfection of way. When they thought of behaviour within the group, comparing one person with another or with the standards of the group, they naturally thought that members could decide to live perfectly in accord with the precepts of the community or to transgress.

For a brief parallel, we turn to Josephus rather than Paul (though Paul shared this view).[57] In his view, Moses required prayers of thanksgiving twice each day. Josephus' summary focuses on God's grace:

> Let all acknowledge before God the bounties which He has bestowed on them through their deliverance from the land of Egypt: thanksgiving is a natural duty, and is rendered alike in gratitude for past mercies and to incline the giver to others yet to come. They shall inscribe also on their doors the greatest of the benefits which they have received from God and each shall display them on his arms; and all that can show forth the power of God and His goodwill towards them, let them bear a record thereof written on the head and on the arm, so that men may see on every side the loving care with which God surrounds them. (*Ant.* 4.212f.)

The same author, of course, emphasized the importance of following the law and believed that God took account of deeds by rewarding obedience and punishing disobedience:

> people who conform to the will of God, and do not venture to transgress laws that have been excellently laid down, prosper in all things beyond belief, and for their reward are offered by God felicity; whereas, in proportion as they depart from the strict observance of these laws, things [otherwise] practicable become impracticable, and whatever imaginary good thing they strive to do ends in irretrievable disasters. (*Ant.* 1.14)

The sectarians emphasized (1) that humans were worthless bits of nothing and depended absolutely on God's grace, and (2) that they were capable of becoming and remaining perfect. These statements are more radical than Josephus', but they are not fundamentally different.

The world is still full of people who will focus on one of these themes, usually human effort in attaining perfection, and conclude that the sectarians in particular and Jews in general believed in the sort of meritorious achievement that is called legalistic self-righteousness. And they will maintain that holding this position excludes reliance on God's goodness and mercy. Scholars who work in the area of Bible and related topics are often fixated on the kind of dogmatic consistency that seldom appears in real life: they think that people who believed in human effort

---

[57]Note his admonitions to upright behaviour, which presuppose human ability: e.g. 1 Thess 4:1; 5:21f.

and moral achievement must have renounced grace. Ancient Jewish groups, just like modern Jewish and Christian groups, had diverse religious thoughts and practices. To this day, when Jews or Christians pray to God, they thank him for calling them to follow him and for giving them the strength and ability to live as they should, and they recognize that in comparison to God humans are weak creatures who must rely on the strength and goodness of God. Yet when these same people falter, they do not blame God, they blame themselves. They seek to return to the path of righteousness, and they know that they must exert effort to do so. Humans are dependent on grace and they are accountable for their deeds. This is a common and in fact a virtually universal view in both Judaism and Christianity, and it is puzzling that many Christian scholars who accept both aspects of religion in their own lives believe that in the ancient world these were mutually exclusive alternatives. They are simply different perspectives that arise in slightly different circumstances. One set of thoughts arises in prayer or meditation, the other in considering the practicalities and difficulties of daily life. The two can combine in one sentence, as in this passage from the Hymns: 'No man can be righteous in your judgment or [innocent] in your trial, though one man may be more righteous than another' (1QH 9:14f.).

Conclusions on the Five Cases

On all these topics – Temple, festivals and sacrifices; sabbath; purity; determinism/free will; dependence on God/self-reliance – the Qumran Scrolls exaggerate and radicalize activities and views that were common in Judaism, many of which also appear in Pharisaism, Rabbinic literature, Josephus and the New Testament, as well as in Jewish literature that I have not cited, such as the apocryphal and pseudepigraphical works and the writings of Philo. What applies to these five points applies to numerous points. The Qumran community had much in common with other Jews of the same place and time. It was, however, a very radical group, and in numerous ways it was distinctive, so distinctive that it separated itself from other Palestinian Jews.

Comments on Other Points

The views that I have offered on commonalities and differences explain my views on other themes of the conference, and clever extrapolation from the main part of the paper would allow the reader to know how I see other topics. But it will be simplest if I write a brief account of the other questions that we were asked to consider. I hold most of the following views more lightly than the positions sketched above, but the main issue below is extremely important for students of Judaism in general and the Scrolls in particular. I refer to the question of whether or not we should construct a composite picture of the Essene party by collecting evidence drawn from the Scrolls, Josephus and Philo.

I shall first put the main question generally: were the Qumranians Essenes? It does not bother me that the DSS do not precisely conform to what Josephus and Philo tell us about the Essenes. Josephus and Philo were outsiders, and they probably had a source or sources written by other outsiders. In the case of Josephus, we may guess his source: the work of Nicolaus of Damascus.[58] I do not regard the text that is now in *J.W.* 2.119–161 as a fantasy, nor even as very inaccurate. But if Josephus derived most of this passage from Nicolaus, we should expect it to reflect Nicolaus' day (the lifetime of Herod) rather than Josephus'. The Essenes, of course, did not change completely in the intervening decades, from late in Herod's reign (let us say 10 BCE) to the fall of Jerusalem (70 CE), but there may have been some differences. Thus this description may not have been 100 per cent accurate when it was written, and most especially it need not be regarded as perfectly describing all Essenes at all times and in all places. If, therefore, we allow for some variety within the Essene party (Josephus mentions

---

[58]It is striking that in his two summaries of the parties (in *J. W.* 2.119–216 and *Ant.* 18. 11–25) Josephus does not tell us very much about the two parties that he knew best, the Sadducees and the Pharisees. His knowledge of these parties, as they were during his lifetime, must have been close to perfect. Occasionally one catches a glimpse of the detail that he could have offered, as in his discussion of the Pharisee Simon son of Gamaliel in *Life* 190–98, where he also refers to three other Pharisees. But instead of putting into his summaries what he knew about these two parties, he offers sketches of their views on the philosophical problem of fate and the speculative issue of life after death. Both aspects of his summaries (what he does not tell and the peculiarity of what he does mention) incline me to the view that he is here, as frequently, using a source, probably Nicolaus of Damascus, a Gentile who had good general information about the parties, but who was probably not expert in Jewish law and who therefore might have had less than perfect knowledge. (Nicolaus had been Herod's courtier and spokesman. He was a learned philosopher and historian, who wrote a massive work, only fragments of which survive, called *The Universal History*. Josephus mentions Nicolaus, but he gives us no idea of how much he depended on this source – following here the custom of ancient historians.) If the work of Nicolaus was Josephus' source, this would also explain why the Essenes receive so much attention in *J. W.* 2: they were not very important in the war (Josephus' subject), but they were quaint and curious, and therefore probably interesting to Nicolaus' audience. Postulating Nicolaus as Josephus' source for much of his descriptions of the parties, however, poses the further question of Nicolaus' source for the long description of the Essenes that appears in *J. W.* 2. I assume that he had a source, which he may have reworked. And, of course, Josephus could have reworked it as well; he certainly added 2.152f., on the bravery of the Essenes when captured by the Romans. As James McLaren has pointed out to me, Josephus also decided where to put the summary of the parties. The possibility that Nicolaus was the source of Josephus' descriptions of the parties is, of course, too large an issue to be dealt with here, but I offer a few further comments below.

single and married groups of Essenes), and also for some changes over time, we may reasonably consider the Qumran community to be a branch of the Essene party. I shall return to the question when we consider a specific issue, defecation, but for now I shall simply propose that the Scrolls conform to the literary descriptions of the Essenes closely enough that the simplest conclusion is that much of the library from Qumran represents the monastic (or celibate?) Essene order.[59]

Next, are all the finds in Qumran equally representative of the monastic sect that lived there? From very early days it has been evident that the library included works that the sect read but had not composed. Copies of parts of *1 Enoch* (for example) were found among the Scrolls, but no one thinks that the Qumran sect composed this work, which was well known and widely available outside of Qumran. Some scholars would put 11QTemple in the same category: it was read at Qumran but was not an explicitly sectarian treatise. I agree with those who think that it was as sectarian as 1QS, 1QH, 1QM and 1QpHab. It is true that there are various features in 11QTemple that call this into question, but assuming an origin of this Scroll in Qumran still seems to me the most satisfactory position. One must remember that a religious movement can easily contain people who have divergent views on speculative questions, such as Jerusalem in the age to come. Very rarely does hard doctrine govern speculative topics, especially in a group that endures for several decades. We should not expect that all Qumranian had precisely the same views of the future age.[60]

The *Damascus Document* presents a quite different problem. It

---

[59]It is possible to distinguish 'monastic' from 'celibate'. According to Josephus, as just noted, some Essenes married, some did not (*J. W.* 2.120, 160f.); this implies celibacy (we need not consider concubines and prostitutes). The Qumran documents do not require members not to marry. On the other hand, 1QS is completely silent about women and children, and it legislates for men who live communally with one another. This has led many scholars to regard the sect of 1QS as the Essenes who did not marry: they were monastic (as in 1QS) and celibate (as in Josephus). As Morton Smith pointed out long ago, however, it is conceivable that the Qumranians had wives who lived in the area but not communally with the men ('The Dead Sea Sect in Relation to Ancient Judaism', *NTS* 7 [1960–61] 347–60; cf. *P&B* 529 n. 6). We may now note that the *Temple Scroll* envisages wives as living at least most of the time outside of the city (to keep Jerusalem free of the impurities caused by semen, menstruation and childbirth). It is therefore possible that the Qumranians believed in a *monastic* life (communal, no contact with families on a daily basis) rather than in a *celibate* life (no wives). The description in Josephus, to be sure, focusses on marriage itself (though it also contains hints of communal life, for example at mealtime, 2.129). It seems to me that we cannot entirely resolve these questions (monastic communal life, marriage, Josephus and 1QS), but at least in principle a group could be monastic but not celibate. Josephus' Essenes are celibate and there are only hints of a monastic life, while the 1QS sectarians are monastic and possibly celibate.

[60]Unanimity on the future would be explicable if a specific future expectation were the *raison d'être* of the community – but even so there would be a few variations over time, as well as some diversity of emphasis from one person to another.

contains a lot of rules and regulations that are not in the other Scrolls, and particularly not in the other Rules (the chief of which is 1QS). Although members of a religious society may harbour different expectations of the future, they cannot obey two competing laws simultaneously. Thus *legal* differences among the Scrolls must be investigated very carefully. But we should again recall that not all Essenes lived at the same time and in the same place. Some aspects of CD and 1QS are completely incompatible, since the former legislates for married people who live in towns and take offerings to the temple, while the latter governs sectarians who live apart from the rest of society. But this difference partly coincides with Josephus' report that some Essenes were celibate (apparently the majority) while some married. That is, legal incompatibility may correspond to the view that there were two groups of Essenes. Thus part of Josephus' account can readily be harmonized with CD: there were some married Essenes who lived in towns. But then we immediately encounter another problem. According to Josephus all the Essenes, both celibate and married, lived in towns, not in a secluded monastery near the Dead Sea. Nowhere in his writings does he mention a habitation like Qumran. Yet even this problem may be resolved if Josephus' summary of the parties was dependent on Nicolaus' history. We noted above that a description of the Essenes written in the time of Nicolaus (Herod's lifetime) might be at least a little different from one written during Josephus' lifetime. Now we shall note what was probably the most important change between those two periods. Archaeology reveals that the settlement at Qumran was unoccupied during part of Herod's reign. The dates of desertion and reoccupation are debated, but we may be confident that the site was abandoned prior to or as a result of an earthquake in 31 BCE. The date of reoccupation is less certain. Some place it after Herod's death (4 BCE) and some earlier.[61] In any case, during at least part of Herod's reign, and perhaps during most of it, Qumran was not occupied. This makes it at least plausible that *when Nicolaus* wrote the Qumranians lived in towns and cities. We know that Herod was friendly towards the Essenes (*Ant.* 15.371–9). Therefore it makes sense to think that the Qumranians were Essenes; that the monastic residential area at Qumran was destroyed at a time when they had a friend on the throne; that they therefore moved to Jerusalem (and other towns and cities); and that Nicolaus correctly described the Essenes – both unmarried and married – as living in

---

[61]The best brief evaluation of Qumran archaeology is by Magen Broshi, 'The Archeology of Qumran – a Reconsideration', *The Dead Sea Scrolls. Forty Years of Research* (ed. Devorah Dimant and Uriel Rappaport, STDJ 10; Leiden: Brill, 1992) 103–15; on chronology, see 105–11. Convenient summaries of the archaeological evidence are F. F. Bruce, 'Qumran', *Enc. Jud.* 13, cols. 1429–1435; John J. Collins, 'Essenes', *ABD* 2. 619–26.

towns. Josephus did not bother to revise his source. He neither added that some Essenes after Herod's time lived near the Dead Sea nor did he improve the inadequate summaries of the Pharisees and Sadducees.

Another complication arises because the two principal futuristic documents, 1QM (the *War Scroll*) and 11QTemple, contain *rules*. If divergences between CD and 1QS lead to the conclusion that they did not both regulate the same group of people at the same time, must the rules in 1QM and 11QTemple agree with each other and also with 1QS for us to consider them all as equally 'sectarian' – that is, equally representative of the Qumran community? It seems to me not. This is, of course, a question of the degree of difference. Rules for the future would not be completely different from the rules for the present. But I think that it is quite possible for an author thinking of the future war and armed camps to have a *few* rules that are different from his own present practice. They might be only improvements that he fondly hopes will be introduced in the better time, when the twelve tribes of Israel are reassembled and angels lead the army. Or, reading the biblical stories of war, he might conform some rules to them. I would even more strongly expect the author of 11QTemple to make some modifications. Why think that the present mean camp on the shores of the Dead Sea was governed in precisely the same way as the Holy City would be when the sect possessed it and rebuilt it in grandeur? Besides, the author of 11QTemple was a kind of genius (in my estimation). Possibly he was one of the few who could actually think of something different, something that was not only bigger than what already existed.

These considerations are not decisive, but I do regard them as heuristically useful. We should not refuse to think that some of the sectarians could envisage legal changes in the new and better age. I note that, in the US, congressmen often vote for revisions to the tax code that do not correspond to the longed-for simple and perfect tax code that they discuss when campaigning. The future does not have to be just a replay of the present.

I shall now take one example of the problems that arise when various sources, all possibly Essene, mention the same legal topic but do not agree. Is it better to explain legal differences as being intra-Essene or to posit different groups or sub-groups? I have already indicated my own inclination to regard the Qumran documents as Essene and CD as coming from a sub-group of the Essene party, but I shall now consider a more complicated case. At nn. 51–52 above, in discussing defecation, I followed Yadin in combining information from 1QM, 11QTemple, CD and Josephus, on the ground that they all seemed compatible (1QM, latrines 2,000 cubits away from the camp; 11QTemple, latrines 3,000 cubits outside Jerusalem; CD, a sabbath journey could be no

further than 1,000 cubits; Josephus, the Essenes defecated in remote
spots and did not 'go to stool' on the sabbath (possibly because they
would not carry or dig with their mattock on that day). I cited all of this
evidence in making the simple point that the Qumran sect wished to
treat Jerusalem as especially pure, and I pointed out that it also
indicated that the sectarians would not defecate on the Sabbath – apparently in the present as well as in the future Jerusalem. Albert
Baumgarten has written an article on defecation in 11QTemple and
Josephus' description of the Essenes. He proposes that the differences
prove that the documents came from separate groups.[62] I did not design
this discussion as an argument with my long-time friend and colleague,
and I first wrote it without having his article in the forefront of my
mind: I read it so long ago that I had forgotten the details. Although I
have now re-studied the article, I have decided to describe the problems
as I see them, without arguing with Baumgarten, and at the end to add
a note indicating why his extremely interesting article does not entirely
persuade me. I hope to publish a fuller discussion of this matter in the
not-too-distant future.

The combination of evidence above (at nn. 51–52) has several difficulties. (a) Since CD does not represent the community at Qumran, we
do not know that the Qumranians accepted a sabbath limit of 1,000
cubits. (b) Neither 1QS nor CD, which presumably prescribe behaviour
in the 'present tense', deals with defecation. (c) Josephus does not say
that the Essenes had latrines (as in 1QM and 11QTemple), but rather
that each individual dug a pit in a remote place. (d) The distances of
2,000 cubits in 1QM and of 3,000 cubits in 11QTemple are obviously
not the same. What shall we make of all this? What I do *not* conclude
is this: there were five different groups: (1) CD: its group could travel
only 1,000 cubits on the sabbath, but they could defecate wherever and
whenever they liked (CD does not mention the act of defecation, though
it may refer to feces in 10:11 and 11:3[63]); (2) 1QS: the sectarians could
travel any distance on the sabbath and defecate wherever and whenever
they liked (1QS mentions neither sabbath limits nor defecation); (3)
1QM: the followers of this Scroll had latrines 2,000 metres outside their
residential areas and could walk to them on the sabbath (no sabbath
limit is specified); (4) 11QTemple: its champions had latrines 3,000
cubits outside their residential areas and could walk to them on the
sabbath (no sabbath limit is specified); (5) Josephus: the Essenes could

---

[62]Baumgarten, 'Toilet Practices', n. 52 above. This article does not contrast Josephus and
Qumran in general, since he did not wish to assume that 11QTemple either is or is not a
Qumranian document. The question is only whether or not 11QTemple and Josephus
represent the same group.

[63]So Baumgarten, 'Toilet Practices', n. 27.

walk as far as they liked on the sabbath but nevertheless did not move their bowels on that day (Josephus does not specify a sabbath limit, nor does he explain the prohibition of defecation on the sabbath; as Baumgarten pointed out (n. 52 above), carrying and digging would have been forbidden on the sabbath).

This is, of course, a caricature of what happens if one interprets evidence too atomistically. Jacob Neusner introduced into Jewish studies the ideas that each ancient Jewish document represents a different social group and that each document presents a complete system, with nothing omitted.[64] The latter view means that silence indicates opposition or lack of concern (e.g. a document that does not mention sacrifice shows that the separate social community that produced it opposed sacrifice). These views are the ones that I caricature in the previous paragraph. Specialists on the Dead Sea Scrolls are not this exreme, and they do combine evidence from various Scrolls, rather than proposing that each document represents a different group. There are, nevertheless, even in this generally prudent and thoughtful field, recurrent tendencies to find diverse groups where, it seems to me, we should allow for internal and individual variation. I think that it is extremely important to grant that we must sometimes combine information from the Scrolls and that we should not suppose that the sect, throughout its history, had only one set of unchanging practices and opinions. Some of the Scrolls (e.g. 1QM) were revised. We should also allow for individuals to assert their own opinions.

This does not mean that we should become uncritical synthesizers of all sorts of divergent evidence. No two scholars will agree precisely on what 'critical' analysis means and what its results are. Some incline more towards harmonization, others more towards atomization. This is as it should be. We all draw lines in different ways. I am willing to put Ephesians in the Pauline camp, but I do not consider it when I am writing about Paul himself. To make my own position on this vexed and important issue clear, I shall review the sources above on the question of defecation. (1) CD's sabbath limit of 1,000 cubits may or may not have been in force at Qumran. The Rabbis (as noted above) accepted a limit of 2,000 cubits, and we should expect that the Qumranians were stricter. Thus it seems *reasonable* (not indisputable) to apply CD's limit to Qumran.[65] (2) The fact that CD and 1QS lack rules about when not

---

[64]E.g. *Judaism* (n. 37 above) 3, 236; *Messiah in Context* (Philadelphia: Fortress Press, 1984) 3; 'Parsing the Rabbinic Canon with the History of an Idea. The Messiah', *Formative Judaism: Religious, Historical and Literary Studies*, 3rd series: Torah, Pharisees and Rabbis (BJS 46; Chico, CA: Scholars Press, 1983) 173. See on all of this *JLJM* 312, 324–6.

[65]As noted above, many of CD's rule would not apply in Qumran – e.g. those that discuss familes and relations with Gentiles.

to defecate and whether or not to wash or immerse after defecation proves nothing at all. Neither one is a complete system, and each omits more possible topics than it includes. We noted above that 1QS mentions a meal called 'the Purity' but says very little about impurities and purification. This does not prove that the sectarians lacked precise and detailed views. We simply do not know. (3) The difference of latrines located 2,000 cubits away (1QM) and 3,000 cubits away (11QTemple) is not very serious. Yadin suggested that the subject is slightly different: military camps in 1QM and Jerusalem in 11QTemple. Various dates and authors would also account for the divergence. I can imagine people trying to outdo one another in strictness, and it is especially easy to understand the view that defecation should be removed farther from Jerusalem than from a military camp. (4) The fact that Josephus envisages individual Essenes as digging their small pits, rather than utilizing group latrines, is more noteworthy. Surely he himself knew what the Essenes who lived in Jerusalem did. But we do not know that this is what he is describing. He may be – and I think that he was – using someone else's report of what the Essenes in Palestine did at some other time (Herod's).

Scholars frequently forget what sort of historian Josephus was. Wherever possible, he had his assistants copy sources, and we not infrequently find an accurate description in one of his works and an inaccurate description elsewhere, while on other topics there are two diametrically opposed views.[66] Moreover, we must also remember that Josephus knew the Bible, including Deut 23:12f. (Heb 23:13f.): 'You

---

[66]This view of Josephus as historian is at a polar extreme from that of Steve Mason, who thinks that he fully meant everything in his work; if he used sources, he shaped them 'to reflect his own agenda, interest, and style' (p. 47); he exercised 'control over his literary productions': Mason, *Flavius Josephus on the Pharisees* (SPB; Leiden: Brill, 1991) 48; see further 41–8; 113f.; 372. I note that Mason asserts this view but does not demonstrate it by examining some of the most obvious self-contradictions in Josephus' work. I offer a couple of examples that illustrate the fact that Josephus sometimes just copied his sources, not altering them so that they would agree with his own view: (1) his description of the Temple is in some respects quite different in *J. W.* 5.184–227 and *Ant.* 15.410–20 (see *P&B* 59). I suspect that the description in *J. W.* 5 is based on Roman military notes (*P&B* 59f.), which explains its accuracy. Either he had a different and less reliable source in *Antiquities* or he simply did not bother to look up the earlier account. If the latter, he mis-remembered a place that he should have known well. (2) Josephus gives various lists of Herod's buildings, sometimes (*J.W.* 1.401–428) citing them as evidence of his piety and the 'grandeur of his character' (1.400, 408, probably from Nicolaus; cf. the praise in *Ant.* 16.136–49), while elsewhere we read that some of Herod's buildings were part and parcel of his corruption of Judaism; they are evidence of his 'unlawful acts' (*Ant.* 15.266–76) (presumably from an otherwise unknown pietist critic; similarly *Ant.* 15.328; 16.153–9). We have no idea what Josephus' 'own' view was. In describing and especially in evaluating the life of Herod, it is plain that he had at least two diametrically opposed sources, and that he had his secretaries copy them into his work. On Mason and the Pharisees, see the review by Rebecca Gray, *JTS* 43 (1992) 217–20.

shall have a designated area outside the camp to which you shall go. With your utensils you shall have a trowel; when you relieve yourself outside, you shall dig a hole with it and then cover up your excrement.'

Therefore if Josephus himself did compose the description of individual Essenes digging their own pits, he could have borrowed it from Deuteronomy. Or Nicolaus' source borrowed it from Deuteronomy. Or, still more likely, in Nicolaus' day the Qumranians had moved into Jerusalem and had changed their practice (as I suggested above).

In short, we do not know the source of *J. W.* 2.148f. with complete certainty; we do not know precisely what the Qumranians did; we may be reasonably confident that at some time or other Essenes in Jerusalem dug individual pits some distance from the city; we do not know whether the practices of either the Qumranians or the Jerusalem Essenes changed over time. Change over time, and even back and forth, should not be ruled out. We could, for example, imagine the following sequence: a few hundred sectarians lived at Qumran for several decades, each using his own mattock; it became increasingly difficult for each sectarian each day to find a new spot for his pit; this led them to build a few latrines with deep pits; after some decades the latrines filled up; they again took up their mattocks. I intend this to be at least faintly amusing. My serious suggestion is to look at Nicolaus as the source of the summaries of the parties. We should also grant that our knowledge will remain imperfect. Still seriously: I do not wish to minimize the conflict between Josephus on the one hand and 1QM and 11QTemple on the other by arguing that the futurists dreamt up latrines even though past and present practice was to dig individual pits. I assume that the latrines of 1QM and 11QTemple were based on some use of latrines at the time of composition (or possibly in the recent past), and I also assume that at some time or other Essenes in the cities went outside the city boundaries and dug individual pits.

There are real problems in sorting out the evidence, in which we should rejoice: if only we were equally overwhelmed with evidence on the Sadducees! I understand why many scholars today would solve some of the problems by positing three groups, one represented by 1QM, one by 11QTemple, and one by Josephus. Others would be happy to combine 1QM and 11QTemple and thus to posit two groups. But manifold groups with such similar practices are also a problem. If one says that Josephus describes the celibate Essenes (since his discussion of toilet behaviour comes well before he mentions married Essenes) and that 1QM represents the monastic (and probably celibate) Qumranians, who were not Essenes, we have two very similar groups, both apparently substantial in numbers, but only one name for them. This strikes me as odd. If Josephus describes the groups perfectly accurately (which would mean that all Essenes had always lived in towns and had always dug individual pits), why did he not flesh out his account of the parties by adding some information on the community at Qumran?[67]

Are our only options either to use the evidence atomistically (each document represents a different group) or to declare our total ignorance? It seems to me not. The evidence *could* come from different groups, instead of from different sub-groups of the Essenes and/or from different chronological periods. No one should be too certain of the answer to this question. But in either case, we are not completely ignorant: it is highly likely that both the Essenes and the Qumranians (if they were not Essenes) had toilet practices that made them stand out from most Jews, and that these practices bore a family resemblance. This seems to me to be *knowledge*. It is only a small point, and it will not settle the question of how many groups there were, but I still think that family resemblances are important and that patient compilation and study of individual points pays off.

I hope that this explains why I am comfortable with the *very* careful use of CD in dicussing the Scrolls (I have a greater problem with combining CD and Qumran than with considering 11QTemple as Qumranian), why divergences among the Qumran Scrolls do not incline me to think of separate groups (e.g. one for most of the Scrolls and one for 11QTemple), why I am happy to call both CD and the other main Scrolls 'Essene' (there were two Essene groups), and why Josephus' description of the Essenes seems compatible with the Scrolls (the Qumranians had moved to Jerusalem during Herod's reign, and Josephus' source was probably written when Herod was king). There are definitely problems; but the other choices also give us problems, and they make it difficult to explain the numerous overlaps with regard to

---

[67]Three disagreements with Al Baumgarten's 'Toilet Practices' prevent me from being persuaded: (1) I do not share his view of Josephus' perfect reliability in describing the parties (since he used a source that may have been less than perfect), and in particular I doubt that Josephus was a meticulous reporter of purity rules; this certainly lay within his capacity, but he repeatedly passed up the opportunity to discuss them. The account of the Essenes in *J. W.* 2 is the exception, not the rule. (2) I do not think that we know that there was once a group that 'lived according to the Temple Scroll' (p. 13). The fact that it describes the Holy City in a new age must have resulted in some differences from present practice. (3) I do not agree with him that 'to appeal (as a last resort) to the multiform nature of Essenism, is to empty the term Essene of all distinctive meaning' (p. 13). If we know that it was multiform, we have *some* knowledge. And even according to Josephus it was multiform; consideration of Philo would expand the possible variations. Moreover, Josephus' references to the Essenes cover a period of about 174 years (from the time of Aristobulus I, 104 BCE, to the conclusion of the revolt, 70 CE). I believe that in this period of time there must have been changes, probably some that were quite substantial. (The usual view of the Essenes places the date of the party appreciably earlier than 104 BCE, and the period of 170+ years refers only to Josephus' accounts.)

very radical or very striking practices. I trust that it is also clear that I think that dogmatism is not helpful. Our evidence is not perfect, it allows competing explanations to co-exist, and it positively fosters academic work. We should all want to avoid the two extremes: uncritical combination of competing or divergent sources and the proposal that every difference proves the existence of another group. If we agree that the issue is actually how to strike the balance between the two extremes, we shall probably find that the problems are becoming less rather than more severe.

Finally: if it is correct that the Qumran sectarians were Essenes, we can say something about the influence of the Qumran community in wider society (this was one of the questions of the conference). The isolated Qumran wing of the Essenes cannot have been very influential, but the broader Essene party could have had some influence from time to time. An examination of the places where Josephus mentions Essenes in his discussions of events (not his summary descriptions of the parties) will reveal that they were a good deal less influential than the Hasmoneans, Herodians, chief priests, Sadducees and Pharisees, but that they still played a role in common activities – such as the revolt against Rome.[68] The Qumran wing of the Essene party, on this view, remained isolated, but its members shared opinions with other Essenes, who were at least a little more socially active.[69]

Because of the intervening pages (called 'Comments on other points'), I wish to return to the main topic of the paper. The Qumran community was an extremist sect. It dealt with and had opinions about the *common* issues of second- and first-century Palestinian Judaism: God, angels, the people of Israel, election, covenant, the Mosaic law, and so on. Its opinions about these topics sometimes overlapped with those of other Jews and were sometimes unique. The Scrolls give us a marvellous first-hand look at a Jewish sect. It is not, however, the model that we should use in considering other Jewish groups.[70] In particular, it stands apart because it was *separatist*. The Pharisees did not, contrary to some

---

[68]The passages may readily be found in the Concordance to Josephus or in the index to the Loeb edition. I have reviewed them, together with some of the evidence from Philo, in *P&B* 345–9.

[69]Baumgarten makes the interesting suggestion (which he describes as speculative, since it is based on an analogy with English Puritans) that 'ordinary Jews might have respected the devotion of sectarians, but also resented their exclusivist attitudes somewhat, regarding them with at least some disdain, and believing (1) that sectarian ideas were new-fangled inventions ... and (2) that if traditional practice had been good enough for generations past there was no need to change it': *Jewish Sects* 62.

[70]See Baumgarten's discussion of the use of Qumran as the lead example in his study of sects: *Jewish Sects* 31–3.

opinions, exclude all other Jews from the commonwealth of Israel. Other groups, as far as we know, did not have the equivalent of Qumran's *mevaqqer* (Guardian or Overseer, 1QS 6:12, 20). In other groups, the path to full membership was not as long, involved and demanding.[71] The other parties did not have to have their own sets of priests (who blessed the obedient) and Levites (who cursed backsliders). Most important, no other group, as far as we know, entirely refused to participate in worship at the temple – not even the sub-group represented by CD. The Qumran documents are brilliantly illuminating for the study of Jewish groups at a general level – what their topics were, how they came to distinctive positions, and so on. But in some ways Qumran can be quite misleading if it is taken as the model for understanding other groups, such as the Pharisees; the other groups were not separatist monastic communities, and we should assume that on every single point they were less extreme and less radical.

---

[71]I do not regard the promises required of second century CE *ḥaverîm* (e.g. *m. Dem.* 2:3) as representing the admission rite for pre-70 Pharisees, but even if they did, they would pale in comparison to 1QS 1:11–2:18; 5:7–11; 6:13–23.

2

THE WICKED PRIEST OR THE LIAR?

Timothy H. Lim

In an article published recently in *Revue de Qumrân*,[1] Adam van der Woude responded to my criticisms of his theory that there are six wicked priests to be identified sequentially in the Habakkuk Pesher. While I am unconvinced by his counter-arguments, and our differences will have to stand, we do agree that more than one wicked priest is to be found in the Habakkuk pesher.

Rather than going over the same ground, let me move the discussion in different directions by using van der Woude's theory as a foil for considering important issues connected with the figures of the Teacher of Righteousness, the wicked priests and the liar. I should like to confine myself primarily to the question: Do the titles 'the wicked priest' and 'the Teacher of Righteousness' occur together in column 1 of the Habakkuk Pesher?

The Wicked Priest in 1QpHab Column 1?

The appellation 'the wicked priest' occurs five times in the Habakkuk Pesher (8:8; 9:9; 11:4; 12:2 and 12:8) and once in 4QpPs[a] 1–10 iv 7–10.[2] It is always understood in a titular sense and is a slur based upon the punning of the Hebrew title 'the high priest', הכוהן הראש[3] Two other references in 1QpHab 8:16 and 9:16 have sometimes been interpreted to refer likewise to the wicked priest, but the two partially mutilated phrases do not include any title. They read 'the priest who rebelled . . .' in 8.16 and 'the [priest] who . . .' in 9:16.

Of the passages in 1QpHab that have been reconstructed to read 'the wicked priest', the one in column 1 line 13 is arguably the most important, since it will determine how one interprets the whole of the

---

[1]'Once Again: The Wicked Priests in the Habakkuk Pesher from Cave 1 of Qumran', 17 (1996) 375–84. Van der Woude first published his theory of six sequential wicked priests in the Habakkuk Pesher in *JJS* 33 (1982) 349–59. This view became one of the pillars of the Groningen Hypothesis and was criticized by me in 'The Wicked Priests of the Groningen Hypothesis', *JBL* 112 (1993) 415–25.

[2]References and readings are those of Maurya P. Horgan, *Pesharim: Qumran Interpretations of Biblical Books* (Washington, DC: Catholic Biblical Association of America, 1979).

[3]Karl Elliger, *Studien zum Habakuk-Kommentar vom Toten Meer* (Tübingen: J. C. B. Mohr [Paul Siebeck], 1953) 266.

Habakkuk Pesher and the relationship between the wicked priest and the liar. Does the sobriquet 'the wicked priest' appear from the beginning of the pesher or is this title to be found for the first time in column 8?

Column 1 of the Habakkuk Pesher is badly mutilated; only the left side of the column is preserved. But enough has survived to allow one to reconstruct the alternating lemma and commentary pattern that is evident throughout the pesher. In line 12, the preserved words near the left margin allow us to reconstruct the citation of Hab 1:4 which, in the MT, reads as 'a wicked one surrounds the righteous'. Below those words in line 13 is the phrase 'he is the Teacher of Righteousness', which is clearly part of the interpretation of the biblical quotation.

Almost all editions of the non-biblical scrolls, whether in their original Hebrew or in a modern language, restore the rest of the mutilated line 13 to read 'the wicked priest'.[4] For example, the recently published bilingual study edition by Florentino García Martínez and Eibert J. C. Tigchelaar restores the line to read: פשרו הרשע הוא הכוהן הרשע.[5] A translation like 'Its interpretation: the *wicked* is the wicked priest' would reflect well the atomization of the quotation and the correlation of the 'wicked' of the biblical lemma with the negative nickname of the denounced pontiff.[6]

The reasons for the popularity of this restoration are not far to find. The MT of Hab 1:4 mentions that 'a wicked surrounds the righteous' and it is likely that the mutilated pesherite quotation originally had the same reading.[7] The extant title 'the Teacher of Righteousness'

---

[4]See, e.g., Elliger, *Studien*, p. 30 and insert; E. Lohse, *Die Texte aus Qumran. Hebräisch und Deutsch mit masoretischer Punktation: Übersetzung, Einführung und Anmerkungen* 2nd ed. (Munich: Kösel-Verlag, 1971) 228; Johann Maier, *Die Texte vom Totem Meer* (München/Basel: Ernst Reinhardt Verlag, 1960) 149; William H. Brownlee, *The Midrash Pesher of Habakkuk* (Missoula, Montana: Scholars Press, 1979) 45; Horgan, *Pesharim*, p. 12 and part I; Bilha Nitzan (1QpHab) מגילת פשר חבקוק ממגילות מדבר יהודה (Jerusalem: Bialik, 1986) 150; Michael Wise, Martin Abegg, Jr. & Edward Cook, *The Dead Sea Scrolls. A New Translation* (San Francisco: HarperCollins, 1996) 116; and Geza Vermes, *The Complete Dead Sea Scrolls in English* (London: The Penguin Press, 1997) 478. Michael Knibb, *The Qumran Community* (Cambridge: Cambridge University Press, 1987) 222, begins his extract of 1QpHab in line 16 of column 1. A. M. Habermann, עדה ועדות מגילות קדומים ממדבר יהודה (Jerusalem: Mahbaroth Le-Sifruth, 1952) 43, restores the line as [פשרו על הצדיק] הוא מורה הצדק, but this is too short for the width of the column.

[5]*The Dead Sea Scrolls Study Edition. Volume One 1Q1–4Q273* (Leiden: Brill, 1997) 10.

[6]The English translation in this study edition is identical with that found in an earlier publication, *The Dead Sea Scrolls Translated. The Qumran Texts in English* (Leiden: E. J. Brill, 1994) 198, which itself is a further rendering of the Spanish edition, *Textos de Qumrán* (Madrid: Editorial Trotta, 1992) 248. Unfortunately, the English does not bring out the lexical identification evident in the Hebrew: 'Its interpretation: the evildoer is the Wicked Priest'.

[7]For a comparison between the MT and the pesherite lemmata generally, see my *Holy Scripture in the Qumran Commentaries and Pauline Letters* (Oxford: Clarendon Press, 1997) ch. 5.

(מורה הצדק) in the next line suggests that the biblical figure of 'the righteous' (הצדיק) had been identified with the authoritative interpreter of the Qumran community. Moreover, it is also widely held that 'a wicked one' (רשע) of Hab 1:4 was regarded by the pesherist as a reference to 'the wicked priest' (הכוהן הרשע).

The restoration of Hab 1:4 is undoubtedly correct, given the lemmatic structure of column 1 and indeed of the entire pesher. Moreover, the equation of 'the righteous' in the biblical text with 'the Teacher of Righteousness' also seems uncontestable. It is the reconstructed identification between 'a wicked one' of the biblical quotation and 'the wicked priest' that gives pause for reflection.

This reconstruction of line 13 to read 'the wicked priest' is based primarily upon the interpretation of another biblical passage in a different pesher. In 4QpPs^a (4Q171), 1–10 iv 7–10 the lacunose lemma of Psalm 37:32–33 can be filled in with the help of the MT: 'a wicked one spies upon a righteous and seeks [to put him to death]'. Both biblical figures of 'a wicked' and 'a righteous' are interpreted as references to an apparently historical incident when the wicked priest spied on the Teacher of Righteousness and sought to put him to death (פשרו על [הכו]הן הרשע אשר צנפה למור[ה] הצד[ק ויבקש ל[המיתו).

But it is uncertain whether the Habakkuk pesherist would interpret the biblical material in the same way. First of all, the Habakkuk pesherist does not always exploit what appear to be lexical opportunities presented to him in the biblical quotations. For example in column 12, lines 10–14 there is just such a missed opportunity when the alternating citation and commentary reach Hab 2:18. The biblical quotation reads as follows:

10 מה הועיל פסל כיא פסל יצרו
11 מסיכה ומרי שקר כיא בטח יצר יצריו עליהו
12 לעשות אלילים אלמים פשר הדבר על כול
13 פסלי הגוים אשר יצרום לעובדם ולשתחוות
14 להמה והמה לוא יצילום ביום המשפט

10 *What profit does an idol bring, when its maker has shaped it?*

11 *A molten image and mry shqr ? For the craftsman trusts in the things he has crafted,*

12 *making dumb idols* (Hab 2.18). The interpretation of the verse concerns all

13 the idols of the nations which they have made in order to serve them and to bow down

14 to them, but they will not save them on the day of judgement

Of the phrase מרי שקר, the last word is clearly שקר or 'falsehood'. The question is what does מרי mean. The MT has מורה שקר, 'a teacher of falsehood', equating the phrase with 'a cast image', מסכה, immediately prior to it. Some scholars have understood מרי too as 'teacher' and explained the spelling as a variant form of מורה. But this is unlikely. Had the pesherist understood מרי as מורה, then we would have expected a comment on 'a teacher of falsehood' in opposition to *the* Teacher of Righteousness'.[8] Instead, we have a typical and uninspired criticism against the inability of idols to save those who worship them. Vermes translates it as 'a fatling of lies'.[9]

Second, the Habakkuk pesherist does not reserve the adjective רשע for 'the wicked priest' alone. In column 5, lines 8–12, 'the wicked' and 'the righteous' of the biblical quotation are identified with the 'Teacher of Righteousness' and 'the man of the lie'.

למה תביטו בוגדים ותחריש בבלע	8
רשע צדיק ממנו פשרו על בית אבשלום	9
ואנשי עצתם אשר נדמו בתוכחת מורה הצדק	10
ולוא עזרוהו על איש הכוב אשר מאס את	11
התורה בתוך כול עצתם	12

8   *Why do you regard, O traitors, and keep silent[10] when*
9   *a wicked one swallows up one more righteous than he?* (Hab
         1:13) Its interpretation concerns the house of Absalom
10   and the men of their congregation who were reduced to
         silence by the reproof of the Teacher of Righteousness
11   and did not help him against the man of the lie who rejected
12   the torah in the midst of their congregation.

There are several difficulties in the Hebrew of Hab 1:13 that a translation will have to resolve, however unsatisfactorily. In the MT, both second person imperfects of the verbs 'to regard' and 'to keep silent' are in the singular and the subject is Yahweh. Forming part of Habakkuk's second complaint, the prophet asks why it is that Yahweh will look on and keep silent while a wicked man consumes another more righteous than he. In the pesherite lemma, however, תביטו is plural, referring either to an unidentified group or better 'traitors' as subject. The question is

[8]Chaim Rabin, 'Notes on the Habakkuk Scroll and the Zadokite Documents' *VT* 5 (1955) 153.
[9]*Complete Dead Sea Scrolls*, 484. This translation is based upon the reading of מרי for מריא. Others translate the word as 'rebellion' (מרי) or 'appearance' (מראה; cf. LXX).
[10]I examined the grammatical incongruity of the singular and plural verbs elsewhere, 'Eschatological Orientation and the Alteration of Scripture in the Habakkuk Pesher', *JNES* 49.2 (1990) 191–2.

not asked of why Yahweh looks on traitors, but why the traitors regard the engulfing of the righteous by the wicked one.

A second difficulty is that the verb 'to keep silent' remains in the singular. Literally, the Hebrew can be translated as follows: 'why do you regard (plural) traitors and keep silent (singular) when a wicked one swallows up one more righteous than he?' As it stands, the biblical lemma appears to be referring to two different subjects, one in the plural and and the other in the singular. In the commentary, the Teacher of Righteousness is clearly the righteous of the biblical lemma. There are also two further subjects, the house of Absalom with the men of their congregation on the one hand and the man of the lie on the other. It is unlikely, however, that the plural and singular subjects of the biblical lemma and intepretation are correlated, since the singular verb 'to keep silent' in the quotation corresponds in meaning to the plural נדמו 'to be reduced to silence'[11] of the commentary. Moreover, the singular 'the man of the lie' does not keep silent, but actively rejects the torah.

English translations of the Hebrew often take either Yahweh or traitors as the subject of both singular and plural verbs. While not entirely satisfactory, one solution is to render 'traitors' as the vocative subject of both the plural 'to regard' and the singular 'to keep silent': 'Why do you regard, O traitors, and keep silent'. This rendering has to its credit a patent correspondence to the Qumranian interpretation of the verse: the association of the two verbs with meanings of silence and the implication that 'to regard' or 'look on' is a tacit refusal to help.

What is relatively straightforward in this passage is the equation of 'a righteous' (צדיק) of the lemma with the Teacher of Righteousness (מורה הצדק) of the commentary. Just as the wicked one swallows up one more righteous than he, so the Teacher of Righteousness needed help in opposing the man of the lie. Significantly, 'a wicked one' (רשע) of the biblical citation is equated with the epithet 'the man of the lie' (איש הכזב).

Returning to line 13 of column 1, therefore, the restoration of 'the wicked priest' is possible, but unlikely. If the Habakkuk pesherist did take advantage of the reference to 'a wicked one' in his biblical quotation just as he appears to have used 'the righteous' as a biblical allusion to the Teacher of Righteousness, then it seems more probable that he had in mind 'the man of the lie' rather than 'the wicked priest'. In fact, the adjective 'wicked' occurs only twice in the first two chapters of Habakkuk, here in 1:4 and the other in 1:13. In 1:13, as discussed, it

---

[11]H. G. M. Williamson, 'The Translation of 1QpHab V, 10', *RQ* 9 (1977) 263–5, provides cogent arguments for translating the niphal perfect נדמו not as 'they kept silent' but 'they were reduced to silence'. In this translation the Teacher of Righteousness not only opposed the man of the lie, but also rebuked the house of Absalom and the men of their congregation.

is interpreted as a reference to 'the man of the lie'. This means that apart from the disputed reference in 1:4, the the adjective 'wicked' when it occurs in the biblical lemma is never equated with the title 'the wicked priest' anywhere else in the pesher. Of course, the pesherist uses nominal and verbal forms of the root רשע in the commentary: the phrase במשפטי רשעה 'with judgements of wickedness' (9:1) is connected with 'the priest who rebelled' (8:16); the wicked priest in 9:9 is described as someone who has acted wickedly (הרשיע) against God's chosen ones; and in 10:5 God will condemn him as guilty (ירשיענו), namely 'the priest' of 9:16.[12] But all three cases do not involve an interplay between the biblical lemmata and interpretation. Rather they form part of the commentary made by the pesherist about judging the wickedness of the priest who rebelled, the wicked treatment of God's elect by the wicked priest, and the guilty condemnation of the priest who was involved in illicit building activity.

Given that 'the man of the lie' figures prominently in the immediately following interpretation of Hab 1:5 a few lines later, and that the next reference to 'the wicked priest' does not occur until column 8, the restoration of line 13 of column 1 with 'the man of the lie' is to be preferred:

13   פשרו הרשע הוא איש הכזב והצדיק] הוא מורה הצדק

13   [Its interpretation: *the wicked* is the man of the lie and *the righteous*] is the Teacher of Righteousness

If this suggested restoration is accepted, then it can be said that the title 'the wicked priest' does not occur in the first seven columns of the commentary, which would support the view that the wicked priest and liar are two different individuals.

The Wicked Priest and the Liar

The figure referred to variously by scholars as 'the liar' or 'the man of the lie' (איש הכזב, 1QpHab 2:2; 5:11; 11:[1]; CD 20:15), 'the spouter (or preacher) of the lie' (מטיף הכזב, 1QpHab 10:9; 1QpMic 10:[2]; CD 8:13 and 19:26, or 'the scoffer' (איש הלצון, CD 1:14) is widely held to be a rival expositor of the law. Based upon the 1963 study by Gert Jeremias, entitled *Der Lehrer der Gerechtigkeit*,[13] and Hartmut Stegeman's 1965 *Habilitationsschrift*, *Die Entstehung der Qumrangemeinde*,[14] many

---

[12]Other references not connected with the liar or the wicked priest are כל רשעי עמו ('all the guilty ones of his people') in 5.5, בקץ רשעה ('at the time of wickedness') in 5.7–8, and הרשעים ('the wicked ones') in 13.3.

[13](Göttingen: Vandenhoeck & Ruprecht).

[14](Rheinischen Friedrich-Wilhelms-Universität, Bonn, 1971).

scholars see 'the wicked priest' and 'the liar' as two different opponents of the Teacher of Righteousness, the former being the high priest whom the Qumran community considered to be 'wicked' and the latter a rival teacher who either originally belonged to the community or was an outsider, but in any case whose legal teachings were considered to be 'lies'.

The belief that they are one and the same individual, however, is not without its supporters. For example, it has been argued that the insults 'the wicked priest' and 'the man of the lie' refer to one person and this high priest is Jonathan Maccabee. The connection between the two may be deduced by recognizing that the Qumran community originally considered the wicked priest to have been called by the name of truth before his heart became haughty (1QpHab 8:8–9). He is now considered wicked presumably because he has been teaching what the Qumran community considered to be lies.[15] The Habakkuk pesherist, however, does not make this point. Rather it is his arrogance, amassing of wealth and carrying out of abominable deeds of impurity that make the priest 'wicked' in the eyes of the Qumran commentator.

Are the wicked priest and liar then two different opponents of the Teacher of Righteousness? Jeremias has provided a persuasive case for distinguishing between the sacerdotal function of the wicked priest and the teaching role of the liar. But this thesis is not without its problems. Elsewhere I have argued that in fact the pesherist does not always keep the two separate.[16] In 1QpHab 9:12–10.13 the priest (presuming that he is 'the wicked priest') and the liar are described in similar terms. Drawing from the second and third woes of the prophecy of Habakkuk (2:9–11 and 2:12–14), the pesherist describes both 'the priest' and 'the liar' to be involved in illicit building activities that results in the punishment and judgement by fire.

It could be added to this overlap between the roles ascribed to the wicked priest and the liar that the Habakkuk pesherists describes both as 'wicked'. If the wicked priest and liar are separate individuals, then it has to be said that the Habakkuk pesherist does not always maintain this distinction.

---

[15]Geza Vermes, *Dead Sea Scrolls in English* 3rd ed. (London: Penguin, 1987) 133–4.
[16]'The Wicked Priests of the Groningen Hypothesis' 421–4.

3

WHAT DID YOU GO OUT TO SEE? JOHN THE BAPTIST, THE SCROLLS AND LATE SECOND TEMPLE JUDAISM

J. Ian H. McDonald

What did you go out to see? The question was put by Jesus to the crowds, and it concerned John the Baptist. It was an invitation to recall, an evocation of past experience. What had the crowds expected to see in John, and what did they find?

Scholars have to attempt a similar exercise. But they are at a certain disadvantage, compared to the crowds Jesus was addressing. Unlike them, scholars have no direct experience of John. They can only experience John vicariously, through traditions that rely on others' perceptions, and while they have to face up to Jesus' challenge to assess John's importance, their method is necessarily different. They may even have to deconstruct – or at least modify – the claims and assessments of two thousand years ago, even if these are highly important in certain contexts. Modern, historically grounded critical scholars can move forward only when they have located John in his *Sitz im Leben*, within the socio-historical totality of his world, and identified the horizons of his being. For this purpose, scholars not only need access to the most reliable religio-social mapping of the times but also effective orienteering skills, for John can be meaningfully assessed today only if one can identify the compass points by which he steered his own course.

In practice, this orienteering metaphor is hard to live up to. The essential maps are not available. We have to assemble them as best we can from the patchwork of evidence available to us. The result is creative sketching rather than precise cartography. Even when an unusual amount of evidence gives us more precise definition in one area, its relation to other areas may remain problematic. In consequence, we find ourselves pursuing a different kind of question: to whom will you liken John the Baptist? The problem is that analogy can be both illuminating and misleading. John may be compared to the Cynics, for example.[1] In certain contexts it may be meaningful to do this. But when we try to assess John's cosmic world – what we referred to above as the socio-historical totality of his world and the horizons of his being – the moving force within it is certainly not Cynicism. We are looking at

---

[1]Cf. Ron Cameron, ' "What have you come out to see?" Characterisations of John and Jesus in the Gospels', *Semeia* 49 (1990) 38–45.

the wrong page of the atlas! Similarities do not necessarily constitute identity or even family connection. Even when one finds an accumulation of similarities, one has still to question how they relate to a coherent vision of the world and a corresponding praxis.

In the light of these observations, the aim of this short article is to make a preliminary study of the problem of the Baptist and his world – informed as it is by the Scrolls and late Second Temple Judaism – and try to pinpoint problems of likeness and identity. We begin with brief references to the bolder hypotheses.

Speculative Identifications of John with Qumran

In spite of the fact that the identification of the Qumran community with the Essenes is problematic in itself, some writers have not hesitated to essay even more dramatic feats of identification and – to the delight of the media – have found precisely what they set out to see! Two examples must suffice. In a series of publications culminating in *James the Brother of Jesus* (1997), Robert Eisenmann posited the existence, amid the fluidity of late Second Temple Judaism, of a 'Zadokite' movement which embraced Ezra, Judas Maccabeus, John the Baptist, Jesus and his brother James.[2] It was a kind of opposition front, repudiating any kind of accommodation to the rulers of the age, and uniting Zealots, the Qumranic Essenes/Zadokites and Jewish Christians in messianic zeal. The quislings included the Pharisees, the high priestly section of the Sadducees, the Herodians and those who, like Paul, made overtures to the Gentiles. To generate this scenario, the prejudicial accounts of Josephus, the Gospels, the Talmud and orthodox Christianity and Judaism are heavily discounted, while selected comments from the Fathers are accorded a surprisingly high profile. The Sadducees in the Gospels, it is argued, bear no relation to the true Zadokites, and the Essenes are not mentioned because John, Jesus and their disciples are essentially identified with them. To sustain this picture, the scholarly consensus on the dating of the Scrolls is repudiated and even scientific tests are set aside on the grounds of the imprecision of the instrument and the fallibility of human interpretation. On the basis of priority given to the internal evidence from the documents and his own peculiar mode of interpreting it, the author claims almost unlimited scope to develop his thesis, and interprets dates and similarities accordingly, although he sometimes falls into evident anachronism. Accordingly, we must similarly question his findings; as Bruce Chilton observed trenchantly, 'It is not clear that the

[2]R. Eisenman, *James the Brother of Jesus* (London: Faber and Faber, 1997).

theory explains anything sufficiently important for the obscurity it generates'.[3]

Barbara Thiering (1981, 1992) projects an even more dramatic role for John the Baptist, who is identified as the leader of the Qumran community, while Jesus is the leader of the Hellenists, called the Wicked Priest and Man of a Lie by everyone working for Jewish supremacy.[4] Once again, the scholarly consensus on the dating of the documents is set aside in favour of a later date that fits the hypothesis. In addition, the material – Scrolls, Gospels and other – is treated as if it were an extraordinary cryptogram. The author seems to have found precisely what she wanted to find. Not surprisingly, her approach has been described as 'highly speculative and quite implausible' by Robert Webb[5] and has been comprehensively refuted by Betz and Riesner.[6]

If parallels between John and Qumran are open to speculative exploitation, it is all the more important to make a responsible assessment of the evidence. To whom indeed may we liken John the Baptist? Did he have a connection with Qumran, or with others, and if so what kind of connection was it?

Was John Connected with Qumran?

Many have been convinced that his connection with Qumran is relatively strong. Daniel Schwartz, for example, stated: 'This ascetic community by the Dead Sea shows us the setting according to which [John] is to be understood'.[7] Schwartz and others adduce a number of parallels, of which we select six for consideration here.

Desert / wilderness

The wilderness is the locale of both John and the Essenes. Charles Scobie spoke of John 'sharing the "wilderness eschatology" of the sectarian movement.'[8] Scholars as diverse as John Allegro[9] and Otto

---

[3]B. Chilton, *Judaic Approaches to the Gospels* (Atlanta, GA: Scholars Press, 1994) 19.

[4]B. Thiering, *Jesus the Man* (London: Doubleday 1992); cf. *The Teacher of Righteousness, the Gospels and Qumran* (Sydney: Theological Explorations 1981); *Re-dating the Teacher of Righteousness* (Sydney: Theological Explorations 1979).

[5]R. L. Webb, *John the Baptist and Prophet. A Socio-Historical Study* (Sheffield: JSOT Press 1991) 351, n.4. Important reviews of Thiering's work include B. Z. Wacholder, *JBL* 101 (1982) 47–8; J. C. VanderKam, *CBQ* 45 (1983) 512–14.

[6]O. Betz and R. Riesner, *Jesus, Qumran and the Vatican* (London: SCM Press 1994) 99–113.

[7]D. R. Schwartz, *Studies in the Jewish Background of Christianity* (Tübingen: J. C. B. Mohr (Paul Siebeck) 1992, 3.

[8]C. H. H. Scobie, *John the Baptist* (London: SCM Press 1964) 46.

[9]J. M. Allegro, *The Dead Sea Scrolls* (Harmondsworth: Penguin Books, 1956) 164.

Betz[10] have drawn attention to the significance of Luke 1:80: John was in the wilderness till the day of his public appearance to Israel. Josephus indicated that the Essenes accepted children for instruction (*J.W.* 1.120). The wilderness was therefore John's habitat, and his proximity to Qumran is commonly put forward as an important factor. But how far can we press this kind of argument? It has to be offset against the following:

(a) Data from the birth stories in the Gospels must be treated with reserve. They are celebratory and poetic, rather than strictly historical reminiscence. In particular, Luke 1:18 is editorial, reflecting scriptural precedents (Isaac, Samson, Samuel: Gen 21:8; Judg 13:24 LXX; 1 Sam 2:21).

(b) John's area of operation is variously described as the Jordan Valley, Samaria and Perea, rather than the wilderness of Judaea near the Dead Sea. For that reason, Joan Taylor concludes that he did not share the same desert with the community at Qumran.[11] Such a conclusion may be too sweeping; John seemed to value the wilderness, perhaps for a variety of reasons, some of which are noted below, but it is true that the locations at which we find him seem to have more to do with water than wilderness. It may be that his area of operation had Essenic connections, as Riesner argues, and that it included northern areas – the 'land of Damascus' to which some groups of Essenes seem to have migrated in the belief that the messianic age would dawn there.[12] Riesner suggested that the 'Bethany' where the Fourth Gospel locates the beginning of John's ministry (John 1:28) was in fact the northern province of Batanaea. At any rate, the geographical proximity of John to Qumran is less than convincing as an argument for John having an organic connection with the community there.

Isaiah 40:3

The longer version of the *Community Rule* states:

And when these become members of the Community in Israel according to all these rules, they shall separate from the habitation of ungodly men and shall go into the

[10]O. Betz, 'Was John the Baptist an Essene?' in H. Shanks (ed.), *Understanding the Dead Sea Scrolls: A Reader from the Biblical Archaeological Review* (New York: Random House 1992) 209.

[11]J. E. Taylor, *The Immerser: John the Baptist within Second Temple Judaism* (Grand Rapids/Cambridge: Eerdmans, 1997) 47. See also her article, 'John the Baptist and the Essenes', *JJS* 47.2 (1996) 256–85, although her book alone is cited here. I gladly acknowledge my indebtedness to Taylor, with whom I find myself in substantial agreement at many points.

[12]R. Riesner, 'Bethany Beyond Jordan (John 1:28). Topography, Theology and History in the Fourth Gospel', *Tyndale Bulletin* 38 (1987) 42–3, 53–6.

wilderness to prepare the way of Him; as it is written, *Prepare in the wilderness the way of [the Lord]; make straight in the desert a path for our God*. This (path) is the study of the Law that He commanded by the hand of Moses.' (1QS 8:13–16; cf. 9:19–20).

W. H. Brownlee led the way in claiming that Isa 40:3 shows that John must have been at home with Qumranic views of the coming Messianic era.[13] It is probable that John, like the community, resonated to Isa 40:3. It should be noted, however, that this text represents a well known *crux interpretum*, and it seems likely that John read the text in a different way.[14] In the *Community Rule*, the wilderness is a destination: they must go into the wilderness, apart from 'the habitation of ungodly men'. John, however, did not call on the crowds to stay in the wilderness or to join a desert community (*contra* Webb and Steinmann).[15] They had to go back to their normal homes and occupations and practise righteousness there. Moreover, the Gospels appear to use Isa 40:3 of John's proclamation of the divine summons in the wilderness (from Sinai?), calling for preparation for the coming divine visitation. While this shows how the evangelists and the Christian communities understood John, it provides a straightforward interpretation of John's ministry. All in all, to build a case for an organic connection between John and Qumran on the basis of Isa 40:3 is stretching things rather far.

Asceticism

John has been compared to the Qumran community in terms of a common ascetic discipline. However, the issue is relatively complex, and it is easy to overstate the significance of both correspondences and contrasts.

Diet is one criterion. John may be compared to his later counterpart, Bannus, who, according to Josephus, wore only what the trees provided and ate only what grew of its own accord (*Life* 11). He lived on what was available around him. In John's case, this was locusts and wild honey. Joan Taylor argues that John's 'natural diet' demonstrated his total dependence on what God provided.[16] He did not partake of any dishes contrived by human hands, and we are told that, like the Nazirite, he drank no wine nor strong drink (Luke 1:15; cf.

---

[13]W. H. Brownlee, 'John the Baptist in the New Light of Ancient Scrolls', in K. Stendahl (ed.), *The Scrolls in the New Testament* (New York: Harper 1957) 73.

[14]Cf. Taylor, *The Immerser*, 25–9.

[15]Cf. Webb, *John the Baptist and Prophet*, 197–202; J. Steinmann, *St John the Baptist and the Desert Tradition* (New York: Harper, 1958) 5.

[16]Cf. Taylor, *The Immerser*, 32–42.

Num 6:1–21). However, the diet of the Qumran community included bread and wine (or, at least, *tirosh*). Nevertheless, the *Damascus Rule* contains regulations for the eating of locusts and honey, and it is reasonable to conclude that John's diet also reflected a concern for purity. Like Judas Maccabeus and his group, he may have undertaken his wilderness diet as part of his avoidance of Temple and city (cf. 2 Macc 5:27). Thus, if we must find a correlative to John, it should perhaps be with the *Damascus Document* rather than the *Rule of the Community*.[17] But the similarities fall far short of proving identity with any Qumranic group. The common factor is the requirement to obey the Torah.

Again, in the tradition of Elijah, John 'wore a garment of hair-cloth, with a girdle of leather about his loins' (2 Kgs 1:8). His uniform was that of a desert holy man. As Joan Taylor argued, the hair-cloth is sackcloth, the symbol of repentance, humility and seeking after God.[18] Bannus again yields a further clue. He wore what he found on trees. In the spring season, the trees round the caravanseries picked up lots of camel's hair shed by the animals as they grew their new coats. Hence, as in the case of his diet, John's garments directly reflected his wilderness ambience. The Essenes, however, did not normally wear sackcloth. They dressed in white (Josephus, *War* 2.123, 137). John's *modus vivendi* might suggest that of the wilderness-dwelling Rechabites or Nazirites: an exceptional asceticism that Second Temple Judaism admired but generally did not follow. His garments were also suitable for his main activity, namely immersion in water.

Ritual purity and immersion

Purity was a central concern in Second Temple Judaism. The horizon was defined by Leviticus 11–15. God's people must be holy and pure, and so are obliged to be cleansed of any pollution they incur; hence the emphasis on immersion in running water, the provision of pools and the concern for ritual cleansing in Temple worship, Pharisaic practice and Essene communities. In a community setting, cleansing was essential from the outset; hence immersion was part of initiation, while regular acts of immersion sustained purity. The fundamental requirement, of course, was righteousness, submission to God's commands and persistence 'in the conversion of one's life' (cf. 1QS 3:3–6). Submission and baptism are two sides of the one coin. 'And when his flesh is sprinkled with purifying water and sanctified by cleansing water, it shall be made clean by the humble submission of his soul to all the precepts of God.'

[17]Cf. Riesner, 'Bethany beyond Jordan', 54–5.
[18]Cf. Taylor, *The Immerser*, 35–8.

As Bruce Chilton has observed, Jews of this period would never have contemplated the separation of the moral and the ritual elements.[19]

There are obvious parallels between John's baptism and the practice of immersion in Second Temple Judaism, including the *Community Rule*. There is a similar emphasis on righteousness, repentance and forgiveness, and also on ritual cleansing from all contamination. After all, the prophets looked for 'the way of holiness, a pilgrim's way along which no one unclean would pass' (Isa 35:8). But there were also divergences from Qumranic practice. John was baptizing outside the Qumran community and would not therefore be recognised by it. He was baptizing others rather than exhorting them to do it for themselves. His practice of baptism was not strictly initiatory. His concern was not for a community apart but rather for the people of God, cleansed and prepared for the day of the Lord's coming. H. Lichtenberger aptly quotes Schlatter: 'Among the endless, ubiquitous "washings", John's "baptism" appeared as a strange, new and significantly different phenomenon that astounded the people and also provided them with the rubric characterizing his peculiarity.'[20] We need not at this point enter into the nuances of Robert Webb's emphasis on the priestly nature of John's repentance baptism or Joan Taylor's Protestant-sounding insistence that without repentance the ritual act is null and void.[21] John's practice should be contextualised within the tradition of late Second Temple Judaism as a whole rather than the community of Qumran in particular. Any other conclusion involves special pleading.

Priestly background

Lukan infancy narratives are historically suspect, but the suggestion that John came from a family of priests is given wide credence. Allegro remarked, 'As the son of a priest he would have been welcomed by such a Community (sc. as Qumran) and probably marked out for a leading role in the Sect'.[22] Chilton has dismissed such views as 'an exercise in hagiography'.[23] Priests and Levites in fact occur across the spectrum of Jewish religious tendencies. Webb takes John's concern for forgiveness

---

[19]Cf. Chilton, *Judaic Approaches*, 21.

[20]'The Dead Sea Scrolls and John the Baptist: Reflections on Josephus' Account of John the Baptist', in D. Dimant and U. Rappaport, *The Dead Sea Scrolls. Forty Years of Research* (Brill and The Magnes Press: Leiden and Jerusalem, 1992) 343. Lichtenberger also discusses the importance of John's baptism not only for Jesus but also for the early church, even though the latter held it to be insufficient (Acts19.1–7) 341–2.

[21]Cf. Webb 184–94; Taylor, *The Immerser*, 88–93.

[22]Allegro, *The Dead Sea Scrolls*, 164.

[23]Chilton, *Judaic Approaches*, 26.

as a parallel to Temple sacrifices. 'We could speculate that in his role as baptizer, John the mediator of forgiveness, might have pronounced the person forgiven, just as a priest pronounced a person forgiven after offering a sacrifice in the temple'.[24] Joan Taylor rejects this priestly emphasis: 'John's putative priestly descent means nothing'.[25] There is no indication that John rejected the Temple or was party to the Essenic quarrel with the Temple and, as we have seen, any suggestion that moral reformation rendered cultic atonement redundant is foreign to Second Temple Judaism. All in all, very little can be made of the supposed priestly connection.

The sharing of property

Josephus speaks of community of goods among the Essenes (*J.W.* 2.122). As far as Qumran is concerned, the pattern of ownership is somewhat complex. The Community Rule describes the handing over of property and earnings after one year's successful novitiate, and of merging property after the second year. Deliberate lying about property brings sanctions: one year's exclusion and a 25% reduction in rations (6.24–25). But, as J. M. Baumgarten has shown, changing circumstances appear to have effected modifications of the community's disciplinary code.[26] To be sure, if a member fails in his care of the common property, he must restore the shortfall or do penance (7:6–8). Restoring the shortfall suggests access to private means; another member must not help him out in a case like this. Perhaps, as VanderKam suggests, a member retained some control over his surrendered property, although the interests of the community took precedence. Josephus speaks of members' discretion in almsgiving, but presents to relatives require special permission (*J.W.* 2.134). The *Damascus Document*, on the other hand, required the payment of two days' earnings per month to the community, for 'the poor and needy, the aged sick and homeless, the captive taken by a foreign people, the virgin with no near kin, and the maid for whom no man cares ...' (14:12–16). To help the needy was, of course, part of the Law of Moses, and the Law was reinforced by prophetic insistence (cf. Ezek 18:5–9). John seemed to give far-reaching expression to this imperative, but his teaching is more readily interpreted in terms of scripture rather than as reflecting any form of community rule. In his apparent concern to relate

[24]Webb, *John the Baptist and Prophet*, 193.

[25]Taylor, *The Immerser*, 24.

[26]J. M. Baumgarten, 'The Cave 4 Versions of the Qumran Penal Code', *JJS* 43.2 (1992) 268–76. For a more general picture, cf. J. C. VanderKam, *The Dead Sea Scrolls Today* (Grand Rapids: Eerdmans/London: SPCK, 1994) 172–3.

scriptural requirements to real life, he resembles the Pharisees. It is impossible to envisage the Qumran community advising tax collectors and soldiers as he is said to have done.

To conclude this section: John certainly resembles the Qumran community – and in particular the Damascus tendency – in a number of respects, but similarities do not prove identity and must be balanced by dissimilarities. The resemblance can be accounted for in terms of Jewish tradition and, in particular, the influence of the scriptures. 'The setting according to which John is to be understood' (to recall Schwartz's phrase) is not Qumran nor even the Essenes as a wider movement but late Second Temple Judaism.

John's Distinctiveness within Second Temple Judaism

John was a figure who left his mark on contemporary history, as Josephus shows, even if Christian enthusiasm for the role he played deprived him of continuing recognition in Judaism. This raises a real problem. As Ernst Bammel put it, 'The portraits of John are fundamentally different according to whether they picture John by himself or in relation to Jesus.'[27] Apart from Josephus, our sources are Christian and have their own theological axe to grind. In them John is Elijah, although he is also reported as denying it; he is witness and forerunner to Jesus, the messiah. His denial of messianic status is underlined. It is surprising that so much of this theological picture of John has been interpreted as a sober account of his own self-awareness. The impression has been given that access to John is relatively straightforward, while the figure of Jesus is veiled by complex layers of interpretation and mythology. Even Daniel Schwartz risks a statement such as, 'John the Baptist and Paul are much more accessible [than Jesus].'[28] In fact, John's self-consciousness is as great a problem to us as that of Jesus, and facile comparisons with Qumran or Essenic culture do nothing to alleviate it.

If the setting according to which John is to be understood is late Second Temple Judaism, what are his own distinguishing characteristics? In this briefest of conclusions, emphasis is put on the coherence of the historical sources and on phenomenological appropriateness.

Purification and immersion

In terms of purification, John is broadly in context with Pharisees, Essenes and Temple practice, while apparently immersing others rather

---

[27]E. Bammel, 'The Baptist in Early Christian Tradition', *NTS* 18 (1971–72) 95.
[28]D. R. Schwartz, *Studies in the Jewish Background of Christianity*, 1–2.

than exhorting them to purify themselves. Josephus underlined the fact that this action referred to bodily purification; inward purification came through repentance and forgiveness. There is a suggestion of Hellenistic dualism here,[29] but as noted above Jewish thinking affirmed the inter-dependence of spiritual condition and liturgical practice.

Righteousness

Josephus spoke of John's appeal 'to Jews who practised virtue and exercised righteousness towards each other and towards God.' This is again an emphasis shared across the board; Taylor probably over-emphasizes his affinities with the Pharisees at this point. The righteous will of God is central to all sections of Judaism, and knowing must lead to doing. With this insistence goes the requirement to (re)turn to God; such repentance correlates to divine forgiveness that cleanses the heart.

Interaction with the crowds on the edge of the wilderness

The wilderness locale is important for John, perhaps for its remoteness from the pollution of towns and cities. The crowds are attracted to him; they were 'profoundly stirred by what he said' (Josephus). Preaching, healing, teaching and counselling are all suggested by the sources. It is odd, therefore, to find Taylor describing him as a loner. He had his disciples, who seem at times to have become proactive in his support. The crowds did not represent an invasion of his privacy but an essential part of his mission. However, he did not establish a separate community with them, but sent them back home purified and renewed in their membership of God's people. By contrast Jesus, who apparently recog-nised him as 'a prophet and, indeed, more than a prophet', shared in the discipline of the desert but took his ministry back into the towns and villages of Israel.

His proclamation of the Day of the Lord to Israel

Josephus omits this aspect, possibly for political reasons. Eschatology was readily interpreted by the authorities as subversive. According to the Gospels, John's proclamation was characterised by eschatological urgency, which served to crystallise his message to Israel. Even when we bracket out messianic features of particular concern to Christians, strains of judgement and salvation come through the tradition, both

---

[29]J. Ernst, *Johannes der Täufer* (Berlin: Walter de Gruyter, 1989) 254; cf. Webb, *John the Baptist and Prophet*, 35.

characterised by the symbolism of fire.[30] Perhaps we find John's spiritual successor in his namesake, the seer of Patmos.[31] As always, the emphasis is on action now, before it is too late. His concern is not so much for an elect community as for a purified Israel. This can only come about by the action of God, who does not respect human validations of righteousness and who can raise up a new people out of the rocks of the wilderness. Hence John the purifier is the agent of God for Israel's purification. He stands in the tradition of prophetic proclamation of the Day of the Lord, even if the designation of 'prophet' is not a definitive category in Second Temple Judaism and should be used more sparingly than Webb, for example, used it.[32]

Political significance

The Gospels relate John's antipathy to Herod Antipas for (among other things) his marriage to Herodias, his brother Philip's wife, in breach of Levitical law (Matt 14:3–4; Mark 6:17–18; Luke 3:19–20; cf. Lev 18:16–18; 20:21).[33] John's rejection of this development as polluted and unholy reflected badly on the ruling family. Josephus, with a military historian's eye for political consequences, recognised Herod's unease at John's influence over the people, for in an ancient Palestinian context insurrection always stood round the corner: hence John's arrest, imprisonment and death (*Ant.* 18.5.2). In ancient Judaism, the religious and the political were always intertwined, although this fact does not indicate that John had zealot sympathies. John's place in Second Temple

[30]Cf. S. Mason, 'Fire, water and spirit: John the Baptist and the tyranny of canon', *Studies in Religion/Sciences Religieuses* (1992) 163–80. Mason argued that 'Q' spoke only of fire, Matthew and Luke independently adding 'holy spirit' from Mark. 'There is no good reason to suppose Q's Baptist mentioned spirit at all' (p. 172). The criterion of dissimilarity (from early Christian interpretation) – admittedly an imperfect tool – would support this cautious estimate, but the matter is more complex: cf. 1QS 4:20–1, where divine cleansing is effected 'by a spirit of holiness'; cf. Taylor, *The Immerser* 139–41. It is not incongruous to hold that John may have spoken of the holy spirit, provided his usage is distinguished from later Christian interpretation.

[31]This case is argued at length by J. Massyngberde Ford in her commentary on Revelation in the Anchor Bible series (Garden City, NY: Doubleday, 1975).

[32]Cf. Webb *John the Baptist and Prophet*, Part III (219–378); for a judicious critique, cf. Taylor, *The Immerser*, 223–34; M. Tilly, *Johannes der Täufer und die Biographie der Propheten* (Stuttgart: Kohlhammer, 1994) *passim*.

[33]Taylor is strictly correct in pointing to the Law as the authority for John's action. No explicit reliance on the Damascus Document can be presumed. But since the latter offers an explicit interpretation of Lev 18:16 (CD 5:9), a parallelism or affinity between John's position and that of the Damascus Document cannot be ruled out. In it, fornication is the first of the 'nets of Belial' in which Israel is caught (CD 4:17–19). Perhaps both are simply reflecting shared standpoints within Second Temple Judaism rather than Essenic solidarity, but contact with Essenes outwith Qumran is a distinct possibility.

Judaism is tacitly affirmed by Josephus' observation that in the public mind Herod's subsequent defeat in battle against Aretas was nothing less than divine retribution for John's death.

The above features, even minimally indicated, serve to sketch out the horizons of John's endeavour. John was not a member of the Qumran community, but he was a significant figure in the religious and political life of late Second Temple Judaism. We can relate him to those circles of piety that emphasised purity, cleansing and the practice of righteousness within an ethos of eschatological intensity. Orthodox Christianity took him over as a witness to Jesus the messiah. Orthodox Judaism subsequently ignored him for similar reasons. It is for the historian and critical scholar to restore the balance.

PART II

The Qumran Biblical Texts and the Masoretic Text

4

THE QUMRAN BIBLICAL SCROLLS – THE SCRIPTURES OF LATE SECOND TEMPLE JUDAISM

Eugene C. Ulrich

Was there a standard biblical text, and how does it relate to the Masoretic Text? ... Are the Dead Sea Scrolls marginal and the community standing behind them peripheral to Judaism that existed in the centuries around the turning of the era? Phrased differently, is the Qumran community simply one of several fringe sectarian groups, about whom we now happen to know more than we do about others? Is our picture of nascent Judaism skewed as a result of their chance discovery and intense research into the Dead Sea Scrolls?[1]

The purpose and method of this paper is historical – at least, it is my intent to be purely historical. My aim is to look at the evidence from the past and to present it accurately and neutrally. After fifty years of intense research and voluminous publication on the Dead Sea Scrolls in a broad range of areas, it is appropriate to explore the historical context of the scrolls and of the community or communities that produced or possessed them. It is time to probe the historical solidity of our available shared knowledge, which is a multifaceted web of conclusions drawn from literary, textual, archaeological, historical, sociological, scientific, and religious analyses which are based on data that are often fragmentary and random, based on evidence that sometimes is lacking information regarding its provenance, and based on what we must admit is an unsettlingly high degree of reconstruction.

Part I of this paper will consider the proper perspective and formulation of the question concerning the status of the biblical scrolls from Qumran. Part II will review results of study on the biblical scrolls, and how that evidence fits with other ancient textual evidence. Part III will examine how a revised understanding of the history of Judaism in the late Second Temple period may confirm or throw doubt on conclusions regarding the nature of the biblical scrolls, by reflecting on what the shape of Judaism actually was, in contrast to earlier ideal views of Judaism, at the end of the Second Temple period.

Preliminary considerations

At the outset, a number of preliminary considerations must be discussed.

---

[1]From the preliminary materials by Timothy Lim announcing this conference on 'The Dead Sea Scrolls in Their Historical Context'.

1. The historical period on which our investigation focuses is primarily the first century BCE and the first century CE, with occasional glances at the second century BCE and the second century CE. First, these are the centuries from which most of the scrolls and most of the archaeological data from the sites in the Judaean Desert derive. Secondly, if it should turn out that the answer to the initial question is negative – that there was not a standard biblical text in the first century BCE nor in the first century CE – then we need not dwell too long on the second century BCE. Thirdly, the destruction of Qumran in 68 CE, of the Jerusalem Temple in 70 CE, and of Masada in 74 CE does unfortunately form the end of an era. It does not seem likely that anything in Jewish life was securely established or 'standard' between 70 CE and the end of the first century. And so, for simplicity's sake, we can designate the period under investigation as 'the first centuries BCE and CE', or (near) 'the end of the Second Temple period'.

2. While attempting to operate on a purely historical level, it is important to clarify that the historical level does not necessarily entail a denial of the religious; in fact, the subject of the investigation is a religious phenomenon, and the specific question about 'a standard biblical text' implies a religious attitude, in which a faith community embraces and acknowledges a collection of texts which have claims on them. But, though the object is religious, the approach must be empirical: a wide-open search to find all the relevant evidence (or at least a large sampling of the most important evidence), full and free scope to analyse it clinically, and fresh and precise vocabulary to describe it neutrally and accurately. Moreover, religious or doctrinal views or convictions, whether ancient or contemporary, must not be allowed to influence or color the analysis. What was, in fact, the nature of the biblical text in antiquity?

3. I should also state how I understand the enterprise of historical iniquiry. History is the science-and-art which aims at objective description of phenomena of the past. It aims at objective truth but is always conducted (a) by subjective minds which view a subjective selection of evidence, (b) by subjective minds which are conditioned by cultural presuppositions, partial knowledge, and limited categories as they view the evidence, and (c) by subjective minds which are even liable to faulty conclusions due to the equivalent of optical illusions – we look at one object but interpret it as something else because of our preconditioned categories.

In the case under discussion, we have only highly fragmentary evidence available. I refer not only to the fragmentary scrolls which seldom preserve even 5% of an original MS, but also the fragmentary and whispy nature of the evidence for Judaism in general in the first centuries BCE and CE. History is a science-and-art which deals in large measure with reconstruction. We scientifically analyse the data available, but the data must be interpreted, subjectively interpreted, and we must be aware that the process of interpretation is an art. The data are a bunch of dots, and the significance assigned to the data is a product of intelligence, subjective intelligence – the art of connecting properly the dots which the data mutely provide. History necessarily involves reconstruction, and, in the case of the Dead Sea Scrolls, a great deal of reconstruction.

I. Asking the Right Question

Formulating the question correctly

The question to be addressed here could be stated as announced: 'Was there a standard biblical text' near the end of the Second Temple period? Rumination, however, over the formulation of this question illuminates a presupposition which suggests that we ought to reformulate the question. The question 'Was there a standard text?' implies the existence of a category of 'standard text'. First, with regard to the time-frame, though now we may have the category of 'standard text', was there in the period we are examining a category of 'standard text'? If not, we risk seeing items that did exist in that period according to a pattern or category that did not exist; we may have seen the data correctly but we have not understood them correctly. The question 'Was there a standard text?' implies the existence of a category of 'standard text' which either was already in place in that period or was not yet in place but expected to come into place at a relatively near future date.

Secondly, the term 'a standard text' implies or even denotes a single text which is not only fixed, but is *acknowledged* to be 'the text', as opposed to other forms of the text. Though it need not, it may even imply a critically selected text. One should also distinguish, as when thinking of the MT as 'the standard text', between 'standard' in the sense of normative (the way the text ought to be, the text by which other texts are judged), and 'standard' in the simpler sense of the common, practical, and traditional form that is routinely used – the common, and only, collection of texts fully preserved in the Hebrew language – the only collection readily available for use.

With the word 'biblical' also slips in another presuppostion, that 'The Bible' already exists, and what the question asks is whether 'The Bible' did or did not have a standard text. I do not think that 'The Bible' in our modern sense (whether Jewish, Protestant, or Catholic, or any other) existed as such in the Second Temple period, if by 'Bible' we mean a complete, fixed, and closed collection of books of Scripture. There is sufficient and sufficiently broad reference to 'the Scriptures' or 'the Law and the Prophets' to ensure that certainly there were Sacred Scriptures at the end of the Second Temple period, but the point would have to be demonstrated that 'The Bible' as such was an identifiable reality at the end of the Second Temple period. To filter out those aspects which might possibly constrain or skew our investigation, I suggest that the question be reformulated: what were the texts of the Scriptures like near the end of the Second Temple period?

Three further questions must be posed and answered before we can arrive at a solution:

1. What are the data available for determining the nature and characteristics of the scriptural texts in the first centuries BCE and CE?
2. Even if we have the proper data, are we looking at them through the correct interpretive lenses?
3. Since 'a standard biblical text' normally refers to the MT, what was the MT? What would be an adequate description of it? Was there such a thing as 'a/the standard text'? If so, was it in reality the MT that was 'the standard text'?
4. Was there an identifiable group of leaders in the first centuries BCE and CE that knew of the variety of texts, was concerned about the diversity of textual forms, selected a single form, had the authority to declare a single form to be the 'standard text', and succeeded in having that standard text acknowledged by a majority of Jews? Was there sufficient cohesion in Judaism in the first centuries BCE and CE and sufficiently acknowledged leadership to make it conceivable that a majority of Jews recognized and used a 'standard text'?

Thus, I propose that a preferable, more neutral formulation of the question is: What were the texts of the Scriptures like near the end of the Second Temple period? Having attempted to pose the question correctly, so as not to color the way the answer is formulated, we should next ask whether we are looking at the evidence correctly.

Looking at the evidence correctly: the two spirits

Like the Maskil, I propose that it is salvific to contemplate the two spirits or two mentalities which rule over the Sons of Light and the Sons of Darkness. A spirit of darkness will prevent us from seeing clearly the evidence we are hoping to interpret. On the other hand a spirit of light will lead us to interpret the evidence as it really existed. Despite real advances in one area, sometimes our thinking does not recompute the corollaries in a logically related area. There seems to be general agreement that the idea of 'normative Judaism' prior to the First Revolt has tended to vanish, as more evidence has become available of a richly diversified spectrum of forms of Judaism, all of which were then considered legitimate forms of Judaism. But many of the related views or conclusions based on the idea of normative Judaism have been slow to disappear.

It seems that there are two models for conceptualizing 'The Biblical Text' and two methodologies by which analysts work to interpret the evidence pertinent to 'The Biblical Text'. One model or methodology starts by presupposing that we know what 'The Biblical Text' is – it is long-since known, it is known well from the Masoretic Text. That form of the text has had an amazingly stable existence since about the early second century CE, and much of it can be proved to be based on texts traceable back to the second century BCE or even earlier. New evidence discovered that appears to be biblical or biblically related can be clearly understood and classified because it is known what 'The Biblical Text' is supposed to look like. Our categories are determined by our present knowledge, and data from antiquity is analysed according to these present categories.

A second, contrasting model or methodology acknowledges that conclusions should follow upon data and upon an adequate understanding of the data. It insists on proceeding according to the scientific principle that we must start our intellectual construct from the data as they are, not from our preconceived notions of what historical reality must have been like. According to this second model, the data are first understood on their own terms, in their historical context, according to the categories and vocabulary operative at that time. If that picture clashes with our modern picture, one honestly considers whether it is not our modern picture that ought be revised.[2]

Part of the problem may come from the way we are trained. When we seek 'the Hebrew Bible', what we are handed is the MT. When we study 'Elementary Hebrew', we are taught Tiberian Hebrew, the system of the

[2]See Emanuel Tov, 'The History and Significance of a Standard Text of the Hebrew Bible', *Hebrew Bible/Old Testament: The History of Its Interpretation*, Vol. 1: *From the Beginnings to the Middle Ages (Until 1300)* (Göttingen: Vanderhoeck & Ruprecht, 1996) 49–66. This is an excellent example of how one should think about the evidence of the scrolls. Though the description of the data and the thinking process are good, and though as early as 1988 ('Hebrew Biblical Manuscripts from the Judaean Desert: Their Contribution to Textual Criticism', *JJS* 39 [1988] 5–37, esp. 7) he had rightly affirmed that the Qumran texts have 'taught us no longer to posit MT at the center of our textual thinking', it seems to me that sometimes he does not push far enough in becoming free of the MT or proto-MT categories when he formulates certain of his conclusions.

Masoretes. When we advance, the learned Gesenius explains all the details to us, including contrived explanations of what are some obvious mistakes in the MT. Now that is all (or mostly) good, but is it the whole picture or part of the picture? The Judaism we learn is the Judaism that emerged triumphant as other forms died or disappeared or were metamorphosed. Newly discovered forms of ancient Judaism which differ from rabbinic Judaism are classified as 'sects.' Manuscripts of the Scriptures which differ from the MT are considered 'parabiblical', 'vulgar texts', 'paraphrases', 'rewritten Bible', or even 'nonbiblical'. One must ask whether retrojective judgment is not involved, history rewritten by the winners, history reconfigured according to later categories. We should consider whether the perspective, the categories, the vocabulary – and ultimately our knowledge – are not thereby distorted. Does not that spirit lead us astray to walk in the stubbornness of our heart?

Those on the other hand who walk according to the Sons of Light, when confronted with the same manuscripts, first ask what the Scriptures were really like in the period from which the MSS derive. What is the evidence from antiquity for the shape of the biblical text? If the MSS fit the profile of what the scriptural texts were really like in antiquity, then those very same MSS which were classified above as 'parabiblical' or 'nonbiblical' they accurately classify as 'biblical'. Once these biblical MSS are seen and interpreted correctly, they can help us better understand the nature and the history of the biblical text.

Finally, since 'a standard biblical text' would normally be presumed to refer to the MT, it is important to reflect whether there was such a thing as 'the MT' or 'the proto-MT' which could be identified as 'the standard text'? All would probably agree that 'the LXX' was not a clearly identifiable text but rather a collection of disparate texts and text types. This is so for several reasons, including the following: the Greek books were translated from various Hebrew *Vorlagen*; there were differing forms of the Greek text (including both individual variants and variant editions) for many of the books; and there was no clear and universal agreement regarding exactly which books beyond the Law and the Prophets constituted the LXX. The LXX was not a unit or unity but a haphazard collection of disparate texts and text types. The same may be said regarding the (proto-)MT. It was a haphazard collection of disparate texts and text types, gathered only near the close of the Second Temple period. It was not a unit or a unity but rather resulted from the presumably chance (as opposed to critically selected) collection of one text per book. The category of the (proto-)MT makes sense only from afterward – after the collection has been gathered and used exclusively, in contrast to other text forms, over a period of time.

II. The Evidence of the Biblical Scrolls

Though we have attempted to refine the question carefully, it is also practical to bear in mind the strategic question for many: were the scriptural scrolls found at Qumran those of peculiar 'sectarians' or those of general Judaism? While aware of this practical question, however, we should proceed in the cautious manner begun.

Review and interpretation of the data

The primary and most straightforward evidence available for the nature of the scriptural text near the end of the Second Temple period is provided by the scrolls of the Scriptures from Qumran and other places in the Judaean Desert. Additional sources of evidence are the Samaritan Pentateuch (SP), the Septuagint (LXX), the New Testament (NT), and Josephus. As the editions of the scrolls have been produced, their editors and I have tried to analyse the principal significance they provide and inform the scholarly world of their significance. I shall here give a summary review of some highlights of the evidence and its significance as I interpret it. Again, I aim to proceed neutrally, and I am not aware that I start off with any bias or pre-conceived need to see the evidence turn in any certain direction. I present my interpretation of the data, but with presuppositions announced (insofar as I am aware of them), because any description of the data involves some kind of subjective interpretation in describing and presenting those data.

Earlier evidence: the Samaritan Pentateuch

The Qumran scrolls did not arrive into a vacuum but took their place in the larger context of what was already known concerning the textual situation in Second Temple Judaism. The SP and the LXX had long since provided evidence concerning the state of the Hebrew Bible in that period. The SP and LXX evidence was in itself just as clear as the Qumran evidence, although the details and examples were somewhat different. Thinking back to the two mentalities, clarity of perspective is hightened when one reflects that the evidence of the SP and the LXX had been under-utilized because academic or religious mentalities did not give proper weight to those witnesses, since insufficient respect was given to the Samaritans, and the worth of the LXX was often dismissed as a paraphrase or a 'free' translation. Would more serious weight and study be given to the Samaritan textual tradition if the community were called, not 'the Samaritans' but 'the Samaritan Jews'?

The Pentateuch preserved by the Samaritans clearly presented what could legitimately be labelled a variant edition of the Torah. Apart from the numerous individual textual variants that distinguish the SP and the MT, the Books of Exodus and Numbers display intentionally revised forms of the text which, when viewed comprehensively, may be called a variant literary edition of the Torah.[3] Two main patterns of intentional variants are (1) the frequent intermittent interpolation by the SP of sizable blocks of text into the base text edition as preserved in the MT, and (2) the less frequent but specifically Samaritan tenets: the insertion of the commandment to build the altar on Mt. Gerizim, and the routine contrast in which the SP refers to 'the place I [YHWH] have chosen' where the MT refers to 'the place I will choose' to have my name dwell there.

For the most part, the interpolations are repetitions of text found virtually identical in the MT and the SP at some other point; that is, they are harmonizations of biblical text into biblical text. From another angle, the Hebrew text of the Pentateuch witnessed by the Old Greek (OG) translation sometimes agreed with the MT against the SP, sometimes agreed with the SP against the MT, and sometime correctly or incorrectly disagreed with both. And both the SP and the OG sometimes have sections of the text in an order different from that of the MT. Thus, the variants encountered could be described as additions, omissions, changes, and altered sequences in the texts.

Both of the major types of MT-SP variants were seen as the work of the Samaritans and thus probably not pertinent for the understanding of the Jewish Scriptures. The first has always correctly been considered intentional expansion through supplementation of biblical text from other close or distant parts of the Pentateuch, with minimal grammatical changes necessary to fit the new context. Thus, the SP was not particularly helpful in arriving at 'the original text'; the MT already attested that. The second was viewed as a secondary change as well, confessionally claiming status for Shechem as opposed to Jerusalem as the divinely chosen place for worship. Thus, it is somewhat under-standable that scholars did not see the important clues regarding the pluriform nature of the biblical text offered by the SP.

The Septuagint

Though virtually all the LXX is a rich mine for textual criticism, two very noticeable sections illustrating that value can be mentioned. The entire text and arrangement of the implementation of the commands to establish the cultic set-up in Exodus 35–39 are different in the LXX and

---

[3]There is evidence as well for different editions or 'recensions' in the MT, SP, and LXX for the chronologies in Genesis 5 and 11; see now Ronald S. Hendel, *The Text of Genesis 1–11: Textual Studies and Critical Edition* (New York: Oxford University Press, 1998) 61–80.

in the MT. The prevailing conclusion is that the LXX presents an earlier form of the text and the MT presents a secondary, rearranged edition of the text.[4]

Similarly, it has long been known and generally recognized that the same phenomenon and explanation hold for the entire Book of Jeremiah. The MT routinely exhibits multiple minor expansions as well as a rearranged order of major sections of the book. Thus, the LXX attests an early, short edition of the book with one order, and the MT attests a later, longer edition with a noticeably rearranged order.

The Qumran scriptural manuscripts

Already from the early days of Qumran study, the scrolls' evidence confirmed the picture already offered by the SP and the LXX, while flooding the data pool with numerous other examples. The two-edition schema for the Pentateuch seemed to be confirmed. On the one hand, some scrolls showed a rather close relationship with the text forms of the five books preserved in the MT. On the other hand, scrolls of Exodus (4QpaleoExod[m] and perhaps 4QExod[j]) and Numbers (4QNum[b]) showed that expanded versions of those books were in circulation, and especially in the case of Exodus, the dramatic similarities to the SP were recognized by Patrick Skehan as early as 1955.[5] Upon further examination, however, Skehan realized that the link was not direct but mediated.[6] The interpolations were already in a Jewish edition of the Pentateuch which did not include the specifically Samaritan beliefs.

Thus, it is probably agreed by all now that there were (at least) two textual forms of the Pentateuch in circulation in the latter part of the Second Temple period, the MT and the SP, and that these are seen as two successive literary editions, not just haphazard variant texts. What may not be fully understood or agreed, however, is that the two major editions of the Pentateuch were forms of the Pentateuch within general Judaism. There is no reason, textual or otherwise, to suspect that they were 'sectarian'; indeed, the fact that the Samaritans made use of that textual base for their own version of the Scriptures indicates that it was considered an authoritative form of the text. Confirmation increases

---

[4]Anneli Aejmelaeus, 'Septuagintal Translation Techniques – A Solution to the Problem of the Tabernacle Account', in G. J. Brooke and B. Lindars (eds.), *Septuagint, Scrolls and Cognate Writings (Manchester 1990)* (SBLSCS 33; Atlanta: Scholars Press, 1992) 381–402.

[5]P. W. Skehan, 'Exodus in the Samaritan Recension from Qumran', *JBL* 74 (1955) 435–40. See also the detailed and valuable study of Judith E. Sanderson, *An Exodus Scroll from Qumran: 4QpaleoExod[m] and the Samaritan Tradition* (HSS 30; Atlanta: Scholars Press, 1986).

[6]P. W. Skehan, 'Qumran and the Present State of Old Testament Text Studies: The Masoretic Text," *JBL* 78 (1959) 21–5, esp. 22.

insofar as the Hebrew *Vorlage* of the LXX attests many of those 'proto-Samaritan', or better, 'expanded-edition Jewish' readings.

Now it is possible that yet a third edition of the Pentateuch was circulating within Judaism in the late Second Temple period. It is arguable that the so-called '4QRP' (4Q364–367 plus 4Q158) is mislabelled and should be seen as simply another edition of the Pentateuch. There is still insufficient analysis to determine whether it should be considered an alternate edition of the Pentateuch or a post-Pentateuchal para-scriptural work.[7] But, just as the variants noted above between the MT and SP forms of the Pentateuch could be described as additions, omissions, changes, and altered sequences in the texts, these are exactly the types of variants occurring between the MT and '4QRP'.[8] I think that it is becoming clearer that those types of variants are *characteristic* of the biblical text as it shows up in manuscripts and editions in antiquity, rather than reasons to suspect authenticity. Moreover, for many readings in which the two versions differ those of '4QRP' agree with the SP against the MT.[9] Thus, there were at least two, and possibly three, editions of the Pentateuch circulating in general Judaism at the end of the Second Temple period.

For many of the books of the Prophets and Writings as well, the scriptural MSS found at Qumran provide evidence for the pluriformity of the text and even for variant literary editions. With varying degrees of certainty or probability some can make persuasive claims of being preferable to the textual form preserved in the MT. 4QJosh[a], for example, seems to provide an earlier and more logical form of the Joshua narrative recounting the building of the first altar in the land after the crossing of the Jordan.[10] 4QJudg[a], exhibits an earlier form of Judg 6:2–13 which does not yet include the secondary, Deuteronomistic-sounding reflection of 6:7–10.[11] The large MS of

---

[7]For the argument that it may be an alternate literary edition of the Pentateuch, see E. Ulrich, 'The Dead Sea Scrolls and the Biblical Text', *The Dead Sea Scrolls after Fifty Years: A Comprehensive Assessment* (ed. P. W. Flint and J. C. VanderKam; Leiden: Brill, 1998) vol. 1, 79–100, esp. 88–9. For the presentation of it as a 'parabiblical' work, see the edition of E. Tov and S. White Crawford in DJD XIII 187–351. I am grateful to Dr. Crawford for allowing me to benefit from several of her prepublished papers.

[8]DJD XIII 191.

[9]Ibid. 193–4.

[10]See the edition and the article by E. Ulrich, '4QJosh[a]', in E. Ulrich, F. M. Cross, *et al.* (eds.), *Qumran Cave 4, IX: Deuteronomy, Joshua, Judges, Kings* (DJD XIV; Oxford: Clarendon Press, 1995) 143–52; and '4QJoshua[a] and Joshua's First Altar in the Promised Land', in G. J. Brooke (ed.), *New Qumran Texts and Studies: Proceedings of the First Meeting of the International Organization for Qumran Studies, Paris 1992* (STDJ 15; Leiden: Brill, 1994) 89–104 + pls. IV–VI.

[11]See the edition and the article by J. Trebolle-Barrera, '4QJudg[a]', DJD XIV 161–4; and 'Textual Variants in 4QJudg[a] and the Textual and Editorial History of the Book of Judges', in

4QSam[a], in addition to providing a wealth and variety of textual information, preserves an entire paragraph at the beginning of 1 Samuel 11 missing in the MT and the transmitted forms of the LXX.[12]

Although for the book of Isaiah 1QIsa[b] is quite close to the MT form of Isaiah,[13] the larger, older scroll, 1QIsa[a], constantly shows differences in orthography, morphology, and lexical items as well as textual pluses and minuses in comparison with the text of the MT.[14] Some of these are superior, some inferior; some are earlier readings, some later. Usually the variants are relatively minor, though occasionally they are more substantial. The same general situation obtains for the Isaiah MSS from Cave 4.[15]

When discussing the LXX above, it was noted that the LXX edition of Jeremiah is earlier and shorter than that in the MT, with a different order. Now 4QJer[b] documents the Hebrew form of the book that lay behind the Greek translation, confirming the validity of the Greek witness, and hinting that greater study of the LXX of other books would pay off for those seeking the Hebrew Bible and not just the MT form of it.[16] In contrast, the Daniel MSS agree with the MT in their textual edition,[17] although there are agreements with the Greek against the MT in individual textual variants.[18]

With our revised understanding of what the biblical text was like in

---

F. García Martínez (ed.), *The Texts of Qumran and the History of the Community: Proceedings of the Groningen Congress on the Dead Sea Scrolls (20–23 August 1989)*, 1. *Biblical Texts* (Paris: Gabalda [= *RevQ* 14/2 No. 54–55] 1989), 229–45.

[12]See F. M. Cross, 'The Ammonite Oppression of the Tribes of Gad and Reuben: Missing Verses from 1 Samuel 11 Found in 4QSamuel[a]', in *History, Historiography, and Interpretation*, ed. H. Tadmor and M. Weinfeld (Jerusalem: Magnes, 1983), 148–58; and E. Ulrich, *The Qumran Text of Samuel and Josephus* (HSM 19; Missoula, MT: Scholars Press, 1978) 166–70.

[13]See E. L. Sukenik, *The Dead Sea Scrolls of the Hebrew University* (ed. N. Avigad and Y. Yadin: Jerusalem: Hebrew University and Magnes Press, 1955 [Hebrew edition 1954]). There are additional fragments in D. Barthélemy and J. T. Milik (eds.), *Qumran Cave 1* (DJD I; Oxford: Clarendon Press, 1955) 66–8 + pl. XII.

[14]See M. Burrows (ed.), *The Dead Sea Scrolls of St. Mark's Monastery 1* (New Haven: American Schools of Oriental Research, 1950).

[15]See P. W. Skehan and E. Ulrich, in E. Ulrich *et al.*, *Qumran Cave 4, X: The Prophets* (DJD XV; Oxford: Clarendon Press, 1997) 7–143.

[16]See E. Tov, '71. 4QJer[b]', ibid., 171–6.

[17]Or at least no Aramaic or Hebrew fragments have been identified to date that might provide the basis for any of the Greek additions to Daniel.

[18]See the editions and article by E. Ulrich, 'Daniel Manuscripts from Qumran. Part 1: A Preliminary Edition of 4QDan[a]', *BASOR* 267 (1987) 17–37; 'Daniel Manuscripts from Qumran. Part 2: Preliminary Editions of 4QDan[b] and 4QDan[c]', *BASOR* 274 (1989) 3–26; 'Orthography and Text in 4QDan[a] and 4QDan[b] and in the Received Masoretic Text', in H. W. Attridge, J. J. Collins and T. H. Tobin (eds.), *Of Scribes and Scrolls: Studies on the Hebrew Bible, Intertestamental Judaism, and Christian Origins presented to John Strugnell on the Occasion of His Sixtieth Birthday* (CTSRR 5; Lanham, MD: University Press of America, 1990) 29–42.

antiquity, it has become reasonably clear that 11QPs[a], whose biblical status was long the minority opinion, should be recognized as a scriptural MS containing an alternate edition of the Book of Psalms,[19] and it also seems appropriate to question whether the MSS of the Song of Songs were secondarily 'Abbreviated Texts'[20] or rather variant literary editions of this collection.[21]

Having sketched a brief survey of the scriptural evidence provided by the Qumran scrolls, we can compare this evidence with that known from two other first-century witnesses, the New Testament and Josephus.

The New Testament

The NT draws heavily on the text and diction of the Hebrew Scriptures, primarily through the LXX. It witnesses clearly and massively to the diversity of textual forms circulating in Judaism in the first century CE. That point is so well known that it need only be recalled here, but of the many specific examples that could be elicited there is one that may be especially illuminating.

The narrative of Matthew 1–2 is structured as five vignettes depicting the birth of Jesus. Each vignette is illustrated by a quote from Scripture which tells the reader that this was done 'to fulfill what had been spoken by the LORD through the prophet' (cf. Matt 1:22). Four of the five quotations can be located in our traditional Bible. But the fifth, 'He shall be called a Nazorean' (Matt 2:23), cannot be located. When we assumed that the traditional text was the only text, Bible annotators or commentators would explain that it was 'unidentifiable in any Old Testament passage' (*NAB*). But with all we have learned in the past half-century about the pluriformity of the biblical text in antiquity, it is a reasonable suggestion to propose that, just as the other four citations, this one as well was in the Scriptures being used by the author of Matthew.

The clearly biblical MS 4QSam[a] at 1 Sam 1:22 has a reading shared by no other extant biblical text: ונת[ח]תיהו נזיר עד עולם. Though no other biblical MS as such has this reading, Josephus (*Ant.* 5.347) surprisingly does reflect it in precisely the same place witnessed by 4QSam[a]. He uses the word 'prophet', but that is because the term 'Nazir' would be

[19]See P. W. Flint, *The Dead Sea Psalms Scrolls and the Book of Psalms* (STDJ 17; Leiden: Brill, 1997), esp. 202–27; and E. Ulrich, 'Multiple Literary Editions: Reflections toward a Theory of the History of the Biblical Text', in D. W. Parry and S. D. Ricks (eds.), *Current Research and Technological Developments on the Dead Sea Scrolls: Conference on the Texts from the Judean Desert, Jerusalem, 30 April 1995* (STDJ 20; Leiden: Brill, 1996) 78–105, esp. 99–101.

[20]See E. Tov, 'Three Manuscripts (Abbreviated Texts?) of Canticles from Qumran Cave 4', *JJS* 46 (1995) 88–111.

[21]See E. Ulrich, 'The Qumran Scrolls and the Biblical Text', the 1997 Jerusalem Congress volume [in press].

unknown to his Greek audience; he never uses that word in the singular about an individual, and in fact he calls the Nazirite par excellence, Samson (cf. Judg 13:5, 7; 16:17), not a Nazirite but a prophet (*Ant.* 5.285). It should be noticed that this occurs in a birth narrative, and in the birth narrative of the person chosen to anoint David as king. I am not prepared to claim that this precise passage in 4QSam[a] was the source for Matt 2:23, but all reasonable indicators point toward the occurrence in the Matthaean author's scriptural text of a line, now no longer extant, that could serve as the basis for that quote. Thus, the NT both voluminously attests to the textual pluriformity of the Jewish Scriptures at the end of the Second Temple period and pointedly shows that the text of the Hebrew Bible used by many Jewish authors is frequently quite different from that preserved in the MT. The latter was demonstrably not viewed as 'the standard text'.

Josephus

Josephus has been demonstrated to have known, preserved, and trans-mitted narrative material which is or was in certain biblical texts of his day but which no longer appears in our contemporary Bibles.[22] That is, when the text of Josephus is compared with the *textus receptus*, words, phrases, ideas, and even an entire passage (the Nahash passage at the beginning of 1 Samuel 11) are preserved which do not agree with the *textus receptus* and thus are sometimes classified as 'non-biblical'.[23] They were, however, biblical for Josephus, and he had actually derived them from a 'biblical text'. Thus, Josephus also teaches us to expand our categories when inquiring into the state of the biblical text in the latter part of the first century CE.

Thus, prior to about 100 CE absolutely every source of evidence we have for the nature of the biblical text shows us that the biblical text was pluriform and dynamically growing – the Qumran scrolls, the Samaritan Pentateuch, the Septuagint, the New Testament, and Josephus all show that there were variant literary editions of many of the biblical books. There is no indication of a standard text form. In fact, four of those five Jewish sources use the Scriptures in a Greek form! They saw no requirement to use the Hebrew, which would presumably be an important aspect of 'the standard text'. The point to be emphasized here, however, is that the forms they use, regardless of

---

[22]See E. Ulrich, *The Qumran Text of Samuel and Josephus* (HSM 19; Missoula: Scholars Press, 1978); and 'Josephus' Biblical Text for the Books of Samuel', *Josephus, the Bible, and History* ed. Louis H. Feldman and Gohei Hata (Detroit: Wayne State University, 1989) 81–96.

[23]See, e.g., Marcus in the Loeb edition of the *Jewish Antiquities*, 201 note c; 330–331 note a; 425 note c; 433 note a; and *passim*.

language, attest to differing Hebrew texts behind the Greek texts. Each source shows major disagreement as well as agreement with the MT. There is no strong evidence for the MT as 'the standard text' before the First Revolt.

Other indicators

Perhaps a quick look may be permitted at other possible indicators concerning whether the scrolls found at Qumran are peculiar to Qumran or are typical of the Scriptures of general Judaism. We are examining human artefacts – scrolls – and asking whether they are like or unlike those in general Judaism, or whether they are different, marginal, non-standard, 'sectarian'. But we do not have any other contemporary scrolls from Jerusalem or wider Judea; the scrolls predate by centuries all other biblical MSS.

We do, however, have other artefacts: pottery and coins found at Qumran, and we have pottery and coins from Judea to compare. With regard to the pottery (following Jodi Magness), the type common at Qumran is rare elsewhere, and some pottery common elsewhere in Roman Judea is rare at Qumran. The pottery in the caves was identical in form, material, and date with that in the settlement, though more limited in quantity. De Vaux also thought that the type of clay suggested that it was manufactured locally. Thus it is likely that the pottery is typical of Qumran and different from that in general Judea. With regard to the coins, in contrast, they are basically similar to those in use in wider Judea; there is no reason to think that those coins found at Qumran are unique to Qumran.

With regard to the biblical scrolls, there is no evidence whatsoever in any scroll of any book that the text was changed due to any interest, belief, practice, or polemic connected with the Qumran community. The thesis that the biblical scrolls are thus illustrative of the shape of the Scriptures used in general Judaism at the time is bolstered by a further consideration. There is no detectable difference in scrolls thought to be copied *outside* Qumran (sometimes because the MSS date from before the Qumran settlement) from those possibly copied *at* Qumran. A detailed study of the scriptural texts written in the Palaeo-Hebrew script, analysing them from the four categories of physical features of the manuscripts, palaeography and date, orthography, textual character and affiliation, demonstrated this point.[24] No feature in any of the other

---

[24]E. Ulrich, 'The Palaeo-Hebrew Biblical Manuscripts from Qumran Cave 4', in D. Dimant and L. H. Schiffman (eds.), *Time to Prepare the Way in the Wilderness: Papers on the Qumran Scrolls by Fellows of the Institute for Advanced Studies of the Hebrew University, Jerusalem, 1989–1990* (STDJ 16; Leiden: Brill, 1995) 103–29.

MSS published since argues against extending this conclusion to the remainder of the biblical MSS.

We cannot be certain, of course, but probability does point to the likelihood that a few of the biblical MSS were copied at Qumran, whereas most were copied in Jerusalem or wider Palestine and brought to Qumran. It appears quite likely that 4QSam[c] was copied at Qumran or at least by an influential member of the Qumran community, since the same person copied 1QS – the copy of the developed *Community Rule* which was stored specially in Cave 1 – the *Testimonia* (4Q175), and an insertion in the Great Isaiah Scroll (1QIsa[a] at 40:8); all exhibit the idiosyncratic features of this scribe. But the ability to assign several MSS to a single scribe is rare among the 800 scrolls. Since there appear to be almost as many scribes as there are MSS, the conclusion seems quite plausible that the majority of the MSS, including the biblical MSS, were copied outside Qumran and thus brought to Qumran.

In sum, nothing in any of the biblical scrolls suggests any specific Qumran features or tampering, while everything fits what is known from every other source for the general Jewish biblical text prior to *ca.* 100 CE.

III. Late Second Temple Judaism

Criteria: 'Who ran what?'[25]

Another important matter which must be considered before we can arrive at a solid answer about 'standard texts' is that of leadership in Judaism in the late Second Temple period. What group was 'in charge' that might render a decision in an important matter such as the selection of 'standard texts'. We are concerned with leadership in general, which was always a mixture of political and religious leadership, but we will keep an eye also specifically on the question of the text form of the Scriptures. Who was in charge? Who decided how the religion functioned practically? When there were significant differences and debates, did most people know and care about them? Whom did most people follow? How do we determine whether there was enough of a unified Judaism to ground the concept of a single standard or authoritative text form?

In this period, leadership in Judaism was basically the same as it had been in the earlier period after the return from Babylon: 'an aristocratic oligarchy, headed by the high priest whenever there was no king'.[26] The

---

[25]For this apt phrase I am obviously indebted to E. P. Sanders, who gave that title to his Chapter 21 in *Judaism: Practice and Belief 63 BCE–66 CE* (London: SCM Press/Philadelphia: Trinity Press International, 1992) 458.

[26]Sanders, *Judaism*, 383.

Sadducees were 'a key element in the Hasmonean aristocracy, supporting the priest-kings and joining with the Pharisees in the Gerousia'; they dominated that body 'for most of the reign of John Hyrcanus and that of Alexander Janneus'.[27] The Pharisees arose probably in early Hasmonaean times and 'played a major role during the period from 135 to 63 BCE; they could affect public events very substantially when everything was intra-Jewish'.[28]

Upon the death of Alexander Jannaeus in 76 BCE, during the rule of his wife Salome Alexandra (76-67) and in accord with her wishes, the Pharisees wielded great power. But in 63 BCE, once Rome's power menaced Palestine, matters were increasingly no longer intra-Jewish. 'For the most part, Roman authority was channelled through the high priest and his allies and friends – the chief priests and the powerful. ... The Pharisees on the whole were not in this category ... Rome's policy of ruling through the local aristocracy ... excluded most of the Pharisees from positions of influence'.[29]

Thus, the high priest, the chief priests, the Sadducees, and the powerful exercised the main leadership among Jews throughout most of the late Second Temple period. The Pharisees seem to have played a major (but not necessarily dominant) role from 135 to 76, and to have risen to leadership briefly, from 76 to 63 BCE, but then were eclipsed when the Romans invaded.

Who was 'in charge' of the Scriptures?

For producing copies of the books of Scripture the group that most likely was responsible was the Jerusalem priesthood. And (were one to consider the distinction historically operative) insofar as there might have been a conscious prioritizing of more 'official' texts vs. 'vulgar' texts, again the Jerusalem priesthood would presumably have been the responsible producers of the more 'official' or 'authoritative' texts.

It was presumably also from that Jerusalem priesthood that at least some, including and especially the leadership, of the Qumran settlers derived. Insofar as that be correct, we should expect that the biblical scrolls in the Covenanters' possession would be texts in line with those of the Jerusalem priesthood and Temple.

On the other hand, if one is peering through the antique fog and shadows looking to find 'the proto-MT', it would presumably be in

---

[27]Lawrence H. Schiffman, *From Text to Tradition: A History of Second Temple and Rabbinic Judaism* (Hoboken, NJ: Ktav, 1991) 111.

[28]Sanders, *Judaism*, 383.

[29]Sanders, *Judaism*, 388.

the hands of the Pharisees where one would expect to find it. It is the Pharisees whom one assumes would be listed as those favoring the texts that would eventually become the MT.[30] Now, if the text in the hands of the Pharisees for each book was consciously 'the proto-MT', then it was either the same text as that in the hands of the Jerusalem priesthood, or it was their distinctive text choice. If it were the same as that of the priests, it would be meaningless to refer to it as the proto-Rabbinic text, and it should be similar to the majority of manuscripts or citations from Judaism in antiquity – which is demonstrably not the case. If it were different from that of the Jerusalem Temple and priesthood, it would not (could not?) have been considered the dominant, much less the 'standard', text.

As a condition for claiming that the MT or any single text form was to be considered the authoritative or dominant form, there would have to be several types of awareness required. There would have to be (1) awareness not just vaguely that 'some texts differ', or awareness of a few sporadic 'hot-topic' variants, but awareness of variant textual editions or 'text types' as such, and (2) this awareness would have to encompass each individual book of the collection, because the MT, just as the LXX, is not a unified 'text type' but varies from book to book through the collection. Demonstration – were it possible – of these types of awareness in the Second Temple period would be a significant contribution to scholarship.

Moreover, in addition to (a) an *awareness* of different text forms for each book, there would have to be (b) *conscious concern* that one form ought to be preferred to others, (c) some *authoritative group* who decided one way or the other, and (d) the *acknowledgement* by a reasonably large percentage of Jews of that specific text form. That is: (a–b) if there were no awareness of different text forms and no conscious concern that one form be preferred to others, then the claim for a standard text (in the normative sense) could not be made; simple use does not constitute normativeness.[31] (c) If there were an awareness of different text forms and a conscious concern that one form be preferred to others, but there were no authoritative group who could make a decision one way or the other, then again the claim for a standard text cannot be made; there would simply be different text

[30]I suspect that at this early stage we cannot really focus sufficiently – analogous to the bottom line on the ophthalmologist's chart – to identify text types. But even if such precise focus were possible, it must be remembered that we would have to repeat the procedure for each individual book.

[31]Such a text form might be called 'the standard text', but only in the religiously insignificant sense of the text that people happen to use.

forms that people disagreed over, and the disagreement is the end of the story. (d) Similarly, if there were an authoritative group who did make a decision but there were no acknowledgement by a reasonably large percentage of Jews of that text form, the claim for a standard text cannot be made; that text form would not in fact have achieved the status of 'the standard text'.[32]

Finally, as a condition for claiming that the proto-MT specifically was considered the authoritative or dominant text form, one would have to demonstrate for a significant number of individual books that the *edition* as well as the *specific sub-family* attested by the MT was *consciously preferred* to other known text editions, to demonstrate that the *main leadership group* who decided such matters *concurred* in this conscious selection, and to demonstrate that most influential religious *leaders and authors actually used* those specific texts when they wrote.

Nothing in my text-critical experience supports any of the notions above.

Conclusion

I have attempted to look at a manageable collection of the most significant data concerning the nature of the Jewish Scriptures at the end of the Second Temple period to sketch an answer to our historical question. Examining the presuppositions behind the phrasing of the question as first posed, I made an effort at refining the question in such a way that it does not unduly influence the way that we look at and explore the data. The attempt was to pose the question as neutrally as possible, so that Jews from antiquity answering the question might describe the scene as they really saw it and characteristically thought about it. I have also admitted that any description and explanation of the data necessarily involves interpretation, which, though it may strive for objectivity, is always flavored with subjectivity (subjectivity introduced by the very education, training, mindset, and previous experience of the investigator).

The revised form of the question was: what were the texts of the Scriptures like near the end of the Second Temple period?

To answer that question properly, a number of sub-questions had to be asked and examined one by one.

Both all our previously known sources – the Samaritan Pentateuch, the Septuagint, the New Testament, Josephus – and the evidence from

---

[32]If all these conditions appear to be excessive, I would point to the quotation cited by Sanders (*Judaism*, p. vi) from Macaulay's *Machiavelli*: 'Historians rarely descend to those details from which alone the real estate of a community can be collected'.

the biblical manuscripts found at Qumran point unambiguously in the same direction:

1. Variant literary editions of many individual books.
2. A canon-in-process, but not a canon – i.e., a collection of Sacred Scriptures largely but not completely acknowledged and agreed upon: Certainly full agreement both on the fact that the Torah was canonical in the sense of *norma normans*, and on the five books that constituted the Torah; virtually complete agreement by all except the Samaritans and possibly the Sadducees that the Prophets was a collection of Sacred Scriptures, though the specific contents of the collection was not fixed.
3. No group that engaged in the type of systematic textual analysis that we moderns assume when we speak of a 'standard text', nor any group that has left evidence of awareness of text types or concern that one text type be preferred over another.

Moreover, we searched but found no group in charge that was likely to promote and promulgate any particular text type that was to serve as the 'standard text' in contrast to other textual forms. A fortiori, there was no evidence that such a 'standard text' would have been specifically the proto-MT. The 'proto-MT' appears to be a category in the mind of the modern person who looks back on the ancient forms of biblical texts and sees the later categories present and operative where historically one would call them indiscriminate texts that happen to have been picked up and used without awareness of specific

It appears that the manuscripts of the books of the Scriptures found at Qumran are, as are all witnesses to the scriptural texts until the end of the first century CE, representative of the state of the Law and the Prophets in general Judaism of this period. Though they were *found* at Qumran and some may have been copied there, they represent *the Scriptures of general Judaism*. In the few instances in which we can reasonably conclude that scriptural scrolls were copied at Qumran, there is no trace of alteration in the text due to any kind of concerns specific to that community. Nor is there any necessary connection to a particular text type or text tradition that is specific to Qumran.

Similarly, when looking at the other textual witnesses from various sectors of Judaism outside Qumran in the Second Temple period, I could find no indications – with the exception of the two glaring features characteristic of the (specifically) Samaritan Pentateuch, and possibly the Mt. Gerizim–Mt. Ebal variant – that any of the rival groups altered their scriptural texts on the basis of competing religious ideologies. The various groups and parties debated and fought, but they did so *outside* the boundaries of the scriptural texts. They argued through their own contemporary theological books and pamphets, not by changing the text of the Law and the Prophets. Even in the case of the Samaritan Pentateuch we have seen greatly reduced the amount of creative editing of which the Samaritans had formerly been accused. Most of the intentional editorial changes that had been observed in the Samaritan Pentateuch had already been present in the expanded variant editions of Exodus and Numbers available in general Judaism; the Samaritans made only their two characteristic types of change (plus possibly the third regarding Mt. Gerizim).

The scrolls as well as the other contemporary witnesses bountifully attest to a pluriformity – and as far as we can tell, a fully accepted pluriformity – in the text of the Scriptures. There is no noticeable indication of a widespread concern to have a single 'standard text' or to move toward one. Even if the so-called 'stabilization of the biblical text' is agreed to have been a phenomenon of the second century CE, it should be questioned whether 'stabilization' may not be the wrong word to describe the reality. Should not the '-iz-' morpheme be avoided, since it denotes causal activity? Should not simply the stative notion of 'a uniform text' or 'a single text form' be used instead, since it appears that Talmon's insight remains the best here: that the rabbis simply 'ended up' with only the single collection of texts that now constitute the Masoretic Text? They did not 'establish' or 'stabilize' the texts but 'received' – *Masorah* – a collection of texts of differing characteristics, text type, sequence in the series of successive literary editions, and quality.

In addition to the realization of the situation in which variant literary editions of the different books were common, the Qumran scrolls combine with the other witnesses to show that those were not just synchronically variant literary editions but also diachronically variant. Viewed from the perspective of the individual books, there was a series of successive literary editions. And it is a reasonable hypothesis that the succession of developing literary editions of the books which is documentable in the latter half of the Second Temple period is only the visible part of the literary iceberg, and that the phenomenon is simply the continuation of the series of major redactional growth-spurts that constitute the compositional process for the books of the Bible from their very beginnings.

If accurate, that would mean that the growth of the individual biblical books developed through repeated creative new editions over time, that this process was constitutive of the biblical books from start to end, that the process was still in effect throughout the Second Temple period, and that it came to an abrupt halt as the result of radically new and different outside factors. The Scriptures did not 'achieve final form' due to a natural and internal process, due to a maturation process, or due to 'the fullness of time', but they suffered an abrupt freezing due to the double threat of loss: the threat of loss of their lives, land, and culture to the Romans, and the threat of loss of their ancient identity as 'Israel' to the Christians, the growing majority of whom were now gentile rather than Jewish.

Since Jewish authors were the creative hands behind the revised literary editions, and since there is no evidence to the contrary, we can presume that all major intentional change in the Hebrew texts (though not in the versions) ceased sometime near 100. It then becomes a tricky question which form of the text of each book is to be included in 'The Bible'. It would seem to be a decision based on religious principles to choose the Masoretic collection of texts uniformly.

The evidence strongly indicates that prior to the second century CE there was no 'standard biblical text', but rather that the manuscripts of the Scriptures found at Qumran are representative of the Jewish Scriptures generally.

5

QUMRAN EVIDENCE FOR A BIBLICAL STANDARD TEXT AND FOR NON-STANDARD AND PARABIBLICAL TEXTS

Julio Trebolle-Barrera

The discussion about the Qumran evidence on the biblical text in the Second Temple Period is usually set in terms of a dilemma for *or* against a standard biblical text.[1] The purpose of this paper is twofold: to discuss some aspects of the Qumran evidence for a standard biblical text *and* also for non-standard biblical texts in the period; and to establish a relationship between the new concepts of 'multiple editions' detected in certain biblical books and of 'parabiblical' texts or writings related to these books. The scope of this paper must be limited to some insights on a rather complex subject, connected with others as broad as the history of the formation of the biblical canon, the history of the edition and textual transmission of the biblical books, and the history of the biblical exegesis in the Qumran texts and in the Jewish literature of the Second Temple period.

Before entering into the questions proposed an idea is needed of how the Bible looked in the Qumran period. On the literary level, the Qumran exegetical literature (pesharim, thematic midrashim and targumim) as well as the Qumran parabiblical literature help to delimit the extent of the Bible, as far as this exegetical and parabiblical literature is concerned. On the textual level, the editorial history of the biblical books and the process of standarization of the biblical text help also to delimit two collections of books differently preserved, edited, ordered and interpreted.

I. Two Series of Books Differently Preserved, Edited, Ordered and Interpreted

1. The Torah, Isaiah, Twelve Prophets and Psalms or 'David' (plus Job or 'Solomon')

The books of the Torah, Isaiah, Twelve or Minor Prophets and Psalms present common characteristics, that differ from those of a second series of books: Joshua, Judges, 1–2 Samuel, 1–2 Kings, Jeremiah and Ezekiel plus Daniel.

---

[1] I thank A. Graeme Auld for having suggested the topic of this paper as he kindly transmitted to me the invitation to participate in the Edinburgh Conference. I thank him also for the revisión of my English text.

a. To judge from *the care in preserving the manuscripts and the number of copies preserved*, the books of the first series enjoyed a special consideration in the libraries of the Judaean Desert caves. Among the Qumran biblical manuscripts 39 (+ 2?) copies of Ps have been counted, 32 (+ 3?) of Deut, 22 of Isa and 10 (+ 1?) of Twelve Prophets. Cave 1, characterized by the special conditions of preservation of its scrolls, has delivered 2 copies of Isa (1QIsa^a,b), 3 of Ps (1QPs^a,b,c) and 1 copy each of Gen, Ex, Lev and Deut, as well as of Judg and 2 Sam. Cave 11 also preserved important scrolls, among them 5 copies of Ps, two of them of a particular value (11Q5, 11Q6), 2 of Lev, 1 of Deut, and only 1 copy of a book of the second series (Ezek).[2]

The book of Twelve Prophets was highly valued in the period, particularly by the revolutionaries of Naḥal Ḥever who destroyed by fire all their documents except a well used copy of the Twelve (8ḤevXIIgr) that they buried with their dead in the innermost parts of the Cave of Horror.[3] This book had a special significance, obviously a messianic and eschatological one.

Job is the only book, besides those of the Torah, of which a copy written in a formal Palaeo-Hebrew script has been found at Qumran (4Q101) as well as two copies of a targum (4Q157, 11Q10).

b. The *textual and literary tradition* of the books of the Torah, Isaiah, Twelve Prophets and Psalms is relatively homogeneous, particularly if compared to that of the books of the second collection, transmitted in various editions or textual forms. The so called proto-Samaritan text of the Pentateuch did not develop very much beyond the stage represented by 4QpaleoEx^m, whose date has been shifted from a very early period (ca. 200 BCE) to around 100 years later.[4] Similarly, the proto-masoretic text of the Pentateuch does not seem to have developed very much beyond a stage earlier than that of the proto-Samaritan.[5]

---

[2]Important scrolls were also entrusted to cave 2 (12 copies of books of the Torah, 1 of Ps, 1 of Job, and from the second series, 2 of Ruth, 1 of Jer), cave 3 (1 copy of Ps, 1 of Ezek and 1 of Lam), cave 5 (1 copy of Deut, Isa, Amos and Ps, and from the second series 2 of Lam and 1 of Kgs) and cave 6 (3 copies of books of the Torah and 1 of Kgs, Song and Dan).

[3]'The only other possible tomb genizah of this period, the admitted earliest of its kind, was found at Murabba'at. The only document found in this burial (P.Mur. 88) also happens to be a copy of the Twelve Prophets, this time in Hebrew', B. W. R. Pearson 'The Book of the Twelve, Aqiba's Messianic Interpretations, and the Refuge Caves of the Second Jewish War', *The Scrolls and the Scriptures. Qumran Fifty Years After* (eds. S. E. Porter and C. A. Evans; Sheffield, 1997) 221–39 (234–5).

[4]J. E. Sanderson, '22. 4QpaleoExodus^m', in DJD IX 70.

[5]The manuscripts of Genesis and Exodus from Cave 4 have two types of text; in Exodus there is also a third type which corresponds to a recension, J. Davila, DJD XII 31–78; *idem*, 'Text-Type and Terminology: Genesis and Exodus as Test Cases', *RevQ* 61 (1993) 3–37. As for Exodus, 4QEx^b represents a short text; 4QpaleoExodus^m, instead, as well as 4QNum^b in

The text of the book of Isaiah was known in a rather stable form. Most of the variants of 1QIsaᵃ can be explained in terms of a number of tendencies and exegetical activity in the manner of the pesharim, although some readings of 1QIsaᵃ may still be preferable to the MT.

The text of the 7 copies of Twelve Prophets from cave 4 coincides substantially with that of the MT.[6]

The contribution of the Qumran manuscripts of Psalms to the study of the text of the Psalter seems to be rather meagre. By contrast, it is of the greatest importance for the study of the editorial formation of the Psalter. The book of Psalms is positioned at the borderline between the first and the second series of books, between the Prophetic books and the Writings and also between the biblical status and the liturgical function of its text. The editorial model of Psalms, consisting in a cumulative addition of smaller books, resembles that of Isaiah and Twelve Prophets, more than that of the second series of books. These were re-edited through the introduction of changes in the structure of the book (addition and/or omission of materials and rearrangement of the order of those which make up the book).

The books of the first series were edited by successive additions of independent books: the older books, placed at the beginning of the collection, are assigned to the monarchic period; the more recent books, placed at the end of the complete work, were formed during or after the Exile. In this way, the books of Hosea, Joel, Amos, Obadiah, Jonah and Micah as well as the first book of Isaiah (Isa 1–39) are assigned to the 8th c. BCE, those of Nahum, Habakkuk and Zephaniah to the 7th c. BCE, and those of Haggai, Zechariah and Malachi as well as the second (and third?) book of Isaiah (Isa 40–55; 56–66) belong to the 6th. c. BCE (although the order of books of the Twelve Prophets does not correspond exactly to their chronological sequence). Similarly, the first book of Psalms (3–41) comprises the oldest level of the Psalter, that goes back to the monarchic period. Next comes the second book (42–83), originating in the Northern Kingdom. The last third of the Psalter is later than the Exile, as proved by linguistic analysis. It is also the section with the greatest textual fluidity as shown by some of the Psalters found at Qumran. These add psalms taken from other books of the OT, compositions not included in the Hebrew psalter, and even pieces composed by the Qumran community itself. They also omit some

---

Numbers, have a longer 'proto-Samaritan' text. The variants in Exodus and Numbers seem to be better explained at the level of textual types (LXX, MT and 'proto-Samaritan') than at that of double editions, except perhaps for the final chapters of Exodus (Ex 35–40).

[6] Cf. R. Fuller, DJD XV 221–71.

psalms or give them in a different sequence.[7] The later editorial activity on Psalms comes nearer to the editorial model of the second series of books.

The book of Job, in spite of its great difficulty, is transmitted in a rather stable text. The considerably shorter text of the Septuagint eliminates the difficulties of the more original MT and seems more like a paraphrase than a translation.

c. The *Septuagint* of this collection of books helps more as a source of data for the study of the Jewish exegesis in the period, while the Greek version of the second series contributes more to the recognition of an intensive editorial activity affecting the books of that series.

d. The *Qumran exegetical literature* (pesharim, thematic midrashim and targumim), as well as the sectarian rules (*Damascus Document, Serek Damascus Document, Tohorot*) consider as Bible for their purpose the books of the Torah, Isaiah, Minor Prophets and Psalms.

The *Qumran pesharim* comment only on the books of Isaiah, Minor Prophets and Psalms: Isaiah (3Q4, 4Q161–165), Hosea (4Q166–167), Micah (1Q14, 4Q168), Nahum (4Q169), Habakkuk (1QpHab), Zephaniah (1Q15), Malachi (5Q10) and Psalms (1Q16, 4Q171, 4Q173). Four of these pesharim were kept in the important cave 1: 1QpHab, 1QpMic, 1QpZeph and 1QpPs.

Among *the thematic midrashim from Qumran*, 4QTanhumim (4Q176) quotes from Isaiah (40:1–5; 41:8–9; 43:1–2; 43:4–6; 49:7; 49:13–17; 51:22–23; 52:1–3; 54:4–10), Zechariah (13:9) and probably from Ps 79:2–3 (frg. 1–2 I 1–4). The thematic midrashim with eschatological content quote mainly from this first series of books, although they include a few selected passages taken from books of the second series. 4QCatena[a] (4Q177 = 4QMidrEschat[b]) quotes from Isaiah to interpret some Psalms and particularly Mic 2:10–11 to comment on Ps 11:1–2, Zech 3:9 on Ps 12:7, Ezek 25:8 on Ps 13:5 and Hos 5:8 on Ps 17:1. 4QFlorilegium (4Q174 = 4QMidrEschat[a]) interprets 2 Sam 7:10–14 with the help of Am 9:11, Ps 1:1 with that of Isa 8:11 and Ezek 37:23, and Ps 2:1–2 in relation with Dan 12:10 and 11:32.[8] 4QCatena[b] (4Q182 = 4QMichEschat[c]) adduces for interpretation the text of Jer 5:7. 4QTestimonia (4Q175) cites only from the Pentateuch but ends

[7]G. H. Wilson, *The Editing of the Hebrew Psalter* (Chico, CA, 1985) 139–228; P. W. Flint, *The Dead Sea Psalms Scrolls and the Book of Psalms* (Leiden, 1997) 227.

[8]A. Steudel, *Der Midrasch zur Eschatologie aus der Qumrangemeinde (4QMidrEschat[a,b]): Materielle Rekonstruktion, Textbestand, Gattung und Traditionsgeschichtliche Einordnung des durch 4Q174 (Florilegium) und 4Q177 (Catena[a]) Repressentierten Werkes aus den Qumranfunden* (Leiden 1994).

with a quotation of Jos 6:26. 11QMelchizedek (11Q13) quotes Lev 25:9.13, Deut 15:2, Isa 52:7; 61:2–3, and Ps 7:8–9; 82:1–2.[9]

The Qumran legal literature quotes also almost exclusively from the first collection of books. The *Damascus Document* introduces 20 quotations from the Pentateuch (Gn 1x, Exod 2x, Lev 4x, Num 4x, Deut 9x), 8 from Isaiah, 11 from the Twelve and only one from 1 Sam, Ezek and Prov. *4QSerek Damascus Document* (4Q265) adduces Lev 12:2; 12:4 and Isa 54:1–2. *4QDamascus Document*[a] (4Q266) cites Lev 26:31; Joel 2:12 and 2:13, and *4QTohorot A* (4Q274) has a quotation of Lev 13:45.

The presence of a *targum of Job* among the Qumran manuscripts (4Q157, 11Q10), in addition to other characteristics of this book already noted, proves the special character that the book of Job enjoyed as the 'Solomonic' complement to the first collection.[10]

e. Like the exegetical and legal literature from Qumran, *the New Testament* quotes almost exclusively from the books of the Pentateuch, Isaiah, Twelve Prophets and Psalms. This is particularly the case of the earliest Christian writings (Mark and the double or triple synoptic tradition) and of the quotations they attribute to Jesus, Peter and Stephen, often in the tradition of pesher interpretation.[11] The conception of the OT canon attested in Luke 24:44, 'the Law of Moses, the prophets, and the psalms' seems to be reflected in the oldest

---

[9]4QMessianic Apocalypse (4Q521), clasified as an apocalypse (É. Puech) or as a sapiential work (F. García Martínez), comes near to the exegetical literature as a commentary on Ps 147:7–8 and Isa 61:1 and seems to come from circles close to the Qumran group in which the work could have been composed in the second half of the 2nd. c. BCE. Cf. É. Puech, *La croyance des esséniens en la vie future: inmortalité, résurrection, vie éternelle? Histoire d'une croyance dans le Judaïsme ancien* (Paris 1993) 627ff. F. García Martínez, *The Dead Sea Scrolls Translated* (Leiden/New York, 1994) 394f.

[10]R. Beckwith, *The Old Testament Canon of the New Testament Church and its Background in early Judaism* (London, 1985) 203 and 209.

[11]The problem of distinguishing between direct quotations, on one hand, and allusions, employment of biblical phraseology or references to Old Testament history, on the other, makes difficult to stablish the exact number of quotations present in the NT books. The following numbers, that do not take into account combinations of two or more biblical texts, should for our purpose be not too far from the true state of things:

Matthew, 37 quotations: Torah, 15; Isa, 9 (or 10); XIIProph, 5; Ps, 6. Two quotations of Matthew (Matt 2:18 and 21:13) come from Jeremiah, but the second includes also a quotation of Isaiah, and a third one in Matt 27:9–10 combines texts of Jeremiah and Zechariah. The important passage of Matt 11:10 (Luke 7:27) combines two texts that enclose the whole prophetical tradition: Isa 40:3 (cited also in Qumran) and Mal 3:1: 'He is the man of whom it is written: "See, I send my messenger before you, who will prepare your way before you"'.

Mark, 9 quotations: Torah, 5; Isa, 1; XIIProph, 1; Ps, 2

Luke, 16 quotations: Torah, 9; Isa, 3; XIIProph, 1; Ps, 3

John: 7 quotations: Isa, 2; Ps, 3; XIIProph, 2.

Acts, 23 quotations: Torah, 7; Isa, 5; XIIProph, 4; Ps, 7

Rom: 45 quotations: Torah, 16; Isa, 14; XIIProph, 4; Ps, 9; 1 Kgs 2

collection of books, Torah, Prophets and Psalms, translated in the 1st–2nd centuries CE into Syriac in connection with the Targum tradition, a version possibly and partly at least made by Jews. This may have antecedents in an ancient Jewish conception of the Bible that, at least for exegetical purposes and eschatological interpretation, emphasized the authority of the Torah and the Prophets including Psalms ('David') (cf. *Rule of the Community* 1:2–3; 8:15–16). The letters of Paul as well as the NT Jewish Christian tractates, Hebrews and the epistles of James, 1 and 2 Peter, also employ for authoritative quotations the books of Job and Proverbs ('Solomon').[12] As within certain Jewish communities, there was also among the first Judeo-christians something like a 'canon-within-a-canon'.[13] In view of a christological application the Christian Church also developed a tendency to close the OT canon with the Minor Prophets, a book prone to messianic and eschatological interpretations (see above).

f. *The books of Isaiah and Twelve Prophets follow after those of Jeremiah and Ezekiel* according to the older of the known ancient lists of biblical books. The baraita of the Babylonian Talmud *Baba Bathra* 14b orders the prophetical books in pairs: Joshua *and* Judges, Samuel *and* Kings, Jeremiah *and* Ezekiel, Isaiah *and* Twelve Prophets. This order of books may correspond to that of the list known by Judas Maccabee around 164 BCE. The earliest lists of biblical books open the collection of Writings with the pair Psalms *and* Job (or Job-Psalms), preceded or separated by Ruth, a book that changes position easily in the lists. The position of the book of Isaiah after those of Jeremiah and Ezekiel was later known in the list of 'Oklah we 'Oklah, in the midrashic compilation of Yalqut Shimoni (XIII c.), and especially in German

---

1 Cor: 15 quotations: Torah, 4; Isa, 6; Ps, 3; Jer, 1; Job, 1

2 Cor: 7 quotations: Torah, 3; Isa, 1; Ps, 2; Jer, 1

Gal: 10 quotations: Torah, 8; Isa, 1; XIIProph, 1

Heb: 38 quotations: Torah, 11; Isa, 2; XIIProph, 2; Ps, 18; Jer, 3; 2 Sam, 1 (significantly 2 Sam 7:14 as in 4QFlorilegium); Prov, 1. Cf. E. E. Ellis, 'Old Testament Quotations in the New: A Brief History of the Research', in *The Old Testament in Early Christianity. Canon and Interpretation in the Light of Modern Research* (Tübingen, 1991) 51–74 (with bibliography).

[12]Job and Proverbs are the only books to be explicitly quoted in the NT besides those of the Torah, Later Prophets and Psalms: Job is quoted in Rom 11:34f.; 1 Cor 3:19 and Proverbs in Rom 12:19f.; Heb 12:5; Jas 4:6; 1 Pet 4:18; 5:5; 2 Pet 2:22. From the historical books or Former Prophets only two quotations are found in the NT. 2 Sam 7:14 is quoted in Heb 1:5b, but its joining with Ps 2 into something of a messianic catena as in 4QFlorilegium makes of this passage of the Nathan's prophecy a special biblical source to be quoted only in relation with Ps 2. Rom 11:3–4 quotes 1 Kgs 19:14, 18 ('the scripture says of Elijah') for a eschatological aplication: 'So too at the present time there is a remnant . . .'.

[13]M. Fishbane, 'Use, Authority and Interpretation of Mikra at Qumran', in *Mikra, Text, Translation, Reading and Interpretation of the Hebrew Bible in Ancient Judaism and Early Christianity* (CRINT 2/1; Van Gorcum/Assen/Maastricht, 1988) 339–77 (360).

manuscripts but also in Italian, Franco-German, Spanish, Yemenite, etc. Melito (*Hom.*, 62–64), Origen (*Ser. Mt.* 28 [49,24–26]) and Tertullian (*Scorpiace* 8,3) seem also to have known this order of books.[14] To these Christian sources can also perhaps be added the witness of a Judeo-christian work of ca. 175 CE, the *Adversus Judaeos* of Pseudo-Cyprian, that gives a list of couples of biblical figures in chronological order: Moses-Dathan, Aaron-Abiram, David-Saul, Elijah-Ahab, etc. Number 25 of the list contains the couples Jeremiah-Hananiah and Isaiah-Manasseh against the chronological order of the previous couples and reflecting possibly the sequence of books Jeremiah-Ezekiel-Isaiah.[15]

The books of Isaiah and Twelve Prophets were intimately connected as shown by their common *inscriptio*: 'in the days of Uzziah, Jotham, Ahaz, and Hezekiah, kings of Judah' (Isa 1:1; Hos 1:1). The collection of Twelve Prophets begins with the book of Hosea, a prophet contemporaneous with Isaiah. The final composition of Twelve Prophets has surprising structural and thematic parallels with the final form of the book of Isaiah, such as a common perspective centered in Sion and the vision of a universalistic future.[16] These parallels are better explained because of having formed a pair of books throughout their editorial process rather than because of the chiastic parallelism that can be found in the more recent order of books (Isa-Jer-Ezek-Twelve).

2. *Joshua, Judges, 1–2 Samuel, 1–2 Kings, Jeremiah and Ezekiel (plus Daniel)*

The books of this second series present a textual and literary history that neatly distinguishes them from those of the first series.

a. *The number of copies and the form of preservation* of these books indicate that their importance in the Qumran period was not comparable to that of the books of the first series.

b. These books were affected by *a process of multiple editions*. Given the limited evidence offered by the Qumran manuscripts, it is uncertain whether the scrolls represent a variant edition of a book or only of the extant passages, but the Old Greek and the Old Latin also come into the picture attesting an 'Old Hebrew' that was at variance with the

---

[14]R. Beckwith, *The Old Testament Canon of the New Testament Church* 122ff., 165, 206f. and 450ff.

[15]D. Van Damme, *Pseudo-Cyprian Adversus Iudaeos. Gegen die Judenchristen die älteste lateinische Predigt, Paradosis* (Beiträge Altchristlichen Literatur und Theologie 22; Fribourg-Schweiz, 1969) 54f. and 89.

[16]O. H. Steck, *Der Abschluss der Prophetie im Alten Testament. Ein Versuch zur Frage der Vorgeschichte des Kanons* (Neukirchen-Vluyn, 1991).

masoretic textual tradition, not only at the level of individual textual variants but also at that of different literary editions.

4QJosh[a] preserves a sequence of the narrative of Joshua's building of the first altar that is at variance with and probably prior to that found in the received text of Joshua. 4QJosh[a]–Josephus and MT-LXX display variant editions of the book of Joshua.[17]

4QJudg[a] is ignorant of a literary development in 6:7–10 and shows significant agreements with the OG (proto-Lucianic text) and OL, founding a presumption for the evaluation of the variant forms attested by the MT on one side and by the OG and/or OL on the other alongside the whole book.

4QSam[a] provides a paragraph not found in any other biblical text, though it was present in the text used by Josephus (1 Sam 10:27b–11:1). The MT of 1 Sam 17–18 transmits a 'second edition' of the story of David and Goliath, different from the shorter 'first edition' reflected by the OG.

In 1–2 Kings MT and OG represent two different editions with a different chronological system and a divergent editorial arrangement associated to the introduction of various 'miscellaneous' or 'parabiblical' materials (see below).

The MT of Jeremiah is one-eighth longer than the LXX and the two texts differ in the order of the material which makes up the book. They represent two different editions, both attested in Qumran manuscripts: the first by LXX and 4QJer[b,d] and the second by MT and 4QJer[a,c] and 2QJer.

The book of Ezekiel has also undergone a process of editorial revision, that resulted in the form of text represented by the MT (characterized by the present order of chapters 36–39). The MT has additions of various kinds throughout the book. Particularly important is the omission in LXX[967] of 36:23c–38 in connection with a change in the original order of the text as attested by the Septuagint.

The 8 Qumran manuscripts of Daniel, 1QDan[a,b], 6QDan and 4QDan[a–e], in spite of a whole series of variants to the MT, are nevertheless in line with the MT. The original Greek version reflects, however, a different edition that included passages not present in the previous edition.

These books knew one or various deuteronomistic redactions, or at least a deuteronomic influence, that those of the first series did not experience at least in the same proportion. The books of Joshua-Kings

---

[17]E. Ulrich, '47. 4QJosh[a]', DJD XIV 143–52; '4QJoshua[a] and Joshua's First Altar in the Promised Land', *New Qumran Texts and Studies. Proceedings of the First Meeting of the International Organization for Qumran Studies, Paris 1992*, ed. G. J. Brooke with F. García Martínez (Leiden: Brill, 1994), 89–104, Pl. 4–6; A. Rofé, 'The Editing of the Book of Joshua in the Light of 4QJosh[a]', *NQTS*, 73–80.

compose the 'deuteronomistic history' and those of Jeremiah and Ezekiel contain texts related with the deuteronomic and deuteronomistic literature (Jer 7:1–8:3*; 11*; 18*; 21*; 25*; 32*; 33f.*; 44* and Ezek 11:18–20; 20:27–29.41f.; 28:25f.; 34:23–24; 36:26–28.31f.; 37:13b–14.20–23, 24a; 38:17).

c. The *Septuagint* of these books differs from the MT textual tradition at the level of different literary editions and not only at that of the individual textual variants. Consequently most of these books passed through an early (pre-Aquilanic) recension, the so-called proto-Theodotionic recension, that affected the books of Judges, I–IV Kingdoms, Jeremiah and Ezekiel (Thackeray's β section). This early recension is probably to be distinguished from the properly Theodotionic additions to the LXX of Job and Daniel and the Theodotionic text of other books.[18]

d. The books of this second series, not suitable for commentaries in the pesher form such as those of Isaiah, Twelve Prophets and Psalms and in contrast to these same books, admitted *exegetical additions or parabiblical supplements* and, together with the Torah, they offered the *textual base for the creation of parabiblical developments* now called 'pseudo-', 'apocrypha', 'paraphrases', 'psalms' or 'visions' of biblical figures prominent in the Torah (the giants, the angels, Enoch, Amram, Noah, etc.) or in the books of this second series: *Apocryphon of Joshua, Vision of Samuel, Apocryphon of Jeremiah, Pseudo-Ezekiel, Pseudo-Daniel*, etc. These writings, generally marked by a strong eschatological accent, turn on the questions of the order of the cosmos and the periodization of history. They have an origin previous to the existence of the Qumran community and independent from the Essene groups that could make use of them.[19]

e. Explicit quotations from the books of this second series are very scarce in the *New Testament*. These books offer, on the contrary, abundant material for biblical allusions, employment of biblical phraseology, typological exegesis and references to the history of salvation and eschatology.

Although the earliest Christian writings know an interpretation akin to the Qumran pesher and quote almost exclusively from the books of

---

[18]The presence of proto-Theodotionic characteristics in the Greek scroll of the Twelve of Naḥal Ḥever as well as the possibility that the books of Jeremiah, Ezekiel and Minor Prophets are the work of the same translator seem to go against a clear differentiation of the two collections in this respect. Cf. E. Tov, *The Septuagint Translation of Jeremiah and Baruch. A Discussion of an Early Revision of the LXX of Jeremiah 29–52 and Baruch 1:1–3:8* (Missoula, MN: Scholars Press, 1976) 149.

[19]Cf. D. Dimant, 'Apocalyptic Texts at Qumran', CRC.

the first series, the Christians did not preserve among their literature any Jewish writing of exegetical character such as the Qumran pesharim, thematic midrashim and targumim, nor any work of a legal genre such as the Temple Scroll or 4QOrdinances. The Christians preserved instead many 'apocrypha' or 'parabiblical' writings related to the historical and prophetical books and still relatively more works of apocalyptic character related to prediluvian figures of the book of Genesis.

f. We may safely think that in the third and second centuries BCE *two different forms of arranging the prophetical books* coexisted: Isa-Jer-Ezek-Twelve Prophets, implied by Sir 48–49, and Jer-Ezek-Isa-Twelve Prophets, attested by *Baba Bathra* 14b. Against the supposition that the historical books are arranged in *Baba Bathra* 14b in chronological order, but the non-historical books in descending order of size,[20] is the fact that the books of Jeremiah and Ezekiel, coming after those of Joshua-Judges-Samuel-Kings, follow also a chronological order and the presence of Isaiah and Twelve Prophets at the end of the list can also answer to a chronological perspective. The second book of Isaiah (40–55) makes mention of Cyrus and relates to the Exilic period, as the last books that entered into the Twelve collection (Haggai, Zechariah and Malachi) come also from a time later than that of the prophets Jeremiah and Ezekiel. The order of prophetical books attested in Baba Bathra 14b seems to respond to the synchrony of the historical figures (the historical Isaiah and Hosea / Amos – the Second (and Third ?) Isaiah and Haggai / Zechariah / Malachi) and to the parallel process of edition of the books of Isaiah and Twelve Prophets.

II. 'Standard' and 'Non-standard' Texts and Editions

The concept of 'standard text' cannot be equally applied to the two series of books: in the first the question is basically of a 'standard type of text', in the second of a 'standard edition'.

As for the Torah, Isaiah, Twelve Prophets, and also, with peculiar characteristics, for Psalms, the standardization of the type of text represented by the proto-rabbinic textual tradition was much advanced in the Hasmonaean period.[21] The Qumran exegetical literature seems to

[20]R. Beckwith, *The Old Testament Canon of the New Testament Church*, 162.

[21]A. S. Van der Woude, 'Pluriformity and Uniformity. Reflections on the Transmission of the Text of the Old Testament', *Sacred History and Sacred Texts in Early Judaism. A Symposium in Honour of A. S. van der Woude* (eds. J. N. Bremmer and F. García Martínez; Kampen, 1993) 151–69; L. H. Schiffman, *Reclaiming the Dead Sea Scrolls. The History of Judaism, the Background of Christianity, the Lost Library of Qumran* (Philadelphia and Jerusalem, 1994) 173.

suppose a more or less standard text of these books, established already in the Maccabbean period, although still coexisting with other biblical textual forms (the Palestinian or proto-Samaritan text and the Hebrew type underlying the Septuagint). Among the oldest Qumran biblical manuscripts are those that display a text totally or practically identical to the MT (4QExod-Lev[f] = 4Q17 from ca. 250 BCE; 4QpaleoDeuteronomy[s] = 4Q46, ca. 250–200; 4QJer[a] = 4Q70, ca. 200; 4QpaleoJob[c] = 4Q101 from ca. 225–150 BCE) but also those that preserve a text akin to that reflected by the LXX (as 4QJer[b,d] = 4Q71, 4Q71a, ca. 200–150 BCE) or a text that goes its own way (as 4QJosh[a] = 4Q47, ca. 125–75 BCE; 4QPs[a] (4Q483), ca. 150 BCE). Manuscripts representing non-standard editions belong rather to an early period. Among the more recent copies, those that are virtually identical with the Masoretic text prevail (such as 4QExod[k] = 4Q21 and 4QGen[b] = 4Q2 from ca. 50–68 CE). Nevertheless, copies of independent or non-standard texts and editions continued to be produced until a relatively late period, such as 4QJudg[a] (4Q49) from ca. 50–25 BCE or 4QNum[b] (4Q27) from around 30 BCE–20 CE.[22]

A decisive factor in the standardization of the biblical text was its 'correction' at the hands of scribes eager to make their sacred books more patently 'orthodox', particularly in references to pagan deities. Like Christianity during its first two and a half centuries,[23] Judaism during the last two and a half centuries of the Second Temple period comprised a number of competing understandings of Israel, and competing groups pretending to represent the true Israel before the pagan nations. That sort of 'orthodox revision' affected the text of the Pentateuch, Isaiah and the Twelve, more than the text of the historical and other prophetical books. Psalms is located, in this respect also, between the first and the second series. In this way the MT of Deut 32:43 demythologises an older text that compared in synonymous parallelism 'heavens' and 'gods' and did not refrain from speaking of the 'sons' of gods (LXX, 4QDeut[q]). However, *benê (ha)'elohîm* continues to appear in the mythologized passage of Gen 6:2.4 and in Ps 29:1; 89:7 and Job 1:6; 2:1; 38:7 (cf. also Ps 82:6–7; 1 Kgs 22:19b–22).

The *edition* of the historical books and of Jeremiah that probably

---

[22]The evolution of the Qumran phylacteries reflects the process of standarization of the biblical text. The older 'Essene' phylacteries follow an unspecified text, which at times agrees with the Samaritan Pentateuch or the LXX and at others is completely different (4Q128–9; 4Q134–142), while the later 'Pharisee' phylacteries (4Q130, 4Q133) follow a text very like the later masoretic text.

[23]B. D. Ehrman, *The Orthodox Corruption of Scripture. The Effect of Early Christological Controversies on the Text of the New Testament* (New York: Oxford University Press, 1993).

became standard in proto-rabbinic circles from the Hasmonean period
onwards also shows signs of an early 'orthodox' revision. It contains a
series of artificial Hebrew vocalizations such as *molech, 'aštoret,
melekhet haššamayim, topheth*, etc., that were unknown to the Hebrew
edition of these books represented by the Septuagint version. This has a
transcription or a translation of the original Hebrew term: *milkom,
'ašerâ, malkat haššamayim, tapheth (tapteh ?)*.[24]

Once affirmed that the process of standarization of the type of text
(1st series) and of the literary edition (2nd series) represented by the
proto-rabbinic textual tradition could be very much advanced in the
Hasmonaean period, the question of the 'non-standard' texts and
editions is not resolved by assuming that these were consequently
vulgar, sectarian and out of control deviations from the standard text or
standard edition. Very much on the contrary, the non-standard texts or
editions are usually those that preserve older textual or editorial forms.
This is well known in classical textual criticism and also in the textual
history of the ancient biblical versions. The older texts, as the Old Greek
and Old Latin, were replaced by the standard texts, the Hexaplaric or
Lucianic in the Greek tradition and the Vulgate in the Latin. The older
or original texts were almost lost; and they have now to be traced back
behind the standard text.

As the text and editions of the proto-masoretic tradition were
becoming more and more standard, they displaced biblical and also
parabiblical texts that circulated beforehand towards the textual,
geographical and social margins. This phenomenon at the Hebrew level
occasioned a similar one in the Greek and Latin textual transmission.
The final result was the formation of a Greek recensional text that
became the standard one and the parallel triumph of the Vulgate, more
akin to the Hebrew standard tradition, over the Old Latin texts. The
recensional history of the versions is nothing but a reflection of a similar
process of creation of a standard Hebrew text that expelled other

---

[24]MT *'aštoret*: Judg 2:13; 1 Sam 7:3–4; 12:10; 31:10; 1 Kgs 11:5.33; 2 Kgs 23:13. The
Septuagint preserves the older Hebrew reading in transcription, *astartē* (or as the place name
Astarteion, 1 Sam 31:10), or translation, *ta alsē*.

Similarly, MT *melékhet/mlᵉ(')kt haššamayim*: Jer 7:18; 44:17, 18:19, 25 – LXX *malkat
haššamayim*, 'queen of heaven'.

MT *topheth*: 2 Kgs 23:10; Jer 7:31, 32; 19:6, 14; 19:12, 13. The Greek has the transcription
tapheth or the translation *diáptosis*. Aquila and Symmachus give usually *tapheth*.

Also the Hebrew form *mipleṣet* 'horrible idol' (1 Kgs 15:13 and 2 Chr 15:16, two instances
in each verse), seems also to have been unknown by the Hebrew original of the Septuagint,
that has *synodon* (Kings) and *leitourgousan* (Chr) .

On MT *molech* and the original reading, *milkom*, preserved in the Vorlage of the OG, cf. J.
Trebolle-Barrera, 'La transcripción mlk = μόλοχ. Historia del texto e historia de la lengua',
Aula Orientalis 5 (1987) 125–8.

previous text forms to the fringes of the textual tradition. As a consequence, the way of recovering these text forms, particularly in the case of the historical books, must necessarily proceed back from the Old Latin through the Old Greek to an 'Old Hebrew'.

To illustrate the model of analysis proposed here, the strange Hebraisms or Hebrew transcriptions present in the OL of Kings are a good point of departure.[25] According to 2 Kgs 13:17–19 Elisha said to King Joash who was fighting a war against the Arameans: 'You will destroy Aram in Aphek completely'. The versions follow the MT in the reading *ba'afeq 'ad kallê, en Aphek heos sunteleias* (LXX), *in Afec donec consumas eam (Siriam)* (Vulgate). The only witness here of the OL, the palimpsest Vindobonensis, presents the reading *in Aseroth quae est contra faciem Samariae usque ad finem*.[26] The word *Aseroth* transcribes the place name *ḥaṣerot*, known in Num 11:34; 12:16 (LXX Vulg 13:1); 33:17–18 and Deut 1:1 as a place in the Sinai peninsula, usually identified with 'Ain el Khadra. The story of 2 Kgs 13:15–19.25 refers, however, to a place on the way from Damascus to Samaria. According to the standard text this place is Aphek, identified as Fiq, on the Golan heights. The OL reading *Aseroth* seems to be completely desperate in this textual, literary, geographical and historical context. But it finds an unexpected confirmation, not in a Hebrew Qumran manuscript but, what is more astonishing, in the Samaria ostraca. These mention the place several times, identified by Aharoni with 'Asîreh eš-Šemalîyeh, to the East of Samaria, in an area very suitable to the geography of the battle referred to in 2 Kgs 13. The Samaria ostraca are probably to be dated in the first third of the reign of Jeroboam II (790–750), not much later than the battle referred to.[27] The coincidence of time and place between the OL *Aseroth* and the witness of the Samaria ostraca over a place called *ḥaṣerot* east from Samaria is very surprising and cannot have been an invention of the Latin translator.

This reading is not isolated but belongs to a whole complex of textual variants, additions and omissions attested by the OG and the OL in 2 Kgs 10–13, that correspond to a literary and historical tradition transmitted in a Hebrew edition of Kings different from the standard edition

[25]The Ethiopic version presents similar cases of Hebrew transcriptions identified by E. Ullendorf, 'Hebrew Elements in the Ethiopic Old Testament', *From the Bible to Enrico Cerulli. A Miscellany of Ethiopian and Semitic Papers* (Aethiopische Forschungen 32; Stuttgart, 1990) 42–50.

[26]Bonifatius Fischer with the collaboration of Eugene Ulrich and Judith E. Sanderson, 'Palimpsestus Vondobonensis: A Revised Edition of VL 115 for Samuel–Kings', *BIOSCS* 16 (1983) 13–87 (85).

[27]Y. Aharoni, *The Land of the Bible. A Historical Geography* (London, 1967), 315–27.

represented by the MT. Remains of this Hebrew non-standard edition could reach the OL through the OG (transmitted in 2 Kings by the proto-Lucianic text), obviating all the recensional influences from the Hebrew standard text that affected the Greek and Latin textual tradition and contributed to form the Greek and the Latin standard texts as well.[28]

As the *ḥaṣerot* reading and the whole complex of variants connected with it are present in a biblical text such as that attested by the OG and OL, there is no doubt about the biblical character of such readings and variants. But if every trace of the OG and OL texts had been completely lost and a Qumran Hebrew manuscript had delivered a fragmentary writing with traces of such texts embedded or mixed with portions of the MT of 2 Kgs 10–13, this writing would be classified as 'parabiblical', as much as the Apocryphon of Elisha (4Q481a) or 4QpapparaKings that recast or quote from the Elijah-Elisha stories.

III. Parabiblical Texts, Parabiblical Writings and Double Editions of Biblical Books

The concept 'parabiblical text' cannot be equally applied to the two series of books formerly distinguished; and, furthermore, a distinction should be made between 'parabiblical texts' and 'parabiblical writings'.

A 'parabiblical text' of the Pentateuch like 4QReworked Pentateuch[a,b,c] (4QRP[a,b,c] = 4Q158 and 4Q364–365) comprise a re-working of the 'biblical text' within small limits, characterized by the presence of exegetical additions, omissions or transpositions.[29] Other works that paraphrase the Pentateuch and modify its expressions to the point of making it almost unrecognisable could still be considered parabiblical texts, such as 4QGenesis Pesher[a] (4Q252, or 'Patriarchal Blessings'), 4QPseudo-Jubilees[ab] (4Q225–226), 4QAn Exposition on the Patriarchs (4Q464), 2QExodus[b] (2Q3) and 4QParaphrase of Genesis-Exodus (4Q422).[30]

'Parabiblical writings' are those which no longer keep to the sequence

---

[28]I remember John Strugnell saying that he would have much preferred to have found a complete manuscript of the OL rather than one more copy of an already known fragmentary Qumran Hebrew manuscript.

[29]Texts of the pre- or proto-Samaritan tradition as 4QpaleoExod[m] and 4QNum[b] represent a biblical text and are not separate parabiblical or exegetical works. The text of 4QDeut[j,n] might no longer be a biblical text but rather biblical excerpts, S. White Crawford, DJD XIV 79 and 121.

[30]E. Tov, 'Biblical Texts as Reworked in Some Qumran Manuscripts with Special Attention to 4QRP and 4QParaGen-Exod', *The Community of the Renewed Covenant. The Notre Dame Symposium on the Dead Sea Scrolls* (eds. E. Ulrich and J. VanderKam; Notre Dame, IN, 1994) 111–34.

of the biblical text, as is the case in 1QapGen or *Jubilees*. The parabiblical writings are often described as 'rewritten bible' or exegetical developments 'based' on the biblical books.[31] However, the parabiblical writings are often not based on a biblical text, the standard or whatever, but on literary traditions different from and earlier than those preserved in the biblical texts. This can be particularly true in the case of historical, sapiential and apocalyptic traditions and texts. Chronicles has also been characterized as an exegetical reworking of inherited biblical material. It is however a work by itself and the non-synoptic materials of Chronicles have always raised the question of possible extra biblical sources. The Prayer of Nabonidus not only does not depend on the biblical text of Daniel, but it also belongs to a level of tradition which is earlier than the tradition represented by the biblical text. It has to be taken into consideration that many parabiblical writings (and certainly their sources) come from a period prior to the hellenistic crisis and prior to the constitution of a closed canon and of a standard text. Such is the case with the *Genesis Apocryphon, Pseudo-Moses, Ordinances, Pseudo-Joshua*; and, within the apocalyptic literature, *Jubilees*, the *Astronomical Book* (*1 Enoch* 72:82), the *Book of the Watchers* (*1 Enoch* 1:36), the *Book of Giants, Visions of Jacob*, the Aramaic *Testament of Qahat* and *Visions of Amram*, as well as the Aramaic testaments of Juda, Joseph and Levi.

The concept of 'parabiblical' texts or writings should be combined with that of double or multiple editions in order to advance the analysis of the textual and literary diversity that resulted in the different editions of the historical books. The so called 'supplements' or 'miscellanies' of the LXX in 1 Kgs 2:35+ and 2:46+ should now be considered as parabiblical material that entered the biblical tradition in two different ways prompting the formation of two different editions: that transmitted by the MT and that reflected by the LXX.

As independent parabiblical material these 'miscellanies' formed two collections more or less structured around the topic of Solomon's wisdom and his profane politics. The Hebrew edition represented by the LXX placed these collections at the more suitable point within its own literary structure: near to the beginning of the book according to the old division of books after 1 Kgs 2:11 (cf. LXX[L]); editorial additions and rearrangements are found mostly at the beginning or the end of the books and in the points of juncture between two successive books

---

[31]In the *Temple Scroll*, for example, a distinction is established between 'primary texts', those found in the known biblical texts, and 'secondary texts' that *eo ipso* are labelled as 'sectarian', cf. D. D. Swanson, *The Temple Scroll and the Bible. The Methodology of 4QT* (Leiden: Brill, 1995) and, for the contrary opinion, J. Maier, *Die Tempelrolle vom Toten Meer und das 'Neue Jerusalem'* (München/Basel, 1997) 33.

(Joshua-Judges, Samuel-Kings). The second edition transmitted by the MT scattered the material of these collections through chapters 2 to 10, placing every piece in the more suitable context according to its own content. Chronicles did not know the second collection of parabiblical material (LXX 1 Kgs 2:46+) and a great part of the first (2:35+). As rightly observed by Graeme Auld, the earliest biblical tradition of 1 Kings was centered around the Temple of Jerusalem.[32] Only later, by the insertion of these parabiblical materials, the biblical tradition – as represented differently by the MT and LXX – took on a more sapiential and profane aspect. 'Parabiblical' material put aside in a first edition of some books became 'biblical' when it was incorporated at later stages of the editorial process.

Finally and to judge by the date of the copies of the biblical and parabiblical texts preserved in the Qumran caves, the policy of acquisitions of the Qumran library seems to have developed from a rather perceptible presence of non-standard texts and editions and of early (pre-Qumranic) parabiblical literature to the prevalence of standard texts and editions and of specifically exegetical (Qumranic) literature. If a still further generalization is allowed, there seems to be a gradual shift from Zadokite or (proto-)Sadducean to Pharisaic-rabbinic (and Zealot) influences on a collection of scrolls of a predominant Essenian character. A global explanation of the Qumran evidence on a biblical standard text and on non-standard and parabiblical texts has to take into consideration numerous data and aspects that still need further investigation.[33]

APPENDIX. CHRONOLOGICAL LIST OF QUMRAN EXEGETICAL AND PARABIBLICAL WRITINGS BY DATE OF COPY

Begin II c. BCE:	4QEnoch[a] (4Q201) (The Book of Watchers)
Middle II c. BCE:	4QEnoch[f] (4Q207), 4QVisions of Amram[b] (4Q544)
Second half II c. BCE:	Jubilees[a] (4Q216), 4QTestament of Qahat (4Q542), 4QVisions of Amram[e] (4Q547)
End II c. BCE:	4QReworked Pentateuch[b,c] (4Q364–5), 4QEnoch[b] (4Q202), 4QTestament of Levi[d] (4Q214a, 4Q541),

---

[32]A. Graeme Auld, *Kings without Privilege: David and Moses and the Story of the Bible's Kings* (Edinburgh, 1994).

[33]The Appendix that follows depends on incomplete and still discussed data. For the dates of each manuscript, cf. the editions in DJD or the preliminary editions. I have relied also on F. García Martínez, 'Textos de Qumrán', in G. Aranda Pérez, F. García Martínez and M. Pérez Fernández, *Literatura judía intertestamentaria* (Estella, 1996) 17–241 (65–172).

	4QTestament of Levi[cf] (4Q540, 4Q214b), 4QVision of Samuel (4Q160)
End II/begin I c. BCE:	4QTargum of Leviticus (4Q156)
Begin I c. BCE:	4QPesher Isaiah[c] (4Q163), 4QTestimonia (4Q175), 1QWords of Moses (1Q22), 4QEnoch[e] (4Q206)
First half I c. BCE:	Jubilees[h] (4Q223), 4QApocryphon of Joseph[a] (4Q371), 4QBiblical Chronology (4Q559), 4QTestament of Levi[c] (4Q213b), 6QApocryphon of Samuel-Kings (6Q9), 4QThe Book of Giants[b] (4Q530), 4QAramaic Levi[a,b] (4Q213, 4Q213a), 4QMessianic Apocalypse (4Q521)
Middle I c. BCE:	4QCommentary on Malachi (4Q253a), 4QTanhumim (4Q176a), 1QJubilees[b] (1Q18, 4Q217), 4QEnoch[g] (4Q212), 4QAstronomical Enoch[ac] (4Q208, 4Q210), Book of Giants (1Q23, 4Q203), 4QWork with Placenames (4Q522), 4QNoah (4Q535, 4Q536), 4QParaphrase of Genesis-Exodus (4Q422), 4QCommentary on Genesis B (4Q253), Visions of Amram (4Q543, 4Q548), 4QApocryphon of Juda (4Q538), 4QApocryphon of Joseph (4Q539), 1QAramaic Levi (1Q21), 4QApocryphon of Joshua[b] (4Q379), 4QApocryphon of Elisha (4Q481a)
Second half I c. BCE:	4QPesher Isaiah[b] (4Q162), 4QPesher Isaiah[d] (4Q164), 4QPesher Nahum (4Q169), 1QPesher Habakkuk (1QpHab), 1QPesher Psalms (1Q16), 4QPesher Psalms[a] (4Q171), 11QMelchizedec (11Q13), 4Q4QCatena[a] (4Q177 = 4QMidrEschat[b]), 4QReworked Pentateuch[a] (4Q158), 4QReworked Pentateuch[d] (4Q366), 4QNarrative or Second Exodus (4Q462), 4QFlorilegium (4Q174 = 4QMidrEschat[a]), 4QCommentary on Genesis A (4Q252) 1QJubilees[a] (1Q17), 4QJubilees[c,d] (4Q218–19), 4QJubilees[f,g] (4Q221–2), 4QJubilees[f] (4Q176b), 4QApocryphon of Moses A (4Q374), 4QApocryphon of Moses B (4Q375), 4QExhortation based on the Flood (4Q370), 1QBook of Giants[b] (1Q24), 4QBook of Giants[d] (4Q532), 6QBook of Giants (6Q8), 4QPseudo-Jubilees[b,c] (4Q226–7), 4QPseudo-Ezekiel[a,b] (4Q385–6), 4QPseudo-Moses[a] (4Q385a), 4QPseudo-Moses[b] (4Q387a), 4QPseudo-Moses[c,d] (4Q388a, 4Q389), 4QApocryphon of Joseph[b,c] (4Q372–3), 4QVisions of Amram[d] (4Q546),

	4QAprocryphon of Jeremiah (4Q385b), 4QLiturgy of The Three Tongues of Fire (4Q376), Description of the New Jerusalem (1Q32, 5Q15), 4QDescription of the New Jerusalem[a] (4Q554, 4Q554a), 4QDescription of the New Jerusalem[b] (4Q555), 4QFour Kingdoms[a,b] (4Q552-3), 4QPrayer of Nabonidus (4Q242)
End I c. BCE:	4QPesher Isaiah[a] (4Q161), 4QPesher Isaiah[e] (4Q165), 4QPesher Hosea[a] (4Q166), 1QPesher Micah (1Q14), 4QPesher Psalms[b] (4Q173), 4QJubilees[e] (4Q220), 4QNoah (4Q534 = 4QElect of God), 4QAn Exposition of the Patriarchs (4Q464), 4QEnoch[c,d] (4Q204-5), Astronomical Enoch[b,d] (4Q209 and 4Q211), 4Q531 4QGiants[c], 4QVisions of Amram[c] (4Q545)1, 3QTestament of Juda (?) (3Q7), 4QAramaic Apocalypse (4Q246)
End I c. BCE/begin I c. CE:	1QGenesis Apocryphon, (1Q20) 4Q215, 4QTestament of Naphtali
End I c. BCE/middle I c. CE:	11QTemple[a] (11Q19)
Begin I c. CE:	11QTemple[b] (11Q20), 4QPesher Hosea[b] (4Q167), 4QPesher Micah (4Q168), 4QCatena[b] (4Q182 = MidrEschat[c]), 4QAges of Creation (4Q181), 4QHistorical Work (4Q183), 2QJubilees[a,b] (2Q19, 2Q20), 1QNoah (1Q19), 2QGiants (2Q26), Liturgy of The Three Tongues of Fire (1Q29), 4QPseudo-Daniel[a,b,c] (4Q243-5)
First half I c. CE:	Pesher Malachi (5Q10), Description of the New Jerusalem (2Q24, 11Q18), 4QCommentary on Genesis C (4Q254), 11QJubilees (11Q12), 4QPseudo-Jubilees[a] (4Q225), 4QPseudo-Moses Apocalypse[e] (4Q390), 4QApocryphon of Joseph (2Q22), 2QApocryphon of Moses (2Q21), 4QGiants (4Q533)
Middle I c. CE:	4QTargum of Job (4Q157), 11QTargum of Job (11Q10), 3QPesher Isaiah (3Q4), 5QPesher Malachi (5Q10), 4QAges of Creation (4Q180), 3QJubilees (3Q5), 4QCommentary on Genesis D (4Q254a), 4QPsalms of Joshua[a] (4Q378), 4QApocryphon of Jacob (4Q537), 4QVisions of Amram[a] (4Q543).

6

E PLURIBUS UNUM: TEXTUAL VARIETY AND DEFINITIVE INTERPRETATION IN THE QUMRAN SCROLLS

George J. Brooke

I. Introduction

The focus of this collection of essays is the issue of the distinctiveness of the Qumran community and the wider movement of which it was a part. Furthermore, the task has been set each contributor, having considered the character, if any, of such distinctiveness, to describe the extent to which it may be central or at the edge of Palestinian Judaism in the late Second Temple period. In light of these overall concerns, this contribution addresses some aspects of biblical interpretation in the sectarian scrolls from Qumran in the context of textual pluralism.

The brief remarks in this study fall into three parts which are closely related. In the first some aspects of the pluralism of texts or text-types as reflected in the biblical manuscripts at Qumran are reconsidered. In the second there is an attempt to identify what is distinctive about Qumran biblical interpretation. In relation to both these matters there has to be constant awareness of how the character of the evidence that survives may skew any assessment of the elements of distinctiveness. In the third part there is a brief sketch of the various principles whereby the discussion can be taken forward.

II. Textual Pluralism

The pluralism of texts and text-types in the so-called 'biblical' manuscripts[1] found in the caves at and near Qumran has been widely celebrated and variously described. For the most part the scholarly analysis of the so-called 'biblical' manuscripts has not been inclined to identify any single manuscript as evidence for the existence of a sectarian scriptural version. This has been the case whether the approach was primarily in terms of 'geographical' families or in terms

---

[1]So-called 'biblical' manuscripts because the term biblical is commonly understood to refer to a definitive collection of authoritative works in a single text-type. As such the term 'biblical' is somewhat anachronistic when applied to the scrolls found at Qumran, since although there is reference in the scrolls to the Law and the Prophets (e.g., 1QS 1:3), the precise form and content of the community's canon is not known.

of those groups responsible for textual transmission.[2] There have been some exceptions. For example, W. H. Brownlee pursued the idea that the great Isaiah scroll was more than simply an exemplar of a localized Palestinian text; he argued that it contained variants which reflected narrowly identifiable sectarian eschatological interests, especially messianism.[3]

That the pluralism of texts or text-types amongst the biblical manuscripts found at Qumran was not the result of sectarian intervention has seemed by most scholars to be confirmed notably by 4QpaleoExod[m], a manuscript in the Samaritan tradition but apparently without the highly specific Samaritan sectarian readings which are present in the Samaritan Pentateuch manuscripts deriving from that community itself.[4] In fact, manuscripts like 4QpaleoExod[m] have shown how very little in the Samaritan Pentateuch need be described as narrowly sectarian.

In recent years, however, E. Tov has proposed a thoroughgoing revision of this approach.[5] Tov's distinction between manuscripts written in what he has labelled the Qumran scribal practice and those written defectively is well known; because the Qumran scribal practice, including fuller orthography, is characteristic of most of the manuscripts containing clearly sectarian compositions, Tov has suggested that the majority of, if not all, the manuscripts in such orthography reflect what may be dubbed the Qumran scribal school. Other manuscripts were either penned elsewhere or at Qumran but by scribes trained elsewhere. Captivated by the logic of this analysis Tov has now come to define his own view of the biblical manuscripts as requiring a fivefold classification: proto-Masoretic texts, pre-Samaritan texts, texts close to the presumed Hebrew source of the Septuagint (LXX), non-aligned texts, and texts written in the Qumran practice. This fifth category of Qumran sectarian texts contains all the biblical manuscripts which are written in full orthography and is

---

[2]These approaches are most clearly seen in the collection of essays edited by F. M. Cross and S. Talmon, *Qumran and the History of the Biblical Text* (Cambridge, MA: Harvard University Press, 1975).

[3]See especially, W. H. Brownlee, *The Meaning of the Qumrân Scrolls for the Bible with Special Attention to the Book of Isaiah* (New York: Oxford University Press, 1964).

[4]As has been demonstrated by J. E. Sanderson, *An Exodus Scroll from Qumran: 4QpaleoExod^m and the Samaritan Tradition* (HSS 30; Atlanta, GA: Scholars Press, 1986).

[5]The end result of Tov's reconsideration of the evidence is stated definitively in his *Textual Criticism of the Hebrew Bible* (Minneapolis, MN: Fortress Press/Assen: van Gorcum, 1992) 114–17. He has recently restated the same view in his essay 'L'importance des textes du désert de Juda pour l'histoire du texte de la Bible hébraïque. Une nouvelle synthèse', *Qoumrân et les Manuscrits de la mer Morte: un cinquantenaire* ed. E.-M. Laperrousaz (Paris: Éditions du Cerf, 1997) 215–52.

consistently evident, Tov has argued, in the attestations of the biblical text to be found in the Qumran sectarian commentaries, such as 1QpHab.[6]

In my opinion Tov's fifth column is subversive of the discipline of textual criticism in a dangerous way and should be resisted.[7] For, rather than aligning manuscripts and the textual traditions they may represent according to criteria derived from variant readings, especially according to common secondary errors, it introduces a new and entirely dissimilar criterion which really only divides the manuscripts into two overall groups according to spelling and some other less significant practices, not the five groups that Tov has described. I am yet to be convinced that there is a single narrowly sectarian[8] Bible manuscript in the Qumran collection. If such is the case, then the answer to the first part of the task of this paper is that there is no reason to believe anything other than that the evidence from Qumran is thoroughly representative of what might be the case in Palestinian Judaism more generally. There is no such thing as a Qumran or Essene Bible as there is a Samaritan Pentateuch; there are only various manuscripts of the biblical books in various textual forms found at Qumran.

Having said that, there is the need to make two further important remarks. It seems likely that as an appreciation of the Qumran evidence increases, several of the manuscripts which are now classified as biblical will be reclassified as reflecting clearly secondary and possibly even sectarian uses of the biblical text. This has already been noted clearly for the manuscripts which have been labelled as 4QDeut[j][9] and 4QDeut[n],[10]

---

[6]'En ce qui concerne les textes non bibliques, il se peut que le texte de base de plusiers *pesharim* appartenait aussi à ce groupe' ('L'importance des textes du désert de Juda pour l'histoire du texte de la Bible hébraïque', 236).

[7]Amongst scholars who express reservations about Tov's classification, see the recent survey study by E. Ulrich, 'The Dead Sea Scrolls and the Biblical Text', *The Dead Sea Scrolls after Fifty Years: A Comprehensive Assessment* ed. P. W. Flint and J. C. VanderKam (Leiden: E. J. Brill, 1998) 84–5. Ulrich himself proposes a theory of 'successive literary editions' in which manuscript evidence is viewed diachronically, not according to some supposed textual norm.

[8]I use the label 'narrowly sectarian' to imply something like the Samaritan Pentateuch with its exclusivist readings with regard to Mount Gerizim.

[9]See J. A. Duncan, 'Considerations of 4QDt[j] in Light of the "All Souls Deuteronomy" and Cave 4 Phylactery Texts', *The Madrid Qumran Congress: Proceedings of the International Congress on the Dead Sea Scrolls, Madrid, 18–21 March 1991* ed. J. Trebolle-Barrera and L. Vegas Montaner (STDJ 11; Leiden: E. J. Brill/Madrid: Editorial Complutense, 1992) 199–215.

[10]See, e.g., S. A. White, '4QDt[n]: Biblical Manuscript or Excerpted Text?' *Of Scribes and Scrolls: Studies on the Hebrew Bible, Intertestamental Judaism, and Christian Origins presented to John Strugnell on the occasion of his sixtieth birthday* ed. H. W. Attridge, J. J. Collins, T. H. Tobin (College Theology Society Resources in Religion 5; Lanham, MD: University Press of America, 1990) 13–20.

has been suggested for 4QDeut[q],[11] and could apply to a range of other texts. For example, the penmanship of 4QNum[b] with red letter phrases may indicate some particular usage of the manuscript,[12] 4QCant[a–b] seem to be excerpted texts (though it is difficult to characterize the criteria for selection),[13] other manuscripts may have been written for a specific liturgical function,[14] and so on. In other words, where the biblical text is presented in a somewhat distinctive fashion, such as in very short columns, with red ink, or as excerpts, we may need to be aware that the manuscript and its text is evidently derivative from a more standard form of scripture and should therefore be deemed of secondary interest.

The other clarificatory remark is to note that great care should be exercised before any or all variants are classified as exegetically sectarian,[15] since the character of the process of the transmission of the biblical texts during the late Second Temple period is one of manifold adjustment in minor ways as the texts are copied from one generation to the next. Who is to say where sectarianism begins in this process, unless there is a particular reading which implies group exclusiveness, as in the Samaritan Pentateuch? Even with regard to particular sectarian readings of that sort special care must be taken since sects tend to view themselves not as cut off from their dominant rivals, but as the sole legitimate representatives of the whole religion.[16] Many variants are indeed created deliberately, but deliberate variants are not necessarily sectarian.

III. Particular Interpretation

If there is no such thing as a Qumran sectarian biblical manuscript or witness, how does the interpreter work with the pluralism that remains in the witnesses to most of the biblical books? How do

[11]Because of its contents J. T. Milik juxtaposed 4QDeut[q] with 4QPhylactery N: J.T. Milik, 'Tefillin, Mezuzot et Targums (4Q128–4Q157)', *Qumrân Grotte 4.II* ed. R. de Vaux and J. T. Milik (DJD VI; Oxford: Clarendon Press, 1977) 38, 73.

[12]N. Jastram, '4QNum[b]', *Qumran Cave 4.VII: Genesis to Numbers* ed. E. Ulrich, F. M. Cross, *et al.* (DJD XII; Oxford: Clarendon Press, 1994) 205–67, esp. 210–11 and plate xlix.

[13]E. Tov, 'Three Manuscripts (Abbreviated Texts?) of Canticles from Qumran Cave 4', *JJS* 46 (1995) 88–111; see also Tov's study 'Excerpted and Abbreviated Biblical Texts from Qumran', *RevQ* 16 (1995) 581–600.

[14]See J. Jarick, 'The Bible's "Festival Scrolls" among the Dead Sea Scrolls', *The Scrolls and the Scriptures: Qumran Fifty Years After* ed. S. E. Porter and C. A. Evans; JSPSup 26 (Roehampton Institute London Papers 3; Sheffield: Sheffield Academic Press, 1997) 170–82.

[15]See my comments on this issue in relation to the biblical quotations in the pesharim in 'The Biblical Texts in the Qumran Commentaries: Scribal Errors or Exegetical Variants?' *Early Jewish and Christian Exegesis: Studies in Memory of William Hugh Brownlee* ed. C. A. Evans and W. F. Stinespring (SBL Homage Series 10; Atlanta, GA: Scholars Press, 1987) 85–100.

[16]Thus the term 'Israel' might be understood by some members of a sect as referring only to them, for all that in a biblical text it could have a suitably inclusive meaning.

sectarian interpreters reach the particularities of their interpretations from the multiplicity of texts and text-types? What process takes place in each case whereby the interpreter proceeds from the many forms of scriptural text to a single interpretation, *e pluribus ad unum*? Matters seem to be far less obvious than one might suppose. I give here four examples which may at least highlight the issues suitably, even if they cannot provide us with a satisfactorily complete description of the variety of ways in which the community's commentators made their ways from text to interpretation.

(a) The text of Genesis in 4Q252

4QCommentary on Genesis A has provoked a very wide-ranging discussion concerning its methods and purpose.[17] What kind of commentary is it? What was its compiler trying to achieve? We may never know the answers to such questions, but one observation is especially intriguing. The manuscripts of Genesis from the Qumran caves are considered to represent a remarkable consistency which is almost uniformly to be associated with what can be described as the proto-Masoretic text-form. With one apparent exception J. Davila has noted that there really seems no reason to suppose that any of the Qumran Genesis manuscripts reflect in any persistent way the variant readings visible in the what may be taken as the Hebrew *Vorlage* of the Septuagint.[18] The exception concerns the supralinear glosses in 4QGen[j] one of which agrees once with the Septuagint against the Masoretic Text and Samaritan Pentateuch, the other of which agrees with the Samaritan Pentateuch and Septuagint against the Masoretic Text: 'It looks as though 4QGen[j] was glossed from a manuscript with at least some readings in common with G and M III, but no far-reaching conclusions can be drawn from this small amount of data.'[19] Surprisingly, however, it is clear that in several of its pericopae the text of Genesis reflected in the Commentary on Genesis A shows evidence of being based on the kind of Hebrew text which may have been used in an earlier generation for the Greek translation.

In 4Q252 3:13 Abraham is described as 'your father' (אביכה) reflecting the similar secondary variant of LXX A for Gen 28:4. Not enough context survives to determine whether anything was made of this. In

---

[17]See the bibliography at the start of the *editio princeps* of 4Q252: G. J. Brooke, '4QCommentary on Genesis A', *Qumran Cave 4.XVII* ed. J. C. VanderKam; DJD XXII (Oxford: Clarendon Press, 1996) 185.

[18]J. R. Davila, 'Text-Type and Terminology: Genesis and Exodus as Test Cases', *RevQ* 16 (1993) 3–37.

[19]J. R. Davila, 'Text-Type and Terminology: Genesis and Exodus as Test Cases', 28.

4Q252 4:4 the verb is a second person form (פחזתה) as is also found in the Septuagint for Gen 49:4. Nothing in the commentary hangs on this minor variant. The contentious לא ידור ('will not dwell') of 4Q252 1:2 may reflect a real textual variant, rather than being an interpretative reading.[20] As variant perhaps it is reflected in the Septuagint's οὐ μὴ καταμείνῃ for Gen 6:3. Again, nothing exegetical depends on this variant. There are no unique readings in the text of Genesis in the Commentary on Genesis A which might lead us to suppose that a distinctive sectarian text was being used, as Tov would have us believe.[21]

But the question remains: if nearly all the manuscript copies of Genesis at Qumran belong broadly to a single text family, why should the compiler or exegete of 4Q252 have chosen to follow a text-type which is akin in several ways to the *Vorlage* of the Septuagint? There is no straightforward answer to this question, but the observation encourages us to realize that the plurality of text-types was accepted as a matter of fact, and perhaps in many instances did not bother the Qumran exegete one way or the other.

(b) 1QpHab 11:8–14; Hab 2:16

In this second example we have the *locus classicus* for showing not only that the Qumran commentators were aware of variant readings in biblical texts, but also could use such variants explicitly in their interpretations. 'You have filled yourself with ignominy more than with glory. Drink also, and stagger! The cup of the Lord's right hand shall come round to you and shame shall come on your glory (2:16).'

Interpreted, this concerns the Priest whose ignominy was greater than his glory. 'For he did not circumcise the foreskin of his heart, and he walked in the ways of drunkenness that he might quench his thirst. But the cup of the wrath of God shall confuse him, multiplying his ... and the pain of ...'[22]

---

[20]See T. H. Lim, 'The Chronology of the Flood Story in a Qumran Text', *JJS* 43 (1992) 292: 'a variant attested by the LXX'; on the other hand M. Bernstein', לא ידור רוחי באדם לעולם: 4Q252 i 2: Biblical Text or Biblical Interpretation?' *RevQ* 16 (1993–94) 421–7, declares it to be an exegetical reading.

[21]For more details on these observations, see G. J. Brooke, 'Some Comments on 4Q252 and the Text of Genesis', *Textus: The Annual of the Hebrew University Bible Project* 19 (1998) 1–25.

[22]Trans. G. Vermes, *The Complete Dead Sea Scrolls in English* (London: Allen Lane/Penguin Press, 1997[5]) 484.

In the Masoretic Text the verb is הערל, 'be uncircumcised', but the Septuagint's translation reflects a Hebrew *Vorlage* of הרעל, 'stagger'. In the commentary the interpreter takes advantage of both readings. As Timothy H. Lim has recently reminded us, following Brownlee and others, the interpreter knew the different readings. He privileged one by way of using it in the biblical lemma (הרעל); but he cites the other explicitly in the commentary while not repeating the verb רעל from the biblical verse. 'He may well have had different texts of Habakkuk in front of him, rather than simply remembering variant readings, as he sought to elucidate the meaning of the prophecy.'[23]

What is to be made of the persistence of the pluralism of textual readings in the commentary? At the least we may conclude that for some community commentators the pluralism of textual readings was accepted as a fact of life, not a problem, something of which one could take advantage and pursue, not an embarrassment. Perhaps on occasion this fluidity in the text even encouraged interpreters to create new readings as they worked.

(c) Num 24:17 in 4Q175, CD 7:19–20 (4QD[a] 3 iii 20–21), and 1QM 11:6–7

Numbers 24:17 is preserved in several different sectarian exegetical compositions. Sadly Num 24:17 is not preserved in any copy of Numbers discovered in the Qumran caves, but the Qumran data on the verse can be laid out as follows:

CD 7:19–20: דרך כוכב מיעקב וקם שבט מישראל

4Q175: דרך כוכב מיעקוב ויקום שבט מישראל

1QM: דרך כוכב מיעקוב קם שבט מישראל

MT: דרך כוכב מיעקב וקם שבט מישראל

Is there enough evidence here to suggest that variant forms of the text of Numbers 24 existed at Qumran?

The interpretative problem lies with the verb. וקם in CD 7 may imply that the figure is yet to come, קם of 1QM may best be understood to imply that he has already come or 'comes', and the same can be said for the ויקום of 4Q175, though the force of the *vav* consecutive is neither

---

[23]T. H. Lim, *Holy Scriptures in the Qumran Commentaries and Pauline Letters* (Oxford: Clarendon Press, 1997) 50. Cf. W. H. Brownlee, *The Midrash Pesher of Habakkuk* (SBLMS 24; Missoula, MT: Scholars Press, 1979) 191–2, who cites C. Rabin, 'Notes on the Habakkuk Scroll and the Zadokite Documents', *VT* 5 (1955) 158–9: 'simultaneous interpretation of two variant readings.'

persistent nor consistent at Qumran.[24] G. Vermes translates all three occurrences similarly:

175   A star shall come out of Jacob and a sceptre shall rise out of Israel.
CD   A star shall come forth[25] out of Jacob and a sceptre shall rise out of Israel.
1QM   A star shall come out of Jacob, and a sceptre shall rise out of Israel.[26]

F. García Martínez offers a more biblically-minded variety of readings:

175   A star has departed from Jacob, and a sceptre has arisen from Israel.
CD   A star moves out of Jacob, and a sceptre arises out of Israel.
1QM   A star will depart from Jacob, a sceptre will be raised in Israel.[27]

The translation by M. Wise, M. Abegg and E. Cook runs as follows:

175   A star shall come out of Jacob, and a scepter shall rise out of Israel.
CD   A star has left Jacob, a staff has risen from Israel.
1QM   There shall come forth a star out of Jacob, a scepter shall rise out of Israel.[28]

J. Maier pays similar attention to the verb tenses:

175   Es geht ein Stern aus Jakob auf, ein Szepter erhebt sich aus Israel.
CD   Es ging ein Stern aus Jakob auf, ein Szepter erhob sich aus Israel.
1QM   Es geht ein Stern aus Jakob auf, ein Szepter erhebt sich aus Israel.[29]

What should be made of these detailed differences and the way in which modern translators either let them stand or harmonize their versions? One suspects that in minor ways the text of Numbers 24 was adjusted to fit syntactically the particular contemporary idiomatic usage of verbal sequences by the various interpreters and that their exegetical contexts also played a part in how they variously represented the scriptural text. Whatever the case, there is clear evidence of pluralism either at the textual or interpretative level or both. There does not seem to have been a single Qumran scribal school text of Numbers which is used constantly in the community's exegeses.

[24]See E. Qimron, *The Hebrew of the Dead Sea Scrolls* (HSS 29; Atlanta, GA: Scholars Press, 1986) 72–3; M. Smith, 'The *Waw*-Consecutive at Qumran', *ZAH* 4 (1991) 161–4; M. Smith, 'Converted and Unconverted Perfect and Imperfect Forms in the Literature of Qumran', *BASOR* 284 (1991) 1–17; M. Smith, *The Origins and Development of the Waw-Consecutive: Northwest Semitic Evidence from Ugarit to Qumran* (Atlanta, GA: Scholars Press, 1991).

[25]A possible stylistic inconsistency.

[26]G. Vermes, *The Complete Dead Sea Scrolls in English*, 133, 174, 496.

[27]F. García Martínez, *The Dead Sea Scrolls Translated* (Leiden: E. J. Brill, 1996²) 38, 104, 137.

[28]M. O. Wise, M. Abegg, and E. Cook, *The Dead Sea Scrolls: A New Translation* (San Francisco: HarperCollins Publishers, 1996) 58, 160, 230. Possibly the variety of translations results from the multi-author character of the book.

[29]J. Maier, *Die Qumran-Essener: die Texte vom Toten Meer* (München: Ernst Reinhardt Verlag, 1995) 1.18, 141; 2.108.

(d) Isa 10:22–27 in 4Q161 and 4Q163

There is little overlap between the pesharim preserved from Qumran; indeed, commonly, the general lack of overlap has been taken to indicate that many of the pesharim proper may be autographs.[30] However, there are some doublets, mostly between the pesharim and other texts (e.g., Isa 10:34 – 11:1 in 4Q161 and 4Q285[31]) but also amongst the pesharim themselves.

This fourth example is mentioned to highlight the point that, even if the text-form is uniform, the commentary may not be. In 4Q161 2–4 1–10 and 4Q163 4–7 ii 10–21, both commentaries on Isaiah, there is some overlap in the use of Isa 10:22–27. Frustratingly only a few letters of the biblical text survive in both cases; no variants are visible (but nor need any be expected).[32] However, enough remains overall to allow us to see that the commentaries clearly had different structures and that the interpretations had different contents. 4Q161 has more extensive passages of interpretation and is concerned with 'the return from the wilderness' and 'the prince of the congregation'. 4Q163 has only very brief interpretations between extensive quotations from Isaiah and the interpretation which remains is fragmentary, possibly concerning 'a few'.[33] So the same biblical text can be interpreted variously, not just in very different genres of interpretation (as say Isa 11:1 in 4Q161 and 1QSb 5[34]), but in texts of the same genre. The differences are not contradictory but reveal that there is not an automatic one on one reading of any single authoritative scriptural text, even if the form of the text remains constant.

IV. Distinctiveness

What can be said about the distinctiveness (or lack of it) of the biblical texts and their interpretations in the scrolls found at Qumran? The following general points are offered as a tentative framework for the

[30]As noted summarily, e.g., by J. C. VanderKam, *The Dead Sea Scrolls Today* (London: SPCK, 1994) 96.

[31]And also in 11Q14, 11QSefer ha-Milḥamah 1 i–ii: see F. García Martínez, E. J. Tigchelaar, A. S. van der Woude, *Qumran Cave 11.II: 11Q2–18, 11Q20–31* (DJD XXIII; Oxford: Clarendon Press, 1998) 245–9.

[32]For the text see J. M. Allegro with A. A. Anderson, *Qumrân Cave 4.I (4Q158–4Q186)* (DJD V; Oxford: Clarendon Press, 1968) 11–15, 17–27; M .P. Horgan, *Pesharim: Qumran Interpretations of Biblical Books* (CBQMS 8: Washington, DC: Catholic Biblical Association of America, 1979) Part I, 15–18, 20–33.

[33]If Horgan's proposed reading and understanding is followed: *Pesharim: Qumran Interpretations of Biblical Books*, 98, 111.

[34]On Isa 11:1 in 1QSb 5 see G. J. Brooke and J. M. Robinson, 'A Further Fragment of 1QSb: The Schøyen Collection MS 1909', *JJS* 46 (1995) 120–33.

discussion in light of all the evidence now available. I shall attempt to list the points under the two broad categories of what is probably not distinctive of Qumran practice and what may be distinctive of the community or the movement of which it was a part.

A. *What has little or no distinctiveness*

1. It seems that there is no sectarian form of the biblical books in the manuscripts found in the Qumran caves, that is, of the biblical books as later confirmed through their inclusion in the Jewish scriptural canon. The authoritative status of the *Book of Jubilees* might provide an exception, if the category of authoritative texts is opened up and extended.[35]

It may well be that the manuscripts from Qumran containing biblical texts can be grouped according to scribal practices, but scribal practices alone do not seem to provide sufficient criteria for constructing a distinctive type of biblical text as Tov has asserted.

2. The pluriformity of the texts of the biblical books in the late Second Temple period is established beyond doubt – and it is a pluralism which even exists at one place (Qumran) and for some time. In several books it seems as if the so-called proto-MT is gaining a position of *primus inter pares*, but it is not privileged to the exclusion of other text forms as is the case in later manuscript discoveries elsewhere in the Judaean desert. That there is little or nothing which might be labelled sectarian about the kind of pluralism discernible in the biblical manuscripts from Qumran can be deduced from the citations of and allusions to scriptural texts in the writings of Philo, Josephus and the New Testament authors, even though those writings are all in Greek.

3. Interpretation is based on one or other of these non-sectarian text-forms. In a few instances the biblical text may be adjusted all the better to suit the interpretation, but for the most part the biblical texts represented in various interpretations are what may be deemed to have been generally available at the time. Thus the particular variant form of some texts is found in both the scrolls and the NT,[36] a fact which need not suggest any literary dependence of the latter on the former, or even any other close relationship, but which is merely evidence for the

---

[35]See the oft-cited reference to what seems to be the *Book of Jubilees* in CD 16:3–4 (= 4Q270 6 ii 17; 4Q271 4 ii 5) and also 4Q228 1 i 2–7: J. VanderKam and J.T. Milik, '228. 4QText with a Citation of Jubilees', *Qumran Cave 4. VIII: Parabiblical Texts Part I* (DJD XIII; Oxford: Clarendon Press, 1994) 180–1.

[36]A well-known example of this is the variant form of Amos 9:11 which occurs in 4Q174 1–3 iii 12 and Acts 15:16; see J. de Waard, *A Comparative Study of the Old Testament Text in the Dead Sea Scrolls and in the New Testament* (STDJ 4; Leiden: E. J. Brill, 1965) 24–6.

widespread availability of many or all of the text forms discovered at Qumran.

4. There is little or nothing that is distinctive about the forms of biblical interpretation found in the Qumran scrolls. Whether it is legal interpretation or haggadah, poetic reworking or the exhortatory recollections of the past, examples of similar exegetical forms can be found in contemporary Jewish texts. From the formal point of view even the pesharim can be viewed most suitably as a kind of dream interpretation best illustrated in the Book of Daniel itself. Though often deemed peculiarly characteristic of Qumran sectarian Bible interpretation, the pesharim are really such only in content.

5. There is little or nothing that is distinctive about the methods of biblical interpretation found in the Qumran scrolls. Whether it is a matter of the adjustment of the biblical texts themselves (by omission, addition, rephrasing, or other alterations) or the application of various exegetical methods, from explanation of the plain sense through to the use of techniques which are explicit in similar forms in later rabbinic exegesis, examples of similar methods can be found in contemporary Jewish texts, including the New Testament.[37]

6. There is little or nothing that is distinctive about the setting of biblical interpretation found in the Qumran scrolls. From scribal activity as that may be guessed in other settings to group study of the texts, sometimes under the tutelage of a particularly well-versed or skilled interpreter, examples of similar settings can be found lying behind contemporary Jewish texts.

B. *What is distinctive*

What may be distinctive of the Qumran sect or the wider movement of which it was a part was the particular content of its interpretation. Here it is important to provide both a suitable model for describing the content and also a suitable description of its tendencies and developments, and the elements which provoked them.

1. The appropriate modelling of the community is very significant. To follow Josephus and see Pharisees, Sadducees and Essenes as entirely discrete groups is to misunderstand how much such groups shared and to minimize the significance of diversity and development within the community(ies) and its (their) writings.

It is perhaps easiest simply to mention *Miqṣat Maʿaśe ha-Torah* (4Q394–99), because this is explicitly a text which represents some kind of dialogue. Several of the items are explicitly addressed to another

---

[37]As I tried to show in *Exegesis at Qumran: 4QFlorilegium in its Jewish Context*.

party and refer to yet a third. The use of 'you/we/they' shows that the author and traditors were aware of other positions and did not assert their own solely as the consequence of direct revelation.[38] The dialogical element in the biblical interpretation of the scrolls is often ignored. In general one may suspect that this dialogue is most evident in relation to legal interpretation, but it is implicit in other forms of interpretation too.

2. The dialogue is represented on the Qumran side by several tendencies, and one might suspect that these derive ultimately from the process of exclusion and self-exclusion which led to the posing of the fundamental question concerning how God's covenant with Israel could be realized. The probable observance of a different calendar from that practised in Jerusalem is both cause and symptom of this exclusion, as may have been disputes about priestly rights (though those are not clearly represented in the sectarian compositions from Qumran). The remedy proposed for these circumstances is traditional and prophetic: 'observe the Law strictly' and 'in penitence'. The disenfranchised religious group commonly takes a hard line with the tradition so as to occupy the moral high ground and justify any claim to the places of power. Thus the key tendency in much Qumran community biblical interpretation is its strictness with regard to the practice of the Law whose directions are extended, strengthened, revalued and re-presented: not a new covenant, but a renewed one, as S. Talmon has correctly insisted.[39]

3. The nature of the exclusion itself features in the sectarian interpretations. Here there is a mixture of political, economic, social and religious issues which variously explain the circumstances of the community. Such experiential issues are addressed with urgency and expectation. Following prophetic principles should result in the kind of prophetic fulfilment that the prophets themselves suggest. Thus,

[38]The use of scripture in MMT was largely ignored by its principal editors, E. Qimron and J. Strugnell, *Qumran Cave 4.V: Miqṣat Ma'aśe Ha-Torah* (DJD X; Oxford: Clarendon Press, 1994). This deficit has been made good by two complementary studies: M. J. Bernstein, 'The Employment and Interpretation of Scripture in 4QMMT: Preliminary Observations', *Reading 4QMMT: New Perspectives on Qumran Law and History* ed. J. Kampen and M. J. Bernstein (SBLSymS 2; Atlanta, GA: Scholars Press, 1996) 29–51; G. J. Brooke, 'The Explicit Presentation of Scripture in 4QMMT', *Legal Texts and Legal Issues: Proceedings of the Second Meeting of the International Organization for Qumran Studies, Cambridge 1995, Published in Honour of Joseph M. Baumgarten* ed. M. Bernstein, F. García Martínez and J. Kampen (STDJ 23; Leiden: E. J. Brill, 1997) 67–88.

[39]S. Talmon, 'The Community of the Renewed Covenant: Between Judaism and Christianity', *The Community of the Renewed Covenant: The Notre Dame Symposium on the Dead Sea Scrolls* ed. E. Ulrich and J. VanderKam (Christianity and Judaism in Antiquity Series 10; Notre Dame, IN: University of Notre Dame Press, 1994) 3–24.

eschatology is as much part of keeping the Law as stringency: it is the motivation.

The controlling influence in everything sectarian of unfulfilled prophecies, promises, blessings and curses can be noticed in a way in the structure of the so-called continuous pesharim. Here the prophetic text dominates the presentation in a way which is sometimes ignored because scholarly attention is directed immediately to the atomistic interpretations themselves. But the basic form of the continuous pesharim is the citation of the prophetic lemma which is then followed by the interpretation; the interpretation should not be given inappropriate priority. For the *Habakkuk Commentary*, for example, it is not insignificant that the commentary is sensitive to the overall structure and purpose of Habakkuk: the interpretation is not entirely arbitrary.[40] The unfulfilled prophecies, promises, blessings and curses of scripture are given priority in the eschatological thinking of the community interpreters. This contrasts intriguingly with the kind of proof-texting visible in the Matthaean infancy narrative where the developing story itself is the control and the biblical quotations merely justify or support the story, perhaps providing a few details.

V. Conclusion

I have proposed in this brief contribution that there is nothing particularly distinctive or sectarian about the pluralism of the biblical texts as discernible in the Qumran caves. This pluralism is known and used in interpretation and to some extent is recognized as interpretation itself. What is distinctive belongs to the community interpretations themselves, not in form or method, but in content. This distinctive content is controlled by the eschatological expectation that in the community's experiences God will surely re-establish his covenant so that unfulfilled scriptural prophecies, promises, blessings, and curses may be fulfilled. For the community and its interpreters the multiple forms of the authoritative texts stand, but the yearning for eschatological fulfilment indicates that the divine purpose is ultimately singular and is the very basis of how the community's interpretation is *e pluribus unum*.

---

[40]As was shown by W. H. Brownlee, 'The Composition of Habakkuk', *Hommages à André Dupont-Sommer* ed. A. Caquot and M. Philonenko (Paris: Adrien-Maisonneuve, 1971) 255–75.

PART III

Sectarian Law and Normative Jewish Law

7

HALAKHAH AND SECTARIANISM IN THE DEAD SEA SCROLLS

Lawrence H. Schiffman

Halakhah and Sectarianism in Judaism

From the earliest discussions of the nature of the group which we now term the Dead Sea sect, much attention has been given to issues of Jewish law. The original debates regarding the identity of the sect took place soon after the discovery of the Zadokite Fragments (*Damascus Document*) among the manuscripts of the Cairo genizah.[1] These debates only intensified after the discovery of the Qumran Scrolls in 1947.[2] The publication of the Temple Scroll,[3] 4QMMT,[4] the Qumran manuscripts of the Zadokite Fragments,[5] and soon the remaining halakhic fragments from Qumran, has further placed the subject of Jewish law at the center of the debate regarding the Dead Sea Scrolls.

By Jewish law, we refer to what the Rabbis would later term halakhah.[6] Such English words as 'law', 'legal', etc. imply for Western readers civil and criminal law. For ancient Jews, indeed for Jews throughout the ages until the rise of modernity, the life of Torah, in its various interpretations, was the dominant form of religious expression. The commands of the Bible were understood to encompass all areas of human life, including civil, criminal, political, religious, moral, ritual and familial issues. Proper behavior in all of these areas was believed to be accessible through exegesis of the biblical text and, in the case of the Pharisaic-Rabbinic tradition, from the traditions enshrined in the oral law. Technically, the term halakhah should only be used to describe the legal system developed in Rabbinic literature, representing the

---

[1]L. Ginzberg, *An Unknown Jewish Sect* (New York: Jewish Theological Seminary, 1976) 304–37; J. A. Fitzmyer, 'Prolegomenon', in S. Schechter, *Documents of Jewish Sectaries: Fragments of a Zadokite Work* (Library of Biblical Studies; New York: Ktav, 1970) 14–15.

[2]H. H. Rowley, *The Zadokite Fragments and the Dead Sea Scrolls* (Oxford: Blackwell, 1952).

[3]Y. Yadin, מגילת המקדש (3 vols.; Jerusalem: Israel Exploration Society, 1977) and its English edition, *The Temple Scroll* (3 vols.; Jerusalem: Israel Exploration Society, 1983).

[4]E. Qimron and J. Strugnell, with contributions by Y. Sussman and A. Yardeni, *Miqṣat Maʿaśe ha-Torah* (DJD X; Oxford: Clarendon Press, 1994).

[5]J. M. Baumgarten, *Qumran Cave 4, XIII: The Damascus Document (4Q266–273)* (DJD XVIII; Oxford: Clarendon Press, 1996).

[6]On this term, see M. Elon, המשפט העברי (Jerusalem: Magnes, Hebrew University, 1973) 143–4.

Pharisaic-Rabbinic trend within Judaism in Late Antiquity. However, no English term can possibly describe this system of law and practice as well as the term halakhah and so, with due apologies, for lack of a better term, it will be employed below.

An appreciation for the central role of Jewish law in the study of Second Temple Judaism is crucial to the very definition of a sect in this context. Whereas in the sociology of religion, the use of the term 'sect' implies a normative 'church', to which the sect may be contrasted, it has become customary to use this term for the various competing trends which existed among the Jews in Second Temple times. Among the distinguishing characteristics which separated these groups from one another was their practice of Jewish law.[7]

To some extent, the view that halakhah can be an important key to understanding Jewish sectarianism is best substantiated by taking a long view of the history of the Jews and Judaism. For us, as scholars working in the field of Dead Sea Scrolls, it may already come naturally, since this form of analysis has been utilized since Schechter first published the *Fragments of a Zadokite Work* in 1910.[8] But it is worthwhile to take a brief detour to consider other such controversies. Closest to the problems faced by us in the study of the Dead Sea Scrolls is the later Karaite schism which occurred in the eighth century. Here, an amalgam of sectarian groups, in some cases based to the east of the Babylonian Jewish community, came together in an informal coalition of opposition to the domination of the Babylonian Rabbis and their system of Jewish law and interpretation.[9] Although it was certainly the case that issues of theology, historical self-conception, and eschatology were major factors influencing the coalescence of the Karaite movement, halakhic considerations functioned to define the dissident group as well as to provide approaches by which the Rabbanites and Karaites could express their own self-definitions. Perhaps more importantly, the theory of Jewish law and the understanding by each group of the sources of authority for this law undergirded the entire conflict.[10]

Another example of the very same phenomenon may be seen in the

[7]For the application of sociological method to Jewish sectarianism, see A. J. Saldarini, *Pharisees, Scribes and Sadducees in Palestinian Society: A Sociological Approach* (Wilmington, DE: Michael Glazier, 1988) and A. I. Baumgarten, *The Flourishing of Jewish Sects in the Maccabean Era: An Interpretation* (JSSSup 55; Leiden: Brill, 1997).

[8]S. Schechter, *Documents of Jewish Sectaries: Fragments of a Zadokite Work*, vol. 1; Cambridge: Cambridge University Press, 1910).

[9]On the history of Karaism, see L. Nemoy, *Karaite Anthology* (Yale Judaica Series 7; New Haven: Yale University Press, 1952) xiii–xxvi and S. W. Baron, *A Social and Religious History of the Jews*, vol. 5: *Religious Controls and Dissensions* (New York and London: Columbia University Press; Philadelphia: Jewish Publication Society of America, 1957) 209–40.

[10]Baron, 5.240–51; B. Revel, *The Karaite Halakah* (Philadelphia: Dropsie College, 1913).

rise of the Hasidic movement in the eighteenth and nineteenth centuries. While again, the Hasidic Jews and their opponents, known as Mitnagdim, certainly differed on matters of theology,[11] the expression of the self-definition of the two groups took place primarily in the area of halakhah, that is, Jewish law, and the associated area of custom which, by that time, had become so major a factor in Jewish practice.[12] Early conflicts between Hasidim and Mitnagdim revolved around matters such as required prayer times, the validity of contemplative prayer,[13] ritual slaughter and the role of ritual purity in contemporary Jewish life. To this day, Hasidic followers are distinguished from other Orthodox Jews by specific halakhic practices and customs. While there can be no question that behind some of these issues of halakhah lay economic and social issues that plagued modern East European Jewish society,[14] the expression of these divisions in the context of Jewish sectarian strife was expressed to a great extent in disagreements about the interpretation of Jewish law and its specific application. The same might be said for the rise of the reform movement in Germany in the early nineteenth century[15] and the eventual establishment of Reform and Conservative Judaism in America.[16]

While it may certainly be argued that these examples are anachronistic, I would argue that all these controversies are based on the nature of Judaism defined as primarily a halakhic system (at least up to modern times). While controversies in Christianity would primarily swirl about matters of doctrine and belief, those of the Jewish community would both be based upon and express themselves in issues of halakhah.

It is in accord with this essentially phenomenological understanding of Judaism that we see halakhic issues at the center of Jewish sectarianism in the Second Temple period. Halakhah and its theoretical underpinnings separated the various sectarian groups from one another. As the

---

[11]G. G. Scholem, *Major Trends in Jewish Mysticism* (New York: Schocken, 1965) 325–50; and *The Messianic Idea in Judaism* (New York: Schocken, 1971) 203–27; M. Idel, *Hasidism: Between Ecstasy and Magic* (Albany, NY: SUNY Press, 1995); E. J. Schochet, *The Hasidic Movement and the Gaon of Vilna* (Northvale, NJ: Jason Aaronson, 1994) 49–146.

[12]For a detailed account of the conflict, see S. Dubnov, תולדות החסידות בתקופת צמיחתה וגידולה (Tel-Aviv: Dvir, 1932) 107–69; E. J. Schochet, *The Hasidic Movement and the Gaon of Vilna*, 3–32. On the critique of Hasidic halakhic practice, see Schochet, 33–48.

[13]L. Jacobs, *Hasidic Prayer* (Littman Library of Jewish Civilization; New York: Jewish Publication Society of America, Schocken, 1975) 70–92.

[14]J. Katz, *Tradition and Crisis: Jewish Society at the End of the Middle Ages* trans. B. D. Cooperman (New York: New York University Press, 1993) 183–236.

[15]M. A. Meyer, *Response to Modernity* (New York: Oxford University Press, 1988) 100–224.

[16]Meyer, *Response to Modernity*, 225–384; M. Davis, 'Jewish Religious Life and Institutions in America (A Historical Study)', *The Jews: Their Religion and Culture* (4th ed.; ed. L. Finkelstein; New York: Schocken, 1971) 274–379.

various movements sought to define themselves, they, in turn, intensified their differences in interpretation of Scripture and in the attendant practice which they followed. For this reason, Jewish legal issues must be at the center of all discussions of sectarianism in Second Temple times.

The Dead Sea Scrolls present us with documents composed over a long period of time. In studying the legal traditions preserved at Qumran, we must be mindful of the fact that some texts are pre-sectarian, representing the heritage which the Dead Sea sectarians brought with them when they established their group. Other texts which include halakhic material were composed by the sectarians themselves. Further, important texts argue implicitly or explicitly with legal rulings of other Jews, thereby providing information about competing systems of halakhah with which those who gathered the scrolls would not have agreed. These various texts allow us to reconstruct much about the state of Jewish law in the Hasmonean period and even earlier in the Hellenistic era. These texts indicate how the various groups expressed their particular character through their approach to an interpretation of Jewish law.

Early Study of Halakhah, Pharisees, and Sadducees

When scholars of the *Wissenschaft des Judentums* first turned to the study of the history of halakhah, they were fortunate to have available a much wider set of sources than had been available to pre-modern students of this topic, for important developments had taken place in Jewish and Christian intellectual history. Beginning in the Renaissance, Jews, albeit a small minority of them, once again became conversant with Hellenistic Jewish literature which had been preserved by Christians.[17] The works of Josephus, Philo, the Septuagint, and the Apocrypha provided numerous examples of halakhic material which appeared to be at variance with Rabbinic halakhah and which historically-minded scholars realized pre-dated the collections of Rabbinic material as they have been preserved. In Christian circles a series of expeditions and discoveries in the seventeenth, eighteenth, and nineteenth centuries brought to the attention of European scholars Jewish documents of the Second Temple period, which we today imprecisely term 'pseudepigrapha'. These texts, most notably *Jubilees* and *Testament of Levi*, contain much halakhic material which is at variance in some cases with Rabbinic literature.

The availability of this expanded documentary evidence meant that the study of halakhah and its history in Second Temple times had now

---

[17]See L. A. Segal, *Historical Consciousness and Religious Tradition in Azariah de Rossi's Me'or 'Einayim* (Philadelphia: Jewish Publication Society, 1989) 27–86.

gone way beyond the mining of Rabbinic references to the pre-70 CE period. Attempts to reconstruct Sadducean or other forms of non-Pharisaic law, such as the work of Abraham Geiger,[18] the work of Zacharias Frankel on the Septuagint,[19] the path-breaking study of Jubilees by Chanokh Albeck,[20] and the work of Bernhard Ritter[21] and Samuel Belkin[22] on Philo, had opened up new issues and, in fact, laid a firm basis for the study of Second Temple Jewish law as a field of study truly unthinkable without the newly expanded documentary canon with which these scholars now worked.

It was against this background that we must see the discovery of the first Dead Sea Scrolls, not by a Bedouin boy in 1947 but rather in the medieval manuscripts of the Zadokite Fragments (*Damascus Document*) brought to light by Solomon Schechter in 1896.[23] It is, of course, now a commonplace that the Cairo genizah transformed many areas of Jewish studies, including the history of halakhah. But in the form of the two partial manuscripts of the Zadokite Fragments, the genizah began a revolution in the history of Second Temple Jewish law.[24] The publication of the Zadokite Fragments was accompanied by the pioneering commentary of Solomon Schechter who came to his work with a solid training in traditional Jewish learning but with little of the ideological baggage of his *Wissenschaft* predecessors or their Christian 'colleagues'. Schechter's choice of a title for this document correctly emphasized its Zadokite/Sadducean links,[25] but he incorrectly

---

[18]A. Geiger, *Urschrift und Übersetzungen der Bibel in ihrer Abhängigkeit von der innern Entwicklung des Judentums* (Breslau: J. Hainauer, 1857); Hebrew trans. Y. L. Baruch, הפנימה המקרא ותרגומיו בזיקתם להתפתחותה של היהדות (Jerusalem: Mosad Harav Kook, 1948/9). Cf. S. Heschel, *Abraham Geiger and the Jewish Jesus* (Chicago: University of Chicago Press, 1998) 76–105.

[19]Z. Frankel, *Vorstudien zu der Septuaginta* (1941); *idem*, *Über den Einfluss der palaestinischen Exegese auf die alexandrinische Hermeneutik* (Leipzig: J. A. Barth, 1851).

[20]C. Albeck, *Das Buch der Jubiläen und die Halacha* (Berlin: Siebenundvierzigster Bericht der Hochschule für die Wissenschaft des Judenthums in Berlin, 1934).

[21]B. Ritter, *Philo und die Halacha* (Leipzig: J. C. Hinrichs, 1879).

[22]S. Belkin, *Philo and the Oral Law. The Philonic Interpretation of Biblical Law in Relation to the Palestinian Halaka* (Cambridge, MA: Harvard University Press, 1940).

[23]Cf. Y. Sussman, 'מגילת מקצת מעשי התורה חקר תולדות ההלכה ומגילות מדבר יהודה הרהורים תלמודיים ראשונים לאור', *Tarbiz* 59 (1989/90) 11–22.

[24]The genizah yielded up not only the Zadokite Fragments but other Second Temple texts as well: partial manuscripts of Ben Sira, and parts of medieval copies of the Testaments of Levi (now called the Aramaic Levi Document) and Naphtali. The Testament of Levi should be singled out as a work of halakhic content which, together with its Qumran fragments, has great potential for contributing to the history of *halakhah*.

[25]The text is now known mostly as the *Damascus Document* because of the few references to Damascus, which in our view is a code word for Qumran. See L. H. Schiffman, *Reclaiming the Dead Sea Scrolls* (Philadelphia and Jerusalem: Jewish Publication Society, 1994) 92–4. The designation Zadokite Fragments should have been retained, however, since it correctly indicates the character of the legal traditions in the text.

attributed the document to a group of Sadducean-type Samaritans.[26] It was ironic that Louis Ginzberg, who believed incorrectly that the document was proto-Pharisaic in origin, provided in his commentary on this work the keys to understanding virtually every line of its difficult halakhic section.[27]

While the work of Ginzberg, Schechter and numerous other scholars made possible a fairly thorough understanding of the halakhic content of this text, they were not able to settle the debate about either the historical ramifications of this document, that is to say the identity of the sect described in it, or its significance for the study of the history of Jewish law.[28] Suffice it to say that between the wars, that is, in what we might call the pre-Qumran discovery era, every possible theory was put forth about provenance of the Zadokite Fragments.[29] But in regard to the importance of this material for the study of Jewish law, a great methodological error was made which must be explained at some length as well.

Already in the works of Abraham Geiger, it was implicit that Second Temple halakhic sources cannot be arranged in some kind of linear, chronological fashion. Geiger's work should have shown that competing halakhic trends vied with one another in Second Temple times and that differences in halakhah could not be ascribed simply to differences of date. But perhaps under the influence of the theory of evolution, as it had been transported to the social and historical world from its original place in the natural sciences, most early students of the history of Jewish law, even Geiger himself, had fallen into the trap of what we might call halakhic Darwinism. The notion of a limited historical sequence which, by the way, has now been abandoned in the natural sciences, incorrectly took hold of the scholars of the history of Jewish law. Further, tendencies towards religious reform played a role in this process as well. Scholars simply assumed that the law had progressed from the stricter to the more lenient, clearly a reflection of their desire to see more lenient approaches applied in their own time, a trend common even amongst traditional Jewish scholars. So there was born the הלכה ישנה, the 'old law', a peculiar construct of Jewish scholarship which was assumed to be reflected in such texts as *Jubilees* and the Zadokite Fragments, as well as in some references in Rabbinic

[26]Schechter, XXI–XXVI.

[27]L. Ginzberg, *Eine unbekannte jüdische Sekte* (New York, 1922); English translation with additional chapters, *An Unknown Jewish Sect* (New York: Jewish Theological Seminary, 1976).

[28]Bibliography in Fitzmyer, 'Prolegomenon', 25–34.

[29]For a short survey, see L. H. Schiffman, *The Halakhah at Qumran* (SJLA 16; Leiden: E. J. Brill, 1975) 1–2.

literature to earlier practice (משנה ראשונה), and that this old law had been gradually replaced through an evolutionary process with what we may call a 'new law' – that of the Pharisaic-Rabbinic tradition.

Role of the Scrolls

This entire notion, however, as we now know, was entirely false. Both the canon of documentary evidence and the perspective from which the material was approached were radically altered as the result of the discovery of the Dead Sea Scrolls.

The Cave 1 collection yielded two major scrolls with halakhic content, albeit mixed in with sectarian teachings. The *Rule of the Community* provides, among its initiation rites, information on the purity system of the sectarians[30] as well as about their understanding of the theology of Jewish law.[31] The *Rule of the Congregation*, a messianic document, sets out a kind of eschatological halakhah.[32] The *War Scroll* contains an entire version of the Deuteronomic laws of war as understood by the sectarians.[33] In addition, the *War Scroll* alludes to sacrificial law and rules of ritual impurity. It was Cave 4 that yielded manuscripts of the Zadokite Fragments and other halakhic works describing an entire system of Jewish law concerning Sabbath,[34] marriage, purity, priestly status, etc. The MMT document provided in a sectarian context even Pharisee-Sadducean disputes regarding sacrificial and purification laws. The caves also yielded phylacteries[35] and mezuzot,[36] and the biblical scrolls revealed much information on the scribal halakhah of the times.[37] Cave 11 contained the *Temple Scroll*, a rewriting of the Torah designed to put forward the author's views on a variety of topics of Jewish law, most notably relating to the Temple,

---

[30]L. H. Schiffman, *Sectarian Law in the Dead Sea Scrolls: Courts, Testimony and the Penal Code* (Chico, CA: Scholars Press, 1983) 161–5.

[31]Schiffman, *Reclaiming*, 245–55.

[32]L. H. Schiffman, *The Eschatological Community of the Dead Sea Scrolls: A Study of the Rule of the Congregation* (SBLMS 38; Atlanta, GA: Scholars Press, 1989) 11–71.

[33]Cf. L. H. Schiffman, 'The Laws of War in the Temple Scroll', *RevQ* 13 (Mémorial Jean Carmignac; 1988) 299–311.

[34]L. H. Schiffman, *Halakhah at Qumran*, 84–133.

[35]J. T. Milik, *Qumrân Grotte 4, II, II. Tefillin, Mezuzot et Targums (4Q128–4Q157)* (DJD VI; Oxford, Clarendon Press, 1977) 34–79; Y. Yadin, *Tefillin from Qumran (X Qumran Phyl 1–4)* (Jerusalem: Israel Exploration Society and Shrine of the Book, 1969).

[36]Milik, DJD VI.80–85.

[37]E. Tov, 'Scribal Practices and Physical Aspects of the Dead Sea Scrolls', *The Bible as Book – The Manuscript Tradition* ed. J. L. Sharpe III and J. Van Kampen (London: British Library, 1998) 9–33; E. Tov, 'Scribal Practices Reflected in the Documents from the Judean Desert and in the Rabbinic Literature: A Comparative Study', *Texts, Temples, and Traditions: A Tribute to Menahem Haran* ed. M. V. Fox, *et al.* (Winona Lake, IN: Eisenbrauns, 1996) 383–403.

sacrifices, and purity. This document, however, did not surface until the 1967 War, and it played an exceedingly significant role in the history of research thereafter.

The first generation of Qumran scholars, because of both training and *Tendenz*, did not effectively continue the work of Schechter and Ginzberg but sought to find in the sectarians – identified as Essenes – the monastic proto-Christians. [38] Accordingly, for these scholars, Qumran research was carried on with little or no attention to the entire second half of the preserved genizah manuscripts of the Zadokite Fragments or to the halakhic materials in the remainder of the Qumran corpus, most of which were left unpublished.[39] Despite the virtual ignoring of halakhah by the mainstream of Dead Sea Scrolls researchers in the years between 1948 and 1967, a number of important contributions were made. Most notable are the early papers by the great Talmudist Saul Lieberman,[40] the work of Chaim Rabin,[41] whose edition of the genizah manuscripts of the Zadokite Fragments became standard, and the articles of Joseph M. Baumgarten.[42]

Israeli scholars generally limited their research to the scrolls bought by Israel which are now housed in the Shrine of the Book. The excellent commentaries of Yigael Yadin on the *War Scroll*[43] and Jacob Licht on the *Rule Scroll*[44] certainly dealt with halakhic issues. Yadin's commentary was more influential due to its translation into English[45] and his renowned expertise in military matters. But Israeli scholars did little to investigate the halakhic aspects of those texts published by the international team operating on the other side of the Mandelbaum Gate, and, of course, they were denied access to the unpublished manuscripts.

---

[38]L. H. Schiffman, 'Confessionalism and the Study of the Dead Sea Scrolls', *Jewish Studies* 31 (1991) 5–14; *idem, Reclaiming*, 16–19.

[39]The halakhic section of the text was ignored in the otherwise incisive study of P. R. Davies, *The Damascus Covenant* (JSOTSup 25; Sheffield: Sheffield Academic Press, 1982) although the legal aspects of the Admonition, the text's sectarian ideological introduction, are discussed (105–42).

[40]S. Lieberman, 'The Discipline in the So-Called Dead Sea Manual of Discipline', *JBL* 71 (1951) 199–206; *idem*, 'Light on the Cave Scrolls from Rabbinic Sources', *PAAJR* 20 (1951) 395–404.

[41]C. Rabin, *The Zadokite Documents* (Oxford: Clarendon Press, 1954).

[42]J. M. Baumgarten, *Studies in Qumran Law* (SJLA 24; Leiden: E. J. Brill, 1977). The popular Rabin edition of the Zadokite Fragments was effectively a summary for the wider scholarly world of the halakhic researches of Schechter and Ginzberg with additional comments based upon the Qumran scrolls that had been published in the interim. In its efforts to attain usefulness, this book accidentally obscured from its readers the complexity of the halakhic material and its analysis, a lack partly remedied in Rabin's later book, *Qumran Studies* (Oxford: Clarendon Press, 1957).

[43]Y. Yadin, מגילת מלחמת בני אור בבני חושך ממגילות מדבר יהודה (Jerusalem: Bialik Institute, 1955).

[44]J. Licht, מגילת הסרכים ממגילות מדבר יהודה (Jerusalem: Bialik Institute, 1965).

[45]Y. Yadin, *The Scroll of the War of the Sons of Light against the Sons of Darkness* trans. B. Rabin and C. Rabin (Oxford: Oxford University Press, 1962).

Sectarian Halakhah

Despite all the limitations, the study of this material yielded important results. Even the study of the limited corpus of Qumran texts then available had led to significant conclusions about the halakhah of the Qumran group in the early years after the discovery of the scrolls. Among the important conclusions drawn from this material was a general sense of how the sectarians understood the authority of Jewish law. The sectarians saw the extra-biblical law as derived *in toto* from inspired biblical interpretation, thus denying such concepts as the 'traditions of the elders' of the Pharisees or the later Rabbinic oral Law concept.[46]

Further, scholars had observed that the legal material in the Qumran corpus (to the extent that it was then known) was entirely dependent or at least linked to biblical interpretation. This further distinguished it from the Pharisaic view. This, of course, could not be said about many of the sectarian regulations which appeared to have no link with the biblical traditions. Yet attempts to trace these regulations to Hellenistic origins must be seen as unsuccessful, despite the efforts of some scholars to link them.[47]

The Qumran sectarian texts display a unique combination of halakhic views with the particular sectarian regulations of the Qumran group. While such tendencies are not totally absent from the Pharisaic–Rabbinic tradition, they are certainly much more pronounced in the Dead Sea sectarian corpus.

In the cases we are discussing here, it is not simply that a group follows a particular set of halakhic rulings, as is to be expected. Rather, we are dealing with a use of halakhic rulings, or of an admixture of law and sectarian regulations, which functions to mark off the boundaries of the group. It is not simply that halakhic differences divide groups of Second Temple period Jews. Here legal rulings function as sociological boundary markers, a role that they have also played in later Jewish history and which they continue to play today. We speak here not of boundaries with non-Jews or with Jews who deny the obligation to live according to any halakhic norms. Rather, we are discussing drawing lines between various groups of Torah observant Jews.

Several examples from the Qumran corpus will illustrate this

---

[46]L. H. Schiffman, *Halakhah at Qumran*, 75–6.

[47]M. Weinfeld, *The Organizational Pattern and the Penal Code of the Qumran Sect* (Novum Testamentum et Orbis Antiquus 2; Fribourg, Switzerland: Éditions Universitaires; Göttingen: Vandenhoeck & Ruprecht, 1986) 10–57. Note Appendix E, 'The Recent Monograph of Schiffman', 71–6 in which he disputes my derivation of numerous rules from biblical tradition. Cf. the review of Weinfeld's *The Organizational Pattern* by E. Puech, *RevQ* 14 (1989) 147–8.

phenomenon. We turn first to the rules for entry into the sectarian group. Entry to the sect, as it was also for the *ḥavurah* described in tannaitic texts,[48] was a process of ascending a ladder of increasing ritual purity.[49] Progression through the ranks meant permission to come in contact first with solid foodstuffs and only later with liquids, which were more susceptible to impurity according to sectarian as well as Pharisaic-Rabbinic law. Transgression of sectarian norms involved demotion within the purity context as part of the penalty. The punishment of one year meant exclusion from the liquid foods of the sect until status was regained after the designated period. One penalized for two years was demoted also as regards the pure solid food and had to wait the full two years until re-entry to the pure meals.[50] These meals, governed as they were by sectarian purity regulations, were reflections of eschatological banquets, and so expressed as well the messianic aspirations of the group for a society of perfect holiness.[51]

This example is one in which the sectarian order of affairs is expressly linked to halakhic norms. The same may be said, for example, of the role of the *mevaqqer*, the sectarian overseer, in the collection of charity from the sectarians of the communities (outside Qumran, apparently) described in the Zadokite Fragments (*Damascus Docement*).[52] In this case, as in the description of the Essenes in Philo,[53] the collection and distribution of charity is done in accord with sectarian halakhic norms which differ to some extent from those of the Pharisaic-Rabbinic community. Examples of the interaction of halakhah and aspects of sectarian law extend even to the Sabbath where the presumption of a communal settlement may explain certain details of the Sabbath laws.[54] In the case of civil law, the role of the *mevaqqer* certainly places these laws in sectarian context, and it is most likely that the same courts judged violations of sectarian regulations and offenses

---

[48]A. Oppenheimer, *The 'Am ha-Aretz* (Arbeiten zur Literatur und Geschichte des Hellenistischen Judentums 8; trans. I. H. Levine; Leiden: Brill, 1977) 118–56. Most writers link the *ḥavurah* described in tannaitic sources directly with the Pharisees. However, there is no explicit evidence for such a connection.

[49]Comparisons of the tannaitic laws of purity and their relation to entry into the *ḥavurah* with those of the Qumran sect are found in C. Rabin, *Qumran Studies* (Scripta Judaica 2; Oxford: Oxford University Press, 1957) 1–21; Licht, מגילת הסרכים, 145–8; cf. his discussion of the tannaitic laws of purity, 294–303; S. Lieberman, 'The Discipline in the So-Called Dead Sea Manual of Discipline'.

[50]Schiffman, *Sectarian Law*, 165–8.

[51]Schiffman, *Eschatological Community of the Dead Sea Scrolls*, 53–67.

[52]CD14:12–16; cf. Schiffman, *Sectarian Law*, 37–38.

[53]Philo, *Every Good Man*, 87.

[54]Cf. Schiffman, *Halakhah at Qumran*, 115.

against what the sectarians and other Jews as well considered violations of the Torah's laws or commonly accepted interpretations of them.

One of the most distinguishing features of Qumran halakhah, the division of the law into *nigleh* and *nistar*,[55] is intimately related to the sectarian character of the group. *Nigleh*, the 'revealed' law, refers to the written Torah or the Bible which contains laws available to all Jews. These laws are contained in what later tradition would refer to as the 'plain' sense (*peshaṭ*) of the biblical legal texts. The *nistar* is the 'hidden' law, known only to the sectarians to whom it has been revealed in divinely inspired study sessions as part of the progressive revelation of God's will which the sectarians understood to be taking place. Those outside the sect, the texts tell us, are to be punished for their violation of the 'hidden' sectarian law, even if its prescriptions are unknown to them. Indeed, the sectarians are commanded to keep this part of their teaching secret.

Accordingly, one of the primary features of the sectarian outlook is that only members of the group possess accurate knowledge of the will of God. To be an insider is to have available this esoteric knowledge. To be an outsider is to be denied, or at least to lack, such knowledge. Halakhic knowledge, then, defines or at least is characteristic of members of the group, and outsiders are characterized by ignorance and violation of the true laws of the Torah.[56]

This feature is intimately linked to the eschatological expectations of the sect. The *War Scroll* and related texts expected that in the end of days the sectarians and their heavenly retinue would emerge victorious from the great war of the Sons of Light against the Sons of Darkness. In this war, the sectarians expected the downfall and death of the nations but also of all Israel except for those who would join, or who were predestined to join, the Qumran sect. The rest of Israel had been predestined for its lot and, therefore, lacked the teachings of the sectarian law. Hence, they do not merit to participate in the eschatological banquet of the Rule of the Congregation in the end of days. Thus, halakhah, sectarianism, and eschatology are intimately linked for the Qumran sectarians.

The *Temple Scroll* and MMT

The 1967 War was a turning point for Dead Sea Scrolls studies. In the course of the War, Israel recovered the *Temple Scroll* and took nominal

---

[55]Schiffman, *Halakhah at Qumran*, 22–32.

[56]Cf. N. Wieder, *The Judean Scrolls and Karaism* (London: East and West Library, 1962) 53–7.

control of the unpublished materials still in the Rockefeller Museum. Yadin's preliminary lectures which accompanied the announcement of the recovery of the *Temple Scroll*[57] as well as its publication set before the scholarly world this full-length halakhic work. Even more importantly, Yadin's commentary demonstrated the complexity and significance of this material both for the history of halakhah and for Dead Sea Scrolls research.

The *Temple Scroll* effectively re-energized the study of the history of Second Temple Jewish law and its relation to sectarianism, setting forth what would become an agenda for years to come. Further, the beautiful Hebrew edition of the scroll, replete with Rabbinic quotations and citations, drew the attention of Talmudic scholars and historians of Second Temple Judaism to this fascinating work.

Throughout the analysis of this document, in Yadin's commentary and in the works of other scholars who dealt with the scroll, the Darwinian theory which had spawned the 'old' and 'new' halakhah never reared its head. By this time, students of the history of halakhah in other periods had all made clear the need to recognize that varying opinions and approaches coexisted at the same time and that debate and dispute often characterized the history of Jewish law. Further, by this time, new studies of the law of Jubilees and other Second Temple documents had greatly enhanced the sense that alongside the law of the Pharisees, later enshrined and developed into the Rabbinic tradition, other ideas competed in the halakhic marketplace.

Throughout Yadin's commentary on the *Temple Scroll*, he alluded to the polemical nature of the text. A casual reader of the scroll, however, would have been impressed by the irenic tone of the author or compiler who chose to build his polemics into positive statements of his own views. But this text is correctly seen as a reformist document, calling for changes in the Temple structure, sacrificial practice, even government and military practices in the Hasmonean state in which the author lived.[58] Yadin was correct in observing that numerous statements of the author constituted polemics against what he termed the

---

[57]Cf. Y. Yadin, 'The Temple Scroll', *BA* 30 (1967) 135–9; *idem*, *New Directions in Biblical Archaeology* ed. D. N. Freedman and J. C. Greenfield (Garden City, NY: Doubleday, 1971) 156–66.

[58]For the dating of the scroll, see Yadin, *Temple Scroll* 1.386–90; M. Hengel, J. H. Charlesworth and D. Mendels, 'The Polemical Character of "On Kingship" in the Temple Scroll: An Attempt at Dating 11QTemple', *JJS* 37 (1986) 28–38; L. H. Schiffman, 'The King, His Guard and the Royal Council in the Temple Scroll', *PAAJR* 54 (1987) 237–59; L. H. Schiffman, 'The *Temple Scroll* and the Nature of its Law: The Status of the Question', *The Community of the Renewed Covenant: The Notre Dame Symposium on the Dead Sea Scrolls* ed. E. Ulrich and J. VanderKam (Christianity and Judaism in Antiquity series 10; Notre Dame, IN: University of Notre Dame Press, 1994) 37–55.

הלכה מגובשת (lit. 'the solidified law') of the Sages. Over and over Yadin pointed to such ideas, but most scholars outside the State of Israel had been sufficiently convinced by the work of J. Neusner regarding the late date of Rabbinic traditions, especially those dealing with the pre-70 period,[59] that they implicitly ignored these claims of Yadin. After all, how could a sectarian author writing in the year 120 BCE, using sources that went back to the pre-Maccabean period (as we now know), polemicize against views supposedly formulated in the later first century CE?[60]

The polemics which Yadin had noticed against views inherent in later Rabbinic literature were soon to be understood in light of the MMT document, the significance of which was first announced in 1984.[61] Based on a short allusion to this document and a brief quotation which had been published earlier under the title 4QMishnique,[62] it had already been proposed by J. M. Baumgarten that this document as well as the Temple Scroll included some Sadducean laws.[63] Indeed, at the very beginning of modern Jewish research, Geiger's studies of Jewish law had sought to reconstruct the influence of the Sadducean tradition.[64] Further, early reformers were, for a variety of reasons, fascinated with the Karaite movement which claimed to have inherited Sadducean traditions and which they saw as a predecessor in revolting against Rabbinic authority.[65] As a result, the Sadducees, as the supposed spiritual – even physical – ancestors of the Karaites, had received considerable attention in the early days of the *Wissenschaft des Judentums*. But the only real information on the halakhic differences between the Pharisees and the Sadducees then available was that contained in tannaitic sources. Josephus had reported only theological differences between the Pharisees and Sadducees, not mentioning any specific halakhic disputes. Now, for the first time, in MMT, a Second Temple text was available

---

[59]J. Neusner, 'Rabbinic Traditions about the Pharisees before A.D. 70: The Problem of Oral Transmission', *JJS* 22 (1971) 1–18; *idem, The Rabbinic Traditions about the Pharisees before 70*, 3 vols. (Leiden: E. J. Brill, 1971).

[60]Schiffman, 'The *Temple Scroll* and the Nature of its Law', 46–51.

[61]E. Qimron and J. Strugnell, 'An Unpublished Halakhic Letter from Qumran', *Biblical Archaeology Today: Proceedings of the International Conference on Biblical Archaeology, Jerusalem, April 1984* ed. J. Amitai (Jerusalem: Israel Exploration Society, 1985) 400–7.

[62]J. T. Milik, *Les 'Petites Grottes' de Qumran* ed. M. Baillet, J.T. Milik and R. de Vaux (DJD III; Oxford: Clarendon Press, 1962) 225. He described the text as an 'écrit pseudé-pigraphique mishnique'.

[63]J. M. Baumgarten, 'The Pharisaic Sadducean Controversies about Purity and the Qumran Texts', *JJS* 31 (1980) 157–70. Cf. M. Lehmann, 'The *Temple Scroll* as a Source of Sectarian Halakhah', *RevQ* 9 (1978) 579–88.

[64]Geiger, המקרא ותרגומיו, 84–95.

[65]I. Schorsch, 324, 349; S. Holdheim, one of the earliest reformers, wrote a work on Karaite marriage law, מאמר האישות על תכונת הרבנים והקראים (1861).

which, as its editors showed,[66] discussed numerous halakhic disputes, some of which were directly parallel to the Pharisee–Sadducee disputes of tannaitic texts. Further, other disputes in this document easily lent themselves to interpretation along the same lines for they clearly involved differences of opinion which could be understood as arising from the hermeneutical assumptions of the Sadducees or as a result of their priestly and Temple-centered piety. Clearly, in this document and in the tannaitic material, we were dealing not with Sadducees bent on Hellenization, but rather with highly committed Jews whose homiletical and legal traditions differed from those of the Pharisees.

A number of controversies described in tannaitic literature as Pharisee–Sadducee debates are documented in 4QMMT. In this document, the founders of the Qumran sect take the view associated with the Sadducees and polemicize against that attributed to the Pharisees, or 'sages of Israel' (חכמי ישראל) in the Rabbinic version. In these cases, MMT proves that later tannaitic accounts accurately portray disagreements regarding halakhic matters that took place in the early Hasmonean period.

One such controversy concerns the ashes of the red heifer used to purify those who have contracted impurity of the dead, in accord with Numbers 19. MMT (B13–17) criticizes the present procedure in the Temple, asserting that it is required that those involved in the preparation of the ashes of the red heifer must be fully pure, having experienced sunset on the last day of their ritual purification period. This same view appears in 4QTohorot (4Q277 Frag. 1).[67] We know from tannaitic sources that this was a Sadducean position and that the Pharisees disagreed strongly.[68] To them, if the required sacrifices and ablutions had taken place on the last day, even if the sun had not set, purification was sufficient for preparation of the ashes.

The sectarian opposition to this view is expressed as well in connection with a wide variety of laws several times in the Temple Scroll and in the Zadokite Fragments (*Damascus Document*). It clearly represented a major controversy between the Pharisees and their Sadducean/Zadokite opponents, which had ramifications in many areas of Jewish law.[69]

---

[66]See the halakhic analysis of E. Qimron, in DJD X 123–77 and the appendix by Y. Sussman, 179–200. The full version of that appendix is available in Hebrew in חקר תולדות ההלכה, 11–76.

[67]B. Z. Wacholder and M. Abegg, *A Preliminary Edition of the Unpublished Dead Sea Scrolls: Hebrew and Aramaic Texts from Cave Four*, Fasc. 3 (Washington, DC: Biblical Archaeology Society, 1995) 86.

[68]*m. Parah* 3:7; *t. Parah* 3:7–8.

[69]L. H. Schiffman, 'Pharisaic and Sadducean Halakhah in Light of the Dead Sea Scrolls: The Case of Ṭevul Yom', *DSD* 1 (1994) 285–99; cf. Schiffman, '*Miqṣat Maʿaśeh ha-Torah* and the

MMT(B18–23) also argued against the making of handles for vessels for Temple use out of animal hides and bones.[70] In the case of bones, this implies that the sectarians considered animal bones to be impure. This controversy is recorded in the Mishnah.[71] The Sadducees argued that the bones of animals were impure, but the Pharisees considered them pure. Again, the historicity of the disagreement is confirmed and MMT allows us to date it to at least ca. 150 BCE.

The final example of this phenomenon to be considered here is that of flowing liquids. This controversy concerned the pouring of ritually pure liquids from a pure vessel into an impure vessel. MMT(B55–58) argues that the impurity flows up through the liquid stream (opposite to the direction of the flow) and renders the upper vessel impure. This is a controversy known also from the Mishnah.[72] The Pharisees considered the upper vessel to remain pure, ruling that impurity cannot flow against the direction of the stream. The Sadducees considered the upper vessel impure.[73] Again, MMT shows that the disagreement dates to early Hasmonean times and confirms its being rooted in the halakhic debates of the time.

A few more such passages could be cited, but they raise the possibility that other laws preserved in the scrolls corpus are also polemics against Pharisaic views. We begin with the example of non-sacral slaughter. The *Temple Scroll* 52:14–16 required that all slaughter performed within three days' journey of the Temple be done sacrificially. Non-sacral slaughter is permitted only beyond the three-day limit. This same law seems to be repeated in MMT(B27–28). The opposite view appears in tannaitic literature ruling that non-sacral slaughter is permitted even right outside the Temple precincts. At stake here is the interpretation of the words 'If the place is far from you' (כי ירחק ממך המקום) in Deut 12:21.[74] It seems reasonable to conclude that this Qumran regulation,

Temple Scroll", *RevQ* 14 (1990) 438–42; cf. A. Solomon, 'The Prohibition against Ṭevul Yom and Defilement of the Daily Whole Offering in the Jerusalem Temple in CD 11:21–12:1: A New Understanding', *DSD* 4 (1997) 1–20.

[70]On hides, see Qimron and Strugnell, DJD X 154–6 and Schiffman, 'Miqṣat Maʿaśeh ha-Torah and the *Temple Scroll*', X 442–8.

[71]*m. Yad* 4:6.

[72]*m. Yad* 4:7.

[73]Qimron and Strugnell, DJD X 161–2; Y. Elman, 'Some Remarks on 4QMMT and the Rabbinic Tradition, Or, When Is a Parallel Not a Parallel?' *Reading 4QMMT: New Perspectives on Qumran Law and History* ed. J. Kampen and M. J. Bernstein (SBL Symposium Series 2; Atlanta, GA: Scholars Press, 1996) 105–24.

[74]L. H. Schiffman, 'Sacral and Non-Sacral Slaughter According to the Temple Scroll', '*Time to Prepare the Way in the Wilderness*': Papers on the Qumran Scrolls by Fellows of the Institute for Advanced Studies of the Hebrew University, Jerusalem, 1989–1990 ed. D. Dimant, L. H. Schiffman (STDJ 16; Leiden: E. J. Brill, 1995) 69–84; cf. E. Eshel, '4QLev^d: A Possible Source for the Temple Scroll and Miqṣat Maʿaśe ha-Torah', *DSD* 2 (1995) 1–13.

which fits totally with the Sadducean Zadokite view of the ultimate centrality of Temple worship, is arguing against an already existing Pharisaic practice allowing non-sacral slaughter anywhere outside the Sanctuary.

A related example pertains to the slaughter of pregnant animals. The *Temple Scroll* (52:5–7) forbids the slaughter of pregnant animals, quoting the prohibition on the slaughter of an animal and its young on the same day (Lev. 22:28). The very same law appears in MMT (B36–38)[75] in polemical context and in the Code of Punishments of the Zadokite Fragments (4Q270 2 ii 15).[76] Tannaitic sources indicate that the Pharisees permitted the slaughtering of pregnant animals, ruling that the fetus may be eaten without further slaughter.[77] The occurrence of this law in the polemical MMT together with the appearance of the opposite point of view in tannaitic sources allow us to conclude that the polemic was indeed against the Pharisees who held the view appearing only later in the Rabbinic material.[78]

Common Halakhah

Despite these observations it is important to keep all these halakhic disputes in context. The vast majority of legal rulings regarding the observances of sacrificial law, Sabbath, purity laws, and other halakhic practices were common to Second Temple period Jews.[79] This common Judaism was practised by the masses (later termed עם הארץ[80]) who had little to do with the detailed disputes of the various elites who had enrolled in the sectarian groups. The debates and differences of opinion we observe are often blown out of proportion. It must be remembered that our sources tend to emphasize disagreements over commonalities.

In this respect let me cite one example, the Tefillin (phylacteries) found at Qumran. While indeed these have been shown to reflect some differences with later Rabbinic rules for the making and copying of phylacteries,[81] the basic practice of wearing Tefillin indicated by the finding of numerous Tefillin in the Qumran caves is the same as that of

[75]Qimron and Strugnell, DJD X 157–8. See especially their n. 115 on the views of the Rabbis. Cf. Schiffman, , 'Miqṣat Maʿaśeh ha-Torah and the Temple Scroll', 448–51.

[76]Baumgarten, DJD XVIII 144, 146.

[77]M. Ḥullin 4:5.

[78]L. H. Schiffman, 'The New Halakhic Letter (4QMMT) and the Origins of the Dead Sea Sect', BA 53 (1990) 64–73 and idem, Reclaiming, 86–7.

[79]E. P. Sanders, Judaism: Practice and Belief, 63 BCE – 66 CE (London: SCM Press; Philadelphia: Trinity Press International, 1992) 45–303.

[80]See Oppenheimer, 67–117 for a survey of Rabbinic sources regarding the עם הארץ.

[81]See above, n. 35; A. M. Habermann, 'על התפילין בימי קדם', Eretz-Israel 3 (1954) 174–77.

the Pharisaic-Rabbinic Jews. But two types of phylacteries seem to have existed.[82] One contains the same exact Scriptural passages as required by the Rabbis and these may be termed 'Pharisaic' Tefillin. The other type is based on the same selection of basic texts but add additional material to each passage, something clearly forbidden by the later Rabbis.[83] These phylacteries are apparently reflective of the Qumran sectarian approach or that of some other non-Pharisaic groups. Yet these differences in detail pale when taken in context: the practice of wearing Tefillin transcended sectarian bounds, and the Tefillin of the competing groups were generally constructed in similar fashion. The law was even observed in Egypt in Hellenistic context, although we cannot be certain how widespread it was. Yet if the Nash Papyrus is from a Tefillin,[84] the dissemination of this observance would be even wider.[85]

We cite this example only to show how the disagreements were greatly outnumbered by aspects of common halakhic observance. Numerous such common Jewish practices could be cited from the scrolls, Josephus, the New Testament, and Pharisaic–Rabbinic sources.

Conclusion

The polemics of the Temple Scroll and other halakhic documents from Qumran represent the views of a group whose traditions and interpretations were already to some extent crystallized before the Maccabean Revolt (168–164 BCE). This halakhic trend, known to us as Zadokite or Sadducean, was followed by the Dead Sea sectarians, the author of *Jubilees*, and by other 'sectarian' groups in the Second Temple period. But perhaps, more surprisingly, the aggregate of all such polemics in the halakhic material in the scrolls, whether direct or indirect, points toward the existence, certainly by about 150 BCE, of a considerably developed Pharisaic system of laws against which these particular priestly sectarian circles were arguing. These conclusions are relevant to the question of the identity of the Dead Sea sect. It is widely accepted, even by many of those who still maintain the traditional 'Essene' theory

---

[82]J. T. Milik, DJD VI 47; E. Tov, '*Tefillin* of Different Origin from Qumran?' *A Light for Jacob: Studies in the Bible and the Dead Sea Scrolls in Memory of Jacob Shalom Licht* ed. Y. Hoffman, F. H. Polak (Jerusalem: Bialik Institute; Tel-Aviv: Tel Aviv University, 1997) 44*–54*.

[83]Note that phylactery texts from Qumran generally exhibit harmonistic tendencies. Cf. E. Tov, 'The Nature and Background of Harmonizations in Biblical Manuscripts', *JSOT* 31 (1985) 3–29.

[84]For a summary, see M. Greenberg, 'Nash Papyri', *EJ* 12 (1971), col. 833.

[85]Cf. Schiffman, *Reclaiming*, 305–12.

regarding the sect, that Sadducean-type law lies at the root of both the schism and the laws of the sectarian documents.[86]

Specifically, the Qumran materials have provided us with what we now know to be an entirely alternative system of Jewish law from Second Temple times, dating at least from the Hasmonean period, and in the case of some laws and even texts, to the pre-Maccabean period. These documents point to the Sadducean priestly heritage as the locus from which these traditions originate and have allowed us to understand an entirely different system of biblical interpretation which was previously not available.

Not only has direct evidence for the Sadducean approach been recovered in the scrolls but, more importantly, it has been established conclusively that the Pharisaic-Rabbinic tradition was deeply rooted in the Hasmonean period. In fact, these conclusions are in marked contrast to the claim of radical discontinuity between the pre- and post-70 period that had been put forward by some scholars.

The increase in our knowledge regarding the Pharisees goes hand in hand with some previous conclusions drawn by scholars from the Zadokite Fragments and the pesher literature. These documents had polemicized against a group known as the דורשי חלקות[87] who preached supposedly false teachings under the leadership of the איש הכזב, the 'man of lies'.[88] Among the designations of the דורשי חלקות was that they were said to be 'builders of the wall', בוני החיץ.[89] The term דורשי חלקות is a pun on the word הלכות (loosely translated as 'laws'), and this derogatory sobriquet, best translated 'false interpreters', refers to the Pharisees. Further, the term 'builders of the wall' can be understood in view of the Rabbinic adage עשו סיג לתורה, 'make a fence around the

---

[86]F. M. Cross, *The Ancient Library of Qumran* (3rd ed.; Sheffield: Sheffield Academic Press, 1995) 185–6. Cf. the carefully nuanced arguments regarding the Sadducees in J. C. VanderKam, *The Dead Sea Scrolls Today* (Grand Rapids, MI: Eerdmans, 1994) 93–5. VanderKam agrees to the existence of certain parallels between the Sadducees and the Essenes (whom he sees as equivalent to the Qumran sect) but attributes less significance to these parallels than I do. Baumgarten's view which continues to see greater affinity in halakhah between the Qumran scrolls and the Essenes, does not, in our view, give sufficient weight to certain parallels which indicate decisively the Sadducean trend. See J. M. Baumgarten, 'Sadducean Elements in Qumran Law', *The Community of the Renewed Covenant: The Notre Dame Symposium on the Dead Sea Scrolls* ed. E. Ulrich and J. VanderKam (Christianity and Judaism in Antiquity Series 10; Notre Dame, IN: University of Notre Dame Press, 1994) 27–36; and J. M. Baumgarten, 'The Disqualifications of Priests in 4Q Fragments of the "Damascus Document", a Specimen of the Recovery of pre-Rabbinic Halakha', *The Madrid Qumran Congress* ed. J. Trebolle-Barrera and L. Vegas Montaner (STDJ 11.2; Leiden: E. J. Brill, 1992) 2.503–4.

[87]1QH 2:15, 32; 4QpNah 3–4 i 2, 7; CD 1:18.

[88]1QpHab 2:2, 5:11; CD 20:15.

[89]CD 4:19, 8:12, 18, 19:25, 31.

Torah',[90] to refer as well to the Pharisees. In one passage it was said about this same group אשר בתלמוד שקרם, 'that their teaching (*talmud*) is their falsehood'.[91] The term תלמוד refers here to an early variety of legal methodology practised by the Pharisees already in the Hasmonean period.[92] Taken together, the evidence of the *Temple Scroll*, MMT, the Zadokite Fragments and the pesher literature have, in fact, provided substantial reflection of Pharisaic teaching and law. Along with what we seem now to be learning about Sadducean halakhah, the scrolls have radically altered our picture of Jewish law among the various sects of the Second Temple period.

These documents push back the date of some of the various halakhic debates known from tannaitic sources into the Hasmonean period and also show us that the Pharisaic–Rabbinic tradition, at least in certain areas of law and specific *halakhot*, was well developed and distinct already in the Hasmonean period.

Perhaps most importantly, the new scrolls allow us to abandon the linear or evolutionary approach to the history of halakhah. Rather, we must reckon with the notion that competing trends, what we might call priestly/Sadducean and Pharisaic/proto-Rabbinic were operative throughout the Second Temple period. In this respect some of the earlier studies were correct in emphasizing Sadducean approaches in some of the so-called schismatic or sectarian traditions, and some supposedly 'credulous' scholars were correct in assuming that certain Pharisaic traditions were to be dated much earlier than the tannaitic texts in which they were embedded. The scrolls have shown that Jewish law was a key issue in the interrelation and self-definition of the various sects and groups of Jews in Second Temple times.

From the point of view of halakhah, therefore, the question of the marginal character of the Qumran sect is a two-sided one. To the extent that Qumran texts reflect the wider nature of Sadducean/Zadokite law and polemicize against Pharisaic views, they are in no way marginal. Confirmation of the importance of many of these same issues comes from New Testament reports and tannaitic literature as well.[93] Yet to the extent that such legal views are used by the sectarians to form the basis of the rules and regulations of their particular way of life, in which law, sectarianism, and eschatology are intimately and to a great extent

---

[90]*m. Avot* 1:1. Cf. L. Finkelstein, 'The Maxim of the *Anshe Keneset ha-Gedolah*', *JBL* 59 (1940) 455–69.

[91]4QpNah 3–4 ii 8.

[92]B. Z. Wacholder, 'A Qumran Attack on Oral Qumran Exegesis. The Phrase אשר בתלמוד שקרם in 4Q Pesher Nahum', *RevQ* 5 (1966) 351–69.

[93]Cf. J. Neusner, *From Politics to Piety: The Emergence of Pharisaic Judaism* 2nd ed. (New York: Ktav, 1979) 67–96.

uniquely combined, these texts represent a very small subset of Jewish society in the Jewish world of Greco-Roman times.

But perhaps for us, as scholars of these ancient scrolls, it is of great importance to realize how much influence can be attained by a group that preserves, copies, and interprets a corpus of texts of great interest and importance. That, after all, is our job.

8

THE STORY OF JOSEPH AND THE *BOOK OF JUBILEES*
Calum M. Carmichael

Scholars such as George J. Brooke, James VanderKam, and Ben Zion Wacholder have increasingly affirmed the importance of the *Book of Jubilees* for the Qumran community.[1] Taking stock of how authoritative *Jubilees* is both at Qumran and among other sectarians, Wacholder suggests that we reclassify *Jubilees* as a sectarian document rather than as part of the pseudepigrapha corpus.[2] He puts forward the remarkable thesis that together with the intimately linked work, the *Temple Scroll*, *Jubilees* enjoys greater status than the traditional Pentateuch at Qumran.[3]

I intend not so much to question directly Wacholder's claims, but to probe further the observations about *Jubilees* that lead him to think that it holds a superior status to the Pentateuch. In broader terms I wish to add to the perspective that VanderKam, with Wacholder's agreement, claims for both *Jubilees* and the *Temple Scroll*, namely, that their authors belong to the same exegetical tradition, in my view, a tradition that has its roots in the Pentateuch itself.[4]

I first wish to look anew at the *Book of Jubilees* in relation to the Pentateuch and then to suggest that what is going on in *Jubilees* is even

---

[1]James VanderKam, for example, gives details about the remarkable frequency with which texts from *Jubilees* shows up in surviving manuscripts at Qumran, 'The Jubilees Fragments from Qumran Cave 4', in *The Madrid Qumran Congress Proceedings of the International Congress on the Dead Sea Scrolls* eds. J. Trebolle-Barrera and L. V. Montaner (Leiden: E. J. Brill, 1992) 2.648.

[2]B. Z. Wacholder, 'Jubilees as the Super Canon: Torah-Admonition versus Torah-Commandment', in *Legal Texts and Legal Issues. Proceedings of the Second Meeting of the International Organization for Qumran Studies, Published in Honour of Joseph M. Baumgarten* eds. M. Bernstein, F. Garcia Martinez, and J. Kampen (Leiden: E. J. Brill, 1997) 210.

[3]Note Philip Alexander's measured statement: 'Works such as *Jubilees* and the Temple Scroll present themselves not as commentaries on the Pentateuch, but as supplements to it, possibly even as replacements for it. These writings appear to claim an inspiration and authority equal to that of the canonic text'. See 'Jewish Law in the Time of Jesus: Towards a Clarification of the Problem', in *Law and Religion. Essays on the Place of the Law in Israel and Early Christianity* ed. Barnabas Lindars (Cambridge: Cambridge University Press, 1988) 56. J. VanderKam and J. T. Milik have recently published 4Q228, a text that cites *Jubilees* as authoritative (DJD XIII *Qumran Cave 4. VIII. Parabiblical Texts Part 1* [Oxford: Clarendon Press, 1994] 177–85).

[4]James VanderKam, 'The Temple Scroll and the Book of Jubilees', in *Temple Scroll Studies: Papers Presented at the International Symposium on the Temple Scroll* (ed. G. J. Brooke; Sheffield: Sheffield Academic Press, 1989) 232; also Wacholder, 'Jubilees as the Super Canon', 210. On exegetical methods at Qumran that replicate those in the Bible, see George J. Brooke, *Exegesis at Qumran. 4Q Florilegium in its Jewish Context* (Sheffield: JSOT Press, 1985) 38, 45.

more interesting than Wacholder has imagined. Specifically, I wish to show that the relation between laws and narratives in *Jubilees* is remarkably similar to how laws and narratives in the Pentateuch are related to each other.

When scholars consider the links between the *Book of Jubilees* and the original Pentateuchal legislation concerning the Year of Jubilee in Leviticus 25, they see only that the biblical legislation provides the author of Jubilees with his curious notion of time. The entry for the Year of Jubilee in the *Interpreter's Dictionary of the Bible* states categorically: 'under any condition the Jubilee Year period persisted in Jewish usage only as the larger unit of time reckoning and nothing more'.[5] I beg to differ. There is a great deal more and it amounts to uncovering a major aspect of how the author of the *Book of Jubilees* interprets the Pentateuch.

We are familiar with how certain Pentateuchal laws commemorate events in Israel's history. The institution of the Passover, for example, recalls the dramatic liberation of the Israelites from their enslavement in Egypt. What has not been seen before is that the institutions of the sabbatical year and the integrally related Year of Jubilee in Leviticus 25, while they too recall the slavery in Egypt, also commemorate the immediately preceding events recounted in the Joseph story.[6]

Before the Israelites become enslaved in Egypt, Jacob and his family go there to seek relief from the famine that afflicts Egypt and the surrounding countries. The famine lasts seven years but Joseph administers a policy that has grain stored from the previous seven years of good harvests and set aside for the seven years of want. Each year during the seven years of famine the Egyptian population buys food from Joseph and is saved from starvation. However, as the years go by the Egyptians' money runs out and one year, in addition to the last of their money, they have to give over their livestock in return for grain. The next year their situation is so desperate that they give over their 'bodies and their lands' to obtain food (Gen 47:18). The original family of Israel fares much better. The pharaoh has them dwell in a part of Egypt where they readily obtain food for themselves and their livestock.

The contrast is striking. The native Egyptians end up enslaved to the pharaoh and lose their landholdings. From this point on they are to receive grain from the pharaoh, and when the land is again cultivable they are to keep four fifths of the produce from the harvest and give to the

---

[5]*Interpreter's Dictionary of the Bible* ed. G. A. Buttrick (Nashville: Abingdon Press, 1962) 1002.

[6]In the Judaism of the last centuries BCE other laws in the Pentateuch came to be linked to events recounted in it. Thus the Feast of Weeks commemorates the promulgation of the Law on Sinai, and the Feast of Booths the forty years sojourn of the Israelites in the wilderness. See Bent Noack, 'The Day of Pentecost in Jubilees, Qumran, and Acts', *ASTI* 1 (1962) 73–95.

pharaoh one fifth by way of payment for the initial loan of seed. The family of Israel on the other hand receives at the time of the famine a landholding (*'aḥuzzah*) in 'the best of the land' of Egypt, and some of the brothers are made supervisors of the pharaoh's own livestock (Gen 47:6, 11). The Israelites' state of well-being, however, is temporary. They too are to experience enslavement to a pharaoh when there arises a new king over Egypt 'which knew not Joseph' (Exod 1:8). It is not until their god delivers them from this slavery that they can look forward to living in their own land as slaves of Yahweh their god and with their own landholdings.

The Levitical lawgiver openly declares that he sets down rules with a view to ensuring that the Israelites do not do what is done in the land of Egypt (Lev 18:3). In so admonishing the Israelites, the lawgiver reminds them that they had dwelt there. The lawgiver drafts his rules about the sabbatical and Jubilee years specifically against the background of the Israelites' experience of the famine in Egypt. Every seventh year there is a requirement that the Israelites deliberately impose famine on their land by refraining from sowing any seed that year. They are not even to take from any growth that might come from the previous year's plantings. The lawgiver focuses on seven of these famine-like years because his intent is to recall the seven years of famine in Egypt. During each of these seven sabbatical years, despite the manifest deprivation of food, there will nonetheless be plenty available to feed the population. The lawgiver states that every sixth year God will cause the harvest to be so bountiful that grain can be stored for three years ahead (Lev 25:21).[7] This plenitude of food is a reminder of the situation in Egypt when Joseph under God's direction stored for the forthcoming famine grain from bumper harvests.

For the Egyptians the outcome of the experience of the seven years of famine is a dramatic change in their social and economic conditions. Within the space of a single year they lose their landholdings and they become permanent slaves to the pharaoh. The Levitical lawgiver wants a different social and legal order for the Israelites from that which befell the Egyptians. This is why he introduces the year of Jubilee immediately after the passage of seven sabbatical years. In that one year of Jubilee any Israelite who has lost his ancestral landholding (*'aḥuzzah*) is given it back (Lev 25:13), and any Israelite who has been enslaved is freed.

The Year of Jubilee is announced on the Day of Atonement. The story of Joseph explains why. The narrative is very much taken up with sin and the forgiveness of sin. Joseph's brothers, the first sons of Israel, sinned against him and their father. In a dramatic climax, after they

---

[7]Three years because the forty-ninth and fiftieth years are both fallow years and the planting in the fifty first year will not provide food until the harvest comes in that year.

come to Egypt to obtain relief from famine, the brothers seek and obtain forgiveness for their wrongdoing. It is granted because it is God's doing that reconciliation should come about (Gen 50:17–21). The Day of Atonement prepares the way for the Year of Jubilee because it is the occasion when all the sons of Israel seek and receive forgiveness from God for their transgressions. In the Joseph story, the beneficent economic order that albeit temporarily Jacob's family enjoys in Egypt has as its necessary accompaniment, we can infer, family members at peace among themselves.[8]

The *Book of Jubilees* gives much attention to the topic of atonement – and its focus is the brothers' evil deeds against Joseph and Jacob. For *Jubilees*, the Day of Atonement was ordained for the tenth day of the seventh month precisely because, so its author claimed, the brothers' offense took place on that very day

Therefore it is decreed for the children of Israel that they mourn on the tenth day of the month – on the day when that which caused him to weep for Joseph came to Jacob, his father – so that they might atone for themselves with a young kid on the tenth day of the seventh month, once a year, on account of their sin because they caused the affection of their father to grieve for Joseph, his son. And this day is decreed so that they might mourn on it on account of their sins and on account of all their transgressions and on account of all their errors in order to purify themselves on this day, once a year. (*Jub.* 34:18, 19)

To connect the Day of Atonement with the brothers' misdeed in such a precise way seems so arbitrary on the part of the author of *Jubilees*. The connection he makes, however, continues the focus of the biblical lawgiver who first derived the Day of Atonement from the Joseph story. I shall return to the link.

R. H. Charles described the *Book of Jubilees* as 'Primitive History [the narration of events in Genesis and part of Exodus] Rewritten from the Standpoint of Law [the legal material in the remainder of the Pentateuch]'.[9] For Wacholder the author of *Jubilees* transformed a historical narrative (Genesis and part of Exodus) into 'a divinely etched law code'.[10] While Charles and Wacholder refer only to the *Book of Jubilees*, their assessments also characterize to a remarkable degree the relationship between the story of Joseph in the Book of Genesis and the laws about the sabbatical year and the Year of Jubilee in the Book of Leviticus.

---

[8]For details of the argument about the Year of Jubilee in relation to events in Joseph's Egypt, see Calum Carmichael, 'The Sabbatical/Jubilee Cycle and the Seven-year Famine in Egypt' *Biblica* 80 (1999) 224–39.

[9]*The Apocrypha and Pseudepigrapha of the Old Testament* ed. R. H. Charles (Oxford: Clarendon Press, 1913) 2.v.

[10]Wacholder, 'Jubilees as the Super Canon', 203, 204.

There is, I submit, a much more substantial link between the biblical legislation concerning the Year of Jubilee and the *Book of Jubilees* than has been hitherto realized. *Jubilees* refers to itself as the Divisions of Times because it divides world history into periods of time calculated according to weeks of years and jubilees. My claim is that the biblical institution about the Jubilee presents the original paradigm of a division of time into seven periods of seven years for the purpose of recalling a formative period of seven years of world history. After the manner of the biblical lawgiver when working with the sabbatical years and the Year of Jubilee in relation to the Joseph story, the author of the *Book of Jubilees* uses divisions of time for the recording of history.[11]

The *Book of Jubilees* claims to reveal how certain biblical laws are integrally related to events in biblical history. For example, the author of *Jubilees* associates the laws about defilement applying to males differently from females with the different times when Adam and Eve appear and encounter each other (Gen 2:20–24; Lev 12:1–5; *Jub.* 3:4–14). How laws relate to incidents in biblical narratives is the key to interpreting biblical legal material itself. Issues that arise in biblical history determine the formulation of every biblical law. The lawgiver Moses, however, only cites those incidents that occur during his lifetime. Events before and after he lived receive no explicit mention because, like the *Book of Jubilees*, the biblical material is fictional, being an attempt to invent the nation's law codes. The fictional author does not, understandably so, reveal his method of producing his laws. Wacholder is far from accurate when he states that 'unlike the comparable biblical material, which has but a handful of laws, Jubilees is a Torah in a legal sense'.[12] With a revealing exception, the one difference is that the biblical lawgiver did not weave the laws that he derived from reflection on the history, as *Jubilees* does, into the narrative accounts themselves. He made separate lists of them instead. The exception is a most interesting one. The Levitical lawgiver sometimes inserts into the Book of Genesis certain institutions (circumcision in Gen 17:10–14, the prescriptions to Noah in Gen 9:3–6) as part of the narrative history.[13]

Wacholder draws attention to the larger division of time in *Jubilees*

---

[11]In his assessment of *Jubilees*, O. S. Wintermute states: 'The author believed that there was a theological value inherent in certain special times', *The Old Testament Pseudepigrapha* ed. J. H. Charlesworth (Garden City, NY: Doubleday, 1985) 38. His assessment could equally well apply to the laws about the sabbatical and Jubilee years in the Bible because they focus on Yahweh's protection of Israel in Egypt during and after the seven years of famine there.

[12]Wacholder, 'Jubilees as the Super Canon', 203.

[13]In his discussion of the *Book of Jubilees*, R. H. Pfeiffer states: 'The Priestly author is only the first known instance in Judaism to date certain laws before Moses'. See his *Introduction to the Old Testament* (London: A. & C. Black, 1952) 210.

into past, present, and future.[14] According to him, what he terms the past perspective covers the period of time from the original revelation to Moses until the repentance of the community at Qumran.[15] The present perspective covers the living community at Qumran. The future perspective is the eschaton when God will dwell eternally in the temple at Jerusalem. Sometimes, according to Wacholder, the three-fold division is different. The past covers the period of time from the creation until Moses, the present is the Qumran community in its state of repentance and obedience to the commandments, and the future is the end of time. However we evaluate the stance taken by the author of *Jubilees*, it may be indebted to the stance of the biblical writer. He has a legendary lawgiver, Moses, look at events in the times of his ancestors, at events in his own lifetime, and at events yet to come (the institution of the monarchy in Deut 17:14–20, for example).

It is characteristic of the author of *Jubilees* to note the first occurrence of certain legal practices in Israel's history.[16] Thus he often sets them in the time of the ancients of Genesis, rather than in the age of Moses. For example, as I have already noted, laws about defilement that Moses gave in his lifetime the author of *Jubilees* places in the context of the coming into being of the first husband and wife ever. The focus on first time developments is also the salient feature of how the biblical lawgiver himself worked. When he formulated rules, for example, those concerning the sabbatical and Jubilee years, he focused on the first instance of a problem in the nation's history, in regard to the latter rules, when the first family of Israel faces starvation in Canaan (Genesis 41–47). Moreover, the lawgiver turned to the traditions in Genesis, a book about origins, in raising topics for judgment. Let me give another illustration.

The *Book of Jubilees* claims that the wrongdoing of Joseph's brothers led to the institution of the Day of Atonement. But it is the biblical lawgiver himself who, I suggest, first established the institution in response to what these brothers do. The reason he did so was that their story furnishes the first example in the nation's history when an offense is committed and forgiveness is sought for it and granted.[17]

The brothers' offense and its aftermath do not take place in the time

---

[14]Wacholder, 'Jubilees as the Super Canon', 202–9.

[15]According to *Jub.* 44:5 Moses receives the tables of the law and instruction in past and future matters on the same day of the year as God appears to Jacob on his way to Joseph in Egypt. It has been my contention that the Levitical legislation about the sabbatical and Jubilee years has this revelation to Jacob and subsequent events in Egypt in focus and, further, that the *Book of Jubilees* derives its periodisation of history from events in Joseph's Egypt.

[16]See the entry on *Jubilees* in *Anchor Bible Dictionary* 3.1032; also *The Old Testament Pseudepigrapha*, 38.

[17]Jacob does not acknowledge, never mind seek forgiveness for, his offense against Esau (Gen 27:41–45, 32).

of Moses. Consequently, the biblical lawgiver is not explicit about them in Leviticus 16. The events are from the preceding period when Joseph reconciles with his brothers who had grievously sinned against him, and who had caused him to end up in Egypt before they themselves had to seek food there. The wrongdoing in question is complicated, the process by which the offenders come to acknowledge it is tortuous, but forgiveness is extended to them by Joseph who involves God in it.

Recall how the brothers, pasturing the family flocks, act with hostility against their father's favorite son when he comes to look for them. They deliberate about killing him, but in the end they refrain. Assaulting him instead, they cast him into a pit in the wilderness. Joseph eventually is removed to Egypt where he becomes a slave, is imprisoned for an offense he did not commit, proves himself a master interpreter of dreams, and, on release, ends up as second in command to the pharaoh because he interprets aright the latter's dreams that foretell famine. Joseph's father thinks that he is dead, especially since the brothers present evidence involving a goat – a major part of their wrongdoing – that he is dead.

In the course of time the brothers themselves have to travel from Canaan to Egypt to obtain food because the famine affects neighboring countries as well as Egypt. On the first of two visits Joseph in disguise torments them (treating them as spies, for example). A consequence is that for the first time they acknowledge their sin against him: 'In truth we are guilty concerning our brother, in that we saw the distress of his soul, when he besought us, and we would not listen' (Gen 42:21). They speak of sinning (*ḥaṭa'*) against him and how they face a reckoning for his blood (Gen 42:22). Over time and after more torment from Joseph, the brothers on their second visit reconcile, but it is not until after their father's death that the issue of forgiveness explicitly comes up. Fearing retribution for their original wrong against Joseph, the offending brothers tell him that their late father had commanded them to go to him and seek forgiveness. They ask of him, 'Forgive, I pray you, the transgression [*peša'*] of your brothers and their sin [*ḥaṭṭa't*], because they did evil to you ... forgive the transgression of the servants of the God of your father' (Gen 50:17). Joseph is receptive to their petition. Although he acknowledges that they meant evil against him, he nonetheless gives a positive religious assessment of all that has taken place: 'God meant it [the evil] for good' (Gen 50:20). It is the last and climactic interaction between the brothers and Joseph.

A major feature of the biblical Day of Atonement is the role of the goat that bears the sins of the sons of Israel into the wilderness to Azazel, the supposed mythical demon. Recall that on the Day of Atonement there is not one goat but two, one for Yahweh that is slaughtered as a sin offering – the one cited in *Jub.* 34:18 – and the other that is sent off live to Azazel in the wilderness. This strange ritual with the live goat becomes intelligible, I submit, once we view it as serving to recall how Joseph's brothers use an animal, a goat, to cover up their failure to return Joseph to their father. To deflect attention from themselves as the culprits for his disappearance they point to an animal as responsible for it.

In effect, the brothers transfer their wrongdoing to an animal when they suggest to their father that Joseph has died the victim of a wild beast. That is the first major link between the scapegoat ritual and the story. The lawgiver devised an expiation ritual that exploited the salient features of what the brothers do with the goat. Only his aim was the reverse of theirs. In the law, the sons of Israel, having confessed to their transgressions, seek to be rid of them by transferring them to a goat. In the story, the sons of Israel, having improperly concealed their transgressions, transfer them to a goat. The *Book of Jubilees* has proceeded similarly. The descendants of Israel kill a goat to atone for their sins, because, conversely, the sons of the original Israel offended by killing a goat falsely to suggest the death of Joseph. The model for the reversal of aim in the law and in *Jubilees* will owe much to the story, namely, Joseph's theological claim that whereas the brothers meant evil against Joseph, God turns the evil into good (Gen 50:20). The biblical lawgiver translates God's response to a specific problem, the brothers' offense and the need to expiate it, into a legal construction for the purpose of dealing with the offenses of later Israelites and their need to expiate them. In this regard, however differently expressed in the Levitical ritual, many or most of the features characteristic of the Hittite and Mesopotamian rituals for the elimination of evil show up. We find substitution (the brothers substitute the goat for themselves), analogy (the ritual imitates their ruse with the goat), concretizing (the goat cum beast symbolizes their evil), and annulment (the ritual action represents a reversal of the offense).[18]

The ritual in Leviticus 16 describes how the goat goes not just to the wilderness (*midhbar*) but to an *'eretz gezera*. The Hebrew of the latter expression is usually taken in the sense of a cut-off part of land, that is, isolated and solitary. Both expressions may be picking up on the geographical location where the brothers mistreat Joseph. They were grazing their flocks at Shechem when Joseph went to report on them but they had moved on to a place called Dothan, which is some twelve to fifteen miles from Shechem. It was at Dothan that they strip him of his coat and cast him into a pit in the wilderness (*midhbar*). The wild

---

[18]See D. P. Wright, *The Disposal of Impurity: Elimination Rites in the Bible and in Hittite and Mesopotamian Literature* (Scholars Press: Atlanta, 1987) 37–43.

beast that supposedly preyed on Joseph would, in turn, have its habitat not in the wilderness as such, but in an even more inaccessible region, accurately depicted as *'eretz gezena.*

There are other illuminating links between law and story. The brothers' offense occurs in the wilderness to which they have come with their goats from their father's home territory: 'Cast him into this pit here in the wilderness', says Reuben to his brothers (Gen 37:22). In the ritual the goat is sent off into the wilderness from Israelite home territory without any explanation as to how the action signifies the bearing away of sins.[19] In the story the brothers kill a goat and splatter its blood on Joseph's coat. They then present the coat to Jacob back at his home without explaining how it has come to be in the state that it is in. It is Jacob who draws the conclusion that Joseph has been torn to pieces, not by a goat, but by a wild beast. The two goats in the expiation ritual of Leviticus 16 correspond to the two animals in the brothers' ruse, the slaughtered goat and the goat that is the fictitious wild beast.[20]

In the wilderness the goat goes to Azazel, the demon spirit, an imaginary mythical creature. This aspect of the action is intended, I suggest, to evoke the malevolence of spirit that characterizes the brothers' attribution of their evil deed to an animal in order to avoid suspicion falling on them.[21] The evil of both their deed and their lie about it is being expressed, indeed, re-enacted by the goat that goes to the imaginary evil being, Azazel, in the wilderness. In the narrative the animal, in reality, is a cover for the brothers' sins. Their very act of concealing what they have done brings up more sharply the issue of evil intent, the question to whom or to what the evil should really be attributed, and, because they are lying, the malevolent spirit at work in them.[22]

The brothers speak of an evil beast ('And we will say: an evil beast hath devoured him', Gen 37:20), and the story itself raises the issue of

---

[19]Erhard Gerstenberger finds it remarkable that there are no words of interpretation appended to what he, assuming an ancient origin for the scapegoat ritual, describes as an 'archaic and murky custom', *Leviticus*, OTL (Louisville: Westminster John Knox, 1996), 220.

[20]N. H. Snaith, CB, *Leviticus and Numbers* (London; 1967) 112, points out that in Lev 16:9 only one of the goats is called a sin offering, but in Lev 16:5 both constitute a sin offering. The interplay between the slaughtered goat and the fictitious beast might illumine this puzzle. When Wright tries to view the two aspects of Leviticus 16 that have the appearance of separate histories, the purgation of the sacred areas with blood and the removal of sin by the goat, he admits that the Levitical lawgiver presents them as very much bound together. See *Disposal of Impurity*, 16–19.

[21]In the Hittite Telepinu Myth the ritual removes Telepinu's malice, see *Ancient Near Eastern Texts Relating to the Old Testament* ed. J. B. Pritchard (Princeton: Princeton University Press, 1969) 127, 128.

[22]T. K. Cheyne may well be correct in claiming that Azazel owes its origin 'to the same school of speculative students of scripture to which we owe the names of angels, good and evil, in the later literature'. He dates the naming of angels to the fourth century BCE, 'The date and

ultimate causation when it states that God directs all the actions that take place, the brothers' misdeeds included (Gen 40:32, 40:5, 50:20). In 1 Chr 21:1 the Priestly writer reacts against the attribution of evil to Yahweh in the incident about David's counting the people (2 Sam 24:1), and substitutes Satan in his account. In Leviticus 16 the Priestly lawgiver may similarly not have cared for the notion of Yahweh as the one responsible for evil in the Genesis narrative and attributed it to the Satan-like figure Azazel instead.

The fiction of the goat as the wild beast would explain why Wright finds Azazel to be a figure devoid of personality, in contrast to the demonic figures that turn up in the Hittite and Mesopotamian rituals.[23] Azazel expresses the nastiness of the fiction. In this light Azazel does not function as a live force with a separate, independent existence. The figure points to the brothers' evil in devising the fiction and hence conveys the inner demonic activity that is their wickedness. Wright is correct to note that Azazel does not measure up to the type of demonic personality associated with Hittite and Mesopotamian figures, but he is wrong to think that Azazel once enjoyed such a personality that the Israelites somehow displaced.

In the law, the goat goes off into the wilderness. The brothers' made-up story inspires the idea. Fantastically, an innocent, herbivorous animal becomes an evil devourer of a human being, Joseph. While it may be no more than coincidental, such a transformation has a parallel in the Joseph story. In the pharaoh's dream, in order to convey – so Joseph interprets – the fate that awaits human beings, including Joseph and his brothers, the sleek cows devour the fat ones (Gen 41:17–24).

In order to conceal their misdeed, the brothers splash the goat's blood on Joseph's clothing – from a priestly perspective a serious offense against the sacred order. The ritual of the Day of Atonement is very much involved with the proper splashing of blood for the purpose of 'covering up' (*kipper*) in a different, although still related sense,

---

origin of the ritual of the scapegoat', *ZAW* 15 (1895) 155. The *Book of Enoch* is an example of the later literature in question. Like the Levitical lawgiver who links Azazel to the incident in the Book of Genesis, the author of *Enoch* also connects Azazel to incidents in Genesis. Thus Azazel is the leader of those angels who lust after the daughters of men and whose children, the giants, fill the earth with blood and unrighteousness (Gen 6:1–5; *Enoch* 8:1, 9:6). The personification of evil, or of an evil attribute, has parallels in other biblical texts. The expression 'sons of belial [unprofitableness]' (*bene beliya'al*) designates those who are lawless and deviant (e.g. Judg 19:22; 1 Sam 10:27, 25:25, 30:22; 1 Kgs 21:10, 13). In 2 Cor 6:15 Belial has become a proper name. The Greek development as found in Theophrastus' characters is comparable, for example, Wilful Disreputableness, *Characters of Theophrastus* (ed. J. M. Edmonds; Cambridge, MA: Harvard University Press, 1946) 52-7.

[23]'Azazel does not appear to be an angry deity who needs to be appeased, nor a desert demon who is the custodian of evil'. *Disposal of Impurity*, 72, 73, cp. 24, 25, 69.

wrongdoing of all kinds. The man who physically sends the goat into the wilderness has to wash his clothes after doing so. We may have another example of the lawgiver requiring a later Israelite to engage in an action that is the converse of what happens in the story. In it, the brothers stain Joseph's coat with blood. In the law, the person who actively participates in the ritual of remembrance has to cleanse his clothes.

When the brothers kill the goat they are deliberately and dangerously playing with life and death. They claim Joseph is dead when in fact he is alive. The slaughter of the goat in the law is for the purpose of expiating sin. When human beings present sin offerings they are expressing the hope that their wrongdoing will avoid the danger that death might be visited on them. A Hittite king fearing death presents offerings to the Moon God and states, 'Let these die! But let me not die!'[24] Some such thinking presumably underlies the claim of the author of *Jubilees* that the slaughtered goat on the Day of Atonement expiates for the offense of the brothers.

Jacob Milgrom points out that the term *peša'* (transgression) appears twice in Lev 16:16, 21 but is found nowhere else in the priestly code.[25] It occurs twice in Gen 50:17 when the brothers ask Joseph to forgive them their transgression against him.

On the Day of Atonement the Israelite has to afflict himself, probably by fasting (Lev 16:29, 31). The requirement puzzles critics, but the influence of the Joseph story may again have to be reckoned with. On the Day of Atonement an Israelite has to refrain from eating in order to do the opposite of what the brothers do. Having cast Joseph into the pit in the wilderness they sit down to eat after which they carry out their deception with the goat (Gen 37:25).[26]

---

[24]See *Ancient Near Eastern Texts*, ed. Pritchard, 355; discussed by Wright, *Disposal of Impurity*, 37.

[25]See Jacob Milgrom, 'Day of Atonement', *Encyclopaedia Judaica* (Jerusalem, 1971) 5. 1384; also *Leviticus 1–16* (Garden City, NY: Doubleday, 1991) 1034.

[26]Gerstenberger thinks that putting on sackcloth might be included in the self-affliction (cf. *Jub.* 34:18, 19). If that is the case, it is possibly pertinent that when Jacob learns of Joseph's fate as the prey of the beast he puts sackcloth on his loins and mourns many days (Gen 37:34), *Leviticus*, 226. In my *Law, Legend, and Incest in the Bible* (Ithaca: Cornell University Press, 1997) 119-22, I argue that the cryptic rule in Lev 19:26, 'Ye shall not eat upon ['al] the blood', comes from the lawgiver's reflecting on the brothers indulging in eating and at the same time planning to shed Joseph's blood. Since publishing that argument I have come upon the identical interpretation. M. Rotenberger and B. L. Diamond paraphrase it as, 'Do not indulge in eating which will eventuate in bloodshed'. See their, 'The Biblical Conception of Psychopathy: the Law of the Stubborn and Rebellious Son', *Journal of the History of the Behavioral Sciences* 7 (1971) 36 n. 39. They attribute it to Maimonides, *Guide of the Perplexed* [London: 1885], ed. M. Friedlander, Part 3, Chapters 33, 46 at 159, 233, although I am not so sure that they are entirely accurate.

The legislation concerning the forgiveness of sins on the Day of Atonement is illumined once we see that it harks back to the first occurrence in the history of the nation when forgiveness is sought for an act of wrongdoing. The issues that come up in the story are the issues that the lawgiver has under review. The story is about the concealment of a transgression by the first sons of Israel. There is a move to have them openly acknowledge it when Joseph trips them up by actions (accusing them of acting secretly as spies, wrongly giving them money) that mirror their original actions against him (concealing their treatment of him, seeking money for him). They do recall their wrongdoing and own up to it in his presence when his identity is still hidden from them (Gen 42:21–23). Eventually forgiveness is openly extended to them.

The Day of Atonement too is about concealed offenses, the offenders' owning up to them in a context of giving cryptic expression to them (the ritual involving the goat), and forgiveness extended to those seeking it. The lawgiver focuses on the brothers' method of concealing an offense, namely, by having it transferred to an animal, and formulates the religious notion of covering over offenses by transferring them to an animal. He wishes all future descendants of these original sons of Israel to acknowledge openly all of their wrongdoing by transferring it to an animal. What the brothers do in secret by way of covering up their wrongdoing, the later Israelites do openly by way of declaring theirs.[27] It is a universal phenomenon. One way of countering wrongdoing is to have the culprits – in this instance, their descendants who share the responsibility for the offense just as they share in the promise to their ancestors of future well-being – engage in like actions that recall it. After the Israelites capture the Canaanite king Adonibezek they cut off his thumbs and great toes because in his time he had cut off the thumbs and great toes of seventy kings: 'As I have done, so God has requited me' (Judg 1:7). In biblical law theft of an animal results in the thief having to hand over a number of his (Exod 22:1). In contemporary America one finds sentences of the type where a slum landlord has to live in a building in which he housed tenants until repairs have been made to it.[28] Like the ritual with the goat, the imitation of the initial offense often intends a constructive outcome.

Even more relevant to the ritual with the goat is the ritual with the heifer in the law about the man found slain in the open country (Deut

[27]B. A. Levine points out that the verb *hitvaddah* in Lev 16:21 means 'to reveal oneself' in the matter of one's sins and is the opposite of concealing them. See *Leviticus* (Philadelphia: Jewish Publication Society, 1989) 106.
[28]See Stephen P. Garvey, 'Can Shaming Punishments Educate?' *The University of Chicago Law Review* 65 (1998) 736.

21:1–9). Its intention is also to recall the features of the original offense. The murderer is unknown so nothing can be done about him. What can be attended to, however, is the stain on the land caused by the victim's blood. God has gifted the land to Israel and the blot will cause God to look away and withhold his blessing of life from it. The lawgiver highlights the contamination to the new land. He requires the elders of the town nearest the murder victim to kill a heifer that is brimful of vitality – it has never worked or been mated – on a parcel of ground that is potentially superabundant – it has not yet been plowed or sown and is beside an ever-flowing stream of water. By killing the animal at this spot the elders dramatically re-enact the horror of a human life struck down on the special life-giving land.[29] Like the ritual with the goat, the re-enactment of the offense is for the purpose of calling to mind and expiating wrongdoing. The elders proceed to pray for forgiveness (Deut 21:8).

What prompted the Levitical lawgiver to pay so much attention to the Joseph story? Like other biblical lawgivers he is intent on looking back to first time developments in the nation's history. The brothers commit the first offense for which forgiveness is sought and achieved. From a priestly point of view, however, proper expiation for an offense requires physical-symbolic actions in a cultic context. The Levitical legislator evaluates the situation in the Joseph story and provides the appropriate cultic remedies for the issues that the story raises and that are bound to recur among future generations of Israelites.

Why did the lawgiver pay so much attention to the brothers' ruse with the goat? Their cover-up furnishes a rich source for reflecting on the topic of wrongdoing. For one thing, they conceal theirs. For another, they suggest Joseph has been killed when he has not. Again, they misuse the blood of an animal. Also, they kill an animal in a manner that is wholly unacceptable to the priests. Again, they dishonor a parent in a quite major way. In devising a focus for later Israelites to dwell on when seeking expiation for their own concealed, multifarious transgressions, the lawgiver would note that the brothers' action represents a multi-faceted tapestry of wrongdoing.

In the law, the ritual with the goat serves to trigger historical memory about the brothers' devious conduct. In the story, the brothers receive forgiveness, but they do not openly recount the various sins they have committed. The later sons of Israel are not to conceal their offenses but are to recount them when seeking forgiveness for them. The ritual is commemorative in function and is not, as is generally thought, a relic of

---

[29]See Calum Carmichael, 'A Common Element in Five Supposedly Disparate Laws', *VT* 29 (1979) 129–34; *Law and Narrative in the Bible* (Ithaca: Cornell University Press, 1984) 136–9.

a rite with decidedly magical overtones from pre-Israelite times.[30] There is no need for critics to be bewildered by the ritual and to complain that there are 'absolutely no elements that are specifically Israelite or that derive specifically from the Yahweh religion'.[31] One indication that the ritual is commemorative is its sheer impracticality. How does one cause a goat to go off into the wilderness? Lev 16:21 speaks of how a man 'at hand' (*'itti*) sends the goat away (possibly reflecting the fact that the story does not single out any one brother as coming up with the idea of killing the goat and saying that a wild beast had killed Joseph). No wonder that later Jewish understanding of the ritual has it led away and pushed over a ravine (*m. Yoma* 6:3–6).[32]

Taking up the work of his student David Wright, Jacob Milgrom in his erudite commentary assesses the similarities and dissimilarities between the rites of elimination of evils in Anatolia and Mesopotamia and the biblical rite of the scapegoat. The former rites, for example, are typically of an emergency nature, whereas the biblical one is not. Milgrom is at pains to stress how there is really no good parallel in the Near Eastern sources to the Levitical institution. Nonetheless, he feels constrained to say that a very ancient foreign rite has at some point been adopted and modified in keeping with Israelite needs. His evidence is of the lightest kind. For example, because the term *pešaʿ* (transgression) is only found in the Levitical material in regard to the Day of Atonement its use supposedly constitutes an indication that the material in which it occurs has been transplanted from somewhere else.[33] In point of fact its use comes, as I have indicated, from its use in regard to the brothers' offense against Joseph.

That the Levitical lawgiver might be familiar with some emergency rites of elimination of evil in surrounding cultures, or in his own, I take to be likely. I would stress, however, that it does not follow that he is taking over one of them and modifying it. Rather, the better perspective is to assume that knowledge of customary rites on his part and that of his audience would make the one he devises more readily intelligible.

---

[30]Martin Noth states that the ritual 'makes a distinct impression of antiquity', that 'it doubtless represents a very ancient rite', *Leviticus*, OTL (London: SCM Press, 1965) 119, 124. He is alert to the ambiguity that scholars create for themselves when they wonder how Azazel needs to be appeased by the gift of a goat, yet removes the sins of the sons of Israel. There are extraordinarily tortuous attempts to explain the rite. For an account of some of them, see Nicolas Wyatt, 'Atonement Theology in Ugarit and Israel', *UF* 8 (1976) 425–30.

[31]So Gerstenberger, *Leviticus*, 220. He asks how theologians of the 5th century BCE 'could have allowed this kind of "polytheistic" idea to pass through' (221). For him the entire ritual seems so opposed to early Jewish belief.

[32]*Targum Yerushalmi* on Lev 16:21 also sees the difficulty with the goat when it has it hurled down a precipice to its death by a gust of wind sent by God.

[33]See Jacob Milgrom, *Leviticus 1–16*, 1034, 1071-9.

The Near Eastern comparisons that Wright and Milgrom pursue are important because they can evoke the atmosphere of concern about evil that may have prevailed among ordinary people when the biblical lawgiver was writing. The fact that we can go to so many different cultures – Wright includes Greek, Roman, and even Indian [34] – and find parallel features suggests that it is incautious to conclude that the biblical ritual is a continuation in a modified form of some pre-existing one.

The author of *Jubilees* spells out in plain terms that the Day of Atonement and the Joseph story are very much bound together. It is a connection that continued to enjoy recognition in later Jewish tradition.[35] The one that I came upon to be particularly striking in light of my own analysis is in Maimonides. He states: 'The Sages ... consider the reason for which the congregation is constantly atoned for by means of *se'irim* [goats] is that the whole congregation of Israel committed their first act of disobedience [the brothers' offense against Joseph] with the help of a kid [*se'ir*] of goats'. Equally interesting is Maimonides's observation about the relationship between the brothers' action with the goat and the priests' use of the goat on the Day of Atonement. He comments: 'For the end of all these actions [using goats to atone for sin] is to establish firmly in the soul of every disobedient individual the constant need for remembering and making mention of his sin ... and that he, his descendants ... must seek forgiveness for the sin by an act of obedience belonging to the same species as the act of disobedience'.[36] I argued that the atoning ritual with the goat – Maimonides' act of obedience – imitates the brothers' use of it to convey that a wild beast had killed Joseph – Maimonides' act of disobedience. In the language of Gen 50:20, if forgiveness for evildoing is sought, God will reverse the evil and transform it into good.

These later Jewish sources do not spell out in the precise terms presented in this paper that the role of the goat and Azazel mirrors the brothers' deception. In the *Book of Jubilees*, for example, it is only the slaughtered goat of the Day of Atonement that the author links to the slaughter of the goat in the Joseph story. It does not follow, however,

---

[34]*Disposal of Impurity*, 5, 52.

[35]Contrary to the view of R. H. Charles, *The Book of Jubilees* (London: SPCK 1917) 171: 'The reason [Jacob's mourning on account of what the blood-stained coat signified] here given for the institution of the Day of Atonement (cf. Lev. xvi) seems to be peculiar to our Book'.

[36]Maimonides, *Guide of the Perplexed*, trans. Shlomo Pines (Chicago: Chicago University Press, 1963), Part III 46 (589); also *Siphra* on Lev 9:3. See Louis Ginzberg, *The Legends of the Jews* (Philadelphia: Jewish Publication Society, 1946) 2.27 notes 62 and 65; and E. E. Urbach, *The Sages: Their Concepts and Beliefs* (Cambridge, MA: Harvard University Press, 1975) 1. 521–3 (on how later generations had to atone for the brothers' offense because it had gone unexpiated); Jacob Neusner, ed. *Sifra: An Analytical Translation*, BJS 139. 2 (Atlanta, GA: Scholars Press, 1988) 125.

that the author did not recognize the action involving the live goat and Azazel as one that gave expression to the content of the brothers' deception with the goat. The reason for not citing this particular link could be that the author of *Jubilees* functions much as the biblical lawgivers did. Like them, he sets out rules in light of developments in a biblical narrative, sometimes emphasizing one aspect of a development and sometimes another.

A major feature of biblical laws is that often two similar laws differ only because they take up different facets of the same tradition. A good illustration is how the two Sabbath laws in the decalogues of Exodus 20 and Deuteronomy 5 took up Aaron's offense in the matter of the golden calf (Exod 32). Aaron's proclaiming a special day in its honor prompted the formulation of the rule about the Sabbath day in each decalogue. Exod 20:10, 11, however, cited Yahweh's creation of the world as the reason why the Sabbath day is special, whereas Deut 5:12–15 attributed its special character to Yahweh's deliverance of the Israelites from their slavery in Egypt. The Exodus version focused on the unacceptable claim in the story of the golden calf that the people created a god. The Deuteronomic version, in turn, focused on the negative fact that the people proclaim the golden calf as the agent that brought them out of Egypt.[37] The author of *Jubilees* might be proceeding similarly to the biblical lawgiver. Whereas the Levitical lawgiver paid attention to that aspect of the brothers' action with the goat which makes it into a beast of the wilderness, the author of Jubilees focuses solely on the actual slaughter of the goat by the brothers.

[37]See Calum Carmichael, *The Spirit of Biblical Law* (Athens, GA: University of Georgia Press, 1996) 87, 88.

9

SABBATICAL CHRONOLOGIES IN THE DEAD SEA SCROLLS AND RELATED LITERATURE

James C. VanderKam

A series of texts from Second Temple times use the biblically inspired language of sabbatical weeks and jubilees to encase the events of scriptural history or smaller segments of time, especially the last parts. The purpose of this paper is to examine how these texts employ and develop such units of time and to inquire about the ends toward which the authors directed their sabbatical chronologies. We shall first survey the biblical sources for the units and then turn to a chronological study of the works that use such systems, including the fragmentary Qumran texts that resort to them.

The Biblical Background

The language of sabbaths and jubilees as units of time goes back to the Hebrew scriptures. The priestly creation story in Genesis 1 already suggests a sabbatical structure for time from the very beginning, and such thinking is attested elsewhere in the Bible. The specific details of the legal texts that set forth these ideas need not detain us, but it will be useful to search for aspects of the presentations that might have encouraged later readers to use sabbatical weeks and jubilees periods for chronological and theological purposes.

Sabbatical legislation

The Covenant Code includes provisions for allowing the land to lie fallow in the seventh year, with the same treatment being accorded to vineyards and olive orchards (Exod 23:10–11). That is, the procedure imitates the six days of labor and one day of rest in every week (this subject is mentioned in the next verse, 23:12). The humanitarian purpose for the year without planting or harvesting is 'so that the poor of your people may eat' (v. 11).[1] A slightly more expanded form of the law is found in the Holiness Code (Lev 25:2–7). The text stresses that the sabbath involves 'complete rest for the land, a sabbath for the Lord' (v. 4). Here too humanitarian concerns are to the fore in that owners are

---

[1]Scriptural citations are from the NRSV.

to share the natural growth with their various kinds of servants (v. 6). In this chapter we also encounter the theological significance that lies behind the sabbatarian legislation: 'The land shall not be sold in perpetuity, for the land is mine; with me you are but aliens and tenants. Throughout the land that you hold, you shall provide for the redemption of the land' (vv. 23–24).

The Deuteronomic Code also contains legislation pertaining to the seventh year. In Deut 15:1–11 the emphasis falls on release from debts owed by fellow Israelites. There is to be no one in need in Israel, and Israelites are to give freely to those who require help. Moreover, a Hebrew servant is to be set free in the seventh year (vv. 12–18). This last provision is paralleled in the Covenant Code (Exod 21:1–6). It should also be recalled that the Deuteronomic law was to be read in the seventh year (Deut 31:10–13). According to the passage, "Every seventh year, in the scheduled year of remission, during the festival of booths, when all Israel comes to appear before the Lord your God at the place that he will choose, you shall read this law before all Israel in their hearing' (vv. 10–11). The reference to the autumnal festival of booths suggests that the year of remission began around that time.

These few biblical references to the seventh year and legislation relating to it show that it was associated with redemption of property, release from debts, freedom of slaves, and reading the law (cf. also Neh 10:31). The seventh year marked off a unit of ordinary time and provided a respite from some of the normal patterns and relations of life. All of the legislation was a part, of course, of Israel's covenantal relationship with the Lord. It is worth adding here that the passages deal with a sabbatical year, not with a seven-year sabbatical period. It is the case, nevertheless, that the seventh year marks off a seven-year unit of time that will be followed by another such unit.

The institution of the sabbatical year is brought into connection with Israel's history in Lev 26:34–35, which envisages the nation in exile: 'Then the land shall enjoy its sabbath years as long as it lies desolate, while you are in the land of your enemies; then the land shall rest, and enjoy its sabbath years. As long as it lies desolate, it shall have the rest it did not have on your sabbaths when you were living on it'. However, after the people confessed their sins, the Lord would call to mind the covenant with the three ancestors and would remember the land (vv. 42–43).

Jubilee legislation

Leviticus 25 is devoted in large part to the laws for the year that came after seven units of seven years, that is, with the fiftieth year. It is the only biblical passage which deals at length with the institution and the

laws that governed it. Although some of the details are more complicated, the basic teaching of the chapter is simple: in the fiftieth year
property alienated from the original owners was to revert to them, and
a Hebrew who had become a slave was given freedom: 'And you shall
hallow the fiftieth year and you shall proclaim liberty [דרור] throughout
the land to all its inhabitants. It shall be a jubilee for you: you shall
return, every one of you, to your property and every one of you to your
family' (v. 10). It should be noted that the term יובל is applied in this
chapter only to the fiftieth year, not to the 49–year period that precedes
it (see especially vv. 10–11), but, as with the sabbatical year, it served
to define a longer span.

   In contrast to the situation for the sabbatical year, there is no
evidence that the jubilee legislation was ever implemented in antiquity.
The only other references to it in the Hebrew Bible are in Lev 27:16–25
where the laws of consecrated property are related to it in the sense that
selling prices must be pro-rated, depending on the proximity to or
distance from the year of jubilee; and Num 36:4 where the possible
effect of the jubilee year on the property of the daughters of
Zelophehad, should they marry into another tribe, is noted.

Employment of weeks and jubilees units for chronological purposes

Although the legal portions of the Bible use the terms *sabbath* and
jubilee for a single year, there is evidence already in the Hebrew Bible
that these and related words such as *weeks* came to include in their
meanings the entire units of time that they concluded. This tradition of
using sabbaths/weeks and jubilees in an extended sense carried over into
a number of other texts from the second temple period.

Jeremiah 25 and 29

The prophet Jeremiah, in speaking of the exile, did not have recourse to
the language of weeks of years and jubilees of years, but he did use a
number which suggested it to later interpreters. In chapter 25 he speaks
about the tribes of the north and the divine servant Nebuchadrezzar
who will conquer Judah and surrounding lands and 'will utterly destroy
them and make them an everlasting disgrace' (v. 9). These nations will
serve the king of Babylon for seventy years, after which he and his
nation will share the fate of their victims (vv. 11–12; cf. 27:7). It is
perhaps interesting that Jeremiah's oracle includes what the text calls
'all the kingdoms of the world that are on the face of the earth' (v. 26);
all of them will drink the wine of the Lord's wrath. Or, later in the same
chapter, he writes about the Lord: 'he will roar mightily against his fold,

and shout, like those who tread grapes, against all the inhabitants of the earth. The clamor will resound to the ends of the earth, for the Lord has an indictment against the nations; he is entering into judgment with all flesh, and the guilty he will put to the sword, says the Lord' (vv. 30b–31). Verses 34–38 call the leaders of the nations their 'shepherds'.

In Jeremiah 29 the same seventy years appear, this time in a letter from the prophet to the Judeans who had already gone into exile with King Jehoiachin. After telling them to settle down where they were and not listen to optimistic prophets and diviners, he wrote: 'For thus says the Lord: Only when Babylon's seventy years are completed will I visit you, and I will fulfill to you my promise and bring you back to this place' (v. 10).

Thus, in Jeremiah's prophecies the seventy years are first and foremost the seventy years that the Lord has allotted to Babylon to rule and punish Judah and other peoples. The language used by the prophet is that of a universal judgment carried out by Babylon and its allies, the tools of the deity in his judgmental work. After that will come a great turn of affairs, when the Lord restores his people. 2 Chr 36:21, which refers to Jer 25:11–12; 29:10, ties the seventy-year exile directly with sabbatical units: the exile which was imposed by the Babylonians and which extended until the rise of Persia came about 'to fulfill the word of the Lord by the mouth of Jeremiah, until the land had made up for its sabbaths. All the days that it lay desolate it kept sabbath, to fulfill seventy years'. As S. Japhet notes, the passage combines the views of the exile found in Leviticus 26:34–35, 43 and in Jer 25:11–12; 29:10: Leviticus supplied the notion of the land's sabbaths, and Jeremiah furnished the temporal duration of the period.[2] A question that is not settled by the existing text of 2 Chronicles is whether every year of the seventy-year desolation was regarded as a sabbatical year; perhaps that is what it implies. If so, the period intended would be seven times as long as seventy years. Williamson adds that the seventy years in the context of sabbaths for the land may be meant to cover the entire period of the monarchy or 490 years: 'Thus the Chronicler seems to suggest that the whole legacy of neglect which the land had suffered has been fully "paid off" by the period of exile'.[3] Such thoughts are certainly suggestive for later readings of the biblical material.

---

[2] *I and II Chronicles: A Commentary* (OTL; Louisville: Westminster John Knox Press, 1993) 1075–76. See also H. G. M. Williamson, *1 and 2 Chronicles* (NCB; Grand Rapids: Eerdmans/London: Marshall, Morgan & Scott, 1982) 417; M. Fishbane, *Biblical Interpretation in Ancient Israel* (Oxford: Clarendon Press, 1985) 479–89.
[3] *1 and 2 Chronicles*, 418.

Daniel 9:24–27

The four verses that constitute part of the angelic reply to Daniel's prayer show further development of the earlier scriptural statements about sabbaths and exile. Daniel was, of course, studying Jeremiah's prophecy: 'I, Daniel, perceived in the books the number of years that, according to the word of the Lord to the prophet Jeremiah, must be fulfilled for the devastation of Jerusalem, namely, seventy years' (v. 2) Perhaps the reference to 'books' means that Daniel was looking not only at Jeremiah but other pertinent passages as well. Fishbane thinks that, in Daniel 9, Leviticus 26 is being used in connection with Jeremiah's prophecies: 'The compiler of Dan. 9 thus produced a skilful exegetical ensemble. He had Daniel turn the oracle of Jer. 25:9–12 into a confessional prayer – that is, into precisely that type of prayer required by Lev. 26:40 for the remission of sins and the termination of the sabbatical cycles of doom and desolation for the land'.[4]

Gabriel, after Daniel's prayer of confession and supplication, came to offer the explanation Daniel had not requested. The fundamental claim in it is the reinterpretation of Jeremiah's seventy years as seventy weeks of years.[5] These seventy weeks of years would also be, although the author does not specifically state the point, ten jubilees of years, if a jubilee is taken to be a period of forty-nine years. The angelic oracle does assert, however: 'from the time that the word went out to restore and rebuild Jerusalem until the time of an anointed priest, there shall be seven weeks' (v. 25), that is, a jubilee of years. Fishbane's interpretation of the entire passage is useful to cite:

This interpretation was presumably stimulated by 2 Chron. 36:21 which, owing to its reuse of Lev. 26:34–5, seems to have understood the seventy years of Jeremiah's oracle as ten sabbatical cycles. Another influence on Dan. 9:24–7 was undoubtedly the jubilee computation of Lev. 25:1–55 as a whole, wherein it is taught that a jubilee cycle of forty–nine years marked both the maximal period of indentured servitude and the maximal period wherein land may be alienated – due to economic distraints – from its ancestral heirs. It is quite striking that Dan. 9:25 apportions one entire jubilee cycle to the period from the assumed effective onset of the Jeremian oracle to the end of the exile and Cyrus' decree (the years 587–38). This period thus marks the first of ten jubilees, and so the first stage of release from foreign hegemony. In short, the initial period of Jerusalem's servitude was interpreted to be of forty-nine years' duration, so that its subsequent restoration to Israelite

[4]*Biblical Interpretation*, 489. As J. Collins remarks, Lev 26:18 may have played into the reinterpretation of seventy years as seventy weeks of years because it contains a threat that the people will be punished sevenfold for their sin (*Daniel* [Hermeneia; Minneapolis: Fortress Press, 1993] 352).

[5]See Collins, *Daniel*, 359, where he calls the passage a midrash on Jeremiah's prophecy of seventy years.

ownership would constitute a דרור, or the return of ancestral patrimony to its rightful heir (cf. Lev. 25:10). It is intriguing to suppose that the references in Isa. 61:1 to the post-exilic restoration as a release of prisoners may reflect an even earlier exegetical application of Lev. 25:1–55.[6]

The period of time covered by the prophecy has now been made to extend over the entire exilic and post-exilic period, a circumstance that will be repeated in some other reuses of Jeremiah's prophecy.

Pre-Qumran Sources

The next texts to be considered are approximately contemporaneous with Daniel 9 and show an ongoing interest in the sabbatical or jubilean periodization of Jewish history or parts of it.

The Apocalypse of Weeks (1 Enoch 93:1–10; 91:11–17)

This short apocalypse is perhaps the earliest Jewish work to employ weeks as a unit of time for ordering the course of biblical history. It appears to be a pre-Maccabean work[7] which divides all of history and the stages of the judgment into ten weeks that are to be followed by many weeks without number. The weeks are not called *weeks of years* but are simply segments of time that seem not to have a uniform length. In fact K. Koch has raised the issue whether it is appropriate to translate the Aramaic שבוע as 'week'; for him it means rather '*siebent*' or '*eine feste Zeitsiebent*'.[8] Enoch who was associated with the 364–day calendar in the earlier Astronomical Book of Enoch – a calendar that is based on sabbatical principles – was a natural candidate to receive revelations about such a chronological system. He learned of the system from visions, angels, and the heavenly tablets (93:2) and notes that he himself had been born the seventh in the first week – a reference to his being the seventh from Adam in the Genesis 5 genealogy.

Because the writer drops clues about the periods included in each of the first seven weeks, it is possible to see how he segments biblical history. The flood comes in the second unit of seven, Abraham in the

[6]*Biblical Interpretation*, 482–3. In a footnote he refers to 11QMelchizedek and its use of Isa 61:1 and Dan 9:24–25 (n. 63).

[7]For the date of the work, see VanderKam, 'Studies in the Apocalypse of Weeks', *CBQ* 46 (1984) 511–23.

[8]'Sabbatstruktur der Geschichte: Die sogenannte Zehn-Wochen-Apocalypse (1Hen 93,1–10; 91,11–17) und das Ringen um die alttestamentlichen Chronologien in späten Israelitentum' in his *Vor der Wende der Zeiten: Beiträge zur apokalyptischen Literatur Gesammelte Aufsätze 3*, ed. U. Glessmer and M. Krause (Neukirchen: Neukirchener Verlag, 1996) 48. The essay first appeared in *ZAW* 95 (1983) 403–30.

third, the law in the fourth, Temple and kingdom in the fifth, Elijah and
the destruction/exile in the sixth, and the author's own time in the
seventh. The description of the seventh 'week' reminds one – at its end
– of the first: 'And after this in the seventh week an apostate generation
will arise and many (will be) its deeds, but all its deeds (will be)
apostasy. And at its end the chosen righteous from the eternal plant of
righteousness will be chosen, to whom will be given sevenfold teaching
concerning his whole creation' (93:9–10).[9] The small Aramaic
fragments surviving from the Apocalypse of Weeks suggest that the text,
after mentioning the chosen righteous, also referred to 'witnesses of
the truth' (4QEn[g] 1 iv 12). The Aramaic (4QEn[g] 1 iv 13) preserves the
words די שבעה פועמין at the point where the Ethiopic text names the
'sevenfold teaching'.[10] The expression is interesting in that it reproduces
words from Lev 25:8 where instructions are given for counting the
jubilee unit (שבע שנים שבע פעמים). The description of the seventh week
seems to be continued in 91:11 where destruction of iniquity, sinners,
and blasphemers is the theme.

Koch has made the plausible suggestion that the purpose of the work
and its regular sequence of epochs is to allow the author and his readers
to find their own place in world history.[11] He has also argued at length,
although the numbers are problematic in places, that the units of seven
in the Apocalypse of Weeks encompass fixed periods of 490 years each.
This would entail that the seventh jubilee, dealing with the exilic and
post-exilic ages, would contain the same number of years that Daniel 9
anticipates.[12]

The significant point for the present purposes, and one made in the
Apocalypse itself, is that the time from creation to the judgment is seven
units of seven, or a jubilee – a point seemingly suggested by the wording
of the Aramaic fragment. History is apparently calculable, and the
faithful, the chosen ones from the righteous plant, are able to tell that
they are living near the time when evil will be destroyed permanently. A
predictable pattern of history, expressed in the language of sevens and
forty-nines, thus serves a consolatory, reassuring function.

In this brief text the new step is taken of extending the sabbatical
method of reckoning time over the full extent of history and also over
the stages of the final assize. Milik thinks that the most ancient text in
which history is divided into seventy ages is *1 Enoch* 10:11–12 which

[9]The translation is from M. Knibb, *The Ethiopic Book of Enoch* 2 vols (Oxford: Clarendon
Press, 1978) vol. 2.
[10]The readings come from J. T. Milik, *The Books of Enoch: Aramaic Fragments of Qumrân
Cave 4* (Oxford: Clarendon Press, 1976) 265.
[11]'Sabbatstruktur', 58.
[12]'Sabbatstruktur', 58–65.

he translates, on the basis of the surviving Aramaic material and the other versions, as:

[And the Lord said to Michael: 'Go then, Michael, and] make known to Šemiḥazâ and to all his companions who have joined with [women in order to defile themselves with them in their impurity, that when] their children have perished and (when they themselves) have seen the destruction [of their loved ones, they will be chained up for] seventy generations [in the vales] of the earth until the great day [of their judgement . . .].[13]

From this reference he moves through a rather speculative survey of other such texts, some of which will be treated below. In the case of *1 Enoch* 10:12, however, it should be said that the seventy generations extend, not over all of sacred history to the judgment, but only over the time from the first judgment of the angels to their definitive punishment. In that sense it is not a precise parallel to the Apocalypse of Weeks.

The Animal Apocalypse (1 Enoch 85–90)

The Animal Apocalypse, in distinction from the Apocalypse of Weeks, does not divide all of sacred history into sevens. This revelation which may have been written in the late 160s BCE – perhaps during or shortly after the Maccabean revolt[14] – traces biblical history and its sequel, but the author does not resort to sevens until he arrives at a time much later in the scriptural drama. At 89:59–60, in a context where he is describing how God had delivered his disobedient flock to the ravages of carnivorous animals, one reads: 'And he [= God] called seventy shepherds and cast off those sheep that they might pasture them; and he said to the shepherds and to their companions: "Each one of you from now on is to pasture the sheep, and do whatever I command you. And I will hand (them) over to you duly numbered and will tell you which of them are to be destroyed, and destroy them" '. Exactly what this point in history might have been is not said explicitly, but it occurs after the removal of Elijah (89:52) and before the destruction of Jerusalem and its Temple (89:66). The shepherds remain a crucial part of the revelation until 90:25 when they are judged for having exceeded the terms of their commission.

The section in the Animal Apocalypse dealing with the seventy shepherds indicates that their rule was divided into seventy parts. The seventy parts are distributed into four segments. The first twelve are

---

[13]*The Books of Enoch*, 248. His survey is on pp. 248–56.

[14]On the dating, see P. Tiller, *A Commentary on the Animal Apocalypse of* 1 Enoch (SBLEJL 4; Atlanta: Scholars Press, 1993) 61–79.

termed 'hours' (89:72: 'I saw how the shepherds pastured for twelve hours'), and the period ends with the return from exile and rebuilding of the Temple. The second unit should, judging from other numbers in the text, consist of twenty-three parts, but 90:1 implies twenty-five (the number 'thirty-seven' seems to include the first twelve units of 89:72). Here the author refers to thirty-seven shepherds, each pasturing in his own time. The third unit has twenty-three, and again this is the number of the shepherds, with each herding the sheep in his own time (90:5). The last number – twelve (90:17) – is also the number of shepherds. It has been suggested that the periods involved correspond generally with the times when the Babylonians, Persians, Ptolemies, and Seleucids controlled the Jewish people, but the text is at times too unclear to be sure. What is unmistakable is that the time of the seventy shepherds extends from before the Babylonian destruction to the end of history.

The meaning of the seventy shepherds has been discussed extensively among commentators, but there can be little doubt that Jeremianic language and imagery lie behind the use of them in the Animal Apocalypse. Jeremiah 25 in particular supplies much of the raw material for the visionary account. The seventy shepherds, since they are human beings, must be angels according to the standard equivalences in the Apocalypse; it seems reasonable to conclude that they are representatives of the seventy nations of the world. Jeremiah had predicted that the people would be exiled among the nations for seventy years; the image of the seventy shepherds expresses his thought in different terms.[15]

The four segments into which the author divided the era of the seventy shepherds do not correspond with meaningful groups of sevens such as weeks of years or jubilees of years. It is more likely that historical periods underlie the division. By using Jeremiah's prophecy of the seventy years in a new way, the writer of the Animal Apocalypse produces a work that resembles Daniel 9 in its reuse of the same prophetic number. The two do not use the same starting point but they do extend Jeremiah's seventy years over the entire last part of history.

Jubilees

As its name 'Jubilees' announces, the book is based upon a heptadic chronology that uses the clumsy categories of weeks of years and jubilees of years (that is, forty-nine year units) to date a large number of events in biblical history. The book may have been written a little after

---

[15]See VanderKam, *Enoch and the Growth of an Apocalyptic Tradition* (CBQMS 16; Washington, DC: CBA of America, 1984) 164–7.

the Animal Apocalypse, although a number of scholars would prefer to date it before the Enochic work.[16]

Jubilees uses weeks of years and jubilees of years as chronological units for the entire period covered by the narrative in the book, i. e. from creation to entry into the promised land (an event that, the author predicts, will occur forty years after the arrival at Sinai). There is no need to deal with the individual dates that the writer offers in such abundance. The crucial passage for our concerns comes near the end of the book. According to the last complete date before this key section (in 48:1) the year for the great events of the exodus is the fiftieth jubilee, the second week, the second year, that is, the year of the world 2410. Once Moses and the Israelites have reached Mt. Sinai in the same year, the narrating angel of the presence says to Moses:

On Mt. Sinai I told you about the sabbaths of the land and the years of jubilees in the sabbaths of the years, but its year we have not told you until the time when you enter the land which you will possess. The land will observe its sabbaths when they live on it, and they are to know the year of the jubilee. For this reason I have arranged for you the weeks of years and the jubilees – 49 jubilees from the time of Adam until today, and one week and two years. It is still 40 years off (for learning the Lord's commandments) until the time when he leads (them) across to the land of Canaan, after they have crossed the Jordan to the west of it. (50:2–4)[17]

If one adds the forty years mentioned in this section to 2410, the year of the revelation, the total is 2450 for entry into the land, that is, the end of fifty jubilee periods of forty-nine years each.

If one keeps in mind the significance of the fiftieth year in Leviticus 25 – the year that comes after the unit of seven times seven years – then the import of *Jubilees*' chronology becomes apparent. Leviticus 25 stipulates that in the fiftieth year alienated land is to be restored to its rightful owners and Hebrew slaves are to be given their liberty. The law has in mind the individual Israelite, but the writer of *Jubilees* takes this concept of the jubilee year, refers it to the fiftieth jubilee unit in his chronology, and applies the laws meant for individuals in Leviticus 25 to the entire nation of Israel. Thus in the fiftieth jubilee period the land that had been promised to the ancestors (the point is heavily emphasized already in the story of the division of the earth among Noah's sons [8:8 – 9:15; 10:27–34] and continued in the patriarchal stories) reverts to its rightful owners, the descendants of the ancestors. And in the

---

[16]For a brief survey of the issue, see VanderKam, *The Book of Jubilees* (2 vols.; CSCO 510–11, Scriptores Aethiopici 87–8; Louvain: Peeters, 1989) vol. 2 v–vi.

[17]The translation is taken from VanderKam, *The Book of Jubilees*, vol. 2.

fiftieth jubilee period the Israelite slaves in Egypt are given their freedom.[18]

The author therefore belongs in the same tradition as the other writers who made use of sabbatical and jubilee units, but with his own understanding of them he employed them to document a profound overall meaning for the early biblical history. The writer speaks only vaguely of what is to happen after the fiftieth jubilee period. He says that the 'jubilees will pass by until Israel is pure of every sexual evil, impurity, contamination, sin, and error. Then they will live confidently in the entire land. They will no longer have any satan or any evil person. The land will be pure from that time until eternity' (50:5). So there will continue to be jubilee periods, but the author does not arrange them or give any further details about them.

Qumran Sources

11QMelchizedek

Thirteen fragments that are remnants from what may have been three columns have survived from 11QMelchizedek. Neither the top nor bottom margin from any of these columns is preserved, and there are no complete lines. Consequently, much remains uncertain about the text and its author's intentions, but it has of course generated a large amount of attention since 1965 when A. S. van der Woude published it.[19] The purpose of this section will not be to interpret the entire work but only to attempt a clarification of the chronology that is mentioned several times in it and the ways in which Melchizedek may have become associated with it.

The surviving text, which van der Woude labelled a midrash,[20] may begin with a citation of Lev 25:12. The words and letters in question are the only remnants of a first column and are found mostly in a vertical note between columns. The mention of Moses and a few words read by the earliest editors seemed to recall Lev 25:12;[21] Puech, however, reads the line differently and without any specific links to Lev 25:12.[22] The

---

[18]For a detailed treatment of this theme, see VanderKam, 'Das chronologische Konzept des Jubiläenbuches', ZAW 107 (1995) 80–100.

[19]'Melchisedek als himmlische Erlösergestalt in den neugefundenen eschatologischen Midraschim aus Qumran Höhle XI', OTS 14 (1965) 354–73.

[20]'Melchisedek', 357.

[21]This is Milik's reading of the intercolumnar addition; see his 'Milkî-ṣedeq et Milkî-reša' dans les anciens écrits juifs et chrétiens', JJS 23 (1972) 95–144. Cf. van der Woude, 'Melchisedek', 356.

[22]E. Puech, La croyance des Esséniens en la vie future: Immortalité, résurrection, vie éternelle? (EBib 22; Paris: Gabalda, 1993) 522. He offers: ... hmwrh (?) hr'yšwn(?) ky'

first identifiable words of col. 2 certainly introduce and quote Leviticus 25 (v. 13). The same chapter reappears at 2:7 where Lev 25:9 is under consideration. It seems significant that the last surviving lines of col. 2 also cite from Leviticus 25 (v. 9), the chapter about sabbatical years and jubilees. This means that the surviving text contains at least three allusions to this chapter, thus establishing its significance for understanding what is being said in it. As Fitzmyer has written:

The thread which apparently runs through the whole text and ties together its various elements is Lv 25. Parts of three verses of that chapter are quoted.... The fragmentary text begins *in medias res* with a reference to a jubilee year; it is part of a quotation of Lv 25:13, the first part of the thread running through the text. Into this context of a jubilee year and the regulations prescribed for it in Lv 25 the figure of Melchizedek is introduced. He is apparently being given a special role in the execution of divine judgment which is related to a jubilee year.[23]

The citation from Lev 25:13 in 2:2 is followed immediately by one from Deut 15:2 which deals with the remission of debts every seventh year. Once he has adduced the passages from Leviticus 25 and Deuteronomy 15, the author turns to the interpretation of these verses through use of Isa 61:1. M. Miller has argued that the various scriptural citations in 11QMelch – citations that come from the Torah, prophets, and writings – are commented upon by means of Isa 61:1–2. 'Though it is never quoted at length, this latter passage stands behind our document and appears in the form of *Stichwörter* at crucial points'.[24] Isa 61:1 provides a new setting for clarifying the texts from the torah: '[The interpretation of it for the e]nd of days concerns *the captives* who' (2:4). The phrase 'e]nd of days' which is fully preserved except for the first letter establishes the context in which the material about sabbatical years/jubilees and remission of debts is to be read. These institutions have been transformed from recurring historical and sociological entities to eschatological realities. Although the context is badly broken here, it seems that the captives alluded to in Isa 61:1 are

d(?)[br, but he translates it as if he has read something quite different: ... *le prem]ier(?) [instructeur(?)] Moïse, parce qu'il a d[it* ... (524). His correct reading appears in his 'Notes sur le manuscrit de XIQMelkîsédeq', *RevQ* 12 (1987) 488. There he properly places *mwsh* before *ky'*.

[23]'Further Light on Melchizedek from Qumran Cave 11', *Essays on the Semitic Background of the New Testament* (London: Chapman, 1971; Missoula: Scholars Press, 1974) 251. The essay was originally published in *JBL* 86 (1967) 25–41; it has now again been reprinted in the combined volume of his essays *The Semitic Background of the New Testament* (The Biblical Resource Series; Grand Rapids: Eerdmans/Livonia, MI: Dove, 1997). On Leviticus 25 in the text, see also P. J. Kobelski, *Melchizedek and Melchireša'* (CBQMS 10; Washington DC: CBA of America, 1981) 3–4, 49–50. Translations of the text are from Kobelski's edition.

[24]'The Function of Isa 61 1–2 in 11Q Melchizedek', *JBL* 88 (1969) 467; see also 469.

the ones who will experience release in the last days.[25] It appears that
they are part of Melchizedek's lot and that they are the ones whom he
will restore (or will restore something to them). Use of the verb ישיבמה
at the beginning of line 6 is presumably a play on the word שבויים from
Isa 61:1. It is interesting that their debt from which they will be freed
is called '[the burden] of all their iniquities' (2:6)[26] – another reinterpretation of the biblical laws about what was to happen every seventh
year and a hint that the day of atonement is lurking in the author's
mind.

In this context one meets the first reference in the extant text to a
more specific unit of time. 'And [thus will] this event [happe]n in the
first week of the jubilee (that occurs) after [the n]ine jubilees. Now the
D[ay of Expia]tion i[s the en]d of the tenth [ju]bilee, when expiation
(will be made) for all the sons of [light[27] and] for the m[e]n of the lot of
Mel[chi]zedek' (2:6–8). The remainder of line 8 is highly uncertain, but
lines 9–10 read 'it is the time *for Melchiz[edek]'s year of favor*, [   ] in
his strength he will raise up the holy ones of El for deeds of judgment,
as it has been written concerning him in the songs of David, as it says:
"Elohim [st]ands in the assembly [of El,] in the midst of Elohim he
judges" '. The fact that the text describes the tenth jubilee as the one that
follows the nine jubilees presupposes that the preceding parts of the
work dealt with or assumed these other jubilees. In the passage just
quoted it seems that the tenth jubilee is still under consideration and
that it is being interpreted with reference to Isa 61:2 where the phrase
שנת רצון ליהוה occurs in the context of the captives/prisoners of v. 1 and
the day of divine vengeance in v. 2. The notion of judgment suggested
by Isa 61:2 in turn called forth Ps 82:1 in the author's mind. The result
is that the jubilee/sabbatical year release is tied in with the judgment in
the latter days, and Melchizedek is inserted into this highly charged
environment.

The remainder of 11QMelch deals with judgment for the evil and
salvation for those of Melchizedek's lot. There are only a few other
references to chronological units. 2:15 mentions the day, and the text is
probably to be filled out with 'of salvation' from Isa 49:8. 11QMelch
2:18 brings Daniel into the picture, and although the passage that the
writer intended is not preserved, it has been plausibly suggested that
Dan 9:25 with its mention of an anointed prince and seven weeks (of
years) is the verse that would have appeared here had the text

[25]Miller, 'The Function', 467–8.
[26]Kobelski, *Melchizedek*, 14.
[27]Puech (*La croyance*, 523) reads בני אל where Kobelski (*Melchizedek*, 5, following van der
Woude, 'Melchisedek', 358) has בני ואור.

survived.[28] 11QMelch 2:20 has an intriguing allusion to our subject: '*to comfo[rt the] m[ourners of Zion]* to [in]struct them in all the ages of the wo[rld]'. Isa 61:2–3 is the scriptural peg for the thought which highlights the fact that the text is concerned with understanding the epochs of world history. 11QMelch 2:25, the last preserved line of the column, ends with a quotation from Lev 25:9: 'And as for what he has said, 'You will blow the [signal-ho]rn in the [seventh] m[onth]'. The seventh month was the time when the jubilee year began; the shofar was blown on the day of atonement (7/10) to signal the inception of the special year. The remaining fragments of the manuscript contain a few words that suggest the text was concerned with chronology elsewhere as well: 3:16 two hundred[; 3:17 the week[; 5 4 y]ears; 11 4 at the appointed times of [; 11 7] the end of the j[ubilee.

An obvious question that arises is why Melchizedek is the one selected for the context and roles assigned to him in this text. The obvious places to begin looking are the two passages in the Hebrew Bible relating to him. The first is, of course, Genesis 14 where Abram meets Melchizedek as the patriarch is returning from defeating the kings. This chapter follows a passage in which the promise of the land is repeated to the patriarch (Gen 13:14–17). The four kings had taken the property of the kings of Sodom and Gomorrah and had also captured Lot and his possessions (Gen 14:11–12). Abram sprang into action when he learned that his nephew had been taken captive (נשבה; 14:14) and brought back (וישב; 14:16) all the property; he also brought back (השיב) Lot and his property, the women, and the people.

Abram's dealings with the king of Sodom surround his encounter with Melchizedek. That is, he meets the king of Sodom in Gen 14:17, the episode with Melchizedek occurs in 14:18–20, and the conversation with the king of Sodom is presented in 14:21–24. It appears from the biblical text, therefore, that we are to imagine these two encounters as part of the same scene, with all three characters present and Abram speaking first with Melchizedek and next with the monarch of Sodom. Or, in other words, the passages are to be read together, and the Melchizedek verses are not to be read in isolation from their immediate context.

Melchizedek is introduced as the king of Salem who brings out bread and wine for Abram; he is also called a priest of El Elyon. Melchizedek seems to be the one who blesses, and he blesses Abram in the name of El Elyon, maker or possessor of heaven and earth. He also blesses El Elyon who had delivered Abram's enemies into his hand. Someone, presumably Abram, gave the priest a tenth of all.

---

[28]So Fitzmyer, 'Further Light', 265–6; Milik, '*Milkî-ṣedeq*', 107; Kobelski, *Melchizedek*, 21.

There follows the dialogue with the king of Sodom. The conversation has to do with what Abram has captured from the four kings. The king of Sodom demands the people Abram had freed from their captors but offers the property to Abram. Abram swears by El Elyon, maker or possessor of heaven and earth, that he will take nothing belonging to the king of Sodom apart from what his men had eaten and what belonged to his three allies. Perhaps playing on the consonants of the word מעשר which he had given to Melchizedek, Abram tells the king that he does not want him to claim he has made Abram rich (העשרתי).

For the purpose of elucidating 11QMelch, it is interesting that the Melchizedek-king of Sodom pericope revolves about the subject of returning people and property to their proper owners. These are, of course, the heart of what the sabbatical and jubilee legislation is all about, and Melchizedek figures in the middle of this story. Also, some terms and ideas that play a role in the cave 11 text come from Genesis 14, e. g., the word captive and the notion of returning or restoring.

It may be that such associations played in the mind of the author of 11QMelch as he brought the ancient priest-king into connection with sabbatical year and jubilee legislation. The special role of Melchizedek in the final judgment and application of a term such as אלוהים to him are more directly related to the way in which the writer read Psalm 110 and associated it and Melchizedek with judgment. It should be recalled that Genesis calls him a priest of אל עליון who is קנה שמים וארץ. Moreover, his name is highly suggestive, meaning 'king of justice' or 'my king is justice'. His city of Salem was generally interpreted to be Jerusalem, in line with the parallelism of Ps 76:3.

Psalm 110 contains one clear reference to Melchizedek in v. 4. But the psalm was capable of being understood in different ways. One approach is familiar from the Epistle to the Hebrews where the argument builds on the interpretation that Melchizedek was the founder of a non-levitical priestly order. Another, however, is to take the entire psalm as referring to him in the second person. D. Flusser seems to have been the first to apply this point to 11QMelch.[29] J. Kugel, in his recent book *The Bible as It Was*, sets out the argument in this way. The consonants of the Hebrew text in Ps 110:4 could be read as saying 'you are a priest forever by my order [or "on my account"], O Melchizedek'. 'If this is the right translation, then it is Melchizedek who is being addressed

---

[29]'Melchizedek and the Son of Man' in *Judaism and the Origins of Christianity* (Jerusalem: Magnes, 1988) 189 (the article was originally published in *Christian News from Israel* [April 1966] 23–9). He finds the same conception behind Heb 7:3 in which Melchizedek is a priest forever.

throughout the psalm, and everything else in the psalm that refers to "you" must therefore be talking about Melchizedek'.[30] One such place is the first verse where the term אדני is addressed to him. Hence he sits at God's right hand and God has given him his kingly scepter. In addition, God promises to make his enemies his footstool (v. 1), he will rule among them (v. 2) and lead his forces. 'The Lord is at your right hand; he will shatter kings on the day of his wrath. He will execute judgment among the nations, filling them with corpses; he will shatter heads over the wide earth' (vv. 5–6).

Flusser[31] (and Kugel) also points to an ambiguity in Ps 110:3 that may have been exploited by the author of 11QMelch. The MT reads: מרחם משחר לך טל ילדֻתיך. The final word was understood by the septuagintal translators as a verb and rendered ἐξεγέννησά σε (I have begotten you).[32] 'If so, then this "son of God" who sits at God's right hand, must have been an angel charged with executing divine justice on earth, the angelic king of justice'.[33] The eternity of Melchizedek's priesthood perhaps also contributed to the general picture of him as eschatological judge.

As Flusser wrote, 'If the Sectarians understood that Psalm 110 was speaking about Melchizedek, they could also relate Psalm 82 to him, as they did in the present new text, which speaks of God's judgment'.[34] Psalm 82, which focuses on the judgment, did indeed make its contributions to the growing portfolio of Melchizedek. Gen 14:18 called him a priest of אל, and this is the term for God in Psalm 82. The interesting point is that אל seems to be differentiated from אלהים in the first verse of the poem in which אלהים takes his stand in the council of אל.[35] One wonders whether the next clause could have been read as saying 'in the midst אלהים judges'. In v. 6 someone says to a group 'I say, "you are gods"'; however, these children of the Most High (עליון) as they are called in the next line are to die, but in v. 8 אלהים is summoned to rise and judge the earth because the nations belong (תנחל) to him.

It is clear from 11QMelch 2:9–10 that the writer understood the word אלהים in Psalm 82 as a reference to Melchizedek. We should attempt to follow his thought process as he works through the different passages that form the basis of his exposition. This may have been

---

[30]Kugel, *The Bible as It Was* (Cambridge/Harvard: Belknap, 1997) 154.

[31]'Melchizedek and the Son of Man', 190

[32]It should be pointed out that the LXX, while it does have ἐξεγέννησά σε, does not take v. 4 as addressed to Melchizedek in the second person. Rather it renders על דברתי מלכיצדק as κατὰ τὴν τάξιν Μελχισεδέκ.

[33]Kugel, *The Bible as It Was*, 156.

[34]'Melchizedek and the Son of Man', 190.

[35]The LXX switches the terms around: ὁ θεὸς ἔστη ἐν συναγωγῇ θεῶν.

adumbrated already in line 6 where he writes that the remission that would occur in the last jubilee would be a remission of sins (עוונותיהמה), not of monetary debts. He speaks of the day of atonement as 'the en]d of the tenth [ju]bilee when expiation (will be made) for all the sons of [light and] for the m[e]n of the lot of Mel[chi]zedek'. While the reading is not certain in all places, it is secure for the action of atonement.

It is understandable that the day of atonement would come under consideration in a context that speaks about jubilee units because of Lev 25:8–10:

You shall count off seven weeks of years, seven times seven years, so that the period of seven weeks of years gives forty-nine years. Then you shall have the trumpet sounded loud; on the tenth day of the seventh month – on the day of atonement – you shall have the trumpet sounded throughout all your land. And you shall hallow the fiftieth year and you shall proclaim liberty [דרור] throughout the land to all its inhabitants. It shall be a jubilee for you: you shall return, every one of you, to your property and every one of you to your family.

The day of atonement was thus the starting point for the events of the jubilee, that is, for the return of property and people to their rightful status.

The associations of the day of atonement are also worth exploring in more detail. In 11QMelch a central topic is the judgment in which Melchizedek plays a central role. Those who belong to his lot (his גורל – a term familiar from Lev 16:8–10 where it is used in connection with the two goats, and where one lot is for the Lord, the other for Azazel) receive atonement for their iniquities and the others – those of Belial's lot – are condemned. The connection of the day of atonement with the forgiveness of transgressions also associates it with the notion of remission in the sabbatical legislation. As we have seen above, the context of the Melchizedek pericope in Genesis includes the idea of returning people and property to their rightful owners.

What was supposed to happen on the day of atonement, and what role might Melchizedek have in such a ceremony? It should be recalled that in some traditions Melchizedek was a high priest,[36] and it was, of course, the high priest who officiated during the ceremonies on the day of atonement. It seems that at some point the day took on themes having to do with judgment. This is only natural because Leviticus 16 speaks frequently of atoning for the sins of the priests and people. It is interesting that the Mishnah, in its familiar list of four new years, says

[36]See Kugel, The Bible as It Was, 154–5.

that the first of Tishri (7/1) is the new year for reckoning the regnal years of foreign rulers, years of release (i.e., sabbatical years), jubilees, and for planting trees and vegetables (*m. Roš. Haš.* 1:1). The next mishnah says that the world is judged four times in the year. For New Year's day (7/1) it relates: 'all that come into the world pass before him like legions of soldiers, for it is written, *He that fashioneth the hearts of them all, that considereth all their works* [= Ps 33:15]'.[37] This seems peculiar when we consider that the day of atonement, which does not figure in the mishnaic list but is the obvious time for removal of sins, is just ten days after the new year. E. Urbach comments on the problem:

But it is surely not possible that a man's sentence should be passed before his sins are forgiven! The solution of these difficulties already forms a subject of dispute among the Tannaim: 'Everything is judged on the New Year, and their sentence is sealed on the Day of Atonement – this is the view of R. Me'ir. R. Judah says: Everything is judged on the New Year, but the sentence of each is sealed in its due season: at Passover (sentence is passed) on the produce, at Pentecost on the fruit of trees, at the Festival (of Tabernacles) on water, while man's sentence is sealed on the Day of Atonement'.[38]

So it seems that the writer of 11QMelch used a series of biblical passages and themes that allowed him to connect Melchizedek, the day of atonement, and sabbatical and jubilee periods. The last jubilee, when the judgment takes place, is the tenth one. It may be that the author divided all history into these ten periods, but that is never said, although 11QMelch 2:20 which refers to instructing people in all the times (קצי) of eternity or the world would favor this inference. We hear explicitly only of the first nine jubilees and a tenth which is the last when judgment takes place. Milik did notice that frg. 11 mentions the wall of Jerusalem, the end of a jubilee, and a time of peace (?), but the text does not preserve an indication of which jubilee is meant.[39] However, it is not clear from the fragment how these entities are related.

4Q180–81

Milik suggested that 11QMelchizedek and 4Q180–81 are copies of a work that was entitled Pesher on the Periods.[40] It seems that we are hardly in a position to decide whether there was such a work and whether these three manuscripts are copies of it, but it is worth noting

---

[37]The translation is from H. Danby, *The Mishnah* (Oxford: Oxford University Press, 1933).
[38]E. E. Urbach, *The Sages: Their Concepts and Beliefs* (Cambridge/London: Harvard University Press, 1987) 470. The words that he cites are from *t. Roš. Haš.* 1:13.
[39]'*Milkî-ṣedeq*', 100–101.
[40]'*Milkî-ṣedeq*', 95–126.

that 4Q180 (The Ages of Creation) says that it is a work regarding 'the ages [or: times] which God has made' and that before 'creating them he determined their operations [according to the precise sequence of the ages,] one age after another. And this is engraved on the [heavenly] tablets [for the sons of men,] [for] /all/ the ages of their dominion' (frg. 1:1–4). The fragmentary text apparently surveys biblical history in the rest of this piece and in frgs. 2–6. 4Q181 2:3 refers to 'Israel in the seventieth week' if that is what the phrase means. The suggestive remains of these two works are insufficient to allow any significant conclusions about their chronologies.

4Q384–90

Whether all of these 4Q numbers are part of a single text or constitute several texts is a matter under discussion.[41] A few of them do contain chronological notices but the system that underlies them is not clear enough to interpret. Apart from a few scattered references (seventy is mentioned several times), the more important notices are a reference to rebellion and the ten jubilees in which God will abandon his people (4Q387 3 ii 3–4) and the seventh jubilee of the devastation of the land (4Q390 7–8). The context suggests that the seven jubilee periods begin with the exile. How these two numbers fit together is not said, but it may be that the seven are a part of the ten so that the ten-jubilee span would also have begun with the exile.

Some Conclusions and Observations

The survey suggests some conclusions about the chronological system involved.

1. The biblical laws about sabbatical and jubilee years and the periods they define, combined with Jeremiah's prophecies (the two entities were associated already in the biblical period as 2 Chr 36:21 and Daniel 9 show) stand at the beginning of the tendency to use these units to measure and divide longer chronological periods of history.
2. The time spans measured or encompassed by the sabbatical and jubilee schemes differ considerably within the literature. The following options are attested:

[41]For one approach, see D. Dimant, 'New Light from Qumran on the Jewish Pseudepigrapha – 4Q390", in J. Trebolle-Barrera and L. Vegas Montaner, eds., *The Madrid Qumran Congress: Proceedings of the International Congress on the Dead Sea Scrolls, Madrid 18–21 March 1991* (STDJ 11; Leiden: Brill/Madrid: Editorial complutense, 1992) 405–48.

a. All of history and the phases of the judgment (Apocalypse of Weeks and possibly 11QMelch).[42]
b. Very long stretches of biblical and post-biblical history *(1 Enoch* 10:12; cf. *T. Levi* 16–17)
c. Only the earlier parts of sacred history (*Jubilees*)
d. The last part of history, especially the exilic and post-exilic periods (Daniel 9; the Animal Apocalypse, 4Q384–90?).

3. The writers of the texts do not dwell on the purposes they had in resorting to sabbatical and jubilee language for their chronologies, but some goals can be inferred.

a. As the past is orderly and calculable because it has been arranged by God, the future too can be discerned and one can see one's own place in the divine plan of history.

b. The particular language of sabbaths/weeks and jubilees had the advantages not only of being familiar markers of longer units of time but also came with richly suggestive associations such as the themes of redemption, freedom, release, restoration, judgment, and pardon. These could certainly be put to good use both for historical analysis (*Jubilees*) and for eschatological predictions.

4. The use of such chronological language seems largely confined to the tradition that produced and was continued by the writers at Qumran.

---

[42]Although they have not been treated here, some of the mishmarot texts from Qumran cave 4 suggest that the group had worked out a jubilee chronology beginning with creation. See, for example, 4Q320 (Mishmarot A) 2 i 5–6; 4 ii 12–13.

10

QUMRAN CALENDARS: THEORY AND PRACTICE
Sacha Stern

In his preface to *The Calendars of Ancient Egypt*, Richard Parker wrote: 'Calendars and chronology are not in themselves difficult subjects, but they are frequently made so by the assumption of their devotees that everyone understands always what they are talking about'.[1] Studies on Qumran calendars are no exception to this – sometimes they frighten off even calendar devotees like myself. In this paper, I shall avoid technical detail and focus instead on the broader historical context of the calendar texts which form a considerable proportion of Qumran literature.

A number of different calendars are represented in various Qumran sources, and often in painstaking detail. They can be grouped, however, into two main categories: the 364-day calendar of *Jubilees*, and the three-year (or six-year) lunisolar cycle. The question I would like to address in this paper, which is neither original nor new, is whether any of these calendars were reckoned and followed in practice by the Qumran community.

Let us begin with the calendar of *Jubilees*. This calendar is described in detail in 4Q320–1 and 4Q325. It consists of a year of 364 days, which is exactly fifty-two weeks; this year is divided into four seasons of thirteen weeks each. Every year, every season and every festival begins, therefore, on the exactly same day of the week.[2] The appeal of this calendar is its mathematical simplicity.

Because this calendar is prescribed as normative in the *Damascus Rule* (CD 16:2–4), and also perhaps, by allusion, in the *Community Rule* (1QS 10:5), it was originally assumed that this was the calendar observed at Qumran in practice.[3] This would have explained why the calendar of *Jubilees* was assumed in the Temple Scroll (4Q325), the Flood story (4Q252), and perhaps also the Psalm Scroll (11QPsᵃDavComp).[4]

---

[1] R. A. Parker, *Calendars of Ancient Egypt* (Univ. of Chicago Press, 1950) v.

[2] See *Jub.* 6:23–32.

[3] G. Vermes in E. Schürer, *The History of the Jewish People in the Age of Jesus Christ (175 BC – AD 135)* (revised and edited by M. Black, G. Vermes and F. Millar; Edinburgh: T&T Clark, vol. I, 1973) 599–601; *idem*, *The Dead Sea Scrolls in English* (3rd ed.; London: Penguin, 1987) 46–8.

[4] Y. Yadin, *The Temple Scroll*, vol. 1 (1983) 116–19; T. Lim, 'The Chronology of the Flood Story in a Qumran Text (4Q252)', *JJS* 43 (1992) 288–98; *idem*, 'Notes on 4Q252 fr.1, cols.i–ii', *JJS* 44 (1993) 121–6; J. A. Sanders (ed.), *The Psalm Scroll of Qumran Cave 11, DJD* vol. 4 (1965) 91–3.

In the last fifteen years, however, this assumption has been questioned on the grounds that in spite of its simplicity, the calendar of *Jubilees* would have been completely impractical. This calendar, indeed, is almost but not quite a solar calendar, because the solar year – as we know from our own, Gregorian calendar – is actually almost $365\frac{1}{4}$ days long. Because of this discrepancy of $1\frac{1}{4}$ days, the calendar of *Jubilees* gradually falls behind the solar year and the annual cycle of seasons. There is no provision, in this calendar, for occasional adjustments or intercalations – in spite of various attempts, by modern scholars, to conjecture that there must have been.[5] Consequently, observance of this calendar over a period of years would have caused the annual, biblical festivals to occur in the wrong agricultural seasons, in clear violation of Mosaic law. This is unlikely to have been tolerated either by the Qumran or any other Jewish community.

As a result, Schiffman has expressed the view that 'this calendar was never really put to the test except perhaps for a short period'.[6] Beckwith, however, has argued that this calendar may still have been used at Qumran, because discrepancies with agricultural seasons, while not going unnoticed, would not have troubled excessively the Qumran community. Such discrepancies could have been justified on the basis of a passage in *Enoch* 80:2–8 according to which God would punish mankind by disrupting the seasons and causing vegetation and rain to occur at the wrong times. The Qumran community could thus have justified the observance of Passover in the winter, by invoking this *Enoch* passage and claiming that this situation was not due to inaccurate calendar reckoning, but rather to God's disruption of the seasons.[7]

The lunar, three-year cycle calendar is represented in a number of calendar texts from Cave 4,[8] including the Aramaic *Enoch* fragments published by Milik[9] – all of which appear to refer to various aspects of the same calendar. Just like the calendar of *Jubilees*, with which this

---

[5]For a general survey, see R. Beckwith, 'The Modern Attempt to Reconcile the Qumran Calendar with the True Solar Year', *RevQ* 7 (1970) 379–96. For a more recent attempt, see U. Glessmer, 'The Otot-Texts (4Q319) and the Problem of Intercalations in the Context of the 364–Day Calendar', *Qumranstudien: Vortrage und Beitrage der Teilnehmer des Qumranseminars auf dem internationalen Treffen der Society of Biblical Literature, Muenster, 25–26. Juli 1993* ed. H. J. Fabry, A. Lange, & H. Lichtenberger (Schriften des Institutum Judaicum Delitzschianum, Bd. 4, Göttingen, 1996) 125–64. Glessmer emphasizes that this attempt is only hypothetical, as it is not supported by any explicit statement in the text (*ibid.* 156–7).

[6]L.Schiffman, *Reclaiming the Dead Sea Scrolls* (Philadelphia: Jewish Publication Society, 1994) 304.

[7]Beckwith, 'Modern Attempt' 392–5.

[8]4Q259 (= 4QSᵉ), 4Q293, 4Q317–37.

[9]Especially 4QEnastrᵃ⁻ᶜ = 4Q208–11: J. T. Milik, *The Books of Enoch – Aramaic Fragments of Qumran Cave 4* (Oxford: Oxford University Press, 1976).

cycle is often synchronised, the three-year cycle calendar is characterized by its mathematical simplicity. It consists of an alternation of
twenty-nine day and thirty-day lunar months; there are twelve lunar
months in the year, but every three years an additional thirty-day month
is added so as to keep up with agricultural seasons and the solar year.
At the end of each cycle, the New Year recommences on the same day
of the week.[10]

This lunar (or lunisolar) calendar is, in a sense, even more impractical
than the calendar of *Jubilees*. In common with the latter, the three-year
cycle assumes an average year length of 364 days; which as we have seen,
is discrepant from the solar year and would cause biblical festivals to occur
in the wrong agricultural seasons. In addition, however, this calendar
assumes an average lunar month of twenty-nine and a half days, which is
significantly too short. Every three years, this cycle would fall behind the
actual lunar cycle by approximately half a day; so that after only a few
decades the calendar month would begin a number of days before the
actual new moon – a discrepancy too obvious to be ignored.[11] Again, there
is no provision in this calendar for adjustments or intercalations.

Because both types of calendar (*Jubilees* and the three-year lunar cycle)
share in common considerable discrepancies from astronomical reality,
and hence are equally impractical, I would favour the view that both were
intended in Qumran sources as purely theoretical models. Calendar
sources from Qumran may be regarded as perpetuating a literary tradition
going back to the book of *Enoch*, in particular to the section sometimes
called the *Astronomical Book* (chaps. 72–82 of Ethiopic *Enoch*), which
according to Milik dates from the third century BCE, and in which the
cycles of the sun and the moon are reduced to simple mathematical models
that are not readily applicable to actual reality. Neugebauer regarded this
text as reflecting an 'extremely primitive' concept of astronomy;[12] but his
view has recently been challenged by Albani and Glessmer on the basis of
contemporary Babylonian astronomical compendia where similar,
simplified astronomical models were assumed.[13] Even so, the purpose of

---

[10]For a full tabulation, see for instance B. and S. Wacholder, 'Patterns of Biblical Dates and
Qumran's Calendar: the Fallacy of Jaubert's Hypothesis', *HUCA* 66 (1995) 1–40, esp. 32–5.

[11]See R. Beckwith, 'The Essene Calendar and the Moon: a Reconsideration', *RevQ* 15
(1992) 457–66, esp. 459–61; and with more accurate figures in *idem*, *Calendar and
Chronology, Jewish and Christian* (Leiden: Brill, 1996) 119.

[12]O. Neugebauer, appendix A to M. Black, *The Book of Enoch or I Enoch* (Leiden: Brill,
1985) 386–419, esp. 387–9. A similar interpretation is implicit in M. Stone, 'Enoch, Aramaic
Levi and Sectarian Origins', *JSJ* 19 (1988) 159–70, esp. 161 and 164.

[13]M. Albani, *Astronomie und Schöpfungsglaube: Untersuchungen zum astronomischen
Henochbuch* (WMANT 68; Neukirchen-Vluyn, 1994) 155–272 (*n.v.*); U. Glessmer,
'Horizontal Measuring in the Babylonian Astronomical Compendium MUL.APIN and in the
Astronomical Book of 1En', *Henoch* 18 (1996) 259–82.

the *Astronomical Book* would not have been more than theoretical or didactic.[14]

The relationship between Qumran calendars and the books of *Enoch* has long been noted: Milik went as far, indeed, as identifying some of the Qumran calendar fragments with an original, Aramaic version of *Enoch*.[15] Whether this identification is correct remains debatable: as pointed out by Knibb, Milik's *Enoch* calendar fragments are so different from the Ethiopic text that it is almost impossible to bring them into direct relationship with it.[16] But even if 4QEnastr texts do not belong to an original Aramaic *Enoch*, they certainly belong to the same literary genre as *Enoch*'s *Astronomical Book*. In this respect, Qumran calendar texts are more plausibly interpreted as theoretical models, similarly to the astronomical models of *Enoch*, than as calendars that would have been observed at Qumran in practice.[17]

The theoretical nature of Qumran calendars is also evident if we consider their synchronisation with priestly courses in 4Q320–1. Priestly courses were probably of little practical relevance to the Qumran community, because of their intrinsic association with the Jerusalem Temple cult. The synchronisation of the three-year cycle calendar with priestly courses suggests perhaps that this calendar was viewed as a theoretical blueprint for an ideal world order.

If, as I am suggesting, none of the calendars represented in Qumran sources as actually used in practice, what calendar did the Qumran community observe? Baumgarten has argued that it is likely to have been lunar, because the liturgy of the *Daily Prayers* text (4Q503) appears to be structured according to a lunar month.[18] These prayers are unlikely to have been 'only theoretical': if they were recited at Qumran in practice, a lunar month must also have been reckoned.

The question is, however, which lunar calendar did they use? We know from a number of sources (especially Philo and the Mishna) that the Jewish calendar in this period was normally based on the empirical observation of the new moon. At Qumran, however, things may have been different. The obvious interest of the Qumran community in

---

[14]See Milik's pertinent comments (*Enoch*, pp. 14 and 277).

[15]Milik, *Enoch*.

[16]Milik does not clarify the criteria he must have employed to distinguish between Qumran calendar fragments which he identified with 'Aramaic *Enoch*' and those which he did not. But his identification of other fragments with other sections of the book of *Enoch* is far more plausible. See M. Knibb, *The Ethiopic Book of Enoch* (Oxford: Clarendon Press, 1978) vol. 2, 11–13.

[17]Models of this kind might have been used as the theoretical basis for the design and construction of more practical calendars; on this, see further below.

[18]J. M. Baumgarten, '4Q503 (Daily Prayers) and the Lunar Calendar', *RevQ* 12 (1986) 399–407; *idem*, 'The Calendar of the Book of Jubilees and the Temple Scroll', *VT* 37 (1987) 71–8. See also Beckwith, 'The Essene Calendar' 457–66; Schiffman, *Reclaiming* 304–5.

theoretical mathematical calendars suggests perhaps that in their practical life they also based their calendar on a mathematical calculation, rather than on the empirical observation of the moon and of the seasonal cycle. It is quite possible, therefore, that the Qumran community reckoned a calculated calendar that was derived from the theoretical three-year lunar cycle, but with adjustments or intercalations to make up for its considerable discrepancies.[19] Adjustments of this kind are not accounted for in Qumran sources, but this does not mean that they did not exist in practice.

A calculated calendar may also have been preferred at Qumran for purely practical reasons. Observation and sighting of new moons, which formed the basis of other Jewish calendars in this period, would have been particularly arduous at Qumran. This is because the new moon is only visible along the Western horizon, shortly after sunset and just before the moon, soon after, sets. Now the site of Qumran is located in the Dead Sea depression, some 300 metres below sea level, and is flanked along the West by the Judean hills that rise to hights of at least 600 metres above sea level.[20] This exceptional elevation (almost 1000 metres over a relatively short distance) cuts off the view, at Qumran, of the Western horizon, and this renders observation of the new moon virtually impossible. In order to obtain a clear horizon and hence a reasonable view of the new moon, the inhabitants of Qumran would have needed to travel some distance to the West up mountainous paths, waited for sunset, and then – having sighted the new moon after sunset – found themselves stranded and unable to return till the next morning.[21] This may explain why at Qumran calculated calendars such as the three-year cycle might in practice have been preferred.

This is not to say, however, that the Qumran community could not have based their calendar on the empirical sighting of the new moon. This may have meant relying on other people's observations of the new moon and on their decisions as to when the month should begin. Alternatively, members of the Qumran community could have made the effort of climbing the mountains and sighting the new moon on their

[19]As many have suggested; see above note 5.

[20]The altitude of Qumran is given as 1000 feet (over 300 metres) below sea level in G. A. Smith and J. G. Bartholomew, *Atlas of the Historical Geography of the Holy Land* (London, 1915) 29. Towards the East, Qumran faces the Northern Moab mountain range which rises to over 500 metres above sea level (with Mount Nebo above 800 metres); for the same reasons, this would cut off visibility of the old moon.

[21]Solar observations, on the other hand, would not have been hindered in this respect. See M. Albani and U. Glessmer, 'Un Instrument de Mesures Astronomiques à Qumran', *RB* 104 (1997) 88–115.

own. In either case, however, their calendar would have been essentially the same as that of all other Jews in the Hasmonean period and beyond.

This suggestion would contradict the widespread opinion that the calendar was one of the main features of Qumran sectarianism (a view developed in particular by Talmon).[22] But evidence of calendar sectarianism at Qumran is actually rather slim. There is a condemnation in the Hosea *pesher*, 4Q166, of those that follow the festivals of the nations, and there are references in the *Damascus Rule* to the notion that those outside the remnant of the faithful have gone astray in the observance of Sabbaths and festivals (CD 3:13–15), and that members of the Covenant should observe the Sabbath, festivals and the day of fast as according to the findings of the New Covenant (CD 6:18–19). However, these passages do not necessarily refer to the *dates* of the festivals: they may refer instead to their rituals and specific acts of worship.

In the *Community Rule* we do find an explicit prohibition to bring forward or postpone any of the festivals (1QS 1:13–15, and cf 3:9–10), but this may simply mean that the calendar must be reckoned correctly – a statement which any Jew could have made in this period, without necessarily implying sectarian diversity.

The juxtaposition of the 364-day calendar of *Jubilees* with one version of the polemical text 4QMMT (4Q394) may be interpreted as an indication that the calendar was a sectarian issue; but Schiffman has argued on the contrary that the absence of reference to the calendar in the main text of 4QMMT indicates that it was not central to Qumran sectarianism.[23] Moreover, the occurrence of 4QMMT and the calendar of *Jubilees* in the same manuscript (4Q394) does not necessarily mean that they constituted a single literary composition.

Finally, the Habakuk *pesher* (11:2–8) speaks of the Wicked Priest's visit to the Teacher of Righteousness and to his followers on their Day of Atonement, in an attempt to disrupt their fast and day of rest. This story implies that they observed the Day of Atonement on different dates – a discrepancy which the Wicked Priest exploited to his own advantage. This is probably the closest we can get to evidence of calendar sectarianism;[24] but even here, there are alternative interpretations. The Teacher of Righteousness and the Wicked Priest could have reckoned the same lunar calendar, based on sightings of the new moon, except that on this occasion they happened to have sighted the new

---

[22]'The Calendar of the Covenanters of the Judean Desert', *Aspects of the Dead Sea Scrolls, Scripta Hierosolymitana* eds. C. Rabin and Y. Yadin, 4 (Jerusalem: Magnes Press, 1958) 162–99; reprinted in S. Talmon, *The World of Qumran from Within* (1989) 147–85.

[23]Schiffman, *Reclaiming*, 305.

[24]As assumed by S. Talmon, 'Yom Hakippurim in the Habakkuk Scroll', *Bib* 32 (1951) 549–63, reprinted in Talmon (1989) 186–99.

moon on different days; or alternatively, they may have differed on the question of whether to intercalate that year (with the addition of a thirteenth month), so that they would have observed the Day of Atonement, on that occasion, one month apart. Arguments such as these would not have meant that fundamentally different calendars were observed.[25] Thus although there is plenty of interest, in Qumran sources, in alternative calendars such as that of *Jubilees*, there is little evidence, if any at all, that calendar reckoning was a centrepiece of Qumran sectarianism.

External evidence of calendrical sectarianism among the Jews of this period is also remarkably slim. There are passages in the Mishna regarding the Boethusians of the Second Temple period, but the argument is confined to the date of the Omer and of Shavuot (Pentecost), and does not appear to concern the rest of the calendar.[26] There is also the book of *Jubilees* itself, where calendar reckoning is an explicitly sectarian issue.[27] This is important, because if the book of *Jubilees* originated from the early Qumran community or some related group, as some scholars have suggested,[28] this book could be regarded as evidence of calendar sectarianism at Qumran, at least in some early stage of the community's history.

But besides the Boethusians of the Mishna and the book of *Jubilees*, there is nothing to suggest calendar sectarianism among the Jews of the Hasmonean or of the early Roman periods. Most significant is Josephus, who is generally interested in sectarian diversity (and has much to say, in particular, about the Essenes), but does not refer in any of his works to any disagreement about calendar reckoning. I would take his silence as indicative that by his period, at least, calendar sectarianism had ceased.

In this light, it is quite possible that the calendar that was reckoned in practice at Qumran was lunar, based on sightings of the new moon, and thus essentially the same as that of all other Jews in Judaea. The reason why this calendar would not have been mentioned or described in Qumran sources is perhaps that the latter tended to be more concerned with theory than with actual practice. It must also be noted that the

---

[25]A similar argument is recorded between two rabbis in the Mishna (*m. Roš Haš* 2:9): they disagreed as to whether the new moon had been seen, and consequently as to when the Day of Atonement should be observed. It should also be noted that the stress in the Habakkuk *pesher* is not on the Wicked Priest's calendrical error, but rather on his violent treatment of the Teacher of Righteousness and his followers, and his deliberate disruption of their observances. The calendar is not, in this passage, the central polemical issue.

[26]M. *Menaḥ* 10:3, cf *m. Ḥag* 2:4.

[27]See 6:31–8, 49:7–8, 49:14.

[28]Indeed, numerous fragments of *Jubilees* have been discovered in the caves of Qumran: see the following paper by Charlotte Hempel in this volume.

lunar calendar based on sightings of the new moon was not exclusive to the Jews of this period. It was modelled on the Babylonian lunar calendar, which until the arrival of the Romans had been shared by all the peoples in the Near East, initially in the Seleucid empire, and then in its successor kingdoms[29] – for instance, the Nabataean kingdom on the other side of the Dead Sea. This calendar was so well established throughout the Near East that its observance at Qumran could easily have been taken for granted and considered not worthy of any special mention.

The purpose of this paper has not been to draw any definitive conclusion. The suggestion of Beckwith that the calendar of *Jubilees* could still have been used in spite of its inaccuracies remains a possibility, even if I would lean in favour of Baumgarten's argument that the calendar observed in practice at Qumran must have been lunar. This lunar calendar, as we have seen, could have been a modified version of the three-year lunar cycle; but alternatively, it could have been the same empirical calendar as observed everywhere else in the Near East. It is not impossible, finally, that different calendars were simultaneously reckoned, as is perhaps suggested by the synchronisation of different calendars in a number of our sources.

Our difficulty in establishing actual practice at Qumran is not confined, however, to calendar reckoning, but extends to all areas of life in the Qumran community. Paradoxically, the abundance of written material from the site of Qumran, including detailed descriptions of a range of calendars, has obfuscated these questions rather than resolved them.[30]

---

[29]See A. E. Samuel, *Greek and Roman Chronology. Calendars and Years in Classical Antiquity* (Munich: Beck, 1972) chap. 6 and esp. p.182 n.1.

[30]I am particularly grateful to Uwe Glessmer, Charlotte Hempel, and James VanderKam, for their kind assistance.

11

THE PLACE OF THE *BOOK OF JUBILEES* AT QUMRAN AND BEYOND

Charlotte Hempel

In this paper I should like to offer a number of reflections on the significance of the *Book of Jubilees* at Qumran and beyond in the light of the recently published material.[1]

The Ancient Manuscripts

Fragments of fifteen copies of the *Book of Jubilees* have been discovered in five Qumran caves.[2] Milik and VanderKam disagree on the identification of one of these, 4Q217 (Jub[b]), and in the DJD edition its identification as a copy of *Jubilees* is accompanied by a question mark.

---

[1]For earlier treatments of the relationship between *Jubilees* and Qumran see P. R. Davies, *Behind the Essenes. History and Ideology in the Dead Sea Scrolls* (Atlanta: Scholars Press, 1987) 107–34; M. A. Knibb, *Jubilees and the Origins of the Qumran Community*, An Inaugural Lecture (London: King's College London, 1989); B. Noack, 'Qumran and the Book of Jubilees', *SEÅ* 22–23 (1958) 191–207; M. Testuz, *Les idées religieuses du Livre des Jubilés* (Geneva: Droz / Paris: Minard, 1960) 179–99; J. C. VanderKam, *Textual and Historical Studies in the Book of Jubilees* (Missoula: Scholars Press, 1977) 255–83. The latter provides additional bibliographical details on p. 259 n. 95. More recently VanderKam has returned to this question in J. C. VanderKam, 'The Jubilees Fragments from Qumran Cave 4', *The Madrid Qumran Congress* ed. J. Trebolle Barrera and L. Vegas Montaner (Leiden: Brill, 1992) 2.635–48.

[2]The Cave 1 copies have been published in D. Barthélemy and J. T. Milik, *Qumran Cave 1* (DJD I; Oxford: Clarendon Press, 1955) 82–4 and Plate XVI. The editions of the cave 2 copies of *Jubilees* appear in M. Baillet, J. T. Milik and R. de Vaux, *Les "petites grottes" de Qumrân* (DJD III; Oxford: Clarendon Press, 1962) 77–9 and Plate XV. 3Q5 was initially published as 'une prophétie apocryphe' and subsequently identified as another copy of *Jubilees*; cf. M. Baillet, 'Petites grottes', 96–8 and Plate XVIII; R. Deichgräber, 'Fragmente einer Jubiläen-Handschrift aus Höhle 3 von Qumran', *RevQ* 5 (1965) 415–22; A. Rofé, 'Fragments from an Additional Manuscript of the Book of Jubilees in Qumran Cave 3', *Tarbiz* 34 (1965) 333–6 [Hebrew]; and M. Baillet, 'Remarques sur le manuscrit du Livre des Jubilés de la grotte 3 de Qumran', *RevQ* 5 (1965) 423–33. For the Cave 4 manuscripts, see J. C. VanderKam, in H. Attridge *et al.*, *Qumran Cave 4.VIII. Parabiblical Texts. Part I* (DJD XIII; Oxford: Clarendon Press, 1994) 1–140 and Plates I–IX. See also VanderKam, 'Jubilees Fragments'. A further Cave 4 copy was initially published as belonging to 4QTanḥumin (4Q176) but 4Q176 19–21 was subsequently recognized by M. Kister as another copy of *Jubilees* from Cave 4; cf. M. Kister, 'Newly-Identified Fragments of the Book of Jubilees: Jub. 23:21–23,30–31', *RevQ* 12 (1987) 529–36. Finally a cave 11 copy of *Jubilees* has been published by A. S. van der Woude; cf. A. S. van der Woude, 'Fragmente des Buches Jubiläen aus Qumran Höhle XI (11QJub)', *Tradition und Glaube: Das frühe Christentum in seiner Umwelt* ed. G. Jeremias, H. W. Kuhn, and H. Stegemann (Göttingen: Vandenhoeck & Ruprecht, 1971) 140–6 and Plate VIII.

Even if 4Q217 does not constitute a copy of *Jubilees* it clearly refers to the Hebrew title of the book as known from the Prologue (cf. 4Q217 2:1) and may thus belong to the sizeable group of *Jubilees*-like works to be considered below. Even on the conservative count of fourteen copies preferred by VanderKam it is noteworthy that *Jubilees* is one of the most popular works to have emerged from the eleven Qumran scroll caves.[3] Only a handful of biblical books are more numerously attested. Moreover, its presence in Caves 1, 2, 3, 4, and 11 indicates that the work is not only present in high numbers but also over a broad area of the library. Devorah Dimant has recently published a table of the non-biblical Qumran corpus that clearly sets out the number of copies of each text in the various caves.[4] A perusal of this table reveals that only *Jubilees* and the *New Jerusalem Scroll* are attested in five caves not counting the entries of sundry fragments collected under single headings. VanderKam has given an assessment of the implications of this for 'the status of Jubilees at Qumran', when he notes that *Jubilees* should be seen as 'one of the most authoritative or "biblical" texts at Qumran'.[5] According to VanderKam one of the factors that contributed to this reverence for the work may have been its claim to divine revelation. He may well be right, although one invariably thinks of the *Temple Scroll* in this connection. The latter work makes claims to divine revelation that are even more 'immediate' than *Jubilees*. Whereas *Jubilees* claims to contain divine revelation to Moses via the medium of the angel of the presence, the *Temple Scroll* famously does away with an intermediary figure and is presented as a direct first-person revelation by God to Moses. There is no reason to believe that the *Temple Scroll*'s claims were not accepted in the Qumran milieu. However, in contrast to *Jubilees*, the *Temple Scroll* has survived in three copies (11Q19, 11Q20, and 4Q524) to which two tentatively identified copies may be added (4Q365a and 11Q21) which seems to indicate that this claim to divine authority alone did not suffice to arouse the amount of interest in the *Book of Jubilees*.[6] It seems likely that its emphases addressed contemporary concerns at Qumran.

---

[3]For a recent overview over the most numerously attested books from Qumran, see G. J. Brooke, '"The Canon Within the Canon" at Qumran and in the New Testament', *The Scrolls and the Scriptures. Qumran Fifty Years After* (ed. S. E. Porter and C. A. Evans; Sheffield: Sheffield Academic Press, 1997) 242–66, 245.

[4]D. Dimant, 'The Qumran Manuscripts: Contents and Significance', *Time to Prepare the Way in the Wilderness. Papers on the Qumran Scrolls by Fellows of the Institute for Advanced Studies of the Hebrew University, Jerusalem, 1989–1990* (ed. D. Dimant and L. H. Schiffman; Leiden: Brill Academic Publishers, 1995) 23–58.

[5]'Jubilees Fragments', 648.

[6]F. García Martínez, '11QTemple[b]: A Preliminary Publication', *The Madrid Qumran Congress*, vol. 2 363–90; F. García Martínez, E. J. C. Tigchelaar, and A. S. van der Woude,

Before moving from the ancient manuscripts to works that resemble *Jubilees* or contain an explicit reference to it I should like to comment on the material evidence of the oldest of the *Jubilees* manuscripts, i.e. 4Q216 (Jub[a]).[7] As the editors have noted, this manuscript is made up of two sheets that were written by two scribes with a considerable interval of time having passed between both palaeographical dates. Most unusually fragment 12 preserves portions from both sheets as well as the seam holding them together. Thus, according to VanderKam and Milik the earlier script preserved on the second sheet may be dated to the second half of the second century BCE whereas the later script found on the first sheet should be dated to around the middle of the first century BCE. VanderKam has offered the following explanation,

Apparently the outer sheet of the scroll became too worn or damaged and had to be replaced. A scribe then recopied the text on it in a later style, and the new first sheet was sewn to the older scroll. The fact that the scroll was repaired, not discarded, may imply that the text was treated with respect.[8]

This situation mirrors Yadin's observations on the first sheet of 11Q19 which goes back to a different scribe from the rest of the scroll.[9] The difference in the case of 11Q19 is the presence of a certain amount of textual overlap between the end of the first sheet (11Q19 5) and the beginning of the second (11Q19 6).

It may be worth considering a number of further possibilities or scenarios that could explain the material evidence. For example, is it to be ruled out that we may be witnessing the compositional growth of *Jubilees*? Scholars differ in their dating of the book. In any event, it is clear that we are dealing with a manuscript the early sheet of which goes back in the opinion of the majority of scholars to the same century as the composition itself. It seems entirely legitimate, therefore, to take the physical remains very seriously and to consider various possibilities. There is no justification, to my mind, to approach the material evidence of the *Jubilees* manuscripts any less rigorously than is currently the case

Qumran Cave 11.II. 11Q2–18, 11Q20–31 (DJD XXIII; Oxford: Clarendon Press, 1998) 357–414 and Plates XLI–XLVIII; E. Puech, 'Fragments du plus ancien exemplaire du Rouleau du Temple (4Q524)', *Legal Texts and Legal Issues. Proceedings of the Second Meeting of the International Organization for Qumran Studies, Cambridge 1995. Published in Honour of Joseph M. Baumgarten*, ed. M. Bernstein, F. García Martínez and J. Kampen (Leiden: Brill, 1997) 19–64; S. White, '4Q365a. 4QTemple?' in *Qumran Cave 4. VIII*, 318–33 and Plates XXXIII–XXXIV; and Y. Yadin, *The Temple Scroll* (3 vols, Jerusalem: Israel Exploration Society, 1983).

[7] I am grateful to Professor Michael A. Knibb and Dr. Eibert J. C. Tigchelaar for reading and commenting on a draft of this section.

[8] *Qumran Cave 4. VIII*, 1.

[9] This was brought to my attention by E. J. C. Tigchelaar. Cf. Yadin, *Temple Scroll*, I.9,11–12,19–20 and III Plates 17–20.

with regard to the *Community Rule*, for instance. Thus, is it not conceivable that one of the components of the Book at one point began with chapter 2, the point at which the more ancient part of our manuscript sets in? The beginning of chapter 2 in some ways constitutes a new beginning. After various preliminaries that set the scene for the Book contained in the Prologue and chapter 1, chapter 2 begins with a command by the angel of the presence to Moses to write down the divine revelation beginning with creation. In terms of content this chapter begins the rewritten story proper from creation to Sinai that makes up the bulk of the *Book of Jubilees*. The beginning of chapter 2 is also a stylistic turning point since the narrative now begins to be told in the first person address by the angel of the presence to Moses. The Prologue and chapter 1, by contrast, are formulated as an introductory narrative interrupted by a dialogue between God and Moses.[10] Alternatively, if the new sheet is replacing an earlier sheet the version of the Prologue and chapter 1 that is attested in this first-century copy may differ from the text it is replacing.

The reference to *Jubilees* in CD 16:2–4 par. 4QD[e] 6 ii 17 and 4QD[f] 4 ii 4–5 is phrased similarly to and seems to presuppose the Prologue. The same is true of 4Q228 (*Text with a Citation of Jubilees*) which is reminiscent of the Prologue. These ancient references to the Hebrew title of the *Book of Jubilees* as known from the Prologue and chapter 1 suggest that the Book or the traditions contained within it, and perhaps also the traditions handed on in the wider cycle of *Jubilees*–related works, were known as 'the divisions of the times' (מחלקות העתים) or an expression incorporating this phrase.[11] It seems clear, therefore, that a version of the Prologue and chapter 1 was known by the first century BCE since explicit references to those opening parts of the Book are attested already in works that have been dated to roughly the same palaeographical period as the second, later scribe of 4QJub[a]. [12]

It is in the nature of reflections such as these that it is impossible to prove or disprove various options in the absence of further clear-cut evidence. I am well aware of this and offer the above merely as a way of thinking through and perhaps opening a debate on a number of

---

[10]Note also the way in which the topic of the sabbath frames the story told in the *Book of Jubilees* in chapters 2 and 50; cf. Ch. Albeck, *Das Buch der Jubiläen und die Halacha* (Berlin: Siegfried Scholem, 1930) 7, and VanderKam, *Textual and Historical Studies*, 242.

[11]B. Z. Wacholder has also recently drawn attention to this in 'Jubilees as the Super Canon', *LTLI*, 195–211, 195.

[12]The earliest 4QD manuscript, 4QD[a] or 4Q266, has been dated to the first half or the middle of the first century BCE; cf. the palaeographical analysis offered by A. Yardeni in J. M. Baumgarten, *Qumran Cave 4. XIII. The Damascus Document (4Q266–273)* (DJD XVIII; Oxford: Clarendon Press, 1996) 26–30. According to the editors, 4Q228 dates from around the middle of the first century BCE; cf. VanderKam and Milik in *Qumran Cave 4. VIII*, 177.

alternative explanations for the evidence in front of us. At the end of the day VanderKam's initial assessment may well hold the day, but it should do so only after all alternatives have been shown to be unlikely.

Jubilees-Related Works and Works that Contain References to the Book

In addition to the fourteen undisputed copies of *Jubilees* and the possible fifteenth copy 4Q217, a number of further manuscripts have at one point been identified as copies of *Jubilees*, although their identification is disputed. These are 4Q482–483 and two fragmentary manuscripts from Masada.[13] Not much can be made of the very fragmentary remains of 4Q482–483. As far as the Masada fragments are concerned, on the other hand, enough distinctive terminology is preserved in one of these (Masada 1276–1786) to leave little doubt that we are dealing with *Jubilees*-type material even if, as has been argued by VanderKam, it is not a copy of *Jubilees*.[14] Compare especially the preserved reference to 'the prince of Mastema' (שׂר המשׂטמה, Masada 1276–1786 i 6). The second (Masada 1039–317) mentions a number of the patriarchs by name and thus shares with *Jubilees* and a wealth of texts from Qumran an interest in the patriarchal period.

What is more, three texts that resemble the *Book of Jubilees* have been published alongside the recent edition of 4QJub[a–h] by VanderKam and Milik.[15] These texts have been classified by Milik as 4QPseudo–Jubilees[a–c] (4Q225–227), and have been defined by the editors as texts which, '. . . employ language that is familiar from and to some extent characteristic of *Jubilees*, but the documents themselves are not actual copies of *Jubilees*'.[16]

By speaking of texts and documents in the plural I have retained the terminology of the editors. However, the interrelationship of the three texts of *Pseudo-Jubilees* is not entirely clear. Are we to think of three copies of the same work or rather of three works that are related to each other because of their resemblance of *Jubilees*? The latter is implied by VanderKam's assessment of the doubtful Jubilees[b] manuscript (4Q217) as perhaps belonging to a 'pseudo-Jubilees *category*' [emphasis

---

[13]Cf. M. Baillet, *Qumran Cave 4. III* (DJD VII; Oxford: Clarendon Press, 1982) 1–2 and Plate I and S. Talmon, 'Hebrew Written Fragments from Masada', *Eretz Israel* 20 (1989) 278–85 [Hebrew]. See also *idem*, 'Hebrew Written Fragments from Masada', *DSD* 3 (1996) 168–77, esp. 169–72.

[14]'Jubilees Fragments', 642–43 n. 27.

[15]For the editions of 4Q225–227 (4QPseudo-Jubilees[a–c]) see VanderKam and Milik in *Qumran Cave 4. VIII*, 141–75 and Plates X–XII.

[16]*Qumran Cave 4. VIII*, 142.

mine].[17] On the other hand, the editors have identified overlapping text between 4QPseudo-Jubilees[a and b] which may suggest that they are two copies of the same work, cf. 4Q226 7 and 4Q225 2 ii 8–14. Should 4QPseudo-Jubilees[c] be regarded as a third copy? The nomenclature, i.e. a shared name 'Pseudo-Jubilees' followed by a-c in suprascript, suggests as much. By contrast, the use of the plural when speaking about these 'documents' and the reference to a 'pseudo-Jubilees category' suggests otherwise. In his review of DJD XIII, Moshe Bernstein airs his unease with the designation 'Pseudo-Jubilees'.[18] Of interest in the present context is his reference to these texts as separate documents when he notes, 'There are three such documents, two of which are possibly related to each other based on an apparent textual overlap'.[19] If, as seems to be implied by VanderKam and Bernstein, the three texts are not three copies of the same work the nomenclature is confusing, and it might have been preferable to designate the Pseudo-Jubilees texts analogously with 4QCommentary of Genesis A-D.[20] The fragmentary state of the material and the lack of context for the preserved texts makes it difficult to assess this question with confidence, and on the basis of the limited evidence it may well be that some of these questions can never confidently be answered.

A further question worth raising is the relationship of these Pseudo-Jubilees works to the Book of Jubilees. Should we assume that they presuppose and somehow imitate Jubilees as the term Pseudo-Jubilees seems to suggest? Or should we think of them in terms of works drawing on a set of traditions that also lies behind the Book? This seems to be Vermes's thinking when he refers to Pseudo-Jubilees 'simply as an alternative account'.[21] It seems that, just like there is evidence for a cycle

[17]'Jubilees Fragments', 640.

[18]M. J. Bernstein, Review of H. Attridge et al., Qumran Cave 4. VIII (DJD XIII; Oxford: Clarendon Press, 1994) in DSD 4 (1997) 102–12.

[19]Ibid., 106.

[20]Cf. G. J. Brooke in idem et al., Qumran Cave 4. XVII. Parabiblical Texts. Part 3 (DJD XXII; Oxford: Clarendon Press, 1996) 185–236.

[21]G. Vermes, The Complete Dead Sea Scrolls in English (Harmondsworth: Allen Lane, 1997) 507. See also idem, 'New Light on the Sacrifice of Isaac from 4Q225', JJS 47 (1996) 140–46, 140 where he comments on 4QPseudo-Jubilees[a] as follows, '... it may as well be an independent version of the pseudepigraphon previously known from Ethiopic, Greek and Latin translations'. Vermes's viewpoint thus questions the criterion of identifying copies of Jubilees on the basis of their closeness to the Ethiopic as established by VanderKam. VanderKam has argued in a note appended to his list of works previously, and in his view unjustifiably, proposed as copies of Jubilees, 'The reason for rejecting their identification as copies of Jubilees is their failure to correspond closely with the Ethiopic text' ('Jubilees Fragments', 642–3 n. 27). In support of VanderKam one can point to the presence of a sizeable group of manuscripts that do by and large correspond to the Ethiopic which seems to indicate that by the turn of the era (the suggested palaeographical date for Pseudo-Jubilees[a]) the text of Jubilees was established.

of Danielic and Enochic works, a *Jubilees*-cycle is attested in the late Second Temple period.

Apart from works that resemble *Jubilees* the Hebrew title of the Book is referred to in a number of Qumran texts. Firstly, there is the long-known reference to the *Book of Jubilees* in the *Damascus Document* (cf. CD 16:2–4 par. 4QD^e 6 ii 17 and 4QD^f 4 ii 4–5). Secondly, 4Q228 (*Text with a Citation of Jubilees*) refers to *Jubilees* as an authoritative work (cf. 4Q228 1 i 9).[22] It is noteworthy that the introductory formula 'for thus it is written' (כי כן כתוב) is here used to introduce the partially preserved reference to *Jubilees*.[23] Finally, the recently published 4QApocryphon of Jeremiah B? (4Q384) contains the remains of a further probable reference to the Hebrew title of *Jubilees* (cf. 4Q384 9:2).[24]

Apart from texts that contain explicit appeals to *Jubilees* a host of works draw on the ideas and language of the Book. Let me give just two examples. Firstly, the partly and preliminarily published text 4QPseudo–Moses (4Q390) displays close affinities to the *Book of Jubilees* as has been shown by Dimant and Knibb.[25] Secondly, the language and ideas of *Jubilees* lie behind a great many passages in the *Damascus Document*, as a glance at the index in Schechter's *editio princeps* or C. Rabin's edition reveals.[26]

A Context Rediscovered

No less significant than the discovery of the ancient manuscripts of *Jubilees* and related works is the discovery of a new context for the Book. Although the *Book of Jubilees* was almost certainly cherished beyond the confines of the Qumran library, the latter revealed a host of comparative material that provides us with a newly-discovered literary context for the study of the Book over and above the limited

---

[22]VanderKam and Milik, *Qumran Cave 4. VIII*, 178–85 and Plate XII.

[23]Cf. VanderKam and Milik, *Qumran Cave 4. VIII*, 182–3.

[24]Cf. M. Smith in M. Broshi *et al.*, *Qumran Cave 4. XIV. Parabiblical Texts Part 2* (DJD XIX; Oxford: Clarendon Press, 1995) 137–52 and Plate XVI. See also G. Brooke, 'The Book of Jeremiah and Its Reception in the Qumran Scrolls', *The Book of Jeremiah and Its Reception* ed. A. H. W. Curtis and T. Römer (Leuven: University Press, 1997) 183–205, 188.

[25]Cf. D. Dimant, 'New Light from Qumran on the Jewish Pseudepigrapha – 4Q390', *MQC*, 2.405–48, esp. 437–9 and M. A. Knibb, 'A Note on 4Q372 and 4Q390', *The Scriptures and the Scrolls. Studies in Honour of A. S. van der Woude on the Occasion of His 65th Birthday* ed. F. García Martínez, A. Hilhorst and C. J. Labuschagne (Leiden: Brill Academic Publishers, 1992) 164–77, esp. 175–6.

[26]Cf. S. Schechter, *Documents of Jewish Sectaries. Volume I. Fragments of a Zadokite Work* (Cambridge: Cambridge University Press, 1910) lxiii–lxiv and C. Rabin, *The Zadokite Documents. I. The Admonition II. The Laws* (Oxford: Clarendon Press, 1954) 82.

comparative material available previously. In many ways the post-Qumran phase of *Jubilees* studies parallels the post-Qumran phase in the study of the *Damascus Document*. In both cases Qumran revealed ancient copies and related works as well as providing an ancient literary context. By way of illustration let me mention two areas in which the discovery of a context is making an impact on our understanding of the *Book of Jubilees*.

1. A sizeable portion of the Qumran corpus is made up of works dealing with the period of the patriarchs. George Brooke has recently shown the pervasive representation of works based on the traditions contained in Genesis-Exodus and the patriarchal period.[27] Moreover, he further notes twelve texts that have an association with Moses.[28] The presence of such works has led Devorah Dimant to observe, 'the existence at Qumran of a well-established and rich literary tradition attached to the figure of Moses'.[29]

2. A host of halakhic texts have appeared in recent waves of publications starting with the *Temple Scroll*.[30] The legal positions underlying the *Jubilees* narrative can now be examined alongside a wealth of comparative material.[31] Thus, *Jubilees* (*Jub.* 7:35–37), the *Damascus Document* (4QD^a 6 iv 4, cf. also 4QD^e 2 ii 6), the *Temple Scroll* (11QT^a 60:3–4), 4QMMT (4Q396 1–2 iii 2b–3) and the *Genesis Apocryphon* (1QapGen 12:13–15) all reflect the same position on the fourth-year produce, to name but one specific example.[32]

---

[27]'Canon Within the Canon', 248–9, 251–2.

[28]*Ibid.*, 249. Cf., however, the cautious remarks by García Martínez with regard to 4Q375–376 and 4Q390 and their association with Moses (cf. F. García Martínez, 'Nuevos Textos no Bíblicos procedentes de Qumrán (I)', *Estudios Bíblicos* 49 [1991] 97–134, esp. 128, 131 and n. 63).

[29]'New Light from Qumran on the Jewish Pseudepigrapha', 410.

[30]Yadin's *editio princeps* of the *Temple Scroll* includes numerous references to correspondences in matters of halakhah between the *Temple Scroll* and *Jubilees*. See also the review by J. M. Baumgarten of Yadin's Hebrew edition of the *Temple Scroll* in *JBL* 97 (1978) 584–9; G. J. Brooke, 'The Temple Scroll: A Law Unto Itself?', *Law and Religion. Essays on the Place of the Law in Israel and Early Christianity* ed. B. Lindars SSF (Cambridge: James Clarke, 1988) 34–43, esp. 37–8; and J. C. VanderKam, 'The Temple Scroll and the Book of Jubilees', *Temple Scroll Studies* ed. G. J. Brooke (Sheffield: Sheffield Academic Press, 1989) 211–36 and further literature referred to there.

[31]On the halakhah in *Jubilees* cf. Albeck, *Das Buch der Jubiläen und die Halacha*.

[32]This is dealt with at length by J. M. Baumgarten, 'The Laws of ʿOrlah and First Fruits in the Light of Jubilees, the Qumran Writings, and Targum Ps. Jonathan', *JJS* 38 (1987) 195–202. See also M. Kister, 'Some Aspects of Qumranic Halakhah', *MQC*, 2.571–88, esp. 575–88 and Y. Sussman in E. Qimron and J. Strugnell, *Qumran Cave 4. V* (DJD X; Oxford: Clarendon Press, 1994) 189–90.

Conclusion

In sum, a very large section of the Qumran corpus is made up of *Jubilees* manuscripts and *Jubilees*-like texts. In fact, the *Book of Jubilees* emerges as one of the most numerously and widely distributed texts in the collection ranking only behind a small number of biblical texts. It further lies behind a great many texts and is at times explicitly and more often implicitly appealed to. There is no reason to believe that *Jubilees* is a sectarian text. Although unfortunately it is not possible to know how widely it was cherished beyond Qumran, it seems likely that it goes back to the circles from which the *yaḥad* emerged as suggested by Knibb and others.[33] As we saw, we now have a newly-discovered literary context for the study of the Book. Though *Jubilees* is not sectarian, it is clearly a literary pillar of the library. In recent years it is has become clear that the library contains less sectarian material than non-sectarian compositions, a fact that clearly emerges from Devorah Dimant's overview to which I referred above.[34] It is therefore no longer legitimate to label *Jubilees* as anything other than a part of the Qumran library. This brings me to the question of the appropriate categorization of the *Book of Jubilees*. The question of the classification of the pseudepigrapha is a difficult one, and I will limit myself to the question of the classification of *Jubilees* on this occasion.[35] The fact that *Jubilees* was handed on by later Christian communities and thus known prior to the discovery of Qumran is an accident of history that should not be determinative for our classification of the Book.[36] It is as little sectarian as the

[33]Cf. Knibb, *Jubilees and the Origins of the Qumran Community*, 16–17. See also Dimant, 'New Light from Qumran on the Jewish Pseudepigrapha', 445–7; García Martínez, 'Nuevos Textos', 102; Testuz, *Les idées religieuses*, 183; and VanderKam, *Textual and Historical Studies*, 282–3.

[34]Cf. Dimant, 'Qumran Manuscripts', 58. Dimant's tables are illuminating. Although one may disagree about the classification of individual texts, the larger picture that emerges from her survey seems accurate.

[35]On this question see the reflections offered by M. E. Stone, 'Categorization and Classification of the Apocrypha and Pseudepigrapha', *Abr–Nahrain* 24 (1986) 167–77 and *idem*, 'The Dead Sea Scrolls and the Pseudepigrapha', *DSD* 3 (1996) 270–95. See also J. C. VanderKam, *The Dead Sea Scrolls Today* (London: SPCK, 1994) 42–3 where he introduces the category of 'New Pseudepigrapha'. Further, K. Schubert in K. Schubert and J. Maier, *Die Qumran Essener* (München: Reinhardt, 1992) 10–19 where he distinguishes between 'Sektenschriften (solche Pseudepigraphen, die bisher noch durch keine Sekundärübersetzung bekannt wurden)' (10) and 'Solche Pseudepigraphen, die bisher schon durch Sekundärübersetzungen oder mittelalterliche hebräische Abschriften bekannt waren' (17). Note also the critical remark by J. Maier on the categories of apocrypha and pseudepigrapha, '... doch ist diese einseitig biblizistische Einbahnstraße schwerlich realitätsgerecht' (J. Maier, *Die Qumran-Essener: Die Texte vom Toten Meer* [München: Reinhardt, 1996] 3.12).

[36]Cf. the apposite observation by Stone, 'Intriguingly, the channel of transmission is the dominant criterion for inclusion of a writing in the Pseudepigrapha', 'The Dead Sea Scrolls and the Pseudepigrapha', 271.

majority of the Dead Sea Scrolls and more ubiquitous in the Qumran library than most. The Book is therefore appropriately included at least partially in most recent translations of the scrolls.[37] The editorial decision by Wise, Abegg and Cook to include the three *Pseudo-Jubilees* texts but leave out *Jubilees* seems an absurd way to proceed.[38] The customary way of arranging the place of *Jubilees* in the indexes of scholarly works is another interesting question. Is it legitimate to have the *Temple Scroll* listed as a Dead Sea Scroll and the *Book of Jubilees* elsewhere?[39] In any event, it is clear in the light of the recently published material that *Jubilees* is a central text in the Qumran collection. Like the majority of the Qumran corpus it sheds light also on Judaism outside of Qumran although the scope of the latter is much harder to assess.

[37]Cf. F. García Martínez, *The Dead Sea Scrolls Translated. The Qumran Texts in English* (Leiden: Brill Academic Publishers, 1994) 238–45; J. Maier, *Die Qumran-Essener: Die Texte vom Toten Meer* (Basel: München, 1995) 2.172–9. Vermes, *Complete Dead Sea Scrolls*, 507–10 includes a translation of only one of the Cave 4 manuscripts (4Q220) and parts of 4Q225–227 Pseudo-Jubilees[a-c].

[38]M. Wise, M. Abegg Jr., and E. Cook, *The Dead Sea Scrolls. A New Translation* (London: HarperCollins, 1996). Their in my view misguided reasoning seems to be that anything not previously known reveals more about the Qumran collection than previously known works also attested in the caves; cf. the following remarks from the introduction, 'But it is the texts that no one knew existed that give the Qumran collection its special quality [....]. They are the texts that are translated here ...' (13). Their collection does, however, include the *Damascus Document*.

[39]In essence the same question as the one dealt with here has been raised by Wacholder, 'Jubilees as the Super Canon', 210 with the significant difference that he employs the term 'sectarian' in this context; cf. the following remarks, 'The fundamental position of *Jubilees* at Qumran gives rise to an ideological question: Should not *Jubilees*, and similar works, such as *Enoch*, now classified as pseudepigrapha, be reclassified as sectarian documents?'

PART IV

*Theology of the Qumran Community, Second Temple
Judaism and Early Christianity*

12

THE NATURE OF MESSIANISM IN THE LIGHT OF THE DEAD SEA SCROLLS

John J. Collins

Messianic expectation has been one of the areas where the Dead Sea Scrolls have engendered liveliest discussion, and this has been especially true since the full corpus became generally available in 1991.[1] There remain, however, some fundamental disagreements as to what it is that we are talking about. 'Messianism', like all '-isms' is a modern scholarly construct. It is not for that reason invalid. If we did not construct analytical categories and synthetic concepts we could not conduct academic discussion at all. But we do well to re-examine such constructs from time to time, to remind ourselves that the data are always more complex than our concepts, and to make sure that hypotheses and assumptions do not cause us to lose sight of the specificity of the texts.

The Concept 'Messiah'

The word 'messianism' is derived from the Hebrew משׁיח, 'anointed one'. In the Dead Sea Scrolls and in later Jewish texts it is often used with reference to an eschatological figure, who would play a significant role in the drama of the end-time, especially the king who would restore the line of David and the kingdom of Israel.[2] The word משׁיח is not used in this future sense in the Hebrew Bible. It is used some thirty times with reference to kings, but it can also be used of other figures, notably the High Priest.[3] Also in the Scrolls, a משׁיח is not necessarily a king, and is not necessarily a future figure. Conversely, the future king can be

---

[1]F. García Martínez, 'Messianische Erwartungen in den Qumranschriften', *Jahrbuch für biblische Theologie* 8 (1993) 171–208; J. VanderKam, 'Messianism in the Scrolls', *The Community of the Renewed Covenant* ed. E. Ulrich and J. VanderKam (Notre Dame, IN: Notre Dame University Press, 1994) 211–34; E. Puech, 'Messianism, Resurrection and Eschatology in Qumran and the New Testament', *ibid.*, 235–56; J. J. Collins, *The Scepter and the Star* (New York: Doubleday, 1995); K. Pomykala, *The Davidic Dynasty Tradition in Early Judaism* (Atlanta: Scholars Press, 1995) 171–216; 231–46; M. Abegg, 'The Messiah at Qumran. Are We Still Seeing Double?' *DSD* 2(1995) 125–44; H. Stegemann, 'Some Remarks to 1QSa, to 1QSb and to Qumran Messianism', *RevQ* 17(1996) 479–505; J. Maier, 'Messias oder Gesalbter? Zu einem Übersetzungs- und Deutungsproblem in den Qumrantexten', *ibid.*, 585–612.

[2]For a sampling of definitions, see G. S. Oegema, *Der Gesalbte und sein Volk* (Göttingen: Vandenhoeck & Ruprecht, 1994) 26–7.

[3]For the references, see F. Hesse, '*Chrio*, etc.', *TDNT* 9 501–9.

identified in other ways, such as 'Branch of David', or 'Prince of the Congregation'. The modern usage of 'messiah', then, is related to, but not identical with, ancient usage of מָשִׁיחַ. I have suggested that 'messiah' be used to mean 'an eschatological figure who is sometimes, but not necessarily always, designated as a מָשִׁיחַ (or translation equivalent) in the ancient sources'.[4] It is not unusual for scholars to object that a particular figure cannot be a messiah because he is not called מָשִׁיחַ in the text.[5] This is to confuse the concept with the word, a logical error to which some philologists are especially prone. What is at issue is not simply the usage of the Hebrew word מָשִׁיחַ, but the structure of authority in the eschatological future, or utopian age. Specifically, messianism concerns the roles in the end-time of the king and the High Priest, the figures who are most frequently called מָשִׁיחַ, and to a lesser degree the role of the eschatological prophet.[6]

Anointing with oil had various connotations in ancient Israel. Oil was used to strengthen, to cleanse or purify, or simply for pleasure.[7] The anointing of kings has been explained as strengthening or empowering. The practice is usually thought to have been taken over from the Canaanites, although clear documentation is lacking. Kings were not anointed in Mesopotamia or in Egypt, but they were anointed among the Hittites. There is also evidence for the anointing of non-royal officials in Egypt and of Egyptian vassals in Syria. In Israel, anointing is associated with monarchy from the beginning. In Jotham's fable in Judges 9 we are told that 'the trees once set out to anoint a king over themselves'. Saul and David are anointed by Samuel. Then in 2 Samuel 5 David makes a covenant with the people at Hebron and they anoint him king over them. There has been some dispute as to whether the anointing signified election by the people or by God, or simultaneously by both.[8] Even in cases where the anointing is said to be by the people, we must assume that the rite was performed by an individual agent, either a priest or a prophet. In 1 Kings 1, Solomon is anointed by Zadok, although in

[4]Collins, *The Scepter and the Star*, 12.

[5]E.g. J. A. Fitzmyer, 'The Aramaic "Son of God" Text from Qumran Cave 4', *Methods of Investigation of the Dead Sea Scrolls and the Khirbet Qumran Site* ed. M. O. Wise *et al.* (New York: The New York Academy of Sciences, 1994) 171; A. Steudel, 'The Eternal Reign of the People of God – Collective Expectations in Qumran Texts (4Q246 and 1QM)', *RQ* 17(1996) 518.

[6]The eschatological prophet will not be taken up here. See Collins, *The Scepter and the Star*, 116–22.

[7]E. Kutsch, *Salbung als Rechtsakt im Alten Testament und im Alten Orient* (BZAW 87; Berlin: Töpelmann, 1963). See also M. Karrer, *Der Gesalbte* (Göttingen: Vandenhoeck & Ruprecht, 1990) 95–213.

[8]For a summary of the discussion see T. Mettinger, *King and Messiah* (Lund: Gleerup, 1976) 185–8.

1 Chron 29:22 we are told that '*they* made Solomon king ... and they anointed him'. The usurper Jehu is anointed by a prophet from the guild of Elisha (2 Kgs 9:3, 6, 12). Even where the king is acclaimed by the people, the anointing should be taken to signify divine election. It has been noted that our sources, which come to us through southern editors, never denote a northern king as מָשִׁיחַ, except for Saul.[9] But they do report the anointing of Jehu, and Elijah is even commanded to anoint Hazael king of Aram (1 Kgs 19:15). Not all kings are explicitly said to be anointed. But since anointing is reported in the cases of some relatively obscure kings (Jehoash in 2 Kgs 11:12, Jehoahaz in 2 Kgs 23:30) we can safely infer that it was standard practice in Judah, at least.

From the time of the Babylonian exile we find a metaphorical usage of 'anointing' to signify divine election. Second Isaiah famously refers to Cyrus of Persia as the Lord's anointed. In this case the anointing is clearly metaphorical – nobody suggests that Cyrus was actually anointed by a priest or prophet of the God of Israel. This is also the case in Isaiah 61, where the prophetic speaker claims that the spirit of God is upon him and that God has anointed him. Similarly, in eschatological texts from the Second Temple period, an anointed person is one who has been chosen by God for a particular task, regardless of whether they have been ritually anointed.[10] So, for example, 11QMelchizedek refers to an eschatological herald as 'the anointed of the spirit' (משוח הרוח) and CD 2:12 refers to the prophets as 'those anointed with his holy spirit' (מְשִׁיחֵי רוח קדשׁו). In both cases there is an allusion to Isaiah 61.[11]

The practice of anointing was not revived by the kings of the Hasmonean dynasty. None of these kings is ever called a מָשִׁיחַ. Whether they were legitimate kings was a matter of dispute, but their case shows that the concepts of anointing and kingship were not inseparably linked. It was certainly possible, then, to conceive also of future Jewish kings (such as the Herodian line) who would not be 'anointed', either literally or metaphorically. When texts from this period speak of a future king who would be a מָשִׁיחַ, however, or when modern scholars speak of a messiah, there is always an implicit contrast with such kings of dubious legitimacy. (This contrast is very explicit in *Psalms of Solomon* 17, where the psalmist prays for a king from the Davidic line in place of the Hasmoneans). Metaphorical anointing, or the status of 'messiah', is not only a matter of kingship. It is also a matter of legitimacy and of the status of this king in the fulfillment of history. Nowhere in the extant

[9]Mettinger, *King and Messiah*, 191.
[10]See Karrer, *Der Gesalbte*, 214–66.
[11]J. J. Collins, 'A Herald of Good Tidings. Isaiah 61:1–3 and its Actualization in the Dead Sea Scrolls', *The Quest for Context and Meaning. Studies in Biblical Intertextuality in Honor of James A. Sanders* ed. C. A. Evans and S. Talmon (Leiden: Brill Academic Publishers, 1997) 230.

literature, however, do we find legitimate eschatological kings who are not anointed as distinct from those that are, just as there is no mention in the historical texts of any king of the Davidic line who was not anointed. The claim of Joseph Fitzmyer that it is possible to conceive of a legitimate Jewish king in the eschatological time who would not merit the title 'messiah' can not in my view be sustained.[12] A legitimate Jewish king in an eschatological context is by definition a messiah.

The Promise to David

In Jewish, and older Judahite tradition, the legitimacy of a king was bound up with the promise to David recorded in 2 Samuel 7. There Nathan dissuades David from building a house for the Lord, but tells him:

the Lord declares to you that the Lord will make you a house. When your days are fulfilled and you lie down with your ancestors, I will raise up your offspring after you, who shall come forth from your body, and I will establish his kingdom. He shall build a house for my name, and I will establish the throne of his kingdom forever. I will be a father to him and he shall be a son to me. When he commits iniquity, I will punish him with a rod such as mortals use, with blows inflicted by human beings. But I will not take my steadfast love from him as I took it from Saul, whom I put away from before you. Your house and your kingdom shall be made sure forever before me; your throne shall be established forever. (2 Sam 7:11–16)

This passage is part of the Deuteronomistic history, edited in the Babylonian exile or shortly thereafter. The unconditional character of the promise is atypical of Deuteronomic theology, and it is reasonable to suppose that Nathan's oracle was part of an earlier edition of the history, which originally served as propaganda for King Josiah and his reform.[13] But the claim of a divine guarantee to the Davidic line is older than the time of Josiah. It is reflected in the royal psalms.[14] In Psalm 2, God makes common cause with his 'anointed':

You are my son; today I have begotten you. Ask of me and I will make the nations your heritage, and the ends of the earth your possession. You shall break them with a rod of iron and dash them in pieces like a potter's vessel.

The sonship in question is generally recognized as adoptive, and does not imply the degree of divinization that we find, for example, in Egypt.

[12]J. A. Fitzmyer, '4Q246: The "Son of God" Document from Qumran', *Bib* 74 (1993) 173–4; 'The Aramaic "Son of God" Text', 172–3.

[13]F. M. Cross, *Canaanite Myth and Hebrew Epic* (Cambridge, MA: Harvard University Press, 1973) 284–5; P. K. McCarter, *II Samuel* (AB 9; New York: Doubleday, 1984) 209–31; A. Laato, *A Star is Rising. The Historical Development of the Old Testament Royal Ideology and the Rise of the Jewish Messianic Expectations* (Atlanta: Scholars Press, 1997) 33–8.

[14]Mettinger, *King and Messiah*, 254–86. See the classic treatment of the royal psalms by S. Mowinckel, *The Psalms in Israel's Worship* (Nashville: Abingdon Press, 1967).

But it should not be dismissed as inconsequential rhetoric. It implies that the king enjoys a status above his fellow human beings. In Psalm 110, the king is invited to sit at the right hand of God, while God is said to be at his right hand in battle. In Psalm 45 the king is even addressed as an *elohim*, a god, even if he remains clearly subject to the Most High:

Your throne, O God, endures forever and ever. Your royal scepter is a scepter of equity; you love righteousness and hate wickedness. Therefore God, your God, has anointed you with the oil of gladness beyond your companions. (Ps 45:6–7)[15]

Only in Psalm 132 do we find the idea that the kingship of the Davidic line may be conditional:

The Lord swore to David a sure oath
from which he will not turn back:
'One of the sons of your body
I will set on your throne.
If your sons keep my covenant
and my decrees that I shall teach them,
their sons also, forevermore,
shall sit on your throne'. (Ps 132:11–12)

Some scholars have argued that this conditional covenant was the original understanding of the monarchy, and represents a transitional stage between the charismatic leadership of the judges and the fully institutionalized monarchy.[16] In my own view, Psalm 132 is more likely to represent a Deuteronomic correction; a chastened view of the monarchy from the latter years of the Davidic dynasty.[17]

The Deuteronomic history claims that there was ambivalence about the monarchy in Israel from the beginning. Some of that ambivalence may have developed with hindsight. Samuel's scathing catalogue of the abuses of the kingship in 1 Samuel 8 was surely formulated by the Deuteronomist in the light of experience. From the Assyrian period onward, the Davidic dynasty lived somewhat precariously, until it was finally brought to an end by Nebuchadnezzar of Babylon. For anyone who relied on the unconditional promise of Nathan's oracle, the demise of the Judean monarchy must have created a situation of cognitive dissonance: there was a manifest gap between what was supposed to be and what was actually the case. We find a number of distinct responses to this crisis in the literature from around the period of the exile.

---

[15]H. J. Kraus, *Psalms 1–59. A Commentary* (Minneapolis: Augsburg Publishing House, 1988) 451, 455.

[16]Cross, *Canaanite Myth*, 232–3; Laato, *A Star is Rising*, 36–8; 84–8.

[17]So also Mettinger, *King and Messiah*, 256–7.

Reactions to the demise of the monarchy

Perhaps the simplest response to the downfall of the Davidic dynasty was to predict that God would gloriously restore it. Some of these predictions may pre-date the actual end of the dynasty. Psalm 132, which we have already quoted, asks God 'for your servant David's sake, do not turn away the face of your anointed one', a prayer that would scarcely have made sense when there was no longer a king on the throne. The psalm concludes:

I will cause a horn to sprout up for David;
I have prepared a lamp for my anointed one.
His enemies I will clothe with disgrace,
but on him, his crown will gleam. (Ps 132:17–18)

What is at issue here is the restoration of the monarchy to its full glory. This may also be the case in the famous prophecy in Isaiah 11, which begins: 'A shoot shall come out from the stump of Jesse ...'. Some scholars argue that this oracle is quite intelligible in the Assyrian crisis in the time of Hezekiah.[18] Marvin Sweeney has recently made a strong case for a date in the time of Josiah.[19] The idealized character of the future reign could be read as a criticism of the shortcomings of previous historical kings. But the reference to the stump of Jesse is probably most easily explained if the oracle was composed after the line was cut off by the Babylonians. In any case, we are dealing here with a genuinely messianic oracle, which predicts not only the restoration of the Davidic line to its full glory, but a definitive restoration.[20] Oracles such as Isaiah 11, Amos 9 and Micah 5, all of which are of uncertain date, would surely have been read in the exilic period as guarantees that God would honor the promise to David by restoring a monarchy that would bring the idealized, even mythological claims of the dynasty to fulfillment.[21]

The oracles of Jeremiah are especially interesting with regard to the development of messianic prophecy. Jeremiah was an outspoken critic of the historical monarchy. His oracle against Jehoiakin ('a despised, broken pot') could be read as the death-knell of the Davidic dynasty:

---

[18]J. J. M. Roberts, 'The Old Testament's Contribution to Messianic Expectations', *The Messiah. Developments in Earliest Judaism and Christianity* ed. J. H. Charlesworth (Minneapolis: Fortress Press, 1992) 45; H. Seebass, *Herrscherverheissungen im Alten Testament* (Neukirchen-Vluyn: Neukirchener Verlag, 1992) 34–6.

[19]M. A. Sweeney, 'Jesse's New Shoot in Isaiah 11: A Josianic Reading of the Prophet Isaiah', *A Gift of God in Due Season. Essays on Scripture and Community in Honor of James A. Sanders* (ed. R. D. Weis and D. M. Carr; Sheffield: Sheffield Academic Press, 1996) 103–18.

[20]So also Laato, *A Star is Rising*, 120–3.

[21]Collins, *The Scepter and the Star*, 24–5.

Record this man as childless,
a man who shall not succeed in his days;
for none of his offspring shall succeed
in sitting on the throne of David,
and ruling again in Judah. (Jer 22:30)

Yet in the next chapter we read:

The days are surely coming, says the Lord, when I will raise up for David a righteous
Branch, and he shall reign as king and deal wisely, and he shall execute justice and
righteousness in the land. In his days Judah will be saved and Israel will live in
safety. and this is the name by which he will be called: 'The Lord is our righteousness.' (Jer 23:5–6)

The name at the end is clearly a play on the name of Zedekiah, the ill-
fated uncle of Jehoiakin who was installed as king by the Babylonians.
What is unclear is the implication of the word-play. Robert Carroll
reads the passage as 'an inaugural celebration of Zedekiah's legitimate
claim to be king'.[22] William Holladay, in contrast, notes that the
Hebrew phrase יהוה צדקנו is a reversal of the name צדקיה, and argues that
'the reign of the new king will reverse the characteristics of the reign of
Zedekiah'.[23] Zedekiah was a Babylonian puppet; the new king would be
a legitimate heir to the Davidic line. Carroll's interpretation is more in
accordance with Jeremiah's usual attitudes to the Davidic line and
Babylonian rule; he seems unlikely to have attached much importance
to the strict line of Davidic succession. But it is by no means certain that
the passage comes from Jeremiah himself.

This oracle is taken up again in Jer 33:14–18:

The days are surely coming, says the Lord, when I will fulfill the promise I made to
the house of Israel and the house of Judah. In those days and at that time I will cause
a righteous branch to spring up for David; and he shall execute justice and righteousness in the land ... And this is the name by which it will be called: 'The Lord
is our righteousness.' For thus says the Lord: David shall never lack a man to sit on
the throne of the house of Israel, and the levitical priests shall never lack a man in
my presence to offer burnt offerings ... If any of you could break my covenant with
the day and my convenant with the night, so that day and night would not come at
their appointed time, only then could my covenant with my servant David be
broken, so that he would not have a son to reign on his throne, and my covenant
with my ministers the Levites. (Jer 33:14–22)

---

[22]R. P. Carroll, *Jeremiah* (Old Testament Library; Philadelphia: Westminster John Knox Press,
1986) 446. Cf. H. Strauss, *Messianisch ohne Messias* (Frankfurt am M.: Lang, 1984) 62–3.

[23]W. L. Holladay, *Jeremiah 1. A Commentary on the Book of the Prophet Jeremiah.
Chapters 1–25* (Philadelphia: Fortress Press, 1986) 617. For Near Eastern parallels to the
metaphor of the branch implying legitimacy, see *ibid.*, 618; Laato *A Star is Rising.* 163.

This oracle is not found in the Greek of Jeremiah, and is almost certainly a late addition. It clearly responds to the fact that the earlier oracle in Jeremiah 23 had not been fulfilled. Hope is sustained, but deferred: the oracle will be fulfilled in due time. Most notable, however, is the manner in which the covenant with David is now paired with the covenant with Levi. Carroll has associated this oracle with the time and perhaps the circle of the Chronicler.[24] Whether the Chronicler entertained any messianic or royalist hopes seems to me doubtful.[25] He idealizes David's reign, but he is far more interested in the cult than in the monarchy. In this respect, the Chronicler conforms to a widespread trend in Second Temple Judaism, to subordinate the monarchy to the cult.

Not all the Jewish responses to the downfall of the monarchy focused on the fulfillment of the promises. The Book of Deuteronomy, while it did not question the legitimacy of the kingship, repudiated much of the traditional royal ideology. Instead, it envisioned a king who would be subject to the Torah:

When he has taken the throne of his kingdom he shall have a copy of this law written for him in the presence of the levitical priests. It shall remain with him and he shall read in it all the days of his life, so that he may learn to fear the Lord his God, diligently observing all the words of this law and these statutes, neither exalting himself above other members of the community nor turning aside from the commandment, either to the right or to the left, so that he and his descendants may reign long over his kingdom in Israel. (Deut 17:18–20)

In effect, the kingship was conditional, and its demise could be explained by the neglect of the Torah.

Another modification of the kingship had even more far reaching implications in the Second Temple period. Ezekiel prophesies the restoration of the Davidic line on a number of occasions. Typically, however, he refers to the Davidide as a 'prince' (נשיא, Ezek 34:23–24; 37:25), the title used in the Priestly source to refer to the lay leader of the tribes. (David is also called 'king' in Ezek 37:24). In the vision of a new order in Ezekiel 40–48, the role of the נשיא is reduced to providing for the cult. He becomes an apolitical messiah, subordinate in importance to the Zadokite priesthood.[26]

---

[24]Carroll, *Jeremiah*, 638.

[25]See Pomykala, *The Davidic Dynasty Tradition*, 110–11.

[26]J. D. Levenson, *The Theology of the Program of Restoration of Ezekiel 40–48* (Missoula, MT: Scholars Press, 1976) 75–101. The assertion by Pomykala that the נשיא in Ezekiel 40–48 is not necessarily Davidic or even likely to be so (*The Davidic Dynasty Tradition*, 32), posits an implausible discontinuity between these chapters and the rest of the book.

The Eclipse of Kingship in the Second Temple Period

In general, the Second Temple period is characterized by a transfer of focus away from the monarchy and aspirations to independence, and toward the priesthood and the cult. The process can be illustrated from the books of Haggai and Zechariah.[27] Haggai hailed Zerubbabel as a 'signet ring', the authorized representative of the Lord (Hag 2:21–24), and Zechariah refers to him as 'the branch' (Zech 3:8; צמח), a common Near Eastern metaphor for the legitimate king. Zechariah links the authority of this figure with that of the High Priest Joshua. They are depicted as two 'sons of oil', represented by two shoots of olive trees in 4:12. Again chapter 6 prophesies the coming of a man 'whose name is Branch ... There shall be a priest by his throne with peaceful understanding between the two of them' (Zech 6:12–13). But in this passage the prophet is told to make a crown and set it on the head of Joshua the High Priest. Actually, the Masoretic Text reads 'crowns', and most probably envisaged two crowns, one for Zerubbabel and one for Joshua, but at some point Zerubbabel was edited out of the text. The potential king disappears, and authority is vested only in the High Priest. Zerubbabel disappears abruptly from the pages of history, and one suspects that his disappearance was due to Persian concern for the status of the province.

One other kind of response to the demise of the monarchy in the Babylonian period should be noted. The prophet we know as Second Isaiah hailed Cyrus of Persia as the משיח of the Lord.[28] Thereby he repudiated native monarchist aspirations. Instead, he transferred to the whole Jewish people the promises made to David: 'I will make with you an everlasting covenant, my steadfast, sure love for David. See, I made him a witness to the peoples, a leader and commander for the peoples' (Isa 55:3–4). Israel is the servant of the Lord, the light to the Gentiles. We may reasonably speak here of 'collective messianism', insofar as the promises are applied to the people as a whole. But such 'collective messianism' does not exclude a role for an individual as agent of God. In Second Isaiah, this role is filled by the Persian king.

There is little evidence for any active messianic expectation in Judah in the period between 500 and 200 BCE. It was not necessarily non-existent. We have a few messianic oracles of uncertain provenance, such as Jeremiah 33 and Zechariah 9, and older prophecies such as Isaiah 11 were still copied. But on the whole, expectations related to the Davidic line seem to have been dormant in this period. Most telling is the

---

[27]Collins, *The Scepter and the Star*, 29–31; Laato, *A Star is Rising*, 195–207.
[28]Collins, *The Scepter and the Star*, 28–9.

absence of messianic expectation in the literature of the early second century BCE. Ben Sira praises David at some length, but assigns his glory to the past. Sir 45:25 contrasts the Davidic covenant with that of Aaron, and suggests that it is inferior in some respects.[29] Messianic expectation is conspicuously lacking in the apocalypses of the Maccabean era, where we might well have expected to find it. Daniel speaks of a kingdom that will be given to 'the people of the Holy Ones of the Most High'. However, the individual agent who receives this kingdom is not a human king, but a human-like figure who comes with the clouds, and is most satisfactorily identified with the archangel Michael.[30] When Daniel speaks of a משיח, in Dan 9:25, 26, the reference is to the High Priest. In the collection of writings that make up 1 Enoch, we find a messianic figure only in the Similitudes,[31] the one section of the work that is not found at Qumran, and that is probably no earlier than the first century CE.

Yet in several texts from Qumran that date from the early or middle first century BCE we find references to messianic figures that assume that they were well known. While messianic expectation is hardly central to the sectarian scrolls, it is much more prominent here than in other literature of the period. Given the absence of messianism in so much of Second Temple Judaism, the question arises, why should the Dead Sea sect have concerned itself with messianic expectation at all?

Messianic Expectation in the Scrolls

Before we attempt to answer that question, it is necessary to recall briefly what kinds of messianic expectation we find in the Scrolls. Some passages, like the famous one in 1QS 9:11 that mentions a prophet and messiahs of Aaron and Israel, say little about these messiahs except that they will come. But the association of messiahs with Aaron and Israel is significant. While the Damascus Document speaks of משיח אהרון וישראל in a way that can be construed as singular, I subscribe to the view that the phrase Aaron and Israel always implies a duality. Balaam's Oracle is taken to refer to two figures in CD 7, a passage attested at Qumran,[32] and it is difficult to see why a priestly messiah should not be called simply 'messiah of Aaron'.[33] In any case there is plenty of evidence that

[29]See now Pomykala, The Davidic Dynasty Tradition, 131–52.

[30]J. J. Collins, Daniel (Hermeneia; Minneapolis: Fortress Press, 1993) 304–10.

[31]1 Enoch 48:10; 52:4.

[32]4Q266 3 iii. See J. M. Baumgarten, Qumran Cave 4. XIII. The Damascus Document (4Q266–273) (DJD XVIII; Oxford: Clarendon Press, 1996) 44.

[33]F. M. Cross, 'Some Notes on a Generation of Qumran Studies', The Madrid Qumran Congress ed. J. Trebolle Barrera and L. Vegas Montaner (Leiden: Brill Academic Publishers, 1992) 14.

the authority of the royal messiah would be qualified, in accordance with the tendency we have seen in Deuteronomy and Ezekiel. In the Temple Scroll, the king 'may not go out before he has come into the presence of the High Priest ... on his instructions he shall go out and on his instructions he shall return home, he and all the Israelites who are with him' (11QT 58:18–19). A pesher on Isaiah interprets the phrase, 'he shall not judge by what his eyes see' to mean that the messiah will defer to the teachings of the 'priests of renown'. In the *Florilegium*, the Branch of David is linked with the Interpreter of the Law, and in CD 7:18 the Prince of the Congregation is similarly associated with the Interpreter.[34] It seems fair to conclude that the future lay ruler would have a chastened role, like that allowed for the king in Deuteronomy and Ezekiel. In several passages he is called a נשיא as in Ezekiel, although he is to restore the kingdom of Israel according to the Scroll of Blessings (1QSb) and he is given the kingship of his people in 4Q252. We read of a future מלך only in the Temple Scroll. In CD 7:16–17, the מלך of Amos 5:26 is interpreted as the assembly.

Given the prominence of the priesthood in the Dead Sea sect, it is axiomatic that there would be a High Priest in the eschatological age and that he would take precedence in some situations over the messianic king. The real point at issue in the debate as to whether there was a consistent expectation of two messiahs at Qumran is whether at any time the sectarians envisaged a polity without a king, in which all authority would be vested in the chief priest. We have seen that the apocalypses of the Maccabean era had no role for a messianic king. There is no a priori reason why the Dead Sea sect might not have entertained a similar scenario in its early stages. The famous reference to the prophet and the messiahs of Aaron and Israel is missing from 4QSᵉ, which Milik regarded as the oldest manuscript of the Community Rule.[35] Both the date of the manuscript and the significance of the omission are disputed,[36] but it is reasonable to suppose that the ideas of

[34]The priest also takes precedence over the messiah of Israel in 1QSa, the Messianic Rule, but here the precedence may be explained by liturgical reasons. For a table of Qumran texts that involve a diarchy, see D. Goodblatt, *The Monarchic Principle. Studies in Jewish Self-Government in Antiquity* (Tübingen: Mohr-Siebeck, 1994) 70.

[35]J. T. Milik, *Ten Years of Discovery in the Wilderness of Judaea* (London: SCM Press, 1959) 123. It appears, however, that there was confusion over the identity of 4QSᵉ. The manuscript that F. M. Cross had identified as the oldest exemplar of the Rule was not in fact the manuscript that lacked the reference to the messiahs. I am indebted to Philip Alexander for clarifying this matter.

[36]F. M. Cross dates this manuscript later than 1QS. See his discussion of the paleography of the Rule manuscripts in J. H. Charlesworth, *The Dead Sea Scrolls. Hebrew, Aramaic, and Greek Texts with English Translations. Volume 1. Rule of the Community and Related Documents* (Louisville: Westminster John Knox Press, 1994) 57.

the sect developed over time. It is difficult, however, to document any specific development from the extant texts.

I do not think that the concept of a single priestly messiah can be inferred from the phrase משיח אהרן וישראל in CD.[37] There are some hints, however, of a combination of kingship and priesthood in a single office in the Levi tradition.[38] In the Aramaic Levi apocryphon, Levi is consecrated priest of El Elyon, as Melchizedek, priest-king of Salem was (Gen 14:18; cf. Ps 110:4). The Greek Mt. Athos manuscript of the *Testament of Levi* says of Kohath, grandfather of Aaron, that 'he and his seed will be the beginning (or rule) of kings, a priesthood for Israel'. The statement about 'the beginning (or rule) of kings' however is not found in the Aramaic. Whether the Aramaic text intended to associate Levi with the kingship remains uncertain. But in any case, the Aramaic Levi apocryphon is a pre-Qumran text, which is representative of the circles from which the sect emerged rather than of the sect itself.

The distinction between the kingly and priestly messiahs in the Scrolls must be seen in the context of the Hasmoneans, heirs of the Maccabees, who served both as kings and as High Priests. The High Priesthood was first assumed by Jonathan in 152 BCE. His son, John Hyrcanus, was said to enjoy the gift of prophecy, in addition to being High Priest and political leader of the people, even though he did not formally declare himself king.[39] We know that some Jews took exception to this combination of offices. Josephus reports that a Pharisee named Eleazar asked John Hyrcanus to give up the High Priesthood 'and be content with governing the people'.[40] The opposition continued in the reign of Alexander Jannaeus. The insistence of the Scrolls on the distinction between royal and priestly authority would inevitably have been read as a criticism of the Hasmoneans. The *Testimonia* (4Q175), which sets out the biblical warrants for expecting a prophet, priest and king, concludes with a curse on the man who would re-build Jericho, and who seems to have been none other than John Hyrcanus.[41] In view of this context, it seems very unlikely that the Scrolls would have vacillated on this subject, or entertained the combination of offices in a single person.

Besides the relationship to the priesthood, two other features of the royal messianism of the Scrolls require comment. First, expectations of the future were grounded in the interpretation of prophetic texts, such

[37]Collins, *The Scepter and the Star*, 74–83.
[38]See Collins, *The Scepter and the Star*, 86–9. Goodblatt, *The Monarchic Principle*, 44–9.
[39]*Ant* 13.299–300.
[40]*Ant* 13.288–292. See D. Mendels, *The Rise and Fall of Jewish Nationalism* (New York: Doubleday, 1992) 61.
[41]H. Eshel, 'The Historical Background of the Pesher Interpreting Joshua's Curse on the Rebuilder of Jericho', *RevQ* 15 (1992) 409–20.

as Balaam's Oracle (Num 24) and Isaiah 11. Second, the role of this messiah was primarily military. He was expected to drive out the Gentiles and restore the kingdom of Israel. Both of these features may be illustrated by the blessing for the Prince of the Congregation in 1QSb:

And he will renew the covenant of the Community for him, that he may establish the kingdom of his people for ever ... May [you strike the peoples] with the power of your mouth. With your sceptre may you lay waste the earth. With the breath of your lips may you kill the wicked (Isa 11:4). [May he shed upon you the spirit of counsel] and everlasting might, the spirit of knowledge and of the fear of God (Isa 11:2); may righteousness be the girdle [of your loins] and may your reins be girdled [with faithfulness] (Isa 11:5). May he place upon you horns of iron and hooves of bronze. May you gore like a bull [... may you trample the peo]ples like mud ...

The violent role of the messianic king, however, seems to have been preparatory for the messianic age. Once the Gentiles were driven out, he would recede into a subordinate role and defer to the authority of the priesthood in matters of cult and teaching.

Communal messianism?

Recently Hartmut Stegemann and Annette Steudel have advanced a new argument that Qumran eschatology was initially communal in character.[42] This argument merits serious consideration, but in my judgment the texts they adduce do not sustain their interpretation.

Stegemann cites three examples: the biblical book of Daniel, the *War Rule* and the fragmentary 4Q491, while Steudel bases her argument on the 'Son of God' text, 4Q246, and also on the *War Rule*. Of these, Daniel at least speaks of a kingdom without a human, Israelite, king, but Daniel can hardly be taken as representative of the Dead Sea sect. Stegemann's third example, 4Q491, is a fragmentary and enigmatic text, but the view that it refers to collective Israel has never been argued in detail and seems gratuitous.[43] The 'Son of God' text, in my view should be interpreted as messianic.[44] This text, 4Q246, says of a ruler,

[42]Stegemann, 'Some Remarks to 1QSa, to 1QSb and to Qumran Messianism'; Steudel, 'The Eternal Reign of the People of God'.

[43]See Collins, *The Scepter and the Star*, 136–53, and, with a different intepretation, M. Abegg, 'Who Ascended to Heaven? 4Q491, 4Q427, and the Teacher of Righteousness', *Eschatology, Messianism and the Dead Sea Scrolls* ed. C. A. Evans and P. W. Flint (Grand Rapids: Eerdmans, 1997) 61–73.

[44]Collins, *The Scepter and the Star*, 154–72; 'Jesus and the Messiahs of Israel', *Geschichte – Tradition – Reflexion. Festschrift für Martin Hengel zum 70. Geburtstag* ed. H. Cancik, H. Lichtenberger, and P. Schäfer (Tübingen: Mohr, 1996) 3.287–303; 'The Background of the "Son of God" Text', *Bulletin for Biblical Research* 7 (1997) 51–62.

in a prophetic context, 'Son of God he will be called and Son of the Most High they will name him'. The messianic interpretation of this text is disputed. Many scholars hold that the figure in question is a Syrian king, and a negative figure in the eschatological drama.[45] After his appearance there are further upheavals, and then there is an indentation in the text, followed by the statement 'until the people of God arise'. The negative interpretation of the Son of God figure assumes that everything prior to the indentation is negative. But this is not necessarily so. The arrival of the Son of God figure and the rise of the people can be read as parallel, and the indentation simply accentuates the final and most extensive account of the time of salvation. By far the closest parallel to the language about the Son of God is found in the New Testament (Luke 1:32, 35), where it is also said that 'the Lord God will give to him the throne of David his father' (1:32). The notion that the Davidic king could be called Son of God was grounded in Psalm 2 and in Nathan's oracle in 2 Samuel 7, and the latter passage is explicitly related to the Branch of David in the *Florilegium* from Qumran.

The *War Rule* is a far more complicated matter. Stegemann contends that the basic draft of the *Rule* was composed about the same time as Daniel, but scarcely anyone agrees with this assessment. The literary history of the *War Rule* is complex, especially in view of the fragments from Cave 4.[46] We now know that at least one edition of the *Rule*, represented by 4Q285, had a role for the 'branch of David' in the final battle.[47] The edition represented by 1QM mentions the נשיא כול העדה in 1QM 5:1. While his role is not clarified, there is no warrant for Stegemann's assertion that he 'is not the Royal Messiah, but only the leader of the troops of Israel in a future war'. What is envisioned in the *War Rule* is not just 'a future war', but the definitive war, and the נשיא here must be assumed to have the same reference as in other sectarian texts from Qumran. It is possible, though by no means certain, that the framing sections of 1QM (columns 1 and 15–19), which describe a war in seven phases, represents an old conception of the eschatological war and an early stage of the *War Rule*.[48] In 1QM 17 Israel is championed by the archangel Michael, as also in Daniel, rather than by a Davidic king. But these sections of the *War Rule* do not describe the kingdom of

[45]The most elaborate argument is offered by E. M. Cook, '4Q246', *Bulletin for Biblical Research* 5 (1995) 43–66.

[46]J. Duhaime, 'War Scroll', *The Dead Sea Scrolls. Hebrew, Aramaic, and Greek Translations* Vol. 2 ed. J. H. Charlesworth (Louisville: Westminster John Knox Press, 1995) 80–203.

[47]M. G. Abegg, 'Messianic Hope and 4Q285: A Reassessment', *JBL* 113 (1994) 81–91.

[48]For the debate on this issue, see J. J. Collins, *Apocalypticism in the Dead Sea Scrolls* (London: Routledge, 1997) 94–5.

Israel on earth, and so it is unclear what role might be played by either a messianic king or a messiah of Aaron. In any case, much work remains to be done on the literary history of the *War Rule* before it can be claimed to represent an early stage of the ideas of the sect. In short, Stegemann's hypothesis is not impossible but it is very far from proven.

A non-Davidic messiah?

Most scholars have assumed that all references to a lay messianic ruler in the Scrolls refer to a Davidic messiah. The Davidic connotation is explicit in several passages (the *Florilegium*, 4Q174; the pesher on Genesis, 4Q252; a pesher on Isaiah, 4Q161, and a fragment of the *War Rule*, 4Q285). A half dozen passages, however, refer to 'the messiah of Israel' or 'the messiah of Aaron and Israel', without mention of David. All of these references are found in rule books, the *Community Rule*, the *Damascus Document* and the 'messianic rule', 1QSa. Recently Kenneth Pomykala has argued that the messiah of Israel should be regarded as a non-Davidic messiah, and that the texts that refer to him represent an early phase of the development of the sect, dating from the Hasmonean period. In contrast, all references to the Branch of David date from the Herodian period.[49] Pomykala argues that the expression 'Prince of the Congregation' was not necessarily Davidic, despite the use of נשיא for a Davidic ruler in Ezekiel. Bar Kochba proclaimed himself נשיא, and we do not know that he claimed Davidic descent. The use of Balaam's Oracle as a messianic proof-text in the *Testimonia* is also taken to point to a non-Davidic messianic ruler.[50]

Pomykala assumes that we can say with some confidence when the various scrolls were written, but this confidence is not well founded. Hartmut Stegemann contends that we have no reliable knowledge that any sectarian scroll was composed (as distinct from copied) later than the pesharim, or biblical commentaries, in the middle of the first century BCE.[51] The oldest copy of the *Damascus Document* also dates from this time, while 1QS, with 1QSa and 1QSb, may be slightly earlier. But even if the chronological periodization is questionable, Pomykala should at least be credited with an interesting observation on the generic distribution of messianic titles in the Scrolls.

A crucial issue for Pomykala's thesis is whether the Prince of the

---

[49]Pomykala, *The Davidic Dynasty Tradition*, 171–216; 232–46. See the critique of Pomykala's thesis by Laato, *A Star is Rising*, 285–9.

[50]*Ibid.*, 245.

[51]H. Stegemann, *Die Essener, Qumran, Johannes der Täufer und Jesus* (Freiburg im Breisgau: Herder, 1993) 192 (= *The Library of Qumran. On the Essenes, Qumran, John the Baptist and Jesus* [Grand Rapids: Eerdmans, 1998] 137).

Congregation in the *Scroll of Blessings*, 1QSb, should be regarded as Davidic. On the one hand, there is no mention of David in the blessing, and while there are several citations from Isaiah 11 there is no mention of the root of Jesse, from Isa 11:1. On the other hand, it was scarcely necessary to mention the root of Jesse: the explicit references to Isaiah 11 ('may you bring death to the ungodly with the breath of your lips') make the allusion transparent. The blessing weaves together allusions to Balaam's oracle ('for God has established you as the scepter') and possibly the blessing of Judah in Genesis 49,[52] in a way that suggests no distinction between Davidic and non-Davidic messiahs. Moreover, the Prince of the Congregation is explicitly identified with the Branch of David in 4Q285, a fragment dealing with the eschatological war that explicitly draws on Isaiah 11. Pomykala notes this identification, but argues that it represents a later development, in the Herodian period.[53]

The question whether the messiah of Israel should be regarded as Davidic presents us, then, with a methodological problem. It is axiomatic in historical critical study that one should not harmonize different ideas, and some scholars take this to mean that even a single expression should be assumed to have different referents wherever possible. But historical reconstruction is always a matter of probability. In my own view, the relative dating of the *Scroll of Blessings* and the *War Rule* fragment 4Q285 is not so secure that we can regard the latter as a later development with any confidence. Moreover, it seems to me that the burden of proof lies on anyone who would argue that a משיח ישראל in the Dead Sea Scrolls is a non-Davidic ruler. There were, to be sure, non-Davidic kings of Judea, first the Hasmoneans and then Herod. But none of them, to our knowledge, claimed to be a משיח, an anointed of the Lord. The *Psalms of Solomon* denounce the Hasmoneans explicitly because they assumed kingship even though they were not of the Davidic line (*Pss. Sol.*17:5–6). We have already suggested that the distinction of messiahs of Aaron and Israel had an anti-Hasmonean *Tendenz*. Should we assume that the revival of Davidic expectation in the Scrolls likewise implied a rejection of the Hasmoneans? Pomykala would argue that the Scrolls fail to make the connection that is so explicit in the *Psalms of Solomon*. But then it is difficult to see why the sectarians should suddenly have felt the need for Davidic legitimacy in the Herodian period, if they had been willing to allow the legitimacy of non-Davidic rulers in the time of the Hasmoneans.

---

[52]Vermes restores: 'and you shall be as a [lion; and you shall not lie down until you have devoured the] prey which nought shall deliver' (G. Vermes, *The Complete Dead Sea Scrolls in English* [London: Penguin, 1997] 377).

[53]Pomykala, *The Davidic Dynasty Tradition*, 203–12.

Pomykala finds further support for the endorsement of a non-Davidic monarchy in the *Temple Scroll*.[54] The Scroll requires that the king be 'one of your brothers', a Judean, not necessarily a Davidide (11QT 56:14–15). Moreover, the monarchy in the *Temple Scroll* is conditional: 'The king whose heart and eye have turned disloyally from my commandments shall have none who shall sit (after him) on the throne of his fathers – never, for I shall disjoin his descendants from further rule over Israel forever' (11QT 59:13–15). A conditional ruler is not necessarily non-Davidic. We have seen a precedent for a conditional understanding of the covenant with David in Psalm 132. Deuteronomy 17, which is a major source for the *Temple Scroll*, also implies that kingship is conditional on observance of the Torah, and it seems unlikely that Deuteronomy envisioned a non-Davidic kingship. An explicitly conditional understanding of the Davidic dynasty is articulated by Josephus.[55] But I agree with Pomykala that such a king should not be called a messiah, in the sense of a definitive eschatological ruler, and that the *Temple Scroll*, while utopian, is not strictly eschatological.[56] Its importance for our theme is that it provides another example of the chastened view of kingship even in utopian Jewish writing of the Hellenistic period.

A limited kingship

I also agree with Pomykala that the Qumran texts portrayed the Davidic messiah 'in a limited fashion, circumscribed his role, relativized his status alongside a priestly messianic figure and subordinated his authority to the priests'.[57] This limited view of the messianic ruler contrasts not only with the exalted Christ of the New Testament, but also with roughly contemporary Jewish portrayals in the *Psalms of Solomon*, where the king is the primary mediator in the future time, or the *Similitudes of Enoch*, which envision an exalted messiah, after the fashion of Daniel's 'one like a son of man'. Also in 4 Ezra, at the end of the first century, more attention is paid to the messianic king, who is allowed a four hundred year reign, even if he is subject to death (4 Ezra 7:28–29).[58] It is noteworthy that in 4 Ezra the origin of the messiah is mysterious. He is 'revealed' in due time, or he rises on a cloud from the

---

[54]*Ibid.*, 234–7.

[55]*Ibid.*, 225. Josephus, *Ant* 7.384–5.

[56]Collins, *The Scepter and the Star*, 109–11.

[57]Pomykala, *The Davidic Dynasty Tradition*, 215.

[58]M. E. Stone, 'The Question of the Messiah in 4 Ezra', *Judaisms and their Messiahs* ed. J. Neusner, W. S. Green and E. Frerichs (Cambridge: Cambridge University Press, 1987) 209–24.

sea (13:3). Nonetheless, he is also said to 'arise from the posterity of David' (12:32). One suspects that if Bar Kochba had been more successful in his messianic adventure, he too might have acquired a Davidic genealogy, just as Jesus of Nazareth did in the New Testament.

The limited role of the Davidic messiah in the texts from Qumran is not contradicted by the one text that might be taken to speak of him in more exalted language, the 'Son of God' text, 4Q246. As we have seen, the interpretation of this text is disputed, but even assuming the messianic interpretation, it should be noted that the Davidic messiah / Son of God is passed over quickly. In the end, the primary emphasis falls on the rise of the people of God. Annette Steudel has recently argued that this text should be regarded as an example, if not of collective messianism, at least of collective expectation.[59] But the rise of the people does not preclude a role for a messianic ruler and the antithesis of messianic and collective expectation is misleading.[60] It is true, however, that this text differs from other messianic texts from Qumran, insofar as it makes no mention of priestly authority. Like many of the Aramaic compositions in the Scrolls, 4Q246 may not be a sectarian composition but simply part of the community library.

Reasons for the resurgence of messianism

We return finally to the explanation of the resurgence of messianism in the Dead Sea Scrolls. The characterization of the Davidic messiah that we have sketched here suggests that three factors played a part. One was biblical exegesis. The Qumran community devoted much of its energy to expounding the Scriptures, and there were several passages that lent themselves to messianic interpretation. But exegesis alone is never a sufficient explanation. Texts that seemed to speak of a present or future king could easily be subverted by the allegorical exegesis of the community. So the 'anointed one' of Psalm 2 is taken as plural 'chosen ones' in the *Florilegium*, and the king of Amos 9 is interpreted as the congregation in CD 7. Both the choice of passages and the interpretation given were influenced by the circumstances of the interpreters. Presumably, then, other factors contributed to the messianic exegesis of the sect. One such factor was Gentile domination. Several texts assign to the messianic ruler the task of driving out the Gentiles. This task was obviously more immediate in the Roman period than under the Hasmoneans, but the inherited biblical tradition was replete with hostility to the Gentiles in any case. Nonetheless, the desire for a

---

[59]Steudel, 'The Eternal Reign', 509–21.
[60]See also the critique of Steudel by Laato, *A Star is Rising*, 315–16.

military ruler to liberate Israel is a factor that should not be discounted in messianic expectation.

In my own view, however, the revival of messianic expectation was prompted initially not by the Romans, but by the Hasmoneans. These non-Davidic Jewish kings had made kingship an issue in the first century BCE in a way that it was not in the Maccabean era.[61] The structure of Qumran messianism, with its emphasis on separate priestly authority, entails a repudiation of the combination of kingship and priesthood by the Hasmoneans. At root, the messianism of Qumran was not a yearning for a monarchical society, as it arguably was in the *Psalms of Solomon*. Rather it was born of respect for tradition, on the one hand, and a sense of military need on the other, but it was not an end in itself. It was only the necessary means to bringing about a society where ultimate authority would be vested in the Torah and the priesthood.

---

[61]Cf. Laato, *A Star is Rising*, 289. In Laato's view the expectation that a messianic king would come from the house of David was self-evident in Judaism, and was emphasized only after it was called into question by the Hasmoneans. In contrast, Goodblatt, *The Monarchic Principle*, 75, discounts the opposition to the Hasmoneans and argues that the dyarchic principle was a way of reconciling the fact of priestly leadership with the biblical pre-eminence of the Davidic monarchy. This view does not seem to do justice to the political realities of the Hasmonean period.

13

JUDAISMS IN THE DEAD SEA SCROLLS: THE CASE OF THE MESSIAH

Philip R. Davies

I have recently begun to explore[1] the Judaisms of the Dead Sea Scrolls. So far, I have compared, though only to a limited extent, the notions of 'Israel', 'Temple' and 'Torah'; and I have focussed in detail only on materials assigned the sigla D or S. I hope to be able to incorporate some other Qumran texts in due course, but first I want to complete the definition for these two sets of documents.

There remain two categories in particular that need to be added to 'Israel', 'Temple' and 'Torah'; one is 'Messiah' and the other 'land'. I am going to take this opportunity to deal with Messiah, though in a short paper the treatment cannot be very full. The topic of messiahs at Qumran has indeed been treated in detail by others, but mostly not very well, largely because of a predilection either to treat the Qumran corpus as a more or less coherent and systematic collection of texts or at least to look in their various statements about messiahs for a systematic belief.[2] One notable exception to these efforts is Lawrence Schiffman's essay in a collection published in 1992.[3] He notes the variety of messianic figures in the Scrolls and that both differences of approach among the authors, and also historical development are factors needing to be taken into account. Recognizing the difficulty of identifying historical development, he decides to go for a synchronic approach, paying great attention to terminology. I think this is right in principle: in both cases what needs to be avoided is a synthetic historical or dogmatic scheme which pays too little attention to the precise wording of texts. That being said, we cannot altogether avoid the problems posed by the existence of the Cave 4 materials, which present different editions of texts from other caves, most notably 1QS, 1QM and CD. These fragments were largely unpublished when Schiffman wrote; now we have to bear in mind the question of the redactional history of texts.

But although he recognizes different documents within CD,

---

[1]Three papers on the topic are scheduled for publication in 1999.

[2]E.g. J. Starcky, 'Les quatres étapes du messianisme à Qumran', *RB* 70 (1963) 481–505; A. Caquot, 'Le messianism qumranien', *Qumran: Sa piété, sa théologie et son milieu* ed. M. Delcor (Paris: Duculot, 1978) 231–47.

[3]L. H. Schiffman, 'Messianic Figures and Ideas in the Qumran Scrolls', *The Messiah* ed. J. H. Charlesworth (Minneapolis: Fortress Press, 1992) 116–29.

Schiffman claims it shows a 'consistent approach to eschatology'. Yet the fact that the biblical prophets are called 'anointed' shows that the 'virtually unequivocal meaning of "Messiah" ' has not yet been acquired.[4] On the question of 'messiah of Aaron and Israel', a distinctive phrase within both D and S material, he concludes that one cannot be certain whether one or two are meant, though in 1QS there are definitely two (1QS 9:11–12; the passage, however, is missing in 4QS[e]).[5] He also notes that in neither D nor S is any messiah linked explicitly with David. After a survey of other major Qumran texts, he concludes that there is 'a variety of motifs and beliefs ... distributed in almost random fashion throughout the texts', reiterating his earlier comment that these are due either to differing approaches or historical development of ideas, or both. He suggests that the most useful matrix for understanding the Qumran data is Scholem's distinction between utopian and restorative messianism, and rejects any attempt to harmonise.[6]

One important implication of Schiffman's treatment is that 'messiah' is not an appropriate category for a taxonomy of 'Qumran Judaisms', because it is not amenable to systematic analysis or to integration with other categories. That seems to me an important challenge from which to proceed.

How has that challenge been met in subsequent scholarship? James VanderKam's treatment of the topic is unsatisfactory in this regard.[7] He starts off with the premise (citing the 'messiah[s] of Aaron and Israel' from CD and 1QS) that there are two messiahs, a priestly and a lay, and assembles all the information in the scrolls under those two categories. His first category is 'The Davidic Messiah', under which he gathers the simple title 'messiah', the 'Branch of David' and the 'Prince of the Congregation'. The second category, 'The Eschatological Priest' is divided between various texts. His essay is not an argument about the number of messiahs but a demonstration of the assumption that there are two, and the conclusion, that 'at Qumran there was a dual messianism, with one messiah being priestly and the other Davidic' is

---

[4]Schiffman, 'Messianic Figures', 117, citing his *Sectarian Law in the Dead Sea Scrolls, Courts, Testimony, and the Penal Code* (Chico: Scholars Press, 1983) 7–9. On the recent work of J. J. Collins, which represents a nuancing of the idea of a 'Qumran messianism', see below.

[5]Noted by Schiffman on the basis of Milik's *Ten Years of Discovery in the Wilderness of Judaea* (London: SCM Press, 1959), 123; see now Sarianna Metso, *The Textual Development of the Qumran Community Rule* (Leiden: Brill Academic Publishers, 1997).

[6]Schiffman, 'Messianic Figures', 128–9.

[7]James VanderKam, 'Messianism in the Scrolls', *The Community of the Renewed Covenant. The Notre Dame Symposium on the Dead Sea Scrolls* eds. Eugene Ulrich and James VanderKam (Notre Dame: University of Notre Dame Press, 1994) 211–34.

merely a restatement of the premise. Of course messianic figures can be divided on the basis of whether they are priestly or not, but this hardly proves that there was a dual messiahship.

The major treatment by John Collins[8] arrives at a similar conclusion, though at greater length and with more discussion and more nuancing. Inspired by the 'star and sceptre' in CD 7:19 (whence also the title of the book) he argues that all the messianic titles in the Scrolls can be explained on the basis of two figures, Davidic and priestly. One departure from VanderKam is that he includes the heavenly figures Melchizedek and 'son of man'. Collins is much more aware of the problem posed by the variety of messianic titles and descriptions at Qumran, but he argues (1) that these can be coherently reduced to two human figures and (2) that messianic expectation is a part of the Qumranic Judaic system. This may represent a somewhat more emphatic statement than his refusal to suggest that 'messianism was the main principle of coherence for the sect revealed by the Scrolls' but it affirms Collins's view that there was a Qumran[9] messianism and that it represents some 'principle of coherence'.

Collins's account is generally well-grounded, but contains a significant omission. For although he devotes a chapter of *The Scepter and the Star* to 'Teacher, Priest and Prophet', he identifies only four messianic offices: king, prophet, priest and angel. Here he does not recognize a Teacher-Messiah as such, but subsumes this role under 'priest'. This procedure is explained partly because one text (CD [ms B] 19:35–20:1) clearly separates the 'teacher of righteousness' from the 'messiah(s) of Aaron and Israel'. And according to the principles on which Collins exegetes, this means that all other texts must do the same. But unfortunately, they do not. Had Collins used a different text as his starting point and argued on the same principle, he would have had to reach a different conclusion.

The issue is especially important because the law of the community constitutes the main theme of both the CD manuscripts (and the Cave 4 fragments taken as a whole). This law is also clearly described as the 'law for the period of wickedness' and its application and *raison d'être* are related to an eschatological expectation. It seems likely, therefore, that the messiah of CD should have some function related to the law of the community, and statements about a teacher-messiah given detailed scrutiny.

[8]John J. Collins, *The Scepter and the Star: The Messiahs of the Dead Sea Scrolls and Other Related Literature* (New York: Doubleday, 1995).

[9]'Messianism in the Dead Sea Scrolls', *Methods of Investigation of the Dead Sea Scrolls and the Khirbet Qumran Site* ed. Michael O. Wise *et al.* (New York: New York Academy of Sciences, 1994) 213–29, esp. 227.

In my previous investigations into the Judaism of Qumran, I have concluded that the topics of 'Israel' and 'Temple' are systematically integrated with 'law': The true Israel is that Israel that possesses and obeys the law, and the Temple is rendered unclean by those who disobey the law, and is fit for use only by those who possess the law. It is therefore unlikely that halakhic and messianic notions in at least some of the Qumran texts will be unrelated. If they were, we could justify Jewish and Christian scholarship on the Scrolls pursuing, as it has tended to do, its respective interest in law and in messianism.[10] But it seems unlikely, *a priori*, that in the Judaisms of Qumran they are in fact so separable.

II

I begin my investigation with CD 12:23–13.1

המתהלכים באלה בקץ הרשעה עד עמוד משוח אהרן וישראל עשרה אנשים למועט

Those who walk in these **during the period** of wickedness until there shall arise the messiah of Aaron and Israel shall be at least ten men.

There are several problems in this passage: what are the 'these'? What is the 'period of wickedness'? How many messiahs? The context helps us not at all in answering these questions, since the preceding text is merely a heading: 'This is the *serekh* of the session of ...' But fortunately the relevant phrases occur elsewhere in CD, so the first procedure is to look elsewhere. We therefore turn to 6:10–11 (again from Cairo manuscript A):

להתהלך במה בכל קץ הרשעה ... עד עמוד יורה הצדק באחרית הימים

To walk in them in all the period of wickedness ... until the rise of one who will teach righteousness at the end of days

Here again we have קץ הרשעה, התהלך and עד עמוד. And, as if we could not already have guessed, התהלך refers to obeying the sectarian laws, called the מחוקקות (which, the preceding text has stated, were introduced by a דורש התורה at some point in the past). It is the community halakhah or law which is at issue. The connection between this sectarian law and

---

[10]An interesting case could be made that 'law' and 'messiah' represent polarities in the developing confrontation of Christianity and rabbinic Judaism: 'Law' is the repressed category of Christianity (which constantly resurfaces in church discipline, in scholasticism and in modern fundamentalistic moralizing on the basis of 'biblical values'), while the messianic undertones of rabbinic Judaism have likewise shown themselves, in Aqiva, in Shabbatai Zevi, and in a disguised form in mediaeval and modern Zionism. This essay, unfortunately, is not the place to pursue such an argument.

the 'period of wickedness' is then underlined in 6:14 with the expression לעשות כפרוש התורה לקץ הרשע. The passages cited so far, then, make a link between (sectarian) law, the present period of time ('period of wickedness') and a future figure who will 'arise'. In one passage this figure is described as teaching צדק, in the other his title is 'messiah'.

The phrase 'law for the period of wickedness' is in some ways quite remarkable, however, because it implies a limited duration. Its validity will cease when the 'period of wickedness' ends, and that will coincide with the arrival of a messiah 'teaching righteousness'. Thus the messianic epithet is explained: teaching righteousness is an indication of the end of the period of wickedness. And why is the sectarian law valid only for the pre-eschatological period? We are not told, but we may conclude that since this law prescribed living in settlements and maintaining a limited connection with the Temple (and whatever else is dependent upon its current relationship with the Judean authorities and other Jews), it would cease with the restoration of true Israel to its Temple; at this time the sect would cease to be a sect, assuming its rightful role as the one true Israel.

When did the 'period of wickedness' begin? This question, I think, cannot be answered definitively, for the sin of Israel, according to CD commenced with the descent of the Watchers (2:17). It can be plausibly argued that 4:2–12 specifies such a period, which begins with the going out from the land of Judah. That passage also refers to the פרוש התורה (i.e., the sectarian interpretation of the Law) עד שלים הקץ (which I would take to be the קץ הרשע because 4:12 refers to Belial being let loose on Israel בכול השנים האלה). But perhaps the beginning of the period does not matter. The essential point is that the sectarian law is to be in force during this period, until it comes to an end. Thus, the sectarian law is to be understood as the Mosaic law as necessarily interpreted for a period in which Israel as a whole is disobedient and the Temple defiled by a rebellious priesthood.

We are left with the third question, whether there are two anointed ones implied in 12:23–13:1 or only one. The parallel between this passage and 6:11 actually suggests only one. Collins, together with a number of other scholars, maintains that there are two messiahs in CD. The phrase משיח אהרן וישראל is certainly ambiguous, though I do think that purely on syntax it is more likely to mean one person than two. But why *should* it be argued that CD expects two? Does CD itself offer any basis for this interpretation? Collins argues the case as well as it can be argued, but is unpersuasive. First, he interprets CD 6 in an impossible way, and then he misinterprets the passage which is reproduced differently in MS A page 7 and MS B page 9. In respect of CD 6, Collins tries to identify the 'interpreter of the law' of line 7 with the 'one teaching righteousness' in line 11.

But this is impossible, because the 'interpreter of the law' is clearly identified with the 'staff' (מחוקק) of Num 21:18, and this staff is referred to in
the perfect tense (חקק); he instituted the laws that the community follows.
The two individuals in CD 6, 'interpreter' and 'one teaching' stand at the
beginning and end of a passage that moves sequentially, even chiastically,
through community history: The one instituted the law for the period of
wickedness and the other will bring that period (and, in some way, that
law) to an end. It continues to baffle me (though strangely, not many
others!) that any exegete can manage to identify two figures so clearly
separated in the text. But the reason for this may be that Collins wishes to
extract a uniform two-messiah doctrine out of these manuscripts.

However, on the basis of the two texts discussed so far, the only
proper conclusion is that CD expects a single messiah, a teacher, who
will bring righteousness and signify the end of the period of wickedness.
While this is not a definitive conclusion as to the nature of the messiah
in D's Judaism, it is a useful starting-point.

There remains, however, one crucial passage to test this provisional
conclusion: CD 7:9b–13a and its equivalent in MS B. A translation of the
passages follows:[11]

> CD 7:10–21 (MS A)
> ... when the saying shall come to pass which is written] among the
> words of the Prophet Isaiah son of Amoz: *He will bring upon you,*
> *and upon your people, and upon your father's house, days such as*
> *have not come since the day that Ephraim departed from Judah* (Isa.
> vii, 17). When the two houses of Israel were divided, Ephraim
> departed from Judah. And all the apostates were given up to the
> sword, but those who held fast escaped to the land of the north; as
> God said, *I will exile the tabernacle of your king and the bases of*
> *your statues from my tent to Damascus* (Amos v, 26–7).
>
> The Books of the Law are the *tabernacle* of the kings; as God said,
> *I will raise up the tabernacle of David which is fallen* (Amos ix, 11).
> The *king* is the congregation; and the *bases of the statues* are the
> books of the Prophets whose saying Israel despised. The *star* is the
> Interpreter of the Law who came[12] to Damascus; as it is written, *A*
> *star shall come forth out of Jacob and a sceptre shall rise out of Israel*
> (Num. xxiv, 17). The *sceptre* is the Prince of the whole congregation,
> and when he comes *he shall smite all the children of Seth* (Num. xxiv,
> 17). At the time of the former Visitation they were saved, whereas the
> apostates were given up to the sword ....

---

[11]The translation follows G. Vermes, *The Complete Dead Sea Scrolls in English* (London
and New York: The Penguin Press, 1997) 132–3.

[12]Here Vermes (followed by Collins) read 'shall come'. The Hebrew reads ambiguously:
either a present participle or a perfect (past) tense.

CD 19:8–13 (MS B)

... when the saying shall come to pass which is written] by the hand of the prophet Zechariah: *Awake, O Sword, against my shepherd, against my companion, says God. Strike the shepherd that the flock may be scattered and I will stretch my hand over the little ones* (Zech. xiii, 7). The humble of the flock are those who watch for Him. They shall be saved at the time of the Visitation whereas the others shall be delivered up to the sword when the messiah[13] of Aaron and Israel shall come, as it came to pass at the time of the former Visitation concerning which God said by the hand of Ezekiel: *They shall put a mark on the foreheads of those who sigh and groan* (Ezek. ix, 4). But the others were delivered up to the avenging sword of the Covenant.

Manuscript A cites Isa 7:17 then Amos 5:26–27 and then interprets Num 24:17 with the 'star' read as the 'Interpreter of the Law' and the sceptre as the 'Prince of the Whole Congregation'. Manuscript B citing Zech 13:7 and Ezek 9:4 refers to the 'messiah of Israel and Aaron'. Thus we seem to have in the former an explicit separation of two messianic figures ('sceptre' and 'star') and in the latter a single (?) 'messiah of Israel and Aaron'.

Several suggestions have been offered to account for the difference in the two texts and to explicate their messianic content. Murphy-O'Connor argued at first[14] that the Amos-Numbers midrash in MS A was an interpolation; the original Zechariah-Ezekiel midrash had been left out through haplography and this midrash inserted at a later stage. He also argued that the opening Isaiah midrash was omitted, again by haplography. George Brooke[15] also accepted the priority of the MS B reading, but suggested that the omission of the Zechariah-Ezekiel midrash and the insertion of the Amos-Numbers midrash were part of a single process within the A text, whereby *two* Messiahs (star and sceptre) replaced the single Messiah (of Aaron and Israel) in the B text. My own position has been to agree with Brooke though for slightly different reasons.[16]

However, Murphy-O'Connor then revised his opinion and argued for the priority of the Amos-Numbers midrash in MS A.[17] Finally, Sidnie

---

[13]Vermes: 'Anointed' (somewhat ambiguously as to number!)

[14]J. Murphy-O'Connor, 'The Original Text of CD 7:9 – 8:2 = 19:5–14', *HTR* 64 (1971) 379–86.

[15]'The Amos-Numbers Midrash (CD 7,13b–8,1a) and Messianic Expectation', *ZAW* 92 (1980) 397–404.

[16]Philip R. Davies, *The Damascus Covenant. An Interpretation of the 'Damascus Document'* (Sheffield: JSOT Press, 1982) 145–55; for a response to Murphy-O'Connor's revised position (defending his original conclusion), see *Behind the Essenes. History and Ideology in the Dead Sea Scrolls* (Atlanta: Scholars Press, 1987) 37–40.

[17]J. Murphy-O'Connor, 'The Damascus Document Revisited', *RB* 92 (1987) 225–45.

White has argued[18] that we have two texts that have coincidentally suffered haplography, and that the original texts contained both the Amos-Numbers and Ezekiel-Zechariah midrashim. Collins agrees with her conclusion. Thus we have a variety of explanations: that A and B are prior; that the differences are deliberate, and they are accidental.

My previous last words on the subject were as follows:

On the whole, it does not seem to me profitable to speculate further. We can be reasonably sure that the history of the transmission of this document is complex, and this particular passage is apparently a victim of this complexity. Thus, any proposed account has a right to be complex itself. It will also, however, be speculative.[19]

That statement probably represents a wise verdict. But on reconsideration, one can estimate degrees of probability among the explanations, and then perhaps even go further. The White–Collins view claims Collins is simpler, but like Murphy-O'Connor's original suggestion, it entails two haplographies. One haplography may be misfortune; two looks like more than carelessness. Brooke's is technically the simplest. The White–Collins theory also supposes that the single original text spoke of *four* figures, an Interpreter of the Law, a Prince of the Whole Congregation, and two Messiahs. We could reduce this to three figures (against Collins) by having a single messiah of Aaron and Israel, but even so the overall effect would have been confusing. Collins identifies the 'Prince of the Whole Congregation' with the Messiah of Israel and the 'Interpreter of the Law' with the Messiah of Aaron. But while the former is certainly conceivable, the latter is not supported textually; and most problematic of all:, the supposed original text did not make this identification itself.

What has not been addressed by any commentator (including me) are two curiosities of the 'messianic' portion of the MS A midrash:

The *star* is the Interpreter of the Law who came to Damascus; as it is written, *A star shall come forth out of Jacob and a sceptre shall rise out of Israel* (Num. xxiv, 17). The *sceptre* is the Prince of the whole congregation, and when he comes *he shall smite all the children of Seth* (Num. xxiv, 17).

The first peculiarity is the *structure*: We have:

interpretation A: star = Interpreter of Law
textual basis (Num 24, mentioning star and sceptre)
interpretation B: sceptre = Prince of the whole congregation

---

[18]S. A. White, 'A Comparison of the "A" and "B" Manuscripts of the Damascus Document', *RevQ* 48 (1987) 537–53.
[19]*Behind the Essenes*, p. 40.

The second peculiarity is that the messianic topic has nothing to with what precedes. The themes of the two passages in MSS A and B are in fact *different*, although they have the same point of departure. The MS A passage is concerned with the exile (escape) of the community to 'Damascus'. There is no basis here for an abrupt introduction of messianic figures at all. By contrast, the theme of the MS B passage is the fate of the wicked, and here the 'messiah of Aaron and Israel' is smoothly introduced together with the Visitation. These considerations certainly raise a larger question mark about the relationship of the two passages, but more acutely about the history of the MS A text, whose original integrity does look questionable. They indicate the danger of making its explicit two-messiah presentation the basis for the interpretation of other texts in CD. In favour of the original integrity of MS B's text is the use of a term attested elsewhere in CD: 'Prince of the Whole Congregation', on the other hand, is used nowhere else in either manuscript.

This line of argument leads us further. The translation by Vermes (followed by Collins) in the MS A passage reads: the 'interpreter of the Law who shall come to Damascus'. This is certainly necessary if a messianic interpretation is to be given to the passage. But could such a figure move from being a past figure in CD 6 to a future one on p. 7? In fact, as represented in the translation given above, the phrase is more plausibly rendered 'who came to Damascus'. But if this is correct, the MS A passage is consistent with the earlier passage, but at the same time can hardly be messianic.

Although any reconstruction must be hypothetical, the following deduction seems fairly sound. The text of CD 7:10–20, which, I have just argued, refers to the time of the founding of the 'Damascus' community, when the righteous 'escaped', might have referred to the founder of the sect, who is known, according to CD 6:7, as the 'Interpreter of the Law'; and this it does, linking him to Num 24. The introduction of the 'sceptre' is secondary, inspired by the Num 24 passage. That addition, however, makes the text eschatological in import. Accordingly, at this layer of expansion, the 'Interpreter of the Law' also becomes a messianic figure. Proof that this person/title is also seen as eschatological in a Qumran text comes from 4QFlorilegium frgs. 1–3, col. 1:11, where he appears with the 'Branch of David'.

This conjectural solution (and *all* solutions to the problem of CD 7:10–21 are conjectural!) implies that the passage has undergone a revision into a messianic passage in which two figures are anticipated. It also implies that an original form of the text might have been consistent with MS B in presenting only one messianic figure, a 'messiah of Israel and Aaron', who was to 'teach righteousness at the end of days'.

The final piece in this jigsaw comes from CD 1:

... In the age of wrath, 390 years after delivering them into the power of Nebuchadnezzar, king of Babylon, he visited them, and caused to sprout from Israel and from Aaron, a root of planting ... and God recognized their deeds, that they sought him with a perfect heart, and raised up for them a teacher of righteousness, to direct them in the way of his heart ....

The 'teacher of righteousness' in this passage is not, indeed, called a 'messiah' and he is spoken of as a past figure. I have explained this in previous publications as due to a redaction of CD by the Teacher's followers, after the Teacher's death.[20] Here, rather than argue the case again, I want simply to point out that we have a group referred to as 'Israel and Aaron' provided with a single personage. In this can be seen a redacted reflection of an earlier expectation of a single messianic teacher from 'Israel and Aaron'.

My concentration on the two passages in CD 7 and 19 has been rather long and rather intricate, but nonetheless necessary in view of the prominence given to 'star and sceptre' in Collins's book. It has been necessary to show that a *single teacher-messiah* is the most consistent representation of the expectation of the Damascus community.

But in arguing for such a view, it has been necessary to concede that CD contains remnants of a different messianic expectation. First, 7:10–21 as we now have it presents two figures, and CD 1 situates the erstwhile teacher-messiah as a past figure. The two developments are related, because the arrival, and then the death, of a messianic figure necessitates either an abandonment or a revision of one's expectations.

To trace this process as reflected in CD we have to turn to 19:35–20:1 (MS B)

מיום האסף מורה היחיד עד עמוד משיח מאהרן ומישראל

From the time of gathering in of the unique teacher [read 'teacher of the *yahad*'] until the rise of a messiah from Aaron and from Israel

Here we have a teacher *and* a messiah of Aaron and Israel, who are not identical. Now this juxtaposition is especially problematic for Collins, who is arguing that the Teacher *is* the 'messiah of Aaron'. It is, of course, possible that we are dealing with different 'teachers' in 6:11 and 20:1. But already we have enough characters without adding more and in any case, in accepting (with most scholars) an emendation from מורה היחיד to מורה היחד, and thus identifying him with the מורה הצדק who

---

[20]Or, to be more precise, after the death of the person claimed by his followers to have been the expected teacher.

appears in CD 1. Given that CD 1 presents a two-stage community formation, with the Teacher arriving within an existing group, it is not difficult to accept that this Teacher is, in retrospect, the one anticipated in CD 6:11 as the figure who would come at the 'end of days', bring to an end the 'period of wickedness' and who is identified in CD 12:23–13:1 as the 'messiah of Aaron and Israel'.

Thus, strictly speaking, CD has *no* consistent view of who bears the title 'messiah'. But it also has no consistent view on whether the 'teacher' is past or future. We can, however resolve both problems with the aid of a fairly simple redactional explanation, and in doing so we can also detect a shift in the messianic expectations of those who preceded and those who followed this 'teacher'.

For from the perspective of the *redacted* CD, the Teacher is not merely a figure of the present time, but one who is now dead. CD 20:13–14 reads :

ומיום האסף יורה היחיד עד תם כל אנשי המלחמה אשר שבו]ע[ם איש הכוב כשנים ארבעים

from the day of the gathering in of the יורה היחיד to the end ' ' all the men of war who returned with the 'man of the lie' (see CD 1:15) is forty years or so.

Here the period following the death of the Teacher is already one of about forty years. I do not place much significance on the reference to 'men of war' because of the presence of scriptural quotation here (Deut 2:14–15), which probably implies that the Teacher was a second Moses. At any rate, a messianic figure who had died and is now referred to in the past is no longer part of the eschaton, and, if any messianic expectation is to continue, he must be replaced. It appears that his followers did indeed provide an illustration of 'cognitive dissonance', namely in confronting a gap that had appeared between reality and their requirements of it, and adjusting their perception accordingly, without apparent detriment to their earlier beliefs.

But the phraseology of CD 19:35 – 20:1 is very significant here. It does not read 'until the arrival of the messiah of Aaron and Israel', but 'until a messiah should arise from Aaron and from Israel'. To me this evokes the famous statement in *1 Macc* 14:41: 'until a faithful prophet should arise', and suggests not a firm deadline, but an indefinite period of time. If so (and one can read too much into texts) it would not be surprising for a renewed messianic expectation in these circumstances to be somewhat tentative. The immediately following passage (CD 20:15–17) might confirm this impression:

ובקץ ההוא יחרה אף אל בישראל כאשר אמר אין מלך ואין
שר ואין שופט ואין מוכיח בצדק

> And in this period [after the Teacher's death] the anger of God will
> be kindled against Israel, as it says, 'no king and no prince and no
> judge and no-one to instruct in righteousness' (Hos 3:4)

The period reflected in the passage is one in which the voice of righteousness is lost with the absence of the Teacher. I am not sure that there
is a sure hope expressed here for another quick messianic appearance.

We can confirm even further that the Teacher was in fact understood
by his followers as the one would bring the period of wickedness to an
end, as anticipated in CD 6:11, from two more texts in CD. In
20:27–28, we find a reference to those who 'hold fast to these rules
(משפטים) by going in and out according to the Law, and listen to the voice
of the Teacher'. The phrasing very clearly adds to the authority of the
law that also of the teacher. The implication in CD 6:11 that this
person's arrival would have an effect on the 'law for the period of
wickedness' seems confirmed; the Teacher was, the phrase implies,
regarded as having an authority alongside the law, perhaps *in effect* even
superior to it. The legal authority of the Teacher is reiterated in 20:32,
where indeed the Teacher's voice now represents what are called חקי הצדק
– and no reference to other laws or commandments here! A question I
will not pursue here is whether the teacher was expected to have the
power to abrogate the law. This passage shows he was accorded the
authority to interpret it and to add to it. But the crucial question is to
what extent the 'law' means a permanent and unalterable divine revelation to Moses (the scriptural law) and how much it also incorporates
the interpretation of the 'Interpreter of the Law' who truly interpreted it
for the Damascus community during the 'period of wickedness'/'period
of wrath'. As I suggested earlier, it seems to me that the role of the
messianic teacher was to oversee the cessation of a sectarian true Israel
and bring in the eschatological period of full restoration, in which full
restoration of the law of Moses would be paramount.

III

The role of the messiah in the Judaism of CD has taken up rather a lot
of time, but I hope to have established that the original expectation of
the Damascus community was of a single anointed figure whose primary
task was related to the restoration of righteousness and the ending of
the period of wickedness when the sectarian law needed to be upheld. I
do not see here a dual messiahship, nor a Davidic figure; even though
there are strong hints of a military style of punishment at the divine
visitation, it is not asserted that the messiah-teacher will personally
wield a sword.

But it is now time to turn to 1QS. In the phrase 'teacher of the *yahad*' in CD we have already been alerted to the authorship of the redactional layer(s); the followers of the teacher refer to themselves as the *yahad*. Thus we may look for some consonance between the messianic expectations of the redactional layer(s) of CD and the Serekh materials.

In 1QS 9:10–12 we have a passage that confirms what was gleaned from CD 20 about the status of the Teacher in the *yahad*:

ונשפטו במשפטים הרשונים אשר החלו אנשי היחד לתיסר בם עד בוא

נביא ומשיחי אהרון וישראל

They shall be judged by the former judgments in which the men of the *yahad* began to be instructed, until the rise of a prophet and the messiahs of Aaron and Israel.

Schiffman rightly contrast this with CD; here there is no question but that we have two messianic figures. The ruling reflects an attitude similar to that found in CD: The present regime will continue until the arrival of the messiah(s). A teaching-judging function still attaches to the messiahs. There remains a realization in the *yahad* that the *legal* regime of the community at any rate, is temporary and is to change with the arrival of a definitive messianic figure or figures.[21] The prophet, too, is absent from CD. We seem to be dealing with an evolution in expectation.[22] But while the expectation is now of two messiahs rather than one, the *yahad* material (the various editions of S) appear relatively uninterested in messianic matters. It may be unwise to judge too conclusively from the selection of material compiled in 1QS and the Cave 4 fragments, but it does not seem that the eschatology of the *yahad* offered much scope for messianic activity. The only explicit eschatological passage in 1QS is the 'two spirits' section in cols. 3–4, and this does not offer any place in its scheme of messianic deliverance. Its dualistic system operates at a different level. Consequently, I am impelled to the startling conclusion that, while the (teaching) messiah is extremely important to the Judaism of the Damascus community, the messianic office is systemically redundant in the S materials. The *yahad* may have had some messianic expectations, but it did not need them, and does not seem to have written much about them. Here, as I have found also in the case of 'Israel', Torah' and 'Temple', there is a distinct difference between the two Judaisms of CD and S; in this case, however, the difference is quite dramatic.

---

[21]For a detailed investigation of this passage and its historical rleationship to CD, see my 'Communities at Qumran and the Case of the Missing Teacher', *RevQ* 15 (1991) 275–86.

[22]That assumption is strengthened by the fact that the section in which the text occurs is missing in 4QS^e.

There remain other texts, of course, to be addressed. In particular, the place of the messiah in 1QSa and 1QM, the *Florilegium* and elsewhere (where the figure occurs) deserves treatment. I have observed previously the curious lack of a role for a warrior messiah in the *War Scroll*, and noted above the transformation of the title 'Interpreter of the Law' into an eschatological figure in the *Florilegium*. But a survey of the remainder of the Qumran texts suggests to me that 'messiah' is *not* a 'principle of coherence' throughout the corpus; indeed, in many texts such a figure is absent. Where a messiah *is* systemically important to a particular text, we may well find considerable variation, as for example if we compare CD with the Melchizedek midrash.

One important conclusion to emerge from a study of the Judaism of the Qumran scrolls is that a comparison of topics (such as messianism) across the various compositions does not generally lead to useful results. Only an analysis of the Judaic *systems*, by which I mean the structural relationships between various elements of which a Judaism is composed, can offer critical access to the history and ideology of the texts and, together with the necessary textual analysis and distinctions between texts, yield a picture of the Judaisms of the Qumran scrolls.

In the case of 'messiah' such an investigation (far from exhaustive as yet) has suggested that only where the messiah is connected to the law do we find the arrival of an anointed figure to be of any particularly systemic significance. This, of course, by no means rules out connections to the New Testament, and in particular the gospel of Matthew. The fact than in all of the gospels the activity of their messiah consists largely in teaching should by no means be overlooked; for an understanding of the Judaism of the gospels, it may be more significant than any 'Davidic' title.

14

THE BRANCH IN THE LAST DAYS: OBSERVATIONS ON THE NEW COVENANT BEFORE AND AFTER THE MESSIAH

Håkan Ulfgard

In this paper I shall focus on some central elements of Qumranite and early Christian self-understanding and theological confession. Not least from the point of view of New Testament exegesis and the study of Christian origins this is a topic which involves concepts of crucial significance. As scholarly research and discussion has developed in recent years, there are strong reasons for intensifying studies on the relationship between the Judaism of the Qumran texts and of the earliest 'Jesus Movement', especially concerning messianic and eschatological ideas. It has also become increasingly clear that the historical questions pertaining to the origins of the Christian Church need to be penetrated anew. What should be discussed, for example, is to which extent the 'post-Easter Jesus Movement' may have been influenced by people, whose messianic, eschatological, ethical and ecclesiological ideas coincide with what we find in the Qumran texts. Or should possible similarities merely be explained as due to the sharing of a common ideological or theological background? These are issues of great relevance not only for the study of early Christianity. They also concern the picture at large of the ideological plurality and development within Judaism in antiquity.[1]

I shall concentrate on Qumranite and early Christian messianism, especially focusing on the expression נצר ('branch', 'shoot') but also taking into account related concepts, against the background of the common Qumranite and early Christian presuppositions of living in 'the

---

[1]Some examples from recent research dealing with these issues include two studies by the French Dominican at the Ecole Biblique in Jerusalem, E. Nodet: *Essaie sur les origines du Judaïsme* (Paris: Cerf, 1992), and *Essaie sur les origines du Christianisme* (Paris: Cerf, 1998) – the last one co-authored with J. Taylor of the Ecole Biblique. The list of relevant studies could easily be prolonged; just let me recall the two volumes edited by J. H. Charlesworth: *Jesus and the Dead Sea Scrolls* (New York: Doubleday, 1992), and *The Messiah: Developments in Earliest Judaism and Christianity* (Minneapolis: Fortress Press, 1992) (the extensive foot-notes in his introductory chapter in the former volume represent a true bibliographical treasury!), and not to forget the important contributions in *Judaisms and Their Messiahs at the Turn of the Christian Era* eds. J. Neusner, W. S. Green and E. S. Frerichs (Cambridge: Cambridge University Press, 1987), and also by J. J. Collins in his *The Scepter and the Star: The Messiahs of the Dead Sea Scrolls and Other Ancient Literature* (New York: Doubleday, 1995).

last days', אחרית הימים, as the elect community of 'the New Covenant'.[2] There will, unfortunately, be no time in this brief presentation to dwell upon related issues of a general kind, such as shared eschatological awareness, or to follow up on the implications concerning other basic presuppositions or characteristics held in common, e.g. actualizing scriptural interpretation or transcendent ecclesiology, nor to comment on the similar, though also different, roles of the Teacher of Righteousness and Jesus as revealers of divine secrets and true *torah*. What has to be borne in mind, though, is the obvious difference in temporal perspective of those who have produced respectively the Qumran scrolls and the New Testament writings: in the one case, the Messiah is still awaited, but in the other, he has already come.

There are two points that I should like to call to special attention concerning the נצר (and related) ideology. The first point relates to the juxtaposition of individual and collective self-understanding and messianic expectation attested both in the Qumran texts and in the New Testament writings. The second point – much more controversial, I think, and involving much more speculation – concerns Jesus' messianic self-consciousness and the history of the Jesus movement in view of the tensions within various strands of the earliest Christian testimony. I shall here get into the subject of Davidic messianism, which is a current 'hot topic'.[3]

I

First, then, Qumranite messianic metaphorical language involving the expression נצר and related concepts.[4] What I especially have in mind is the actualizing, messianic exegesis of the Isaianic prophecies about the saving 'stump' or 'root' which will grow from the family tree of Jesse. Isa 11:1: 'A shoot shall come out from the stump of Jesse, and a branch shall grow out of his roots (וְיָצָא חֹטֶר מִגֵּזַע יִשַׁי וְנֵצֶר מִשָּׁרָשָׁיו יִפְרֶה).' While three nouns, חֹטֶר, נֵצֶר, and שֹׁרֶשׁ are used in the plant metaphor in this text, one

[2] An excellent comprehensive study of the concept of 'the End of Days' in the Qumran literature is found in A. Steudel, 'אחרית הימים in the Texts from Qumran', *RevQ* 16 (1993) 225–46.

[3] I am referring to the online course on mediator figures in the biblical tradition, run by James Davila at St. Andrews University, in which the Davidic traditions have been the subject for study and electronic discussion. Web address: http://www.st-andrews.ac.uk/~www_sd/mediators.html.

[4] A most valuable synthetic presentation of messianic texts from Qumran, with special attention to their significance for the New Testament, is found in C. A. Evans, 'Jesus and the Messianic Texts from Qumran: A Preliminary Assessment of the Recently Published Materials' in *idem, Jesus and His Contemporaries* (Comparative Studies [AGJU 25]; Leiden: Brill, 1995) 83–154.

of them, שֶׁרֶשׁ, reappears some verses later, in 11:10: 'On that day the root of Jesse shall stand as a signal to the peoples; the nations shall inquire of him, and his dwelling shall be glorious (וְהָיָה בַּיּוֹם הַהוּא שֶׁרֶשׁ יִשַׁי אֲשֶׁר עֹמֵד לְנֵס עַמִּים אֵלָיו גּוֹיִם יִדְרֹשׁוּ וְהָיְתָה מְנֻחָתוֹ כָּבוֹד).' Furthermore, closely connected with this metaphorical language there are some expressions that speak of a Davidic 'branch' (צֶמַח), and that likewise carry a clear potential for messianic exegesis. Thus, e.g., Jer 23:5 and 33:15 speak about the 'righteous branch (צֶמַח צְדָקָה/צֶמַח צַדִּיק)' that God will raise for David. In Zechariah the expected saving figure is simply called 'the Branch'; cf. Zech 3:8: 'I am going to bring my servant the Branch' (כִּי־הִנְנִי מֵבִיא אֶת־עַבְדִּי צֶמַח), and Zech 6:12f: 'Thus says the Lord of hosts: Here is a man whose name is Branch: for he shall branch out in his place, and he shall build the temple of the Lord' (כֹּה אָמַר יְהוָה צְבָאוֹת לֵאמֹר הִנֵּה־אִישׁ צֶמַח שְׁמוֹ וּמִתַּחְתָּיו יִצְמָח וּבָנָה אֶת־הֵיכַל יְהוָה). Cf. the 'growth metaphors' in Ps 132:17: ' . . . I will cause a horn to sprout up for David' (אַצְמִיחַ קֶרֶן לְדָוִד), and in David's farewell speech, 2 Sam 23:1–5: 'Will he not cause to prosper all my help and my desire?' (כִּי־כָל־יִשְׁעִי וְכָל־חֵפֶץ כִּי־לֹא יַצְמִיחַ). From later times, other well-known and clear-cut examples of such Davidic messianism are found in e.g. *Pss. Sol.* 17, *T. Judah* 24 and 4 Ezra 12:31–32. But there is also a strong potential for messianic exegesis in the prophetic metaphor describing the coming era of salvation in Isa 4:2: 'On that day the branch of the Lord shall be beautiful and glorious' (יְהוָה לִצְבִי וּלְכָבוֹד בַּיּוֹם הַהוּא יִהְיֶה צֶמַח). Particularly in this passage the plant metaphor allows for both an individual and a collective interpretation. The same goes for the parallel expression about 'the planting of the Lord' (מַטַּע יְהוָה) in Isa 61:3.

In a recent article in *Dead Sea Discoveries*, Patrick A. Tiller has studied the use of the plant metaphor in the Qumran writings.[5] Under the title: 'The "Eternal Planting" in the Dead Sea Scrolls', he briefly accounts for the scriptural background of the expression, followed by a longer analysis of its appearance in para-biblical literature such as *1 Enoch* and *Jubilees* (*1 Enoch* 10:16; 84:6; 93:5 and 10; *Jub.* 1:16; 16:26; 21:24; 36:6), in the manuscripts from Qumran (4Q415–418, 1QS 8:5; 11:8; 1QHᵃ 6(14):15; 8(16):6), and also in CD 1:7–8.[6] In his conclusions, he especially draws attention to the narrowing down of the metaphor in the Qumran literature to refer only to the community of the elect, the true remnant of Israel. He also points out how the metaphor is associated with the concept of the earthly community

---

[5]*DSD* 4 (1997) 312–35.

[6]See also the older article by S. Fujita, 'The Metaphor of Plant in Jewish Literature of the Intertestamental Period', *JSJ* 7 (1976) 30–45, exploring the rich symbolism evoked by the use of this imagery.

participating in the heavenly worship of God, according to the Qumran texts. As to the relationship between the various writings in which the metaphor is used, he thinks that the differing ways in which it is used do not indicate that there can have been any direct historical or socio-logical connections. Rather, he prefers to speak about a shared 'cultural and historical matrix'.[7]

Tiller's article is a significant contribution to the ongoing discussion concerning the conceptual and hermeneutical world of the Qumran writings. However, I should like to broaden his scope, and at the same time to draw some implications for our understanding of the earliest Jesus movement, by focusing on the concepts 'shoot' or 'branch' (especially נצר, but also צמח), and by bringing the New Testament usage of these concepts into discussion. What is especially significant is that the Isaianic prophecies about 'the shoot/branch' of Jesse, together with related sayings such as those about 'the branch of David' in Jer 23:5 and 33:15, belong to a cluster of concepts, related to plant imagery, which evidently must have been very important for expressing not only ideas about a coming messianic figure, but also for expressing the collective 'messianic' self-understanding revealed both in the Qumran scrolls and in the New Testament writings. Thus, for instance, the messianic impli-cations in the stem נ–צ–ר, used as a verb meaning 'to keep', should be noted. In Isa 42:6 and 49:6, the servant of the Lord is told that 'I [God] have ... kept you' (אֶצָּרְךָ) and that one of his tasks is to 'restore the survivors of Israel' (וּנְצִירֵי יִשְׂרָאֵל).[8] The oscillation between individual messianism and collective expectation involving the whole community of the chosen, using a shared imagery, is convincingly analysed by Annette Steudel in her article 'The Eternal Reign of the People of God – Collective Expectations in Qumran Texts (4Q246 and 1QM)'.[9] Steudel's article is closely related to Hartmut Stegemann's recon-struction of the successive stages in the development of Qumranite messianism, according to which there is a historically conditioned shift after the middle of the second century BCE from a – so to speak – collective to an individual messianism.[10]

---

[7]*DSD* 4 (1997) 334.

[8]Among many valuable studies, apart from Tiller's, see especially Collins' *The Sceptre and the Star* (pp. 49–73). Cf. also the short account of the relevant passages in the Qumran texts by J. C. VanderKam, 'Messianism in the Scrolls', in *The Community of the Renewed Covenant* eds. E. Ulrich and J. C. VanderKam (Notre Dame, Indiana: University of Notre Dame Press, 1994) 216–18.

[9]*RevQ* 17 (1996) 507–25.

[10]Cf. his article 'Some Remarks to *1QSa*, to *1QSb*, and to Qumran Messianism' in the same issue of *RevQ* as Steudel's, 479–505; see especially pp. 501–5. See also the earlier and still valuable attempt at reconstructing the history of messianism in the Qumran writings by J. Starcky, 'Les quatre étapes du messianisme à Qumrân', *RB* 70 (1963) 481–505.

Regarding the earliest 'Jesus Movement', then, what I should particularly like to emphasize is the application of the prophetical plant metaphor and its related concepts not only to Jesus, the individual Messiah, but also to the Christian community, which considered itself as the true remnant of Israel in the last days. Especially, this concerns the apparent similarity between the Hebrew word for 'branch' or 'shoot', נֵצֶר, and the designation in Greek of Jesus as ὁ Ναζαρηνός or ὁ Ναζωραῖος.[11] Let me just recall that this last epithet is also used to denote the young Jesus movement in Acts 24:5, where Paul is accused of causing trouble among the Jews throughout the world as the leader of the 'Nazorean sect', ἡ τῶν Ναζωραίων αἵρεσις. In fact, beyond its use as a simple geographical designation to denote where this sect came from, Jesus' followers in the renewed covenant could claim scriptural support for such an appellation in Jer 31. Precisely in this chapter, culminating with the prophecy about God's new covenant with Israel and Judah (31:31), it is stated that there will be נֹצְרִים proclaiming God's salvation and the return to Zion (31:6).[12]

In the Isaiah pesher from Qumran, 4Q161 ([4QpIsᵃ] 8–10 iii 11–25), the passage from ch. 11:1ff about a branch coming out from the root of Jesse is quoted at length. The text is explained as referring to '... the shoot] of David which will sprout [in the final days ...', after which the author goes on to speak about his royal glory, dominion and judgement over the whole world. The same militant imagery involving 'the shoot ... from the stump of Jesse' and 'the bud of David' also appears in the much-discussed text 4Q285 (frg. 5). Robert Eisenman caused some sensation by claiming that this is a text about a 'pierced Messiah', but his reading has been widely – and rightly – refuted.[13] In particular, it should be noted that the whole passage is a demonstration of God's sovereign authority and triumph, taking Isa 10:34ff as its point of departure.

The term צמח דויד ('the Branch of David'), used in the context of

[11]For a comprehensive overview of scholarly discussion and a presentation of the various exegetical possibilities, see R. E. Brown, *The Birth of the Messiah. A Commentary on the Infancy Narratives in the Gospels of Matthew and Luke*, new updated edition (London: Geoffrey Chapman / New York: Doubleday, 1993), 209–13 (bibliography p. 230). Among earlier studies devoted to the 'Nazorean' question, see especially B. Gärtner, 'Die rätselhaften Termini Nazoräer und Iskariot', in *Horæ Sœderblomianæ* 4 (Uppsala: Gleerup, 1957) 5–36.

[12]Cf. E. Zolli, ' "Nazarenus vocabitur" ', ZNW 49 (1958) 135–6.

[13]Cf. G. Vermes, T. H. Lim and R. P. Gordon, 'The Oxford Forum for Qumran Research Seminar of the Rule of War from Cave 4 (4Q285)', JJS 43 (1992) 85–90; L. H. Schiffman, *Reclaiming the Dead Sea Scrolls. The History of Judaism, the Background of Christianity, the Lost Library of Qumran* (Philadelphia/Jerusalem: The Jewish Publication Society, 1994) 344–7, 446; and J. C. VanderKam, *The Dead Sea Scrolls Today* (Grand Rapids, Mich.: Eeerdmans, 1994) 179–80.

expressing the hope for a Davidic Messiah, is also found in 4Q252 (4QpGen^a 5:1–6). Jacob's blessing of his son Judah (Gen 49:10) is interpreted as referring to 'the messiah of justice ... the branch of David'. An eternal 'covenant of royalty' has been given to him and his descendants; these descendants apparently being identified with the 'men of the Community' according to the fragmentary remains of the following text.

But an even more informative text on the messianic 'branch' in the last days is found in the collage of *pesharim* in 4Q174 (4QFlorilegium). In its combination of several scriptural passages in order to put the history of the community into an actualizing eschatological perspective, the prophecy of Nathan in 2 Sam 7:11–14 about a future heir to the throne of David is understood as referring to the 'branch of David' (צמח דויד), who will appear together with 'the Interpreter of the Law' (דורש התורה) in the last days. Cf. col. 1, ll. 11–12: 'This (refers to the) "branch of David", who will rise with the Interpreter of the law who [will rise up] in Zi[on in] the last days ...'

However, the reference to David is not merely used to express the expectation of an individual messianic figure, i.e. the traditional royal and Davidic messianism. It is also associated with the restoration of the *torah*, with an implied collective reference. While the individual Davidic messianism in 4QFlorilegium is supported by quoting from Amos 9:11: 'I will raise up the booth of David which has fallen', a collective implication is found in another central Qumranite text, CD 7:14–18. Here, the author gives a historical account of the 'Damascus Movement' in a combined interpretation of Amos 5:26f and 9:11: 'As he [God] said: "I will deport the Sikkut of your King and the Kiyyum of your images away from my tent to Damascus". The books of the law are the Sukkat of the King, as he said "I will lift up the fallen Sukkat of David". The King is the assembly; and the plinths of the images "and the Kiyyum of the images" are the books of the prophets, whose words Israel despised.' This collective understanding, associated with the restoration of the *torah*, may also be detected in 4QFlor ll. 6–7, declaring God's 'house ... in the last days' (l. 2) to be a מקדש אדם, a 'human temple' (or a 'temple of Adam') in which the 'works of the law' will be offered unto God (cf. the interpretation of Ps 2:1 in ll. 18–19). As regards the concept of מקדש אדם, I agree with the argument of George Brooke in favour of retaining both senses of the Hebrew expression as a way of denoting 'a community anticipating the eschatological sanctuary and as referring to an Adamic sanctuary of Eden restored'.[14]

---

[14]See G. J. Brooke, '4Q500 1 and the Use of Scripture in the Parable of the Vineyard', *DSD* 2 (1995) 275–9 (quotation from p. 278).

In passing, the use of Amos 9:11 in the account of the 'apostle meeting' in Jerusalem in Acts 15:13–21 should be noted. James, the 'brother of the Lord' quotes from Amos 9:11f to support his opinion concerning the inclusion of non-Jews into the Jewish Christian community. Neither the Qumranite nor the Christian versions correspond to the Masoretic Hebrew. But whereas the Qumranite authors take the text to speak about the restoration of the *torah* and research into its deeper meaning, led by the דורש התורה, the Christian author of Acts seems to depend on the LXX version, in which the text from Amos refers to the repentance of the non-Jews. Thus, James is establishing his idea of correct *torah* in the messianic age inaugurated by Jesus, when pagans have begun to seek the Lord, asking to be accepted as members of the true people of God in the era of salvation.

II

Coming to my second point, some reflections on the Davidic messianism among the Christian 'New Covenanters', there are three passages which are illuminated in a special way by the texts from Qumran. In its turn, this will call for some further considerations on the self-understanding of the first Christians. I am here especially referring to the designation 'Nazoreans' for the followers of Jesus in Acts 24:5, which was also the self-designation of the early Syrian Church. Another issue involves the messianic ecclesiology of the Book of Revelation, not least the way in which its use of 'Trito-Isaiah' in the final vision of the 'New Jerusalem' may illuminate the connection between this particular type of early Christianity and the Judaism of the Dead Sea Scrolls.

The three New Testament texts that I should like to draw attention to are Rom 15:12; Rev 5:5 (cf. 22:16) and Matt 2:23. In the focus of the first one is the role of Jesus as the Saviour of both Jews and Gentiles, in the second his role as warrior and victor in the eschatological battle, and in the third his designation 'Nazorean'.

In Romans 15, Paul ends his pleading for the unity of all believers by a catalogue of scriptural quotations in vv. 7–12. Once again salvation for both Jews and Gentiles through Jesus, the Messiah is affirmed, with Gentile participation especially emphasized by four quotations, the last of which is from Isa 11:10 (LXX): '... and again Isaiah says, "The root of Jesse shall come, the one who rises to rule the Gentiles; in him the Gentiles shall hope".'[15] Thus, Paul clinches his

---

[15]καὶ ἔσται ἐν τῇ ἡμέρᾳ ἐκείνῃ ἡ ῥίζα τοῦ Ἰεσσαὶ καὶ ὁ ἀνιστάμενος ἄρχειν ἐθνῶν ἐπ᾽ αὐτῷ ἔθνη ἐλπιοῦσιν. For critical notes on the 'coming' of 'the root of Jesse', according to some modern Bible translations, cf. B. Frid, 'Jesaja und Paulus in Röm 15,12', *BZ* 27 (1983) 237–41.

argument about universal salvation, thereby also legitimizing his gospel and special mission to the Gentiles by making use of the messianic potential of the prophetic text. But it should be noted that Paul never speaks about Jesus as 'the Nazorean' or as 'Jesus from Nazareth'. Though Paul does acknowledge Davidic messianism applied to Jesus (cf. Rom 1:3), this is effected in a way that makes it subordinated under the Pauline idea of universal mission. Within the Pauline orbit, the notice about the Antiochan designation of Jesus' followers as χριστιανοί in Acts 11:26 accentuates the derogatory use of the term Ναζωραῖοι in Acts 24:5. It may be that these details indicate differences and tension among the earliest followers of Jesus, such as outlined by Etienne Nodet and Justin Taylor in their recent *Essaie sur les origines du Christianisme*.[16]

The second text, Rev 5:5, provides a comment on the vision of the slaughtered but victorious Lamb, the only one who is worthy of opening the sealed scroll in which God's secrets are contained. At the end of the book, Jesus himself affirms his messianic dignity in 22:16. Both designations, 'the root of David' (ἡ ῥίζα Δαυίδ) and 'the root and the descendant of David' (ἡ ῥίζα καὶ τὸ γένος Δαυίδ) refer to the prophecies of Isa 11:1 and 10. It is also apparent that the context in Isaiah 11 may give some significant clues for the particular christology of Revelation.[17] Thus, the seven spirits held by the Lamb/Jesus in Rev 5:6 (cf. 1:4; 3:1; 4:9) clearly allude to Isa 11:2f with its prophecy about God's manifold Spirit, the *spiritus septiformans* (in particular if the LXX text is read). Here is the Davidic descendant, invested with the Spirit of the Lord. A few verses further on, the universal scope of Isa 11:10 is reflected in the statement about the saving effect of the blood of the Lamb for people of every 'tribe and language' etc. (cf. 7:9; 10:11; 11:9; 13:7; 14:6; 17:15), evoking similar universal formulations in Dan 4:1 and 6:26, at the same time as there is also an echo of the Isaianic 'Servant Song' in Isa 52:13–53:12.

There are good reasons to look further into the way other scriptural references are interwoven in the fabric of John's text as far as the Davidic messianism of Rev 5:5 and 22:16 is concerned. In 5:5, the allusion to the Isaianic prophecy is combined with Jacob's blessing of the lion-like Judah in Gen 49:9f, and in 22:16 with the prophecy about the star rising out of Jacob and a sceptre out of Israel in Num 24:17. What is especially noteworthy is the similar combined exposition of

---

[16]Pp. 254–65; for bibliographical details, see above, n. 1.

[17]See J. Fekkes III, 'Isaiah and Prophetic Traditions in the Book of Revelation', in *Visionary Antecedents and their Development* (JSNTSup 93; Sheffield, 1994) 150–3; however, he is more concerned with Rev's use of single texts from Isaiah than with christological and ecclesiological issues.

these scriptural passages in CD 7:18–20, in which 'the star' is identified with 'the Interpreter of the Law', whereas 'the sceptre' is understood as 'the Prince of the Community', i.e. the royal Messiah.[18] Similar ideas are also found in *T. Judah* 24 and in *T. Levi* 18:3, and in 1Q 28b there is here a description of a ruler like a lion, combining motifs from Isa 11 and Gen 49.

But perhaps the most consequential perspectives are opened by the third New Testament text, Matt 2:23. For generations, biblical translators and scholars, together with pious Bible readers, have contributed to reducing the potential charge in the messianic formulation 'Jesus of Nazareth'. However, Matt 2:23 reveals the deeper significance of this standard formula, apart from its superficial geographical meaning: 'There he (Joseph) made his home in a town called Nazareth, so that what had been spoken through the prophets might be fulfilled, "He will be called a Nazorean."' (ὅπως πληρωθῇ τὸ ῥηθὲν διὰ τῶν προφητῶν ὅτι Ναζωραῖος κληθήσεται).[19] In the extensive discussion about the meaning of the expression Ναζωραῖος κληθήσεται,[20] it has been argued – with substantial evidence – that this is a reference to the Hebrew expression נזיר. Especially, attention has been drawn to the story about Samson in Judg 13:5, in which his birth is heralded by an angel, declaring that he will be sacred unto God and that he will save Israel.[21] Similarly, strong arguments speak in favour of seeing an allusion to Isaiah's prophecy about the 'branch of Jesse' (11:1; נצר). The wider reference would then also include the verb 'to keep' (נצר), and hence not only refer to the 'branch prophecy' of Isa 11, but to the Servant Song of 42:6 as well.[22] It is an apparent fact that the whole context of the latter passage may be applied to the Jesus figure of the gospels. Here is the birth of the one who is to become a light unto the nations, and who will open the eyes of the blind and liberate those in prison and slavery. The light motif in Isa 42:6 may be seen in combination with the earlier prophecy in 9:2–7 about the

---

[18]See further, Collins, *The Sceptre and the Star*, 63–4.

[19]Apart from the study by Brown, quoted above, n. 11 (and the works cited in his bibliography), see J. A. Sanders, 'Ναζωραῖος in Matthew 2.23', and – though less devoted to this particular text – R. Pesch, "'He will be called a Nazorean": Messianic Exegesis in Matthew 1–2'; both articles appearing in *The Gospels and the Scriptures of Israel* eds. C. A. Evans and W. R. Stegner (JSNTSup 104; Sheffield: JSOT Press, 1994) 116–28 and 129–78.

[20]Cf. the bibliography in Sanders, 'Ναζωραῖος', 117, n 1.

[21]Cf. LXX[A] Judg 13:5: ἰδοὺ σὺ ἐν γαστρὶ ἕξεις καὶ τέξῃ υἱόν· καὶ οὐκ ἀναβήσεται σίδηρος ἐπὶ τὴν κεφαλὴν αὐτοῦ ὅτι ἡγιασμένον ναζιραῖον ἔσται τῷ θεῷ τὸ παιδάριον ἐκ τῆς γαστρός καὶ αὐτὸς ἄρξεται σῴζειν τὸν Ισραηλ ἐκ χειρὸς ἀλλοφύλων. This is the interpretation preferred by Sanders, 'Ναζωραῖος', and, before him (among others), H. H. Schaeder, Ναζαρηνός, Ναζωραῖος, *TDNT* 4, 874–9. However, unlike John the Baptist (cf. Luke 1:15), the Jesus of the gospels is never depicted as a *nazir*; cf. e. g. Matt 11:19; Luke 7:34.

[22]Gärtner, *Die rätselhaften Termini*, 13–18, followed by Brown, *Birth of the Messiah*, 213.

people walking in darkness and the birth of the messianic child, who will rule over David's kingdom. Even more, it may also be connected with the prophecy in Isa 60:3 about universal pilgrimage to the glorified Zion. And just to mention one other passage, Luke's account of Jesus' programmatic appearance in the synagogue of Nazareth (4:18) with its quotation from Isa 61:1f (LXX), shows some clear signs of being related to both the נצר prophecy in Isa 11:2 (the presence of the spirit of the Lord) and to the proclamation of divine healing and liberation in Isa 42:7 (sight to the blind, release of prisoners).

However, the quest for a scriptural background to Matt 2:23 must not be reduced to a question of either–or.[23] It should be noted that the Matthean text just once refers what the *prophets* – in the plural! – have said. Since, in ancient Judaism, the Book of Judges is included among the prophets (the Earlier Prophets), the author may very well have been alluding to both Isa 11 and 42, and to the Samson story in Judg 13, as he makes his claim that Jesus is the fulfilment of Scripture. Furthermore, it is not clear that the author is quoting precisely from a previously existing formulation. At least there is no known text with the same wording as that rendered by Matthew.

What is important, though, is the insistence on Nazareth as the home town of Jesus – with slightly different accounts in Matthew and Luke: whereas, in Matthew, Joseph and his family do not move to Nazareth until after a revelation, the Lukan account presupposes that they were already living there before the story begins. I cannot dwell here on the implications of this detail – which may be significant – but the designation of Nazareth as Jesus' home town opens up for hermeneutical possibilities of mixing geography and messianism. Note, for example, the episode of Jesus' encounter with the blind Bartimaeus outside Jericho (Mark 10:47; Luke 18:37): When Bartimaeus is told that Jesus the Nazorean is passing by, he calls out to him: 'Jesus, son of David, have mercy upon me!'

III

As a conclusion to this paper I should like to comment on how the collective self-understanding of representing the 'true Israel' in the End Time, expressed in plant metaphors, may have influenced the ways in which the followers of Jesus expressed their messianic convictions.

In Acts 24, the lawyer Tertullus accuses Paul of being the leader of the 'Nazorean sect', ἡ τῶν Ναζωραίων αἵρεσις. The same designation, 'Nazoreans', recurs later in Church history, used both by and about

---

[23]This is precisely the point made by Brown, *Birth of the Messiah*, 209.

Oriental Christians (e.g. Syrian or Arabic-speaking Christians). It may also be found in patristic literature as well as in Jewish polemic against deviant groups. Particularly noteworthy is the Mandean self-identification as 'Nazoreans', and likewise the reference by the Church Father Epiphanius of Salamis (towards the end of the fourth century) to a *pre-Christian* Jewish group called 'Nazoreans', which, he is careful to point out, must not be identified with the Jewish-Christian 'Nazoreans'.[24] Already in 1957, these aspects of the self-designation of Jesus and of his early followers were discussed in the article '*Die rätselhaften Termini Nazoräer und Iskariot*' by Bertil Gärtner, with special attention paid to the then newly published texts from Qumran.[25] Gärtner especially points to the oscillation between and individual and a collective perspective in the messianic hermeneutic application of Scripture in both Qumranite and New Testament writings, as well as their striking similarities in respect of messianism and collective self-understanding of being the chosen and holy rest of Israel. The parallelism between 'holy shoot' and 'holy remnant' in the Qumran texts reflects the oscillation between the individual and the collective in the Deutero-Isaianic 'Servant Songs'. It is the word stem נצר which comes into the focus of this messianic application, and the double use of this stem as a noun ('shoot', 'branch') and as a verb ('to keep') may provide an explanation of this oscillation. Thus, the prophecies about God's chosen and preserved in Isa 42:6 (sing.) and 49:6 (plur.) may be viewed in conjunction with the Davidic individual messianism in Isa 11, as well as with the collective identification of the faithful remnant of Israel as 'priests' in 'Trito-Isaiah' (61:6). In Christian interpretation, this oscillation between divinely chosen individual and collective comes to expression in the formulations about Jesus as ὁ Ναζωραῖος and his followers as οἱ Ναζωραῖοι.[26] As I have already hinted at above, I would therefore suggest that the designations Ναζωραῖος and Ναζωραῖοι carry a theological message, rather than they are to be taken as simple notices about geographical origin (though not excluding this 'plain' meaning).

Further illumination of the background for the appellation Ναζωραῖοι on the first Christians may be found in some other instances of נצר

[24]Epiphanius, *Haer.* 29; cf. *b. AZ* 17a. Further examples are found in Schaeder, *TDNT* 4, 874f, but see also the discussion on the Ebionites and Nazorites in J. A. Fitzmyer, 'The Qumran Scrolls, The Ebionites and Their Literature', in *idem, Essays on the Semitic Background of the New Testament* (Missoula: Society of Biblical Literature/Scholars Press, 1974) 437–47.

[25]Gärtner, 18ff. A few years later, Gärtner was one of the first to discuss the Qumranite and early Christian collective self-understanding of representing the temple of God in the End Time in his *The Temple and the Community in Qumran and the New Testament* (SNTSMS 1; Cambridge: Cambridge University Press, 1965).

[26]Gärtner, '*Die rätselhaften Termini*', 24.

ideology in the Qumran writings.[27] 1QH 6:15; 8:6 and 10 speak about a 'shoot' (נצר) growing from 'the everlasting plantation' (מטעת עולם).[28] These formulations closely resemble the description of the early history of the 'New Covenant' in CD 1:7, according to which God 'caused to sprout from Israel and from Aaron a shoot of the planting (ויצמח שורש ... מטעת)', but also the characterization of the יחד in 1QS 8:4–5 (cf. also 1QH 7:10):

When these things exist in Israel the Community council shall be founded on truth, ... like an everlasting plantation (מטעת עולם), a holy house for Israel and the foundation of the holy of holies for Aaron ...[29]

It is most significant that all these Qumranite examples of self-understanding within the community of the New Covenant seem to have been inspired by the metaphoric language about the coming era of salvation in Isa 60:21. Here, immediately preceding the prophecy about the vindication and glorification of the faithful (cf. above on the 'priests' of 61:6), the righteous members of God's renewed and holy people are described as 'the shoot that I [God] planted (נצר מטעו; lQIsa[a]: מטעי)'.

The plant metaphor is also used in the schematic historical survey of the 'Apocalypse of Weeks' in *1 Enoch* 93:1–10 and 91:12–17 (cf. the Qumranite fragment 4Q212 4:12). The 'eternal plant of righteousness' is mentioned in two passages, first pointing to an individual (Abraham) and his offspring in the third of the ten weeks (93:5), and then, in the seventh week — which evidently represents the author's own time — to the holy remnant of God's people living at the end of the old world order (93:10):

After that in the seventh week an apostate generation shall arise; its deeds shall be many, and all of them criminal. At its completion, there shall be elected the elect ones of righteousness from the eternal plant of righteousness, to whom shall be given sevenfold instruction concerning all his flock.[30]

Clearly, there is a connection between this formulation and the self-understanding of those responsible for the 'Damascus Document',

---

[27]Cf. *ibid.*, 21–3.

[28]Note that the context immediately preceding 6:15 describes the communion between the 'men of the council' and the angels; cf. 6:13–14. The text of 8:10 is understood very differently by E. Lohse and F. García Martínez in their translations of the Qumran texts (*Die Texte aus Qumran. Hebräisch und Deutsch ...*, Darmstadt: Wissenschaftliche Buchgesellschaft 1981; *The Dead Sea Scrolls Translated: The Qumran Texts in English* (Leiden: Brill, [2]1996); according to Lohse, it is the holy shoot which makes the 'plant of truth' grow, whereas García Martínez understands the phrase as an impersonal 'he' (= God?), who 'causes the holy shoot to grow in the true plantation'.

[29]Translation García Martínez, *The Dead Sea Scrolls Translated*.

[30]Translation E. Isaac, *OTP* 1.

speaking about themselves as an 'shoot of the planting' (cf. CD 1:7).
Note also the correspondence between the end of the seventh week in
1 Enoch and the *chronomessianic* scheme hinted at in CD 1:7 and
20:13–15: The 'shoot' emerges after 390 years, followed by twenty
years of 'groping for the path' before the appearance of the Teacher of
Righteousness, after whose 'gathering in' forty more years are expected
to pass until God's final act of deliverance and judgement; the sum is
450 years, i.e. leaving a period of forty years for the Teacher's activity
until the completion of a 'complete' period of 490 (70 × 7) years.

This oscillation between individual messianic exegesis and an application of the scriptural passages on the collective community is clearly
to be seen in the Book of Revelation. Its characterization of the holy
people of God at the time of the End and in the era of the new creation
has many elements in common with the Qumran texts referred to
earlier.[31] The self-understanding of representing a 'kingdom' and
'priests' (1:6; cf. 5:10; 20:4–6; 22:5) does not only signal an 'Exodus
perspective' on the Christian community (cf. Exod 19:6), but also the
fulfilment of the prophecy in 'Trito-Isaiah' about the future restoration
of the people of God (cf. Isa 61:6). It is highly important to be aware of
this conflation of scriptural motifs in Revelation, which is one of its
typical features, and which is so common in much of the Qumran
literature. Thus, when in 1:5–6 the addressees of Revelation are told
that Jesus has liberated them from their sins through his atoning
death, and that he has 'made us to be a kingdom, priests serving his
God and Father', the implication goes further than just the establishment of Israel as the particularly chosen and sanctified people of
God at Sinai.

In order to understand what the Book of Revelation has to say about
the Christians as 'priests' it is therefore of special significance to study
its use of 'Trito-Isaiah's' depiction of the glorified faithful remnant of
the people, which shall 'enjoy the wealth of the nations', and 'glory . . .
in their riches' (Isa 61:6). There is a clear allusion to this idea in its final
vision of the redeemed people of God in the New Jerusalem, Rev
21:24–26 (cf. the proclamations of the future glory of Zion, Isa 60:5,
11). Evidently, the particular use of several of the prophecies in 'Trito-
Isaiah' and their application on the followers of the Lamb is an
important part of the self-identification of the author of Revelation.
John is reminding his readers/listeners that they, through their
confession of the Messiah Jesus as the Saviour of the world, constitute
'the planting of the Lord' (מַטַּע יְהוָה; Isa 61:3) in the era of salvation. As
members of this renewed and saved people of God at the End Time they

[31]Cf. the above-mentioned article by Steudel, 'Eternal Reign of the People of God'.

have attained priestly dignity, and it is in this capacity that they are promised to see God's face in the concluding visionary prophecy of the book (Rev 22:4).[32]

It is also important to note the Isaianic reference in 22:3–5, speaking about the eternal rule of God's chosen people in the paradisiac conditions of the New Jerusalem:

Nothing accursed will be found there any more. But the throne of God and of the Lamb will be in it, and his servants will worship him; they will see his face, and his name will be on their foreheads. And there will be no more night; they need no light of lamp or sun, for the Lord God will be their light, and they will reign forever and ever.

Compare Isa 60:19–21 (see also the collective expectation in Dan 7:18, 27):

The sun shall no longer be your light by day, nor for brightness shall the moon give light to you by night; but the Lord will be your everlasting light, and your God will be your glory. Your sun shall no more go down, or your moon withdraw itself; for the Lord will be your everlasting light, and your days of mourning shall be ended. Your people shall all be righteous; they shall possess the land forever. They are the shoot that I planted,[33] the work of my hands, so that I might be glorified.

A matter of particular interest is that the Isaianic נצר concept is thus used in Revelation both to describe the redeemed followers of the Lamb and the Lamb/Jesus himself. Together with other signs of Revelation's heavy indebtedness to a Jewish hermeneutical and conceptual world of thought like that expressed in the Qumran findings, this indicates that the relation between Revelation and Qumran may have been more than just a dependence on similar sources. I should suggest that the author of Revelation himself may have been part of the same hermeneutical and theological/ideological tradition as that represented in the Qumran writings.[34]

To conclude: The application of the scriptural plant metaphors (נצר, צמח, מטע; including the verbal forms) on the collective of the chosen and righteous community of the Qumran texts is of great significance for comprehending early Christian messianism and self-understanding, as well for situating these 'reform movements' in relation to each other and

---

[32]Cf. Fekkes, *Isaiah*, 100f, especially n. 82, with reference to similar ideas in 1Q28b (1QSb) 4.

[33]The BHS emends with מטע יהוה, in accordance with 1QIsᵃ.

[34]See my articles 'Uppenbarelseboken och 'Sabbatsoffersångerna' från Qumran och Masada'; in *Tro og historie. Festskrift til Niels Hyldahl i anledning af 65 års fødselsdagen den 30. december 1995 (Forum for Bibelsk Eksegese 7)*; Copenhagen: Museum Tusculanums Forlag, 1996) 285–300, and 'L'Apocalypse entre judaïsme et christianisme: Précisions sur le monde spirituel et intellectuel de Jean de Patmos', *RHPR* 79 (1999) 31–50.

to other contemporary forms of Judaism. In particular, the formulations about Jesus 'the Nazorean' and about his followers as 'Nazoreans' call for a comprehensive study of the individual and collective application of the Isaianic נצר prophecies in the earliest Jesus movement.[35] Not only are further studies on the relation between Qumranite and New Testament language and theology/ideology needed, but it will also be necessary to reflect anew from a historical perspective on the Jewish-Christian movement and its possible relation to the Judaism of the Dead Sea Scrolls.[36] And even more: the whole question about Jesus' messianic consciousness should also be reconsidered in recognition of the simple but significant etymological analogy between the Isaianic נצר and the combined geographical and hermeneutical/ideological implications of the New Testament ὁ Ναζωραῖος.

[35]The early Christian emphasis on 'keeping/preserving the words of Jesus' and on 'keeping his (or God's) commandments', especially in the Johannine literature, including Rev, may also belong to this complex, since the Greek τηρεῖν equates the Hebrew נצר (cf. John 8:51, 52, 55; 14:23f; 15:20; 1 John 2:5; Rev 3:8 [see also 3:10; 22:7, 9] – John 14:15, 21; 15:10; 1 John 2:3f; 3:22, 24; 5:3; Rev 12:17; 14:12).

[36]As the publication of all Qumranite texts is approaching its completion, and in view of the vivid renewed discussion about the origins of Christianity within its Jewish context, it has become a most important task to reconsider the whole issue of Jewish Christianity, as also the earlier studies by e.g. H.-J. Schoeps, *Theologie und Geschichte des Judenchristentums* (Tübingen, 1949), and J. Daniélou, *Théologie du judéo-christianisme: Histoire des doctrines chrétiennes avant Nicée* 1 (Tournai, 1958) (in English: *The Theology of Jewish Christianity: A History of Early Christian Doctrine Before the Council of Nicaea* 1 [London/Philadelphia, 1977]).

15

THE DEAD SEA SCROLLS AND MERKAVAH MYSTICISM*

James R. Davila

Introduction

In 1987, Lawrence Schiffman published an article in Hebrew which surveyed all the available evidence for connections between the Qumran library and the much later mystical corpus of Hekhalot literature.[1] Since the publication of this article, all the unpublished scroll material has been made available for analysis, and other parallels to the Hekhalot corpus have been noted in the new material as well as in the previously published scrolls. And some parallels remain that have yet to be adequately discussed.

In addition, the field of Hekhalot studies has not stood still between 1987 and 1998. Although the importance of ascent traditions in these texts cannot be denied, more notice has been taken of the important role of theurgy.[2] Some scholars have focused more on the exegetical background to the texts, while others have continued to maintain that an experiential element contributed to their composition.[3]

The time is ripe for a re-evaluation of the complex relationship

---

*All quotations from the Hekhalot literature are based on an eclectic text of the MSS published by P. Schäfer in *Synopse zur Hekhalot-Literatur* (Tübingen: Mohr [Siebeck], 1981) and follow the paragraph numbering in this edition.

[1] L. Schiffman, '*Sifrut Ha-Hekhalot ve-Kitve Qumran*' ('The Hekhalot Literature and the Qumran Writings'), *Meḥqere Yerushalaym Be-Maḥshevet Yisra'el* 6 (1987) 121–38. In an earlier article Schiffman examined the relationship between the Hekhalot corpus and the portions of the *Songs of the Sabbath Sacrifice* which had been published by J. Strugnell along with some information on the unpublished material: L. Schiffman, '*Merkavah* Speculation at Qumran: The 4QSerekh Shirot '*Olat ha-Shabbat*', in *Mystics, Philosophers, and Politicians: Essays in Jewish Intellectual History in Honor of Alexander Altmann* ed. J. Reinharz *et al.* (Durham, NC: Duke University Press, 1982) 15–47; J. Strugnell, 'The Angelic Liturgy at Qumrân – 4Q Serek Šîrôt '*Ôlat Haššabbāt*', *Congress Volume: Oxford 1959* (VTSupp VII; Leiden: Brill, 1960) 318–45.

[2] I note in particular D. J. Halperin, *The Faces of the Chariot: Early Jewish Responses to Ezekiel's Vision* (Tübingen: Mohr [Siebeck], 1988) and the essays by P. Schäfer collected in *Hekhalot Studien* (Tübingen: Mohr [Siebeck], 1988).

[3] M. Himmelfarb, *Ascent to Heaven in Jewish and Christian Apocalypses* (New York/Oxford: Oxford University Press, 1993) esp. 106–14; contrast my online review of this volume in *Ioudaios Review* 4.017 (ftp://ftp. lehigh.edu/pub/listserv/ioudaios-review/ 4.1994/himmelfarb.davila.017). C. R. A. Morray-Jones, 'Transformational Mysticism in the Apocalyptic-Merkabah Tradition', *JJS* 43 (1992) 1–31; J. R. Davila, 'The Hekhalot Literature and Shamanism', *Society of Biblical Literature 1994 Seminar Papers* (Atlanta, GA: Scholars Press, 1994) 767–89.

between the Dead Sea Scrolls and Merkavah mysticism. Inasmuch as the subject is probably worthy of a monograph, the purpose of this article is to outline such a re-evaluation. Using somewhat different categories from Schiffman's, I shall summarize the state of the question in his article, note the advances of the intervening years, and add some observations of my own. My goal is not only to collect and supplement a list of parallels, but also to sharpen the analysis with methodological and theoretical observations and to use the comparisons to assess the centrality or peripherality of the Qumran corpus within Second Temple Judaism.

Technical Terminology and Scriptural Exegesis

Schiffman noted a great deal of technical terminology shared between the Hekhalot texts and the Qumran literature. He concludes that the *Songs of the Sabbath Sacrifice*, which he takes to be sectarian with no clear connection with the cult,

is replete with expressions and motifs met also in the later *hekhalot* traditions. Among the most prominent are: the notion of seven archangels, the idea that the angelic hosts praise God regularly, the notion of the *gevurah*, *kavod*, or *dynamis*, the heavenly sanctuary and cult, the 'gentle voice,' association of fire with the angels, the variegated colors, the 'living God,' the multiple chariot-thrones, and the military organization of the heavenly hosts. Further, the language, terminology, and style of our text are very similar to what we encounter in the later *hekhalot* literature.[4]

He also notes that the Merkavah vision in *1 Enoch* 14, based on Ezekiel 1 and 10 and bearing some relationship to Daniel 7, is attested in Aramaic fragments from Qumran; that in the *War Scroll* angels are arranged in military units; that terminology similar to that found in the Hekhalot literature appears also in the Hymn to the Creator in 11QPsalms[a]; that, although the Hekhalot texts do not share the dualism of the Qumran sectarian literature, the closely related magical literature of late antiquity (on which see below) does contain dualistic elements; and that Michael or the Prince of Light in the Qumran texts is replaced by Metatron (and, we might add, the 'Youth' – see below) in the Hekhalot literature.[5]

The most significant texts published since Schiffman's article which anticipate the technical terminology and exegesis of the Hekhalot traditions are the paraphrase of Ezekiel's Merkavah vision in 4QSecond

---

[4]Schiffman, '*Merkavah* Speculation at Qumran' (note 1 above): 45. Cf. 'The Hekhalot Literature and the Qumran Writings' (note 1 above): 122, 124–6.

[5]Schiffman, 'The Hekhalot Literature and the Qumran Writings', 122–4, 126–8, 132–3.

Ezekiel (4Q385, frag. 4), published in 1990,[6] and the remaining fragments of 4QBerakhot.[7] The reference to the Chariot (מרכבה) in 4QSecond Ezekiel is based ultimately on 1 Chr 28:18, since Ezekiel himself never uses this term. The use of the word נשמה, 'soul' or 'breath' in the sense of 'spirit', in a broken context pertaining to the living creatures, is perhaps paralleled by a description of the celestial throne room in the Hekhalot Zutarti which mentions these creatures individually and then adds 'and the shine of the countenance of His face is like the image of the spirit/wind (כדמות הרוח) and like the formation of soul (כיצירה נשמה)' (§356). The ox (שור) of Ezekiel's vision is called a calf (עגל) in 4QSecond Ezekiel, perhaps foreshadowing latter rabbinic exegesis that tied Ezekiel's ox-faced living creature to the golden calf of Exodus 32. The Hekhalot texts never use the term 'calf' for the ox-faced living creature, although one passage tells us 'and when Israel sinned in the matter of the calf, the face of the ox was hidden away, and He brought the face of the cherub in place of it' (§955). The surviving material in 4QSecond Ezekiel never calls the living creatures 'cherubim', which may indicate that, like the Hekhalot literature, this Qumran text treated them as two different types of angels, despite their apparent identification in Ezekiel chapters 1 and 10.

The relationship between scriptural exegesis in the Dead Sea Scrolls and in the Hekhalot literature is an immensely fruitful area, one whose surface has still barely been scratched. Space permits only a single example, drawn from the *Songs of the Sabbath Sacrifice*. The twelfth song in this document describes the celestial tabernacle (משכן) and is built, as Carol Newsom has shown, around an exegesis of Ezek 3:12, informed by Ezekiel 1 (the Hashmal and the rainbow) and 10 (the cherubim); 1 Kgs 19:12 (the divine silence); Ps 68:17–20; and perhaps Dan 7:10 (the streams of fire). The passage seeks to explain how the *ophannim* of Ezek 3:12 make the sound attributed to them in this verse. The phrase 'sound of a great earthquake' (קול רעש גדול) is tied by the shared word רעש to 1 Kings 19:12 and explained or corrected in the light of the phrase 'a still, small voice' (קול דממה דקה). There is also a reference to 'the camps of the gods' (מחני אלוהים), that is, the angels. Crispin H. T. Fletcher-Louis has

[6] D. Dimant and J. Strugnell, 'The Merkabah Vision in *Second Ezekiel* (4Q385 4)', *RevQ* 14 (1990) 331–48.

[7] B. Nitzan, '4Q Berakhot (4Q286–290): A Preliminary Report', *New Qumran Texts and Studies* (ed. G. J. Brooke with F. García Martínez; Leiden: Brill Academic Publishers, 1994) 53–71 and pl. 3. In *Qumran Prayer and Religious Poetry* (Leiden: Brill Academic Publishers, 1994), Nitzan also discusses, *inter alia*, 4QBerakhot, the *Songs of the Sabbath Sacrifice*, and the *Songs of the Sage*. The official editions of 4QBerakhot and of the *Songs of the Sabbath Sacrifices* (edited by Nitzan and Newsom, respectively) have now been published in *Qumran Cave 4 VI: Poetical and Liturgical Texts, Part 1*, ed. E. Eshel *et al.* (DJD 11; Oxford: Clarendon Press, 1998) 1–74 and 173–401.

also pointed out that the twelfth and thirteenth songs draw on imagery from Exodus 28 to describe both the angelic high priests around the throne-chariot and the divine glory itself.[8] Newsom has suggested that the proximity of the twelfth sabbath of the year to the festival of Shavuot (which comes on the preceding Sunday in the Qumran solar calendar) means that the association of Ezekiel 1 and Psalm 68 in the later Shavuot synagogue liturgy may have more ancient roots than suspected by David Halperin, who dates the association to the third century CE.[9]

The Hekhalot literature frequently ties just this group of scriptural passages together (usually along with Isa 6:1–3) in its descriptions of the heavenly throne room and liturgy. One striking example is found in the complex of Hebrew and Aramaic material on the Youth (הנער), the angelic high priest, found floating in various formulations in the Hekhalot Zutarti and elsewhere (§§384–98 and parallels). The cosmological introduction mentions the Hashmal as well as the four living creatures who come and stand before God while the Youth prostrates himself and the angels recite the benediction of Ezek 3:12 (§384). The Youth goes 'beneath the throne of glory' and directs the angelic praise during the three daily times of prayer. He is called both Metatron and 'Throne' (כסא). A difficult passage (§389) appears to say that he 'is inscribed' with various letters and names of cosmological import arranged in a pattern that alludes to the high priest's ephod in Exodus 28, and it locates him or the object in question in the 'innermost rooms' (the holy of holies?). One living creature descends upon the heavenly 'tabernacle of the Youth' and recites in a 'still, small voice' (1 Kgs 19:12). The *ophannim* and the angels are silent; other angels rush into the river of fire (Dan 7:10) while the Youth places 'deafening fire' into the ears of the four living creatures, presumably so they cannot hear him speak the divine names. The Youth invokes God with a series of *nomina barbara* (§390). Then we are informed that his name is YWPY'L and that 'in the encampments of the holy ones (ובמחנות קודשים) he is called Metatron' and additional *nomina barbara*. The text continues, 'this is his great name that was transmitted to

---

[8]C. H. T. Fletcher-Louis, 'Heavenly Ascent or Incarnational Presence? A Revisionist Reading of the Songs of the Sabbath Sacrifice', *Society of Biblical Literature 1998 Seminar Papers* (Atlanta, GA: Scholars Press, 1998), pp. 267–99.

[9]C. Newsom, 'Merkabah Exegesis in the Qumran Sabbath Shirot', *JJS* 38 (1987) 11–30; Halperin, *Faces of the Chariot* (note 2 above): 262–358. In connection with the statement above, I note that Halperin recognizes the early association of Ezekiel 1 with Psalm 68 in the LXX of Ezekiel (roughly second century B.C.E.). See *Faces of the Chariot*, pp. 55–60 and 'Merkavah Midrash in the Septuagint' *JBL* 101 (1982): 351–63. The fragments of 4QBerakhot published in recent years by Nitzan (see note 7 above) support this conclusion. This document is a liturgy for the annual renewal of the sectarian covenant, perhaps at Shavuot, and it contains hymns with Merkavah terminology and allusions to Ezekiel 1 and 10, Dan 7:9–10, Psalm 68, etc.

Moses on Sinai', and from Moses to a line of leaders and prophets extending to the rabbinic sages. This paragraph (§397) concludes with a quotation from Ps 68:18, reinforcing the connection between Ezekiel 1, the revelation of the Torah at Sinai celebrated at Shavuot, and Psalm 68. The Youth is also compared to Ezekiel's rainbow in the next paragraph (§398). Even the superficial analysis to which we are limited here makes obvious the striking and significant parallels between the two texts. A full-scale study of scriptural exegesis in the *Songs of the Sabbath Sacrifice* and the Hekhalot literature is an urgent desideratum for both corpora.

Physiognomy

Gershom Scholem and Ithamar Gruenwald have published a number of late antique or medieval tractates in Hebrew belonging to the genre of הכרת פנים, 'physiognomy', in which physical features such as height, lines on the forehead or hand, shape of the nose, lips, ears, or face, timbre of the voice, birthmarks, and complexion are supposed to reveal the character and destiny of the bearer. Astrological speculation is also found in some of these works. Both Scholem and Gruenwald have noted parallels to a number of Qumran texts.[10] The use of the biblical word תולדות, 'generations', in the *Community Rule* (1QS[a] 1:17–19; 4:15–16) is similar to its use in the later physiognomic texts according to Scholem, who argues that in both the *Community Rule* and the later documents it has the technical meaning 'nature', The Hebrew text 4Q186, written backward in a secret code, is a physiognomic tractate much like the later ones, which combines astrology and descriptions of physical features with character analyses presented in terms of light-darkness dualism. Gruenwald has also noted shared terminology in the Aramaic text 4QMess ar (4Q534) and the later works.[11] In 1984, Peter Schäfer published another physiognomic fragment that seems to be a redaction of parts of *3 Enoch* which is stratigraphically earlier than the other manuscripts of *3 Enoch* in our possession. In this fragment (which

---

[10]G. Scholem, 'Physiognomy and Chiromancy' in *Sepher Assaf* (Festschrift for Simha Assaf) (Jerusalem: Mossad HaRav Kook, 1953) 459–95 (Hebrew); *idem*, 'Ein Fragment zur Physiognomik und Chiromantik aus der Tradition der spätantiken jüdischen Esoterik', in *Liber Amicorum: Studies in Honour of Professor Dr. C. J. Bleeker* (Leiden: Brill, 1969) 175–93 (all citations of the Physiognomy of R. Ishmael follow the paragraphing in this article); I. Gruenwald, 'Further Jewish Physiognomic and Chiromantic Fragments', *Tarbiz* 40 (1970–1) 301–19, esp. 317–19 (Hebrew). Schiffman surveys their conclusions in 'The Hekhalot Literature and the Qumran Writings' (note 1 above): 128–31.

[11]Gruenwald, 'Further Jewish Physiognomic and Chiromantic Fragments' (note 10 above): 304–6, 317.

is not mentioned by Schiffman), a Hekhalot ascent tradition is combined with physiognomic and astrological speculation.[12]

In a recent article, I have extended the comparisons between 4Q534 and the later physiognomic material (including Schäfer's text), arguing that the Qumran text is another example of the same genre and expressing doubt that the document pertains either to Noah or to the eschatological high priest, although such associations cannot be entirely ruled out and do not affect my thesis as a whole. I have shown that the parallels to the later physiognomic tractates are far more extensive than have been realized before and that 4Q534 also has direct connections with the Hekhalot literature.[13]

The Qumran parallels to later physiognomic tractates are not yet exhausted. Some have argued that two other fragmentary Aramaic MSS (4Q535 and 4Q536), which as far as I know have not yet been published apart from photographs, are copies of the same work as 4Q534.[14] The texts of these two MSS overlap, so they do seem to be copies of the same document. But although there are thematic similarities between them and both 4Q534 and 4Q186, it has hardly been demonstrated that they are the same work as either. 4Q535 contains a reference to the angel Barakiel (frag. 1), to someone's birth (frags. 2 and 3) and perhaps to astrological houses (frag. 2), and to someone's weight (frag. 3). 4Q536 refers to angelic beings, revelations, sages, secrets, perhaps an ascent (frag. 1, col. 1), and includes an admonition having to do with writing the words of the document in a book (frag. 1, col. 2). Frag. 2 refers to someone sleeping 'until the division of days' and includes the phrase 'in the day, until he completes years'. This fragment overlaps with 4Q535 frag. 3. Some connection with the Hekhalot and physiognomic traditions seems likely.

In addition, an Aramaic text (4Q561), not yet published in an official edition, appears to be another example of this genre.[15] Like the others,

---

[12]P. Schäfer, *Geniza-Fragmente zur Hekhalot-Literatur* (Tübingen: Mohr [Siebeck], 1984) 135–9; 'Ein neues Fragment zur Metoposkopie und Chiromantik', *Hekhalot Studien* (note 2 above): 84–95.

[13]J. R. Davila, '4QMess ar (4Q534) and Merkavah Mysticism', *Dead Sea Discoveries* 5 (1998): 367–81.

[14]J. A. Fitzmyer, 'The Aramaic "Elect of God" Text from Qumran Cave 4', in *Essays on the Semitic Background of the New Testament* (Missoula, MT: Scholars Press, 1974) 127–60, esp. 158–9; J. T. Milik with M. Black, *The Books of Enoch: Aramaic Fragments of Qumrân Cave 4* (Oxford: Clarendon Press, 1976) 56; F. García Martínez, '4QMess ar and the *Book of Noah*', in *Qumran and Apocalyptic: Studies on the Aramaic Texts from Qumran* (Leiden: Brill Academic Publishers, 1992) 1–44, esp. 17. 4Q535 can be found on the photographs PAM 41.363 and 43.572; 4Q536 can be found on photographs PAM 41.945, 41.956, and 43.575.

[15]A transliteration and translation have been published by R. Eisenman and M. Wise in *The Dead Sea Scrolls Uncovered* (London/New York: Penguin, 1992) 263–5. 4Q561 can be found on the photographs PAM 41.944 and 43.598.

it refers to physical features (e.g., eyes, nose, teeth, limbs, sole of the foot, voice, hair of the beard and head, fingernails, height, and perhaps birthmarks), although it is not well enough preserved for us to be sure that these are tied to personality or fate.

Mysticism and Ascent to Heaven

In his two articles, Schiffman has relatively little to say about the idea of a mystical ascent to heaven in the Qumran literature. He notes the ascent traditions about Enoch in *1 Enoch* and points out that there is no similar ascent or tour of heaven in the *Songs of the Sabbath Sacrifice*, but he does not discuss any other potentially relevant texts.[16] There are such texts, however, and discussion of them has continued in the intervening years. I have surveyed the problem of ascents to heaven in the Qumran literature in an article, so I will limit my comments here to a brief summary.[17]

The most striking text of this category is the so-called *Self-Glorification Hymn*, which is found in at least two recensions in the Hodayot MSS (4Q491, 4Q471^b, 4Q427 frag. 7, 1QH^a col. 26) and which boastfully describes the enthronement of the writer in heaven among the gods.[18] Various other passages in the Hodayot (1QH^a col. 7.21; col. 23 frag. 2.10; col. 11.19–23a; col. 10.20–30; col. 18.30–35; col. 19.10–14; col. 12) present a similar if more restrained picture of the writer's apotheosis and exaltation, as does at least one passage in the *Songs of the Sage* (4Q511, frag. 35; cf. frag. 2 col. 1.7–10 and frag. 8.6–9). The figure described in 4Q534 (4QMess ar) may also experience an ascent to the celestial realm and certainly has a visionary experience of some sort.[19]

Traditions about the ascent or apotheosis of other figures besides Enoch are also found in the Dead Sea Scrolls. Melchizedek appears as an eschatological warrior angel in 11QMelchizedek and perhaps as a celestial (and eschatological?) high priest in the fifth of the *Songs of the*

[16]Schiffman, 'The Hekhalot Literature and the Qumran Writings' (note 1 above): 122, 124; *idem.*, '*Merkavah* Speculation at Qumran' (note 1 above): 17, 19, 45.

[17]J. R. Davila, 'Heavenly Ascents in the Dead Sea Scrolls', in vol. 2 of *The Dead Sea Scrolls after Fifty Years: A Comprehensive Assessment* ed. P. W. Flint and J. C. VanderKam (2 vols.; Leiden: Brill Academic Publishers, 1998, pp. 461–85). See also J. R. Davila, 'The Hodayot Hymnist and the Four Who Entered Paradise', *RevQ* 17/65–68 (1996) 457–78.

[18]M. Smith, 'Ascent to the Heavens and Deification in 4QM^a', in *Archaeology and History in the Dead Sea Scrolls: The New York University Conference in Memory of Yigael Yadin* ed. L. Schiffman (JSPSS 8; JSOT/ASOR, 1990) 181–8; E. Eshel, '4Q471B: A Self-Glorification Hymn', *RevQ* 17/65–68 (1996) 175–203.

[19]See my article '4QMess ar (4Q534) and Merkavah Mysticism', cited above in note 13.

Sabbath Sacrifice.[20] In Aramaic *Levi*, Levi ascends to heaven, evidently for a priestly investment (see below). According to the *Genesis Apocryphon* (col. 2) Methuselah travels to the angelic realm that Enoch inhabits. And it may be that traditions about the apotheosis of Moses are fragmentarily preserved in 4Q374 and 4Q377 (the story of Moses' ascent to heaven is quite important in the Hekhalot literature).

All in all, then, the Qumran library shows a significant interest in the heavenly ascents and divinization of human beings in texts that have other connections with the Hekhalot literature (Aramaic *Levi*, the *Songs of the Sage*, and 4Q534) as well as in texts in which such connections are lacking or less obvious. Although heavenly ascents can no longer be regarded as the center of the Merkavah mystical experience, they remain an important building block of the tradition, and their presence in the Qumran literature is of considerable interest.

Magic and Theurgy[21]

Schiffman notes that there is a close relationship between Jewish mysticism and Jewish magic. The terminology and praxes found in the Hekhalot literature are similar in many ways to those found in incantation texts (such as the Babylonian magic bowls) and handbooks such as *Harba de Moshe* (the Sword of Moses) and *Sepher HaRazim* (the Book of Mysteries). In his analysis he concentrates on one text, the *Songs of the Sage* (4Q510–511) and he shows its concern with demonological matters.[22]

Since Schiffman's article appeared, two additional magic-related texts have been published, and more work has been done on the material that was already been available. The two new Aramaic texts are 4Q318, an astrological text, and 4Q560, an incantation. 4Q318 preserves fragments of two magico-astrological tables, a *selenodromion*

---

[20]I have discussed this song in detail in my article 'Melchizedek, Michael, and War in Heaven', *Society of Biblical Literature 1996 Seminar Papers* (Atlanta, GA: Scholars Press, 1996) 259–72.

[21]The magical and physiognomic literature from Qumran has also been surveyed recently by P. S. Alexander, ' "Wrestling against Wickedness in High Places": Magic in the Worldview of the Qumran Community', in *The Scrolls and the Scriptures: Qumran Fifty Years After* ed. S. E. Porter and C. A. Evans (JSPSS 26; Sheffield: Sheffield Academic Press, 1997) 318–37. The definition and even viability of the term 'magic' remains a subject of dispute among scholars. For a recent challenge to the use of the term with reference to the Qumran texts discussed in this section, see W. J. Lyons and A. M. Reimer, 'The Demonic Virus and Qumran Studies: Some Preventative Measures', *DSD* 5 (1998) 16–32.

[22]The MSS 4Q510–511 were published by M. Baillet in *Qumrân Grotte 4 III (4Q482–4Q520)* (DJD VII; Oxford: Clarendon Press, 1982) 215–62, pls. lv–lxxi; cf. Schiffman, 'The Hekhalot Literature and the Qumran Writings' (note 1 above): 131–2.

(describing the movement of the moon through the Zodiac during the year) and a *brontologion* (predictions of the future based on the occurrence of thunder in association with a given sign of the Zodiac), both of which can be reconstructed to a large extent thanks to the mathematical regularity of their subject matter, although most of the omens of the *brontologion* are lost and the texts evidently can be reconstructed with either a 360-day year (as in Mesopotamian astrological texts) or a 364-day year (as in the Qumran sectarian texts, the Enoch literature, and *Jubilees*).[23] The relationship of the two sections is open to debate. The names of the signs of the Zodiac correspond to the later western (Palestinian) Jewish tradition. 4Q560 is also fragmentary and is written in extremely difficult Aramaic. Douglas L. Penny and Michael O. Wise are forced to emend it six times in the space of five partial lines and to resort to creative etymologies for some words in order to make any sense of the text. Such difficulties are typical of magical incantations, however, and overall the case made by Penny and Wise that 4Q560 is such a text seems solid. The fragments belong to one or more spells involving childbirth and illness, which adjure at least one spirit and appear to mention several types of demons. Such concerns and contents are typical of the magic bowls and later Jewish incantatory texts and are indirectly related to material in the Hekhalot literature.[24]

More study has been devoted to the *Songs of the Sage*, especially by Bilhah Nitzan, who has drawn attention to verbal and thematic parallels in the later Jewish magical and mystical literature, but she also proposes that there is an important difference between them.[25] According to the theology of the Qumran work, demons can be frightened away temporarily, but their final defeat must wait until the eschaton. Spells in the later magical works, in contrast, claim to have the power to drive away demons forever. Nitzan considers the *Songs of the Sage* to be 'not pure and simple incantations, but actually hymns recited for the purpose of incantation'.[26]

---

[23]M. O. Wise, 'Thunder in Gemini: An Aramaic Brontologion (4Q318) from Qumran', in *Thunder in Gemini and Other Essays on the History, Language and Literature of Second Temple Palestine* (JSPSS 15; Sheffield: Sheffield Academic Press, 1994) 13–50; J. C. Greenfield, M. Sokoloff *et al.*, 'An Astrological Text from Qumran (*4Q318*) and Reflections on Some Zodiacal Names', *RevQ* 16/64 (1995) 507–25.

[24]D. L. Penny and M. O. Wise, 'By the Power of Beelzebub: An Aramaic Incantation Formula from Qumran (4Q560)', *JBL* 113 (1994) 627–50.

[25]B. Nitzan, 'Hymns from Qumran 'לפחד ולבהל' Evil Ghosts (4Q510–511)', *Tarbiz* 55 (1985–6) 19–46 (Hebrew); *idem*, 'Hymns from Qumran – 4Q510–4Q511', in *The Dead Sea Scrolls: Forty Years of Research* ed. D. Dimant and U. Rappaport (Leiden: Brill Academic Publishers, 1992) 53–63. See also J. M. Baumgarten, 'The Qumran Songs against Demons', *Tarbiz* 55 (1985–6) 442–5 (Hebrew).

[26]Nitzan, 'Hymns from Qumran – 4Q510–4Q511': 54.

The most important work done on 11QPsApoc[a] since its publication
is a new edition by Emile Puech.[27] He has also compared the text to
Hellenistic Jewish literature and part of the corpus of magic bowls, but
further analysis in the light of later magical and Hekhalot traditions is
a desideratum for the history of Jewish magic. The songs in
11QPsApoc[a] appear to be attributed to David, although Solomon is
mentioned as well. One or more demons are addressed directly and
defied, and a mighty angel is invoked against the demonic foes.
Comparisons with the *Sar Panim* material (§§623–39) in the Hekhalot
MSS suggest themselves, but more study is needed.

Ritual, Cult, and the Mystical Experience

One area Schiffman did not cover in any detail was the relationship
between rituals described in the Hekhalot literature and comparable
cultic material in the Qumran corpus. He notes the potential connection
between the heavenly liturgy of the *Songs of the Sabbath Sacrifice* but
suggests that it is only in later (i.e., rabbinic) sources that the songs of
the angels are connected to the earthly liturgy.[28] More recent analysis,
however, tends to support the view that the *Songs of the Sabbath
Sacrifice* were used in a sectarian cultus. As has already been noted,
Carol Newsom has drawn attention to the fact that in the Qumran
calendar, the festival of Shavuot fell on the Sunday preceding the twelfth
sabbath of the year, the sabbath whose song describes the vision of the
Merkavah in the *Songs of the Sabbath Sacrifice*. Since the later
synagogue homilies for Shavuot tied Ezekiel 1 to the Sinai narrative
through the use of Psalm 68, it is important to note that exegesis of both
Ezekiel 1 and Psalm 68 appear in the twelfth song, perhaps indicating
that the whole set of Sabbath Songs was used liturgically by the sectaries
in association with the sabbath celebration and scripture readings
leading up to Shavuot. Since the liturgy of 4QBerakhot, a text
associated with the annual covenant renewal ceremony of the Qumran
sect, is also closely tied to Merkavah traditions, Christopher Morray-
Jones proposes that the *Songs of the Sabbath Sacrifice* presents a 'ritual

---

[27]Published originally by J. P. M. van der Ploeg, 'Un petit roleau de psaumes apocryphes
(11QPsAp[a])', *Tradition und Glaube: Das frühe Christentum in seiner Umwelt* (Göttingen:
Vandenhoeck & Ruprecht, 1971) 128–39 and pls. 2–7; new edition by E. Puech in
'11QPsAp[a]: Un rituel d'exorcismes. Essai de reconstruction', *RevQ* 14/54 (1989) 377–408;
and *idem*, 'Les deux derniers psaumes davidiques du rituel d'exorcisme, 11QPsAp[a] IV 4 – V
14', in *The Dead Sea Scrolls: Forty Years of Research* (note 25 above) 64–89. See now
Florentino García Martínez *et al.* in *Qumran Cave 11. 11 llQ2–18, 11Q20–31* (DJD XXIII;
Oxford: Clarendon Press, 1998) 181–205.

[28]Schiffman, 'The Hekhalot Literature and the Qumran Writings' (note 1 above) 126.

construction' of the celestial temple which was completed on the eleventh Sabbath, coinciding with this covenant renewal ceremony.[29]

The exorcism texts 4Q510–511 and 11QApocPsalms, discussed in the previous section, also look to be tied to cultic settings about which we know all too little. The *Songs of the Sage* (4Q510 1.4; 4Q511 2.i.1) mentions the משכיל, a sectarian title, and repeatedly says that the purpose of the songs is to frighten away demons (4Q510 1.4–6 = 4Q511 10.1–3; 4Q511 8.4; 35.7; 48–51.2–3). This work has an intriguing reference to the 'festivals of the year' celebrated by the Yahad (4Q511 2.i.9; cf. 35.8); there is a call to worship in the plural (4Q511 frag. 10.7–9 = 4Q510 1.8–9; note the mention of a lyre), although some material is also in the first person singular (4Q 511 18 ii; 63 ii, iii; 48–51), and there are addresses to God (e.g., 4Q511 52, 54–55, 57–59; 63 ii–iv). Unfortunately, no cultic instructions are preserved (but note 'And on the eighth I will open [my mouth]' in 4Q511 42.4), and it is quite unclear under what circumstances these songs were recited. The songs in 11QApocPsalms sound more like hymns that might actually be used in an exorcism, and some phrases may be instructions for use, but again, the details of the ritual are not yet understood. A comparison with ritual elements in later exorcism texts would probably be quite useful.

A striking parallel to the ritual praxes of the Merkavah mystics is found in the Aramaic *Levi* document. Fragments of at least seven MSS of this work survive in the Qumran library (1Q21, 4Q213, 4Q213a, 4Q213b, 4Q214, 4Q214a, 4Q214b). In addition, medieval fragments of the same work have been recovered from the Cairo Geniza; the Mt. Athos MS of the Greek *Testament of Levi* contains additions that correspond to Aramaic *Levi*; and the Greek *Testament of Levi* (known to us only in a Christian MS tradition – hereafter, *TLevi*) draws on similar material. A great deal of the original Aramaic *Levi* document can be reconstructed with near certainty and some of what remains missing can be inferred with reasonable confidence.[30]

[29]C. R. A. Morray-Jones, 'The Temple Within: The Embodied Divine Image and Its Worship in the Dead Sea Scrolls and Other Early Jewish and Christian Sources', *Society of Biblical Literature 1998 Seminar Papers* (Atlanta, GA: Scholars Press, 1998), pp. 400–31.

[30]See R. A. Kugler, *From Patriarch to Priest: The Levi-Priestly Tradition from Aramaic Levi to Testament of Levi* (SBLEJL 9; Atlanta, GA: Scholars Press, 1996). For the official editions of the Qumran material see J. T. Milik in *Qumran Cave 1* ed. D. Barthelemy *et al.* (DJD I; Oxford: Clarendon Press, 1955) 87–91; J. C. Greenfield and M. E. Stone in *Qumran Cave 4 XVII Parabiblical Texts, Part 3*, ed. George Brooke *et al.* (DJD XXII; Oxford: Clarendon Press, 1996) 1–72, pls. 1–4. Other treatments include Milik, 'Le Testament de Lévi en araméen: Fragment de la Grotte 4 de Qumra3n', *RB* 62 (1955) 398–406; J. C. Greenfield and M. E. Stone, 'Remarks on the Aramaic Testament of Levi from the Geniza', *RB* 86 (1979) 214–30 and pls. 13–14; *idem*, 'The Prayer of Levi', *JBL* 112 (1993) 247–66.

Both *TLevi* and Aramaic *Levi* preserve traditions about one or more ascents of Levi to heaven. The first relevant connected passage in Aramaic *Levi* contains an episode that corresponds very generally to *TLevi* chaps. 2–5.[31] (In *TLevi* it appears between the opening scene at Levi's deathbed [chap. 1] and the destruction of Shechem [chap. 6], but we have no way of determining its context in Aramaic *Levi*.)[32] In Aramaic *Levi*, Levi washes his clothes and bathes in running water, then lifts his eyes to heaven and prays a long prayer asking God to deliver him from sin; grant him the holy spirit, wisdom, and strength; protect him from demonic assault, and to bless him and his line. After praying, he goes on from Abel Mayin (where, according to *TLevi* 2:3, he had been tending flocks) to his father Jacob (in Bethel, as we learn later). Lying down to sleep (perhaps in an incubation ritual?), he sees visions in which he evidently ascends to heaven and is met at the gates of heaven by an angel. The text breaks off at this point.

Another passage preserves the end of a vision that corresponds, again in a general way, to the vision in *TLevi* 8.[33] Until recently, scholars had assumed that two visions were narrated in Aramaic *Levi*, as in *TLevi*, but Robert Kugler has rightly called this assumption into question.[34] Although Levi goes from Abel Maoul (to Shechem?) *between* the two visions in *TLevi*, and thence to Bethel (2:3; 6:1–5), in Aramaic *Levi* he journeys from Abel Mayin to Bethel *before* he has a vision at all. The order of events and details in the two works are clearly different, and there is no reason to reconstruct more than one vision in Aramaic Levi, in which case it appears that the beginning and end of this vision are preserved in the Aramaic fragments. The passage begins with a narrative about the coming 'reign of the sword'. The speakers refer to a lost episode in which they made Levi 'greater than anyone' and granted him 'the anointing of eternal peace'. Then seven beings, presumably the speakers, depart from Levi. He wakes up and marvels at his vision, but tells no one about it. Then Jacob dresses him in priestly clothing and invests him as a priest. This surviving passage is close enough to *TLevi*

---

[31]The passage must be reconstructed from the Greek of the Mt. Athos MS and 4Q213a (4QLevi[b] ar), frag. 1.5–18 + frag. 2.5–10.

[32]Fragments of the Shechem episode survive in Aramaic *Levi*, but their placement in the work as a whole is uncertain.

[33]This passage must be reconstructed from 4Q213b and the Geniza text §§6–9. Kugler also includes 4Q213 frag. 2 as part of the vision, on the ground that parallel material is found in the version of an angelic address to Moses in *Jub.* 30:5–17 which may have Aramaic *Levi* as its source (*From Patriarch to Priest* [note 30 above]: 36–7). Milik's suggestion that the fragment belongs to Isaac's instructions to Levi after the vision (Kugler, *From Patriarch to Priest* 83 n. 83) seems better to me (cf. *TLevi* 9:6–14), but the problem has little bearing on my analysis.

[34]Kugler, *From Patriarch to Priest* 53–59.

8:1–9:5 to justify our using the Greek work to fill in some of the missing material in Aramaic *Levi*. It is very likely that the vision involved the heavenly consecration of Levi as priest by seven angels. This is what happens in *TLevi*, and it coheres well with the references to anointing and to the seven unnamed beings at the end of the vision in Aramaic *Levi*.

This episode in Aramaic *Levi* has some interesting similarities to rituals found in the Hekhalot literature. Although no Hekhalot text describes exactly the same ritual complex, the elements of laundering of clothing,[35] immersion (sometimes in running water),[36] prayer in a set position in an isolated situation,[37] wearing of white garments,[38] and incubation to generate dreams with angelic revelations[39] are all found in the Hekhalot MSS. One example of such a passage is found in the Sar Torah document:

(§299) R. Ishmael said:
Thus said R. Akiva in the name of R. Eliezer the Great:
He who would join himself to the prince of Torah must wash his garments and his clothes and immerse (in) a strict immersion as a safeguard in case of pollution. And he must dwell for twelve days in a room or in an upper chamber. He must not go out or come in, and he must neither eat nor drink. But from evening to evening see that he eats his bread, clean bread of his own hands, and he drinks pure water, and that he does not taste any kind of vegetable.

(§300) And he must insert this midrash of the prince of Torah into the prayer three times in every single day; it is after the prayer that he should pray it from its beginning to its end. And afterward, he must sit and recite during the twelve days, the days of his fasting, from morning until evening, and must not be silent. And in every hour that he finishes it he must stand on his feet and adjure the servants, as well as their King, every single prince twelve times. Afterward he must adjure every single one of them by the seal.

[§§301–302 give *nomina barbara* and angelic names the practitioner should invoke.]

[35]Sar Torah §299 (see below).
[36]Pirqe di R. Nehuniah ben HaQanah §314; Magic Book §489; Maʿaseh Merkavah §560; Sar Panim §623; Merkavah Rabba §682.
[37]Pirqe di R. Nehuniah ben HaQanah §314; Hekhalot Zutarti §424; Magic Book §489; Maʿaseh Merkavah §560; Merkavah Rabba §682.
[38]Magic Book §489. Perhaps the white garment is an echo of priestly garb? Cf. Josephus, *Ant.* III 179. A number of Hekhalot texts refer to the importance of the priestly status of R. Ishmael, one of the heroes of the corpus (3 Enoch 1:3 [§1]; 2:1–4 [§3]; Messiah Aggadah §140; Maʿaseh Merkavah §586; Merkavah Rabba §681).
[39]The Dream Prince §502–11.

(§303) When he completes the twelve (days), he will go forth to all the principles of Torah that he seeks, whether to Bible, or whether to Mishnah, or to the vision of the chariot, for he goes forth in a pure condition and (departs) from grief and from great pain.

This particular unit of tradition includes the washing of clothes and immersion, followed by protracted prayer in isolation. The promised result is either miraculous knowledge of scripture (generally granted by angelic visitants) or the 'vision of the chariot,' that is, a celestial ascent to the throne of God. The vision in Aramaic *Levi* certainly involves a celestial ascent, one or more encounters with angels, and possibly a vision of the throne of God (cf. *TLevi* 5:1). The idea of a priestly investment in heaven is also found in *3 Enoch* 8–15, in which Enoch is transformed into the angel Metatron, who is crowned, given glorious clothing, and enthroned in a ritual that resembles both priestly and royal investitures.[40] Since Enoch remains in heaven thereafter, a passage in the Hekhalot Rabbati provides a somewhat closer parallel. In §§203–37, R. Nehuniah ben HaQanah describes the ritual praxis (recitation of a set number of divine names) by which the mystic summons the angel Suriah to lead him through the perils of the six celestial palaces to the seventh containing the divine throne room. The successful mystic shows the final magical seals to the angels Dumiel and Qaspiel, after which

(§231) At once Qaspiel draws his bow and sharpens his sword and brings to you a wind storm and seats you in a wagon of brightness and causes about eight thousand myriad horns and three thousand myriad trumpets and four thousand myriad clarions to be blown before you. And Dumiel the prince bears a gift and goes before you.

An alternate version (§§233–34) has Dumiel questioning the candidate as to his merits, but in the end the mystic is taken past the angelic hosts to enter the divine throne room and join the celestial choir:

And they enter before the throne of glory and bring before him all kinds of music and song. And they make music and come before him until they bring him up and seat him beside the cherubim, the *ophannim*, and the holy living creatures. Then he sees wonders and mighty acts, majesty and greatness, holiness and purity, awe, humility, and uprightness in that hour.

Conclusion: Sectarian vs. Nonsectarian Origins

I conclude by asking whether the mystical and magical traditions found

---

[40]Himmelfarb, *Ascent to Heaven* (note 3 above) 29–46.

in the Qumran library belong to the wider traditions of late Second Temple Judaism or are specifically sectarian expressions. Schiffman's view seems to have developed over time. In 1982 he wrote,

In light of our study, it is possible to conclude that *merkavah* mysticism had its origin at Qumran or in related sectarian circles. From there it somehow penetrated and was absorbed by Pharisaic and then tannaitic tradition. It would be through these channels that this speculation entered into the mainstream of Judaism.[41]

But by 1987 he had adopted a more cautious view, concluding that the Merkavah mystical traditions were scattered among circles outside the Qumran sect and that there were no grounds for asserting a direct connection between the Qumran library and the later Hekhalot literature. He expressed doubt that such ideas were widespread among the Pharisees, although he granted that he could not rule out the possibility.[42]

My survey of the evidence leads me to a similarly cautious position. Many of these texts have links to sectarian thought, including the exorcism hymns of the *Songs of the Sage*, the Merkavah hymns associated with the sectarian covenant renewal ceremony in 4QBerakhot, the physiognomic traditions of 4Q186, the Hodayot passages that deal with apotheosis and paradisiacal themes, and the *Self-Glorification Hymn* (which appears in two Hodayot MSS). The eschatological exaltation of Melchizedek is also narrated in a sectarian text. It is likely, although not certain, that the *Songs of the Sabbath Sacrifice* was composed by the Qumran sect and, in any case, it follows the sectarian solar calendar. Likewise *1 Enoch*, which preserves ascent traditions about Enoch, is not a sectarian compilation, although parts of it too use the solar calendar. It is not clear to me whether the exorcism hymns in 11QPsApoc[a] are sectarian, although the two possible references to Belial in the fourth song may point in that direction.

At the same time, a number of texts in our corpus show no particular sectarian traits at all. 4Q534 combines physiognomy with visionary experience and perhaps heavenly ascent. 4Q561 contains additional physiognomic traditions. 4Q560 appears to be a relatively generic magical amulet. Aramaic *Levi* describes purificatory rituals combined with an ascent tradition and celestial investment of Levi as priest. The ascent of Methuselah in the *Genesis Apocryphon* and the possible deification of Moses in 4Q374 (and 377?) occur in what appear to be nonsectarian works. It is interesting to note that all but one of these

---

[41]Schiffman, '*Merkavah* Speculation at Qumran' (note 1 above) 46.
[42]Schiffman, 'The Hekhalot Literature and the Qumran Writings' (note 1 above) 133–4.

works are in Aramaic, although I am not sure what implications to draw from this circumstance.

Naturally our sample is skewed, since presumably the collectors of the Qumran library selected works they approved of, but the fact that so many of the works with clear antecedents to Merkavah mysticism do not contain obvious sectarian traits leads me to believe that this magical and mystical conglomeration of ideas belonged to a wider range of Judaism in the Second Temple period than the Qumran sect alone.

SELECT BIBLIOGRAPHY

Abegg, M. 'Messianic Hope and 4Q285: A Reassessment' *JBL* 113 (1994) 81–91.

——. 'The Messiah at Qumran. Are We Still Seeing Double?' *DSD* 2 (1995) 125–44.

——. 'Who Ascended to Heaven?' 4Q491, 4Q427 and the Teacher of Righteousness' in *Eschatology, Messianism and the Dead Sea Scrolls* edited by C. A. Evans and P. W. Flint. Grand Rapids: Eerdmans, 1997. Pp. 61–73.

Aejmelaeus, Anneli. 'Septuagintal Translation Techniques – A Solution to the Problem of the Tabernacle Account' in *Septuagint, Scrolls and Cognate Writings* edited by G. J. Brooke and Barnabas Lindars. Atlanta: Scholars Press, 1992. Pp. 381–402.

Aharoni, Y. *The Land of the Bible. A Historical Geography*. London: Burns & Oates, 1967.

Albani, M. *Astronomie und Schopfungsglaube: Untersuchungen zum astronomischen Henochbuch*. Neukirchen-Vluyn: Neukirchener Verlag, 1994.

——. 'Un Instrument de Mesures Astonomiques à Qumran' *RB* 104 (1997) 88–115.

Albeck, C. *Das Buch der Jubiläen und die Halacha*. Berlin: Siegfried Scholem, 1930.

——. *Sisha Sidre Mishnah (The Six Orders of the Mishnah)*. 6 volumes. Jerusalem: Bialik Institute, 1958–59.

Alexander, P. S. 'Jewish Law in the Time of Jesus: Towards a Clarification of the Problem' in *Law and Religion. Essays on the Place of the Law in Israel and Early Christianity* edited by Barnabas Lindars. Cambridge: Cambridge University Press, 1988. Pp. 44–58.

——. ' "Wrestling against Wickedness in High Places": Magic in the Worldview of the Qumran Community' in *SSQFYA*, pp. 318–37.

Allegro, J. M. *The Dead Sea Scrolls*. Harmondsworth: Penguin Books, 1956.

Allegro, J. M., with Anderson, A. A. *Qumran Cave 4.I (4Q158–4Q186)*. DJD V; Oxford: Clarendon Press, 1968.

Auld, A. Graeme. *Kings without Privilege: David and Moses and the Story of the Bible's Kings*. Edinburgh: T&T Clark, 1994.

Baillet, M. 'Remarques sur le manuscrit du Livre des Jubilés de la grotte 3 de Qumran', *RevQ* 5 (1965) 423–33.

——. *Qumrân Grotte 4.III (4Q482–4Q520)*. DJD VII. Oxford: Clarendon Press, 1982.

Baillet, M., Milik, J. T., and de Vaux, R. *Les 'petites grottes' de Qumrân*. DJD III. Oxford: Clarendon Press, 1962.

Bammel, E. 'The Baptist in Early Christian Tradition' *NTS* 18 (1971–2) 95–128.

Baron, S. W. *A Social and Religious History of the Jews. Volume 5: Religious Controls and Dissensions*. Philadelphia: Jewish Publication Society, 1957.

Barthélemy, D. and Milik, J. T. *Qumran Cave 1*. DJD I. Oxford: Clarendon Press, 1955.

Baumgarten, Albert I. 'The Temple Scroll, Toilet Practices, and the Essenes' *Jewish History* 10 (1996) 9–20.

——. *The Flourishing of Jewish Sects in the Maccabean Era: An Interpretation*. Leiden: E. J. Brill, 1997.

——. 'The Zadokite Priests at Qumran: A Reconsideration' *DSD* 4 (1997) 137–56.

Baumgarten, J. M. *Studies in Qumran Law*. Leiden: E. J. Brill, 1977.

——. Review of Y. Yadin's Hebrew edition of the Temple Scroll in *JBL* 97 (1978) 584–9.

——. 'The Pharisaic-Sadducean Controversies about Purity and the Qumran Texts' *JJS* 31 (1980) 157–70.

——. 'The Qumran Songs against Demons', *Tarbiz* 55 (1985–86) 442–5 (Hebrew).

——. '4Q503 (Daily Prayers) and the Lunar Calendar' *RevQ* 12 (1986) 399–407.

——. 'The Laws of ᶜOrlah and First Fruits in the Light of Jubilees, the Qumran Writings, and Targum Ps. Jonathan', *JJS* 38 (1987) 195–202.

——. 'The Calendar of the Book of Jubilees and the Temple Scroll' *VT* 37 (1987) 71–8.

——. 'The Purification Rituals in *DJD 7*' in *DSSFYR*, pp. 199–209.

——. 'The Disqualification of Priests in 4Q Fragments of the "Damascus Document", a Specimen of the Recovery of pre-Rabbinic Halakha' in *MQC* volume 2, pp. 503–14.

——. 'The Cave 4 Versions of the Qumran Penal Code' *JJS* 43.2 (1992) 268–76.

——. 'Sadducean Elements in Qumran Law' in *CRC*, pp. 27–36.

——. *Qumran Cave 4. XIII. The Damascus Document (4Q266–273).* Oxford: Clarendon Press, 1996.

Beckwith, Roger. 'The Modern Attempt to Reconcile the Qumran Calendar with the True Solar Year' *RevQ* 7 (1970) 379–96.

——. 'The Essene Calendar and the Moon: a Reconsideration' *RevQ* 15 (1992) 457–66.

——. *The Old Testament Canon of the New Testament Church and its Background in Early Judaism.* London: SPCK, 1985.

——. *Calendar and Chronology, Jewish and Christian.* Leiden: Brill Academic Publishers, 1996.

Belkin, S. *Philo and the Oral Law. The Philonic Interpretation of Biblical Law in Relation to the Palestinian Halaka.* Cambridge, MA: Harvard University Press, 1940.

Benoit, P., Milik, J. T., de Vaux, R. *et al. Les grottes de Murabba'at.* DJD II. Oxford: Clarendon Press, 1961.

Bernstein, M., 'לא ידור רוחי באדם לעולם: 4Q252 i 2: Biblical Text or Biblical Interpretation?' *RevQ* 16 (1993–94) 421–7.

——. Review of H. Attridge *et al. Qumran Cave 4. VIII.* DJD XIII (Oxford: Clarendon Press, 1994), in *DSD* 4 (1997) 102–12.

——. 'The Employment and Interpretation of Scripture in 4QMMT: Preliminary Observations' in *Reading 4QMMT: New Perspectives on Qumran Law and History* edited by J. Kampen and M. J. Bernstein. Atlanta: Scholars Press, 1996. Pp. 29–51.

Bernstein, M., García Martínez, F., and Kampen, J. (eds). *Legal Texts and Legal Issues. Proceedings of the Second Meeting of the International Organization for Qumran Studies. Cambridge 1995. Published in Honour of Joseph M. Baumgarten.* Leiden: Brill Academic Publishers, 1997. (=*LTLI*)

Betz, Otto. 'Was John the Baptist an Essene?' in *Understanding the Dead Sea Scrolls: A Reader from the Biblical Archaeological Review* edited by Hershel Shanks. New York: Random House, 1992.

Betz, Otto, and Riesner, R. *Jesus, Qumran and the Vatican*. ET: London: SCM Press, 1994.

Black, Matthew. *The Scrolls and Christian Origins*. New York: Scribner, 1961.

Brooke, G. J. 'The Amos-Numbers Midrash (CD 7,13b–8,1a) and Messianic Expectation' *ZAW* 92 (1980) 397–404.

——. *Exegesis at Qumran: 4QFlorilegium in its Jewish Context*. Sheffield: Sheffield Academic Press, 1985.

——. 'The Biblical Texts in the Qumran Commentaries: Scribal Errors or Exegetical Variants?' in *Early Jewish and Christian Exegesis: Studies in Memory of William Hugh Brownlee* edited by C. A. Evans and W. F. Stinespring. Atlanta, GA: Scholars Press, 1987. Pp. 85–100.

——. 'The Temple Scroll: A Law Unto Itself?' *in Law and Religion. Essays on the Place of the Law in Israel and Early Christianity* edited by Barnabas Lindars. Cambridge: James Clarke, 1988. Pp. 34–43.

——. '4Q500 1 and the Use of Scripture in the Parable of the Vineyard', *DSD* 2 (1995) 268–294.

——. '4QCommentary on Genesis A' in *Qumran Cave 4. XVII.* DJD XXII. Oxford: Clarendon Press, 1996.

——. 'The Explicit Presentation of Scripture in 4QMMT' in *LTLI*, pp. 67–88.

——. 'The Book of Jeremiah and Its Reception in the Qumran Scrolls' in *The Book of Jeremiah and Its Reception* edited by A. H. W. Curtis and T. Römer. Leuven: Leuven University Press, 1997. Pp. 183–205.

——. ' "The Canon Within the Canon" at Qumran and in the New Testament' in *SSQFYA*, pp. 242–66.

——. 'Some Comments on 4Q252 and the Text of Genesis' *Textus* 19 (1998) 1–25.

Brooke, G. J. with F. García Martínez (eds). *New Qumran Texts and Studies*. Leiden: Brill, 1994. (=*NQTS*)

Brooke, G. J., and Robinson, J. M. 'A Further Fragment of 1QSb: The Schøyen Collection MS 1909' *JJS* 46 (1995) 120–33.

Broshi, Magen. 'The Archaeology of Qumran – A Reconsideration' in *DSSFYR*, pp. 103–15.

Brown, R. E. *The Birth of the Messiah. A Commentary on the Infancy Narratives in the Gospels of Matthew and Luke.* New York: Doubleday, 1993.

Brownlee, W. H. 'John the Baptist in the New Light of Ancient Scrolls' in *The Scrolls and the New Testament* edited by K. Stendahl. New York: Harper, 1957.

———. *The Meaning of the Qumrân Scrolls for the Bible with Special Attention to the Book of Isaiah.* New York: Oxford University Press, 1964.

———. 'The Composition of Habakkuk' in *Hommages à André Dupont-Sommer* edited by A. Caquot and M. Philonenko. Paris: Adrien-Maisonneuve, 1971. Pp. 255–75.

———. *The Midrash Pesher of Habakkuk.* Missoula: Scholars Press, 1979.

Burrows, Millar (ed.). *The Dead Sea Scrolls of St. Mark's Monastery 1.* New Haven: American Schools of Oriental Research, 1950.

Cameron, Ron. ' "What have you come out to see?" Characterisations of John and Jesus in the Gospels' *Semeia* 49 (1990) 38–45.

Caquot, A. 'Le messianism qumraniens' in *Qumrân. Sa piété, sa théologie et son milieu* edited by M. Delcor. Leuven: Leuven University Press, 1978. Pp. 231–47.

Carmichael, Calum. 'A Common Element in Five Supposedly Disparate Laws' *VT* 29 (1979) 129–34.

———. *Law and Narrative in the Bible.* Ithaca: Cornell University Press, 1984.

———. *The Spirit of Biblical Law.* Athens: University of Georgia Press, 1996.

———. *Law, Legend, and Incest in the Bible.* Ithaca: Cornell University Press, 1997.

———. 'The Sabbatical/Jubilee Cycle and the Seven-Year Famine in Egypt' *Bib* 80 (1999) 224–39.

Carroll, R. P. *Jeremiah.* Philadelphia: Westminster John Knox Press, 1996.

Charles, R. H. (ed.). *The Apocrypha and Pseudepigrapha of the Old Testament*. Oxford: Oxford University Press, 1913. 2 volumes.

Charles, R. H. *The Book of Jubiless or the Little Genesis*. London: SPCK, 1917.

Charlesworth, J. H. (ed.). *The Old Testament Pseudepigrapha*. New York: Doubleday, 1985. 2 volumes.

——. *Jesus and the Dead Sea Scrolls*. New York: Doubleday, 1992.

——. *The Messiah: Developments in Earliest Judaism and Christianity*. Minneapolis: Fortress Press, 1992.

——. *The Dead Sea Scrolls. Hebrew, Aramaic, and Greek Texts with English Translation. Volume 1. Rule of the Community and Related Documents*. Louisville: Westminster John Knox Press, 1994.

Chilton, B. *Judaic Approaches to the Gospels*. Atlanta: Scholars Press, 1994.

Collins, John J. 'Messianism in the Dead Sea Scrolls' in *Methods of Investigation of the Dead Sea Scrolls and the Khirbet Qumran Site* edited by M. Wise *et al*. New York: The New York Academy of Sciences, 1994. Pp. 213–29.

——. *Daniel*. Minneapolis: Fortress Press, 1993.

——. *The Scepter and the Star: The Messiahs of the Dead Sea Scrolls and Other Ancient Literature*. New York: Doubleday, 1995.

——. 'Jesus and the Messiahs of Israel' in *Geschichte – Tradition – Reflexion: Festschrift für Martin Hengel zum 70. Geburtstag* edited by H. Canick, H. Lichtenberger and P. Schaefer. Tübingen: Mohr, 1996. Volume 3, pp. 287–303.

——. 'The Background of the "Son of God" Text' *BBR* 7 (1997) 51–62.

——. *Jewish Wisdom in the Hellenistic Age*. Louisville: Westminster John Knox Press, 1997.

——. 'A Herald of Good Tidings. Isaiah 61:1–3 and its Actualization in the Dead Sea Scrolls' in *The Quest for Context and Meaning. Studies in Biblical Intertextuality in Honour of James A. Sanders* edited by C. A. Evans and S. Talmon. Leiden: Brill Academic Publishers, 1997.

——. *Apocalypticism in the Dead Sea Scrolls*. London: Routlege, 1997.

Cross, F. M. *Canaanite Myth and Hebrew Epic*. Cambridge, MA: Harvard University Press, 1973.

——. 'The Ammonite Oppression of the Tribes of Gad and Reuben: Missing Verses from 1 Samuel 11 found in 4QSamuel[a]' *in History, Historiography and Interpretation* edited by H. Tadmor and M. Weinfeld. Jerusalem: Magnes Press, 1983. Pp. 148–58.

——. 'Some Notes on a Generation of Qumran Studies' in *MQC*, volume 1, pp. 1–14.

——. *The Ancient Library of Qumran*. Third edition. Sheffield: Sheffield Academic Press, 1995.

Cook, E. '4Q246' *BBR* 5 (1995) 43–66.

Cross, F. M., and Talmon, S. (eds). *Qumran and the History of the Biblical Text*. Cambridge, MA: Harvard University Press, 1975.

Danby, H. *The Mishnah*. Oxford: Oxford University Press, 1933.

Daniélou, J. *Théologie du judéo-christianisme (Histoire des doctrines chrétiennes avant Nicée 1)*. Tournai, 1958. ET: *The Theology of Jewish Christianity (A History of Early Christian Doctrine Before the Council of Nicaea 1)*. London: Darton, Longman & Todd, 1977.

Davies, P. R. *The Damascus Covenant. An Interpretation of the 'Damascus Document'*. Sheffield: Sheffield Academic Press, 1982.

——. *Behind the Essenes. History and Ideology in the Dead Sea Scrolls*. Atlanta: Scholars Press, 1987.

——. 'Communities at Qumran and the Case of the Missing Teacher' *RevQ* 15 (1991) 275–86.

Davila, J. A. 'Review of M. Himmelfarb, Ascent to Heaven in Jewish and Christian Apocalypses' *Ioudaios Review* 4.017.

——. 'Text-Type and Terminology: Genesis and Exodus as Test Cases' *RevQ* 16 (1993) 3–37.

——. 'The Hekhalot Literature and Shamanism' in *Society of Biblical Literature 1994 Seminar Papers*. Atlanta: Scholars Press, 1994. Pp. 767–89.

——. 'The Hodayot Hymnist and the Four Who Entered Paradise' *RevQ* 17/65–68 (1996) 457–78.

——. 'Melchizedek, Michael, and War in Heaven' *in Society of Biblical Literature 1996 Seminar Papers*. Atlanta: Scholars Press, 1996. Pp. 259–72.

———. '4QMess Ar (4Q534) and Merkavah Mysticism' *DSD* 5 (1998) 367–381.

———. 'Heavenly Ascents in the Dead Sea Scrolls' in *The Dead Sea Scrolls after Fifty Years: A Comprehensive Assessment*. Volume 2 edited by Peter Flint and James C. VanderKam. Leiden: Brill Academic Publishers, 1999. Pp. 461–85.

Davis, M. 'Jewish Religious Life and Institutions in America (A Historical Study)' in *The Jews,: Their Religion and Culture* edited by L. Finkelstein. New York: Schocken, 1971. Pp. 274–379.

Deichgräber, R. 'Fragmente einer Jubiläen-Handschrift aus Höhle 3 von Qumran' *RevQ* 5 (1965) 415–22.

Delcor, M. *Les Hymnes de Qumran (Hodayot)*. Paris: Letouzey et Ani, 1962.

de Vaux, R. and Milik, J. T. *Qumrân Grotte 4.II.* DJD VI. Oxford: Clarendon Press, 1977.

de Waard, J. *A Comparative Study of the Old Testament Text in the Dead Sea Scrolls and in the New Testament*. Leiden: E. J. Brill, 1965.

Dimant, D. 'The Qumran Manuscripts: Contents and Significance' in *TPWW*, pp. 23–58.

———. 'New Light from Qumran on the Jewish Pseudepigrapha – 4Q390' in *MQC* volume 2, pp. 405–48.

———. 'Apocalyptic Texts at Qumran' in *CRC*, pp. 175–91.

Dimant, D., and Strugnell, J. 'The Merkabah Vision in Second Ezekiel (4Q385 4)' *RevQ* 14 (1990) 331–48.

Dimant, D., and Rappaport, U. (eds). *The Dead Sea Scrolls: Forty Years of Research* Leiden: E. J. Brill, 1992. (=*DSSFYR*)

Dimant, D., and Schiffman, L. W. (eds). *Time to Prepare the Way in the Wilderness. Papers on the Qumran Scrolls by Fellows of the Institute for Advanced Studies of the Hebrew University, Jerusalem, 1989–1990.* Leiden: Brill Academic Publishers, 1995. (=*TPWW*)

Dubonov, S. תולדות החסידות בתקופת צמיחתה וגידולה. Tel Aviv: Dvir, 1932.

Duhaime, J. 'War Scroll' in *The Dead Sea Scrolls. Hebrew, Aramaic, and Greek Texts with English Translation* edited by J. H. Charlesworth. Louisville: Westminster John Knox Press, 1995. Pp. 80–203.

Duncan, J. A. 'Considerations of 4QDt' in Light of the "All Souls Deuteronomy" and Cave 4 Phylactery Texts' in *MQC* volume 1, pp. 199–215.

Ehrman, B. D. *The Orthodox Corruption of Scripture. The Effect of Early Christological Controversies on the Text of the New Testament.* New York: Oxford University Press, 1993.

Eisenman, R. *James the Brother of Jesus.* London: Faber and Faber, 1997.

Eisenman, R., and Wise, M. *The Dead Sea Scrolls Uncovered.* London/New York: Penguin, 1992.

Elliger, Karl. *Studien zum Habakuk-Kommentar vom Toten Meer.* Tübingen: J. C. B. Mohr, 1953.

Ellis, E. Earle. 'Old Testament Quotations in the New: A Brief History of the Research' in *The Old Testament in Early Christianity. Canon and Interpretation in Light of Modern Research.* Tübingen: 1991. Pp. 51–74.

Elman, Y. 'Some Remarks on 4QMMT and the Rabbinic Tradition, or, When Is a Parallel Not a Parallel?' in *Reading 4QMMT: New Perspectives on Qumran Law and History* edited by J. Kampen and M. J. Bernstein. Atlanta: Scholars Press, 1996. Pp. 105–24.

Elon, M. משפט העברי. Jerusalem: Magnes Press, 1973.

Ernst, J. *Johannes der Täufer.* Berlin: Walter de Gruyter, 1989.

Eshel, E. '4QLevᵈ: A Possible Source for the Temple Scroll and Miqsat Ma'aśe ha-torah' *DSD* 2 (1995) 1–13.

———. '4Q471b: A Self-Glorification Hymn' *RevQ* 17/65–68 (1996) 175–203.

Eshel, H. 'The Historical Background of the Pesher Interpreting Joshua's Curse on the Rebuilder of Jericho' *RevQ* 15 (1992) 409–20.

Evans, C. A. 'Jesus and the Messianic Texts from Qumran: A Preliminary Assessment of the Recently Published Materials' in *Jesus and His Contemporaries* edited by C. A. Evans. Leiden/New York/Köln: Brill Academic Publishers, 1995. Pp. 83–154.

Fekkes, J. *Isaiah and Prophetic Traditions in the Book of Revelation: Visionary Antecedents and their Development.* Sheffield: Sheffield Academic Press, 1994.

Finkelstein, L. 'The Maxim of the *Anshe Keneset ha-Gedolah' JBL* 59 (1940) 455–69.

Fishbane, Michael. *Biblical Interpretation in Ancient Israel.* Oxford: Clarendon Press, 1985.

——. 'Use, Authority and Interpretation of Mikra at Qumran' in *Mikra* edited by M. J. Mulder. Assen/Maastricht: van Goveum, 1988. pp. 339–78.

Fitzmyer, J. A. 'Prolegomenon' in S. Schechter, *Documents of Jewish Sectaries: Fragments of a Zadokite Work.* New York: Ktav, 1970. Pp. 14–15.

——. 'The Aramaic 'Elect of God' Text from Qumran Cave 4' in *Essays on the Semitic Background of the New Testament.* Missoula: Scholars Press, 1974. Pp. 127–60.

——. 'The Qumran Scrolls, The Ebionites and Their Literature' in *Essays on the Semitic Background of the New Testament.* Missoula: Scholars Press, 1974. Pp. 435–80.

——. 'Further Light on Melchizedek from Qumran Cave 11' in *Essays on the Semitic Background of the New Testament.* Missoula: Scholars Press, 1974. Pp. 245–70.

——. '4Q246: The "Son of God" Document from Qumran' *Bib* 74 (1993) 153–74.

——. 'The Aramaic "Son of God" Text from Qumran Cave 4' in *Methods of Investigation of the Dead Sea Scrolls and the Khirbet Qumran Site* edited by M. Wise *et al.* New York: The New York Academy of Sciences, 1994. Pp. 163–78.

Fletcher-Louis, C. H. T. 'Heavenly Ascent or Incarnational Presence? A Revisionist Reading of the Songs of the Sabbath Sacrifice' *Society of Biblical Literature 1998 Seminar Papers.* Atlanta: Scholars Press. Pp. 367–99.

Flint, P. W. *The Dead Sea Psalms Scrolls and the Book of Psalms.* Leiden: Brill Academic Publishers, 1997.

Flusser, D. *Judaism and the Origins of Christianity.* Jerusalem: Magnes Press, 1988.

Frankel, Z. *Vorstudien zu der Septuaginta.* Leipzig: J. A. Barth, 1941.

——. *Über den Einfluss der palästinischen Exegese auf die alexandrinische Hermeneutik.* Leipzig: J. A. Barth, 1851.

Frid, B. 'Jesaja und Paulus in Röm 15,12' *BZ* 27 (1983) 237–41.

Fujita, N. S. 'The Metaphor of Plant in Jewish Literature of the Intertestamental Period' *JSJ* 7 (1976) 30–45.

García Martínez, F. 'Nuevos Textos no Bíblicos procedentes de Qumrán (I)' *Estudios Bíblicos* 49 (1991) 97–134.

——. '4QMessAr and the Book of Noah' *in Qumran and Apocalyptic: Studies on the Aramaic Texts from Qumran*. Leiden: E. J. Brill, 1992. Pp. 1–44.

——. '11QTemple[b]: A Preliminary Publication' in *MQC* volume 1, pp. 363–90.

——. 'Messianische Erwartungen in den Qumranschriften' *Jahrbuch für biblische Theologie* 8 (1993) 171–208.

——. *The Dead Sea Scrolls Translated*. Second edition. Leiden: E. J. Brill, 1996.

——. 'Textos de Qumrán' in *Literatura judia intertestamentaria*. Estella, 1996.

García Martínez, F., Tigchelaar, E. J., van der Woude, A. S. *Qumran Cave 11.II: 11Q2–18, 11Q20–31*. DJD XXIII. Oxford: Clarendon Press, 1998.

Gärtner, B. 'Die rätselhaften Termini Nazoräer und Iskariot' in *Horæ Sœderblomianæ* 4. Uppsala: Gleerup, 1957. Pp. 5–36.

——. *The Temple and the Community in Qumran and the New Testament*. Cambridge: Cambridge University Press, 1965.

Geiger, A. *Urschrift und Übersetzungen der Bibel in ihrer Abhängigkeit von der innern Entwicklung des Judentums*. Breslaus: J. Hainauer, 1857.

Gerstenberger, Erhard. *Leviticus*. Louisville: Westminster John Knox Press, 1996.

Ginzberg, L. *The Legend of the Jews*. Philadelphia: Jewish Publication Society, 1946.

——. *An Unknown Jewish Sect*. ET. New York: Jewish Theological Seminary, 1976.

Glessmer, U. 'The Otot-Texts (4Q319) and the Problem of Intercalations in the Context of the 364-day Calendar' in *Qumranstudien: Vorträge und Beiträge der Teilnehmer des Qumranseminars auf dem internationalen Treffen der Society of Biblical Literature, Münster, 25–26 Juli 1993* edited by H. J. Fabry, A. Lange and H. Lichtenberger. Göttingen: 1996. Pp. 125–63.

Goodblatt, D. *The Monarchic Principle. Studies in Jewish Self-Government in Antiquity*. Tübingen: Mohr-Siebeck, 1994.

——. 'Horizontal Measuring in the Babylonian Astronomical Compendium MULAPIN and in the Astronomical Book of 1 En' *Henoch* 18 (1996) 259–82.

Gray, Rebecca. *Prophetic Figures in Late Second Temple Jewish Palestine. The Evidence of Josephus*. Oxford: Oxford University Press, 1993.

Greenberg, M. 'Nash Papyri' *EJ* 12 (1971) 833.

Greenfield, J. C., Sokoloff, M. *et al.* 'An Astrological Text from Qumran (4Q318) and Reflections on Some Zodiacal Names' *RevQ* 16/64 (1995) 507–25.

Greenfield, J. C., and Stone, M. E. 'Remarks on the Aramaic Testament of Levi from the Geniza' *RB* 86 (1979) 214–30 and pls. 13–14.

——. 'The Prayer of Levi' *JBL* 112 (1993) 247–66.

——. *Qumran Cave 4.XVII Parabiblical Texts, Part 3*. DJD XII. Oxford: Clarendon Press, 1996.

Gruenwald, I. 'Further Jewish Physiognomic and Chiromantic Fragments' *Tarbiz* 40 (1970–71) 301–19 (Hebrew).

Habermann, A. M. עדה ועדות מגילות קדומים ממדבר יהודה Jerusalem: Mahbaroth Le-Sifruth, 1952.

——. 'על התפילין בימי קדם' *Eretz-Israel* 3 (1954) 174–7.

Halperin, D. J. *The Faces of the Chariot: Early Jewish Responses to Ezekiel's Vision*. Tübingen: Mohr (Siebeck), 1988.

Harrington, Daniel J. *Wisdom Texts from Qumran*. London: Routledge, 1996.

Hendel, Ron. *The Text of Genesis 1–11: Textual Studies and Critical Edition*. New York: Oxford University Press, 1988.

Hengel, M., Charlesworth, J. H., and Mendels, D. 'The Polemical Character "On Kingship" in the Temple Scroll: An Attempt at Dating 11QTemple' *JJS* 37 (1986) 28–38.

Heschel, S. *Abraham Geiger and the Jewish Jesus*. Chicago: University of Chicago, 1988.

Himmelfarb, M. *Ascent to Heaven in Jewish and Christian Apocalypses*. New York: Oxford University Press, 1993.

Holdheim, S. מאמר האישות על תכונת הרבנים והקראים. 1861.

Horgan, M. P. *Pesharim: Qumran Interpretations of Biblical Books.* Washington: Catholic Biblical Association of America, 1979.

Idel, M. *Hasidim: Between Ecstasy and Magic.* Albany, NY: SUNY Press, 1995.

Jacob, L. *Hasidic Prayer.* New York: Jewish Publication Society, 1975.

Japhet, S. *I and II Chronicles.* Louisville: Westminster John Knox Press, 1993.

Jarick, J. 'The Bible's "Festival Scrolls" among the Dead Sea Scrolls' in *SSQFYA*, pp. 170–82.

Jastram, N. '4QNumb' in *Qumran Cave 4.VII: Genesis to Numbers.* DJD XII. Edited by E. Ulrich, F. M. Cross, *et al.* Oxford: Clarendon Press, 1994. Pp. 205–67.

Jeremias, Gert. *Der Lehrer der Gerechtigkeit.* Göttingen: Vandenhoeck & Ruprecht, 1963.

Karrer, M. *Der Gesalbte.* Göttingen: Vandenhoeck & Ruprecht, 1990.

Kister, M. 'Newly-Identified Fragments of the Book of Jubilees: Jub. 23: 21–23, 30–31" *RevQ* 12 (1987) 529–36.

——. 'Some Aspects of Qumranic Halakhah' in *MQC* volume 2, pp. 571–88.

Knibb, M. A. *The Ethiopic Book of Enoch.* Oxford: Clarendon Press, 1978. 2 volumes.

——. *The Qumran Community.* Cambridge: Cambridge University Press, 1987.

——. *Jubilees and the Origins of the Qumran Community, An Inaugural Lecture* London: King's College, London, 1989.

——. 'A Note on 4Q372 and 4Q390' in *The Scriptures and the Scrolls. Studies in Honour of A. S. van der Woude on the Occasion of His 65th Birthday* edited by F. García Martínez, A. Hilhorst and C. J. Labuschagne. Leiden: E. J. Brill, 1992. Pp. 164–77.

Kobelski, P. J. *Melchizedek and Melchireša.* Washington: Catholic Biblical Association of America, 1981.

Koch, K. 'Sabbatstruktur der Geschichte: Die sogenannte Zehn-Wochen-Apocalypse (1 Hen 93, 1–10; 91, 11–17) und das Ringen um die alttestamentlichen Chronologien in späten Israelitentum' in *Vor der Wende der Zeiten: Beiträge zur apokalyptischen Literatur* edited by U. Glessmer and M. Krause. Neukirchen: Neukirchener Verlag, 1996.

Kraus, H. J. *Psalms 1–59. A Commentary*. Minneapolis: Augsburg, 1988.

Kugel, J. *The Bible as it Was*. Cambridge, MA: Belknap, 1997.

Kugler, R. A. *From Patriarch to Priest: The Levi-Priestly Tradition from Aramaic Levi to Testament of Levi*. Atlanta: Scholars Press, 1996.

Kutsch, E. *Salbung als Rechtsakt im Alten Testament und im Alten Orient*. Berlin: Töpelmann, 1963.

Laato, A. *A Star is Rising. The Historical Development of the Old Testament Royal Ideology and the Rise of the Jewish Messsianic Expectations*. Atlanta: Scholars Press, 1997.

Lehmann, M. 'The *Temple Scroll* as a Source of Sectarian Halakhah' *RevQ* 9 (1978) 579–88.

Levenson, J. D. *The Theology of the Program of Restoration of Ezekiel 40–48*. Missoula: Scholars Press, 1976.

Levin, B. *Leviticus*. Philadelphia: Jewish Publication Society, 1989.

Lichtenberger, H. 'The Dead Sea Scrolls and John the Baptist: Reflections on Josephus' Account of John the Baptist' in *DSSFYR*, pp. 340–6.

Lieberman, S. 'The Discipline in the So-Called Dead Sea Manual of Discipline' *JBL* 71 (1951) 199–206.

——. 'Light on the Cave Scrolls from Rabbinic Sources' *PAAJR* 20 (1951) 395–404.

Lim, Timothy H. 'Eschatological Orientation and the Alteration of Scripture in the Habakkuk Pesher' *JNES* 49.2 (1990) 185–94.

——. 'The Chronology of the Flood Story in a Qumran Text (4Q252)' *JJS* 43 (1992) 288–98.

——. 'Notes on 4Q252 fr. 1, cols. i–ii' *JJS* 44 (1993) 121–6.

——. 'The Wicked Priests of the Groningen Hypothesis' *JBL* 112 (1993) 415–25.

——. *Holy Scripture in the Qumran Commentaries and Pauline Letters*. Oxford: Clarendon Press, 1997.

Lohse, Eduard. *Die Texte aus Qumran. Hebräisch und Deutsch mit masoretischer Punktation: Übersetzung, Einführung und Anmerkungen.* Second Edition. Munich: Kösel-Verlag, 1971.

Lyons, W. J., and Reimer, A. M. 'The Demonic Virus and Qumran Studies: Some Preventative Measures' *DSD* 5 (1998) 16–32.

Maier, J. *Die Qumran-Essener: die Texte vom Toten Meer.* München: Ernst Reinhardt Verlag, 1995.

——. 'Messias oder Gesalbter? Zu einem Übertsetzungs- und Deutungsproblem in den Qumrantexten' *RevQ* 17 (1996) 585–612.

——. *Die Tempelrolle vom Toten Meer und das 'Neue Jerusalem'.* München/Basel, 1997.

Mason, S. *Flavius Josephus on the Pharisees.* Leiden: E. J. Brill, 1991.

——. 'Fire, Water and Spirit: John the Baptist and the Tyranny of Canon' *SR* (1992) 163–80.

McCarter, P. K. *II Samuel.* New York: Doubleday, 1984.

Mendels, D. *The Rise and Fall of Jewish Nationalism.* New York: Doubleday, 1992.

Mettinger, T. *King and Messiah.* Lund: Gleerup, 1976.

Meyer, M. A. *Response to Modernity.* New York: Oxford University Press, 1993.

Miller, M. 'The Function of Isa 61 1–2 in 11Q Melchizedek' *JBL* 88 (1969) 467–9.

Milik, J. T. 'Le Testament de Lévi en araméen: Fragment de la Grotte 4 de Qumrân' *RB* 62 (1955) 398–406.

——. *Ten Years of Discovery in the Wilderness of Judaea.* ET: John Strugnell. London: SCM Press, 1959.

——. 'Milkî-sedeq et Milkî-resa? dans les anciens écrits juifs et chrétiens' *JJS* 23 (1972) 95–144.

——. 'Tefillin, Mezuzot et Targums (4Q128–4Q157)' in *Qumrân Grotte 4.II. DJD VI* edited by R. de Vaux and J.T. Milik. Oxford: Clarendon Press, 1977.

Milik, J. T., with Black, M. *The Books of Enoch: Aramaic Fragments of Qumrân Cave 4.* Oxford: Clarendon Press, 1976.

Milgrom, J. 'Day of Atonement' *EncJud* Volume 5, p. 1384.

——. *Leviticus 1–16.* Garden City, NY: Doubleday, 1991.

Morray-Jones, C. R. A. 'Transformational Mysticism in the Apocalyptic-Merkabah Tradition' *JJS* 43 (1992) 1–31.

——. 'The Temple Within: The Embodied Divine Image and Its Worship in the Dead Sea Scrolls and Other Early Jewish and Christian Sources' *Society of Biblical Literature 1998 Seminar Papers*. Atlanta: Scholars Press, 1998. Pp. 400–31.

Mowinckel, S. *The Psalms in Israel's Worship*. Nashville: Abingdon, 1967.

Murphy-O'Connor, J. 'The Original Text of CD 7:9–8:2 = 19:5–14' *HTR* 64 (1971) 379–86.

——. 'The Damascus Document Revisited' *RB* 92 (1987) 225–45.

Nemoy, L. *Karaite Anthology*. New Haven: Yale University Press, 1952.

Newsom, C. 'Merkabah Exegesis in the Qumran Sabbath Shirot' *JJS* 38 (1987) 11–30.

Neusner, J. *Rabbinic Trditions about the Pharisees Before 70*. 3 volumes. Leiden: E. J. Brill, 1971.

——. 'Rabbinic Traditions about the Pharisees before A.D. 70: The Problem of Oral Transmission' *JJS* 22 (1971) 1–18.

——. *From Politics to Piety: The Emergence of Pharisaic Judaism*. Second edition. New York: Ktav, 1979.

——. *Judaism. The Evidence of the Mishnah*. Chicago: University of Chicago Press, 1981.

Neusner, J., Green, W. S., and Frerichs, E. S. (eds). *Judaisms and Their Messiahs at the Turn of the Christian Era*. Cambridge: Cambridge University Press, 1987.

Nitzan, B. 'Hymns from Qumran "לפחד ולבהל Evil Ghosts (4Q510–511)"' *Tarbiz* 55 (1985–86) 19–46 (Hebrew).

——. 'Hymns from Qumran – 4Q510–4Q511' in *DSSFYR*, pp. 53–63.

——. '4QBerakhot (4Q286–290): A Preliminary Report' in *NQTS*, pp. 53–71 and pl. 3.

——. *Qumran Prayer and Religious Poetry*. Leiden: E. J. Brill, 1994.

Noack, B. 'Qumran and the Book of Jubilees' *SEA* 22–23 (1958) 191–207.

——. 'The Day of Pentecost in Jubilees, Qumran and Acts' *ASTI* 1 (1962) 73–95.

Nodet, E., and Taylor, J. *Essaie sur les origines du Christianisme*. Paris: Les Éditions du Cerf, 1998.

Noth, M. *Leviticus*. ET. London: SCM Press, 1965.

Oegma, G. S. *Der Gesalbte und sein Volk*. Göttingen: Vandenhoeck & Ruprecht, 1994.

Oppenheimer, A. *The 'Am ha-Aretz*. ET. Leiden: E. J. Brill, 1977.

Pearson, B. W. R. 'The Book of the Twelve, Aqiba's Messianic Interpretations, and the Refuge Caves of the Second Jewish War' in *SSFQYA*, pp. 221–39.

Penny, D. L., and Wise, M. O. 'By the Power of Beelzebub: An Aramaic Incantation Formula from Qumran (4Q560)' *JBL* 113 (1994) 627–50.

Pesch, R. ' "He will be called a Nazorean": Messianic Exegesis in Matthew 1–2' *in The Gospels and the Scriptures of Israel* edited by C. A. Evans and W. R. Stegner. Sheffield: Sheffield Academic Press, 1994. Pp. 129–78.

Pomykala, K. *The Davidic Dynasty Tradition in Early Judaism*. Atlanta: Scholars Press, 1995.

Porter, S. E., and Evans, C. A. (eds) *The Scrolls and the Scriptures. Qumran Fifty Years After*. Sheffield: Sheffield Academic Press, 1997. (= *SSQFYA*)

Pritchard, J. B. (ed.). *Ancient Near Eastern Texts Relating to the Old Testament*. Princeton: Princeton University Press, 1969.

Puech, E. 'Notes sur le manuscrit de XIQMelkîsédeq' *RevQ* 12 (1987) 483–513.

——. '11QPsAp^a: Un rituel d'exorcismes. Essai de reconstruction' *RevQ* 14/54 (1989) 377–408.

——. 'Les deux derniers psaumes davidiques du rituel d'exorcisme, 11QPsAp^a IV 4–V 14' in *DSSFYR*, pp. 64–89.

——. *La croyance des esséniens en la vie future: Immortalité, résurrection, vie éternelle? Historie d'une croyance dans le Judaïsme ancien*. Paris: J. Gabalda, 1993.

——. 'Messianism, Resurrection and Eschatology in Qumran and the New Testament' in *CRC*, pp. 235–56.

——. 'Fragments du plus ancien exemplaire du Rouleau du Temple (4Q524)' in *LTLI*, pp. 19–64.

Qimron, E. *The Hebrew of the Dead Sea Scrolls*. Atlanta: Scholars Press, 1986.

——. 'An Unpublished Halakhic Letter from Qumran' in *Biblical Archaeology Today: Proceedings of the International Conference on Biblical Archaeology, Jerusalem, April 1984* edited by J. Amitai. Jerusalem: Israel Exploration Society, 1985. Pp. 400–7.

Qimron, E., and Strugnell, J., *Qumran Cave 4.V: Miqsat Ma'aśeh Ha-Torah*. DJD X. Oxford: Clarendon Press, 1994.

Rabin, C. *The Zadokite Documents. I. The Admonition II. The Laws*. Oxford: Clarendon Press, 1954.

——. 'Notes on the Habakkuk Scroll and the Zadokite Documents' *VT* 5 (1955) 158–9.

——. *Qumran Studies*. Oxford: Oxford University Press, 1957.

Revel, B. *The Karaite Halakhah*. Philadelphia: Dropsie College, 1913.

Riesner, R. 'Bethany Beyond Jordan (John 1:28). Topography, Theology and History in the Fourth Gospel' *Tyndale Bulletin* 38 (1987) 42–56.

Ritter, B. *Philo und die Halacha*. Leipzig: J. C. Hinrichs, 1879.

Roberts, J. J. M. 'The Old Testament's Contribution to Messianic Expectations' in *The Messiah. Developments in Earliest Judaism and Christianity* edited by J. H. Charlesworth. Minneapolis: Fortress Press, 1992.

Rofé, A. 'Fragments from an Additional Manuscript of the Book of Jubilees in Qumran Cave 3' *Tarbiz* 34 (1965) 333–6 (Hebrew).

——. 'The Editing of the Book of Joshua in the Light of 4QJosh[a]' in *NQTS*, pp. 73–80.

Rowley, H. H. *The Zadokite Fragments of the Dead Sea Scrolls*. Oxford: Blackwell, 1952.

Sanders, E. P. *Paul and Palestinian Judaism*. London: SCM Press, 1977.

——. *Jewish Law from Jesus to the Mishnah*. London: SCM Press, 1990.

——. *Judaism: Practice and Belief*. London: SCM Press, 1992.

Sanders, J. A. *The Psalms Scroll of Qumran Cave 11 (11QPs[a])*. DJD IV. Oxford: Clarendon Press, 1968.

——. 'Ναζωραῖοσ in Matthew 2.23' in *The Gospels and the Scriptures of Israel* edited by C. A. Evans and W. R. Stegner. Sheffield: Sheffield Academic Press, 1994. Pp. 116–28.

Sanderson, J. E. *An Exodus Scroll from Qumran: 4QpaleoExod^m and the Samaritan Tradition*. Atlanta: Scholars Press, 1986.

Saldarini, Anthony J. *Pharisees, Scribes and Sadducees in Palestinian Society: A Sociological Approach*. Wilmington: Michael Glazier, 1988.

Samuel, A. E. *Greek and Roman Chronology. Calendars and Years in Classical Antiquity*. Munich: Beck, 1972.

Schäfer, P. *Synopse zur Hekhalot–Literatur*. Tübingen: Mohr (Siebeck), 1981.

——. *Geniza-Fragmente zur Hekhalot-Literatur*. Tübingen: Mohr (Siebeck), 1984.

——. *Hekhalot Studien*. Tübingen: Mohr (Siebeck), 1988.

Schechter, S. *Documents of Jewish Sectaries. Volume I. Fragments of a Zadokite Work*. Cambridge: Cambridge University Press, 1910.

Schiffman, Lawrence H. *The Halakhah at Qumran*. Leiden: E. J. Brill, 1975.

——. 'Merkavah Speculation at Qumran: The 4QSerekh Shirot 'Olat ha-Shabbat' in *Mystics, Philosophers, and Politicians: Essays in Jewish Intellectual History in Honor of Alexander Altmann* edited by J. Reinharz et al. Durham, NC: Duke University Press, 1982. Pp. 15–47.

——. *Sectarian Law in the Dead Sea Scrolls: Courts, Testimony and the Penal Code*. Chico: Scholars Press, 1983.

——. *Who Was a Jew? Rabbinic and Halakhic Perspectives on the Jewish Christian Schism*. Hoboken: Ktav, 1985.

——. 'Sifrut Ha-Hekhalot ve-Kitve Qumran' (ET: 'The Hekhalot Literature and the Qumran Writings') *Mehqere Yerushalaym Be-Mahshevet Yisra'el* 6 (1987) 121–38.

——. 'The King, his Guard and the Royal Council in the Temple Scroll' *PAAJR* 54 (1987) 237–59.

——. 'The Laws of War in the Temple Scroll' *RevQ* 13 (1988) 299–311.

——. *The Eschatological Community of the Dead Sea Scrolls: A Study of the Rule of the Congregation*. Atlanta: Scholars Press, 1989.

——. '*Miqsat ma'aseh ha-Torah* and *Temple Scroll*' *RevQ* 14 (1990) 435–57.

——. 'The New *Halakhic Letter* (4QMMT) and the Origins of the Dead Sea Sect' *BA* 53 (1990) 64–73.

——. *From Text to Tradition: A History of Second Temple and Rabbinic Judaism*. Hoboken: Ktav, 1991.

——. 'Confessionalism and the Study of the Dead Sea Scrolls' *Jewish Studies* 31 (1991) 5–14.

——. 'Messianic Figures and Ideas in the Qumran Scrolls' in *The Messiah: Developments in Earliest Judaism and Christianity* edited by J. H. Charlesworth. Minneapolis: Fortress Press, 1992. Pp. 116–29.

——. *Reclaiming the Dead Sea Scrolls. The History of Judaism, the Background of Christianity, the Lost Library of Qumran*. Philadelphia: Jewish Publication Society, 1994.

——. 'Pharisaic and Sadducean Halakhah in Light of the Dead Sea Scrolls. The Case of Tevul Yom' *DSD* 1 (1994) 285–99.

——. 'The *Temple Scroll* and the Nature of its Law: The Status of the Question' in *CRC*, pp. 37–55.

——. 'Sacral and non-Sacral Slaughter According to the Temple Scroll' in *TPWW*, pp. 69–84.

Schochet, E. J. *The Hasidic Movement and the Gaon of Vilna*. Northvale, NJ: Jason Aaronson, 1994.

Schoeps, H.-J. *Theologie und Geschichte des Judenchristentums*. Tübingen: Mohr, 1949.

Scholem, G. 'Physiognomy and Chiromancy' *in Sepher Assaf (Festschrift for Simha Assaf)*. Jerusalem: Mossad HaRav Kook, 1953. Pp. 459–95 (Hebrew).

——. *Major Trends in Jewish Mysticism*. New York: Schocken, 1965.

——. 'Ein Fragment zur Physiognomik und Chiromantik aus der Tradition der spätantiken jüdischen Esoterik' *in Liber Amicorum: Studies in Honour of Professor Dr. C. J. Bleeker*. Leiden: E. J. Brill, 1969. Pp. 175–93.

——. *The Messianic Idea in Judaism*. New York: Schocken, 1971.

Schubert, K., and Maier, J. *Die Qumran Essener*. München: Reinhardt, 1992.

Schürer, Emil. *The History of the Jewish People in the Age of Jesus Christ (175* B.C.–A.D. *135)* revised and edited by Geza Vermes, Fergus Millar, Martin Goodman, *et al.* Volumes I – III.2 Edinburgh: T&T Clark, 1973, 1979, 1986, and 1987.

Schwarz, D. *Studies in the Jewish Background of Christianity.* Tübingen: Mohr (Siebeck), 1992.

Scobie, C. H. H. *John the Baptist.* London: SCM Press, 1964.

Seebass, H. *Herrscherverheissungen im Alten Testament.* Neukirchen-Vluyn: Neukirchener Verlag, 1992.

Segal, L. A. *Historical Consciousness and Religious Tradition in Azariah de Rossi's Me'or 'Einayim.* Philadelphia: Jewish Publication Society, 1989.

Skehan, P. W. 'Exodus in the Samaritan Recension from Qumran'. *JBL* 74 (1955) 435–40.

——. 'Qumran and the Present State of Old Testament Text Studies: The Massoretic Text' *JBL* 78 (1959) 21–5.

Smith, Jonathan Z. 'A Matter of Class: Taxonomies of Religion' *HTR* 89 (1996) 387–403.

Smith, Morton. 'The Dead Sea Sect in Relation to Ancient Judaism' *NTS* 7 (1960–61) 347–60.

——. 'Ascent to the Heavens and Deification in 4QM[a]' in *Archaeology and History in the Dead Sea Scrolls: The New York University Conference in Memory of Yigael Yadin* edited by Lawrence H. Schiffman. Sheffield: Sheffield Academic Press, 1990. Pp. 181–8.

Smith, Mark S. 'Converted and Unconverted Perfect and Imperfect Forms in the Literature of Qumran' *BASOR* 284 (1991) 1–17.

——. *The Origins and Development of the Waw-Consecutive: Northwest Semitic Evidence from Ugarit to Qumran.* Atlanta: Scholars Press, 1991.

——. 'The Waw-Consecutive at Qumran' *ZAH* 4 (1991) 161–4.

Starcky, J. 'Les quatre étapes du messianisme à Qumrân' *RB* 70 (1963) 481–505.

Steck, O. H. *Der Abschluss der Prophetie im Alten Testament. Ein Versuch zur Frage der Vorgeschichte des Kanons.* Neukirchen-Vluyn Neukirchener Verlag, 1991.

Stegemann, H. *Die Enstehung der Qumrangemeinde.* Bonn dissertation, 1965.

——. 'Some Remarks to 1QSa, to 1QSb, and to Qumran Messianism' *RevQ* 17 (1996) 479–505.

——. *The Library of Qumran. On the Essenes, Qumran and John the Baptist and Jesus.* Grand Rapids: Eerdmans, 1998.

Steudel, A. 'אחרית הימים in the Texts from Qumran' *RevQ* 16 (1993) 225–46.

——. *Der Midrasch zur Eschatologie aus der Qumrangemeinde (4QMidrEschat^{a.b}). Materielle Rekonstruktion, Textbestand, Gattung und traditionsgeschichtliche Einordnung des durch 4Q174 („Florilegium") und 4Q177 („Catena A") repräsentierten Werkes aus den Qumranfunden.* Leiden: E. J. Brill, 1994.

——. 'The Eternal Reign of the People of God – Collective Expectations in Qumran Texts (4Q246 and 1QM)' *RevQ* 17 (1996) 507–25.

Stone, M. E. 'Categorization and Classification of the Apocrypha and Pseudepigrapha' *Abr-Nahrain* 24 (1986) 167–77.

——. 'The Question of the Messiah in 4 Ezra' in *Judaisms and their Messiahs* edited by J. Neusner, W. S. Green and E. Frerichs. Cambridge: Cambridge University Press, 1987. Pp. 209–24.

——. 'Enoch, Aramaic Levi and Sectarian Origins' *JSJ* 19 (1988) 159–70.

——. 'The Dead Sea Scrolls and the Pseudepigrapha' *DSD* 3 (1996) 270–95.

Strugnell, J. 'The Angelic Liturgy at Qumrân – 4Q Serek Šîrôt 'Ôlat Haššabbat' in *Congress Volume: Oxford 1959.* Vetus Testamentum Supplements 7. Leiden: Brill, 1960. Pp. 318–45.

Sukenik, E. *The Dead Sea Scrolls of the Hebrew University.* Jerusalem: Hebrew University and Magnes Press, 1954. ET 1955.

Sussman, Yaakov. 'The History of Halakha and the Dead Sea Scrolls. Preliminary Observations on *Miqsat Ma'aseh Ha-Torah*' (Hebrew) *Tarbiz* 59.1–2 (1989–90) 11–76.

Swanson, D. *The Temple Scroll and the Bible. The Methodology of 4QT.* Leiden: E. J. Brill, 1995.

Sweeney, M. A. 'Jesse's New Shoot in Isaiah 11: A Josianic Reading of the Prophet Isaiah' in *A Gift of God in Due Season. Essays on Scripture and Community in Honor of James A. Sanders* edited by R. D. Weis and D. M. Carr. Sheffield: Sheffield Academic Press, 1996. Pp. 103–18.

Talmon, S. 'The Calendar of the Covenanters of the Judean Desert' in *The World of Qumran from Within.* Jerusalem: Magnes Press, 1989. Pp. 147–85.

——. 'Yom Hakippurim in the Habakkuk Scroll' in *The World of Qumran from Within.* Jerusalem: Magnes Press, 1989. Pp. 186–99.

——. 'Hebrew Written Fragments from Masada' *Eretz Israel* 20 (1989) 278–85 (Hebrew).

——. 'The Community of the Renewed Covenant: Between Judaism and Christianity' in *CRC*, pp. 3–24.

——. 'Hebrew Written Fragments from Masada' *DSD* 3 (1996) 168–77.

Taylor, J. E. *The Immerser: John the Baptist within Second Temple Judaism.* Grand Rapids/Cambridge: Eerdmans, 1997.

——. 'John the Baptist and the Essenes' *JJS* 47.2 (1996) 256–85.

Testuz, M. *Les idées religieuses du Livre des Jubilés.* Geneva: Droz/ Paris: Minard, 1960.

Thiering, B. *Jesus the Man.* London: Doubleday, 1992.

Tiller, P. A. *A Commentary on the Animal Apocalypse of 1 Enoch.* Atlanta: Scholars Press, 1993.

——. 'The "Eternal Planting" in the Dead Sea Scrolls' *DSD* 4 (1997) 312–35.

Tilly, M. *Johannes der Täufer und die Biographie der Propheten.* Stuttgart: Kohlhammer, 1994.

Tov, E. *The Septuagint Translation of Jeremiah and Baruch: A Discussion of an Early Revision of the LXX of Jeremiah 29–52 and Baruch 1:1 – 3:8.* Missoula, Montana: Scholars Press, 1976.

——. 'Hebrew Biblical Manuscripts from the Judaean Desert: Their Contribution to Textual Criticism' *JJS* 39 (1988) 5–37.

——. *Textual Criticism of the Hebrew Bible.* Minneapolis: Fortress Press/Assen: van Gorcum, 1992.

——. 'Biblical Texts as Reworked in Some Qumran Manuscripts with Special Attention to 4QRP and 4QParaGen-Exod' in *CRC*, pp. 111–34.

——. 'Three Manuscripts (Abbreviated Texts?) of Canticles from Qumran Cave 4' *JSS* 46 (1995) 88–111.

——. 'Excerpted and Abbreviated Biblical Texts from Qumran' *RevQ* 16 (1995) 581–600.

——. 'The History and Significance of a Standard Text of the Hebrew Bible' in *Hebrew Bible/Old Testament: The History of Its Interpretation. Volume 1: From the Beginnings to the Middle Ages (until 1300)*. Göttingen: Vandenhoeck & Ruprecht, 1996. Pp. 49–66.

——. 'Scribal Practices Reflected in the Documents from the Judean Desert and in the Rabbinic Literature: A Comparative Study' in *Texts, Temples and Traditions: A Tribute to Menahem Haran* edited by M. V. Fox *et al*. Winona Lake: Eisenbrauns, 1996. Pp. 383–403.

——. 'L'importance des textes du désert de Juda pour l'histoire du texte de la Bible hébraïque. Une nouvelle synthèse' in *Qoumrân et les Manuscrits de la mer Morte: un cinquantenaire* edited by E.-M. Laperrousaz. Paris: Les Éditions du Cerf, 1997. Pp. 215–52.

——. 'Scribal Practices and Physical Aspects of the Dead Sea Scrolls' in *The Bible as Book – The Manuscript Tradition* edited by J. L. Sharpe III and K. Van Kampen. London: British Library, 1998. Pp. 9–33.

Trebolle-Barrera, J. 'Textual Variants in 4QJudg[a] and the Textual and Editorial History of the Book of Judges' in *RevQ* 14.2 (1989) 229–45.

Trebolle-Barrera, J., and Vegas Montaner, L. (eds). *The Madrid Qumran Congress: Proceedings of the International Congress on the Dead Sea Scrolls, Madrid, 18–21 March 1991*, 2 volumes. Leiden: E. J. Brill, 1992. (= *MQC*)

——. '4QJudg[a]' in *Qumran Cave 4.IX: Deuteronomy, Joshua, Judges, Kings*. DJD XIV. Oxford: Clarendon Press, 1995.

——. '*Tefillin* of Different Origin from Qumran?' in *A Light for Jacob: Studies in the Bible and the Dead Sea in Memory of Jacob Shalom Licht* edited by Y. Hoffman, F. H. Polak. Jerusalem: Tel Aviv University Press, 1997. Pp. 44–54.

Ulfgard, H. 'Uppenbarelseboken och "Sabbatsoffersångerna" från Qumran och Masada' in *Tro og historie. Festskrift til Niels Hyldahl i anledning af 65 års fødselsdagen den 30. december 1995*. Forum for Bibelsk Eksegese 7. Copenhagen: Museum Tusculanums Forlag, 1996. Pp. 285–300.

——. 'L'Apocalypse entre judaïsme et christianism: Précisions sur le monde spirituel et intellectuel de Jean de Patmos' *RHPR* 79 (1999) 31–50.

Ullendorf, E. 'Hebrew Elements in the Ethiopic Old Testament' in *From the Bible to Enrico Cerulli. A Miscellany of Ethiopian and Semitic Papers*. Stuttgart: Steiner Verlag Wiesbaden, 1990.

Ulrich, Eugene C. *The Qumran Text of Samuel and Josephus*. Missoula: Scholars Press, 1978.

——. 'Daniel Manuscripts from Qumran. Part 1: A Preliminary Edition of 4QDan^a' *BASOR* 267 (1987) 17–37.

——. 'Daniel Manuscripts from Qumran. Part 2: Preliminary Editions of 4QDan^b and 4QDan^c' *BASOR* 274 (1989) 3–26.

——. 'Josephus' Biblical Text for the Books of Samuel' in *Josephus, the Bible and History* edited by L. H. Feldman and G. Hata. Detroit: Wayne State University Press, 1989. Pp. 81–96.

——. 'Orthography and Text in 4QDan^a and 4QDan^b and in the Received Masoretic Text' in *Of Scribes and Scrolls: Studies on the Hebrew Bible, Intertestamental Judaism, and Christian Origins Presented to John Strugnell on the Occasion of his Sixtieth Birthday* edited by H. W. Attridge, John J. Collins, T. H. Tobin. Lanham, MD: University Press of America, 1990. Pp. 29–42.

——. '4QJoshua^a and Joshua's First Altar in the Promised Land' in *NQTS*, pp. 89–104, pls. IV–VI.

——. 'The Palaeo-Hebrew Biblical Manuscripts from Qumran Cave 4' in *TPWW*, pp. 103–29.

——. 'Multiple Literary Editions: Reflections toward a Theory of the History of the Biblical Text' in *Current Research and Technological Developments on the Dead Sea Scrolls: Conference on the Texts from the Judean Desert, Jerusalem, 30 April 1995* edited by D. Parry and S. D. Richs Leiden: Brill Academic Publishers, 1996. Pp. 78–105.

——. 'The Dead Sea Scrolls and the Biblical Text' *in The Dead Sea Scrolls after Fifty Years: A Comprehensive Assessment* edited by P. W. Flint and J. C. VanderKam. Leiden: E. J. Brill, 1998. Volume 1, pp. 84–5.

Ulrich, E., and VanderKam, J. (eds). *The Community of the Renewed Covenant: The Notre Dame Symposium on the Dead Sea Scrolls*. Notre Dame: University of Notre Dame Press, 1994. (= CRC)

Ulrich, E., Cross, F. M. *et al. Qumran Cave 4.IX. Deuteronomy, Joshua, Judges, Kings*. DJD XIV. Oxford: Clarendon Press, 1995.

Ulrich, E. *et al. Qumran Cave 4.X. The Prophets*. Oxford: Clarendon Press, 1997.

Urbach, E. E. *The Sages: Their Concepts and Beliefs*. ET. Cambridge: Harvard University Press, 1987.

VanderKam, J. C. *Textual and Historical Studies in the Book of Jubilees*. Missoula: Scholars Press, 1977.

——. 'Studies in the Apocalypse of Weeks' *CBQ* 46 (1984) 511–23.

——. *Enoch and the Growth of an Apocalyptic Tradition*. Washington: Catholic Biblical Association of America, 1984.

——. *The Book of Jubilees*. Louvain: Peeters, 1989. 2 volumes.

——. 'The Temple Scroll and the Book of Jubilees' in *Temple Scroll Studies* edited by G. J. Brooke. Sheffield: Sheffield Academic Press, 1989. Pp. 211–36.

——. 'The Jubilees Fragments from Qumran Cave 4' in *MQC* volume 2, pp. 635–48.

——. 'Messianism in the Scrolls' in *CRC*, pp. 211–34.

——. *The Dead Sea Scrolls Today*. London: SPCK, 1994.

——. 'Das chronologishce Konzept des Jubiläenbuches' *ZAW* 107 (1995) 80–100.

VanderKam, J. C., and Milik, J. T. '228. 4QText with a Citation of Jubilees' in *Qumran Cave 4.VIII: Parabiblical Texts Part I*. DJD XIII. Oxford: Clarendon Press, 1994.

van der Ploeg, J. P. M. 'Un petit roleau de psaumes apocryphes (11QPsAp^a)' in *Tradition und Glaube: Das frühe Christentum in seiner Umwelt*. Göttingen: Vandenhoeck & Ruprecht, 1971. Pp. 128–39 and pls. 2–7.

van der Woude, A. S. 'Fragmente des Buches Jubiläen aus Qumran Höhle XI (11QJub)' in *Tradition und Glaube: Das frühe Christentum in seiner Umwelt* edited by G. Jeremias, H. W. Kuhn, and H. Stegemann. Göttingen: Vandenhoeck & Ruprecht, 1971. Pp. 140–6 and plate VIII.

——. 'Pluriformity and Uniformity. Reflections on the Transmission of the Text of the Old Testament' in *Sacred History and Sacred Texts in Early Judaism. A Symposium in Honour of A. S. van der Woude* edited by J. N. Bremmer and F. García Martínez. Kampen: Kok Pharos, 1992. Pp. 151–69.

——. 'Once Again: The Wicked Priests in the Habakkuk Pesher from Cave 1 of Qumran' *RevQ* 17 (1996) 375–84.

Vermes, G. *The Dead Sea Scrolls. Qumran in Perspective*. London: Collins, 1977.

——. 'Preliminary Remarks on Unpublished Fragments of the Community Rule from Qumran Cave 4' *JJS* 42 (1991) 250–5.

——. *The Complete Dead Sea Scrolls in English*. London: Penguin Press, 1997.

——. 'New Light on the Sacrifice of Isaac from 4Q225' *JJS* 47 (1996) 140–46.

Vermes, G., Lim, T. H., and Gordon, R. P. 'The Oxford Forum for Qumran Research Seminar of the Rule of War from Cave 4 (4Q285)' *JJS* 43 (1992) 85–90.

Wacholder, B. Z. 'A Qumran Attack on Oral Qumran Exegesis. The Phrase אשר בתלמוד שקרם in 4QPesher Nahum' *RevQ* (1966) 351–69.

——. 'Jubilees as the Super Canon: Torah-Admonition versus Torah-Commandment' in *LTLI*, pp. 195–211.

Wacholder, Ben Zion, and Abegg, Martin G. *A Preliminary Edition of the Unpublished Dead Sea Scrolls. Fascicle 3*. Washington: Biblical Archaeology Society, 1995.

Wacholder, B., and Wacholder, S. 'Patterns of Biblical Dates and Qumran's Calendar: the Fallacy of Jaubert's Hypothesis' *HUCA* 66 (1995) 1–40.

Webb, R. L. *John the Baptist and Prohet. A Socio-Historical Study*. Sheffield: JSOT Press, 1991.

Weinfeld, M. *The Organizational Pattern and the Penal Code of the Qumran Sect*. Göttingen: Vandenhoeck & Ruprecht, 1986.

White, S. A. 'A Comparison of the "A" and "B" Manuscripts of the Damascus Document' *RevQ* 48 (1987) 537–53.

——. '4QDt^n: Biblical Manuscript or Excerpted Text?' in *Of Scribes and Scrolls: Studies on the Hebrew Bible, Intertestamental Judaism, and Christian Origins presented to John Strugnell on the Occasion of his Sixtieth Birthday* edited by H. W. Attridge, John J. Collins, T. H. Tobin. Lanham, MD: University Press of America, 1990. Pp. 13–20.

Wieder, N. *The Judean Scrolls and Karaism*. London: East and West Library, 1962.

Williamson, H. G. M. 'The Translation of 1QpHab V, 10' *RevQ* 9 (1977–8) 263–5.

——. *1 and 2 Chronicles*. Grand Rapids: Eerdmans, 1982.

Wilson, G. H. *The Editing of the Hebrew Psalter*. Chico: Scholars Press, 1985.

Wise, M. O. 'Thunder in Gemini: An Aramaic Brontologion (4Q318) from Qumran' in *Thunder in Gemini and Other Essays on the History, Language and Literature of Second Temple Palestine*. Sheffield: Sheffield Academic Press, 1994. Pp. 13–50.

Wise, M. O., Abegg, M. and Cook, E. *The Dead Sea Scrolls: A New Translation*. San Francisco: HarperCollins Publishers, 1996.

Wright, D. P. *The Disposal of Impurity: Elimination Rites in the Bible and in Hittite and Mesopotamian Literature*. Atlanta: Scholars Press, 1987.

Yadin, Yigael. *The Scroll of the War of the Sons of Light Against the Sons of Darkness*. ET: Oxford: Oxford University Press, 1962.

——. 'The Temple Scroll' *BA* 30 (1967) 135–9.

——. *Tefillin from Qumran (X Qumran Phyl 1–4)*. Jerusalem: Israel Exploration Society and Shrine of the Book, 1969.

——. *The Temple Scroll*. ET: 3 volumes. Jerusalem: Israel Exploration Society, 1983.

Zolli, E. 'Nazarenus vocabitur' *ZNW* 49 (1958) 135–6.

INDEX OF NAMES

INDEX OF SUBJECTS

INDEX OF DEAD SEA SCROLLS